ERROR AND THE ACADEMIC SELF

COLUMBIA UNIVERSITY PRESS   NEW YORK

ERROR AND THE ACADEMIC SELF

the scholarly imagination, medieval to modern

SETH LERER

Columbia University Press
Publishers Since 1893
New York   Chichester, West Sussex

Copyright © 2002 Columbia University Press
All rights reserved

Library of Congress Cataloging-in-Publication Data
Lerer, Seth, 1955–
Error and the academic self : the scholarly imagination,
medieval to modern / Seth Lerer.
p. cm.
Includes bibliograhical references and index.
ISBN 978-0-231-12372-3 (cloth)—ISBN 978-0-231-12373-0 (paper)
1. English philology—History.   2. Great Britain—Intellectual life.
3. Scholarly publishing—Great Britain.   4. Errors and blunders, Literary—History.
5. English literature—History and criticism—Theory, etc.   6. American literature—
History and criticism—Theory, etc.   7. Error—History.   I. Title.

PE51.L46 2002
820.9—dc21
2002073501

CONTENTS

ACKNOWLEDGMENTS
VII

INTRODUCTION
The Pursuit of Error: Philology, Rhetoric, and the History of Scholarship
1

CHAPTER ONE
Errata: Mistakes and Masters in the Early Modern Book
15

CHAPTER TWO
Sublime Philology: An Elegy for Anglo-Saxon Studies
55

CHAPTER THREE
My Casaubon: The Novel of Scholarship and Victorian Philology
103

CHAPTER FOUR
Ardent Etymologies: American Rhetorical Philology, from Adams to de Man
175

CHAPTER FIVE
Making Mimesis: Exile, Errancy, and Erich Auerbach
221

EPILOGUE
Forbidden Planet and the Terrors of Philology
261

NOTES
277

INDEX
317

ACKNOWLEDGMENTS

So many individuals and institutions have contributed to this book that I cannot name them all. Joseph Dane has always been a source of knowledge and a stimulating, thoughtful reader of just about everything I have written. Brian Stock has long guided my sense of historical inquiry. Conversations with Timothy Hampton helped me formulate the shape of this book, while R. Howard Bloch, John Ganim, Anthony Grafton, Nicholas Howe, and David Wallace have, at various times, helped me see the implications of its claims. Specific contributions to my work were also made by Brett Bourbon, Hans-Ulrich Gumbrecht, Nicholas Jenkins, Gavin Jones, Coppélia Kahn, Herbert Lindenberger, Stephen Orgel, Marjorie Perloff, Jennifer Summit, Roland Greene, and Alex Woloch.

Portions of this book were read at Berkeley, Brown, Columbia, Fordham, the Huntington Library, California State University at Long Beach, the University of Miami, the University of Oregon, the University of California at Santa Cruz, Stanford, the University of Texas, the University of Toronto, Vanderbilt University, Yale, York

University, and at meetings of the Modern Language Association of America.

Present and former students who have helped with this material include Dorsey Armstrong, Bradin Cormack, Karen Gross, Ryan Johnson, Meg Worley, and especially Deanne Williams.

Stanford University funded several leaves of absence and hosted a conference on Erich Auerbach in 1992, out of which my work on *Mimesis* and émigré philology developed. A fellowship year at the Stanford Humanities Center (2000–2001) and a summer fellowship at the Huntington Library (2001) enabled me to finish the book. I also thank the staffs at the British Library, the Bodleian Library, the Cambridge University Library, the Library at Trinity College, Cambridge, and the libraries at Berkeley, Princeton, and Stanford.

I am also grateful to David Kastan and James Shapiro for sponsoring a visit to Columbia and for putting me in contact with Jennifer Crewe of Columbia University Press, who generously welcomed this book for publication and who has proven to be an insightful and patient editor.

Portions of this book have previously appeared in print. Chapter 2 incorporates some material from a much longer and detailed treatment of George Hickes, "The Anglo-Saxon Pindar: Old English Scholarship and Augustan Criticism in George Hickes's *Thesaurus*," *Modern Philology* 99 (2001): 26–65. That chapter also includes, in revised and self-critical form, sections of my "*Beowulf* and Critical Theory," in *A "Beowulf" Handbook*, ed. Robert Bjork and John D. Niles (Lincoln: University of Nebraska Press, 1997). Chapter 5 revises and expands material originally published as "Making Mimesis: Erich Auerbach and the Institutions of Medieval Studies," in *Medievalism and the Modernist Temper*, ed. Stephen G. Nichols and R. Howard Bloch (Baltimore: Johns Hopkins University Press, 1996), a different version of which was also published as the introduction and "Philology and Collaboration," in *Literary History and the Challenge of Philology: The Legacy of Erich Auerbach*, ed. Seth Lerer (Stanford: Stanford University Press, 1996), pp. 1–10, 78–91. The epilogue is an expanded and annotated revision of my essay "*Forbidden Planet* and the Terrors of Philology," *Raritan* 19 (2000): 73–86. I am grateful to the original editors and publishers for permission to incorporate these earlier materials into this book.

Finally, I have sought to quote accurately from my sources. No texts are normalized. Spelling, capitalization, punctuation, syntax, and phrasing remain (unless otherwise noted) as they appear in the originals, except that single quotation marks have been changed to doubles where appropriate (and vice versa). All unattributed translations are my own—as are, of course, all errors.

For Aaron

ERROR AND THE ACADEMIC SELF

> *I would like to write a book on the scholar's way of life.*
> —Friedrich Nietzsche, *Wir Philologen*

INTRODUCTION

THE PURSUIT OF ERROR:
PHILOLOGY, RHETORIC, AND THE HISTORY
OF SCHOLARSHIP

I do not think I have ever published anything that did not have an error in it. Typos have crept in and escaped proofreading. Miscitations and mistranslations have refused correction. Facts and judgments have, at times, seemed almost willfully in opposition to empirical evidence or received opinion. It is the duty of readers, so it seems, to catch such errors. Referees for publishers and, after them, book reviewers often begin well and well-meaningly. But praise soon shatters into pedantry, and reports and reviews will often end with catalogs of broken lines and phrases: errata uncaught by editor or author, blots on the reputation of the scholar's knowledge or critical acumen.

I'm not alone. All creatures of the academic life subject themselves to such reviewing, and most practice it themselves. To have been savaged and to savage, whether veiled behind the scrim of the anonymous report or displayed in the full acknowledgment of the printed byline, are the marks of my business: the rite of passage and the passing of one's rights. It is as if I've led an erroneous life, as if what should be toted up on the pages of the book of judgment—or, more prosaically, in annual decanal salary reviews—are not achievements but mistakes. We live, in the academy, by blunder.

What are the sources of this life, the origins of such a business? This book began as both a cultural-historical and an autotherapeutic answer to this question. Its working claim is that the origins of error—as an ideology, a practice, a defining mode of scholarly identity—lie in the nexus of the editorial, the academic, and the political that has shaped textual adventures from the Renaissance to the present. My argument is that the professionalization of literary study took shape through such encounters with the erroneous: more specifically, through detailed engagements with the classical inheritance of rhetoric and philology. But my conception of error embraces both the erring and the errant (the Latin word "*errare*" means, of course, "to wander"). Being wrong is also about being displaced, about wandering, dissenting, emigrating, and alienating. The professionalization of the scholar, and, in turn, the pose of the vernacular rhetorician and philologist, was a means by which émigrés, exiles, dissenters, and the socially estranged gained private worth and public legitimacy. This is a book, therefore, about the academic's search for institutional and intellectual belonging. By defining a rhetoric of error in professional self-shaping, by recalibrating the impact of canonical writers and readers, and by resuscitating long-neglected but historically vital early scholars, this book hopes to illuminate the texture of academic culture and the formation of university disciplines. Indeed, it hopes to show how scholarship itself can be a form of personal illumination—an encounter with the sublime, a romance of reading.

I have framed my history of scholarship through specialized case studies of its major methodologies and moments. The chapters of this study, though distinct in focus, should be read in sequence as detailing a trajectory of intellectual development—my own, as well as my subject's. Thus I begin at the beginning of our modern academic culture, with the humanists of Renaissance England and the origins of textual production in print. Errata sheets become, I argue in my first chapter, the sites of authorial self-definition, the places where the writer poses as his own best reader, where confessions of mistake and acts of emendation establish intellectual authority. There is both a poetics and a politics to the erratum in the early modern period. The academic and literary life in print becomes here both a performance and a defense, and my review of its foundational activities (textual criticism, lexicography, epistolary writing, lyric poetry) hopes to contribute to a new account of the self-fashioning long seen as the defining idiom of Renaissance discourse.

"Agnosco fateor" (I admit I was wrong), wrote Guillaume Budé to Erasmus, and I think that I have never been so pressured to admit my wrongs as in my work in Anglo-Saxon literature. My chapter on Old English studies seeks to understand this discipline historically as shaped by scholarly preoccupations with the right and the wrong—but with a difference, for the telos of Old English literary studies has, since its own origins, been not so much the crisis of correction as the search for the sublime. Philology itself becomes a sublime art: an inquiry into word roots or poetic fragments that can lead to illumination of the personal, the social, the aesthetic. My history of Anglo-Saxon studies—perhaps, more accurately put, a counterhistory—seeks therefore to find a new professional as well as personal place for a field once central but now marginal to literary curricula.[1]

The habits of the Anglo-Saxonist remain rooted in nineteenth-century historical philology, and my next chapter calibrates anew the history of that discipline by meditating on its greatest fictional figure of error: George Eliot's Casaubon. Here, I read *Middlemarch* against the *Oxford English Dictionary* (and Casaubon against that dictionary's great instaurator, James A. H. Murray) to expose the errancies and attainments of the Victorian construction of the scholar's life. Both works become essays in authorship. They voice ideals of canonicity and literary history. They are both novels of the philological imagination, and my double reading of these works—fractured into alphabetically arranged subsections miming my own Casaubonian emprise—presents new evidence for understanding both the idioms and ideologies of error in the century that formed many of our scholarly practices.

It was Henry James who said that one had to be an American to "relish the inner essence" of *Middlemarch*, and my following chapter rises to that challenge. What does it mean to be an American philologist? My answer is, in part, that it means to be a rhetorician. Philology and rhetoric go hand in hand in the American tradition: at times competing and at times complementary disciplines that shape the university study of language and literature and construct ideals of academic life. America becomes, in these discourses, a country of tropes, of metaphors and metonymies, of people who have traveled far to find an ever-receding academic home. To read as an American, then, is to read rhetorically, and at this chapter's heart lies a claim for American philology as primarily a rhetorical enterprise and, in turn, for the importance of that philology to the growth of literary theory. But the American rhetorical and philological condition is an *ardent* one—that word shows up repeatedly throughout our history—and what concerns me, in the end, is the emotional condition of the scholar, the burning of a memory or a mission.

My vision of American rhetorical philology thus centers on estrangements: word and meaning, scholar and home, past and present. In my concluding chapters, on the émigré philologist and postwar academic life, I take these tropes literally. Erich Auerbach has long stood for me (and recently for many of my peers) as the quintessential émigré intellectual. His *Mimesis* compiles tales of wandering and exile, homecoming and alienation, parents and children. Its seeming random choices of great literary works and isolated passages constitute a controlling narrative about the scholar's place in a suspicious world. Criticism becomes political allegory. Scenes of domestic harmony fracture into dispersal. And the women of *Mimesis* (Euryklea, Eve, Fortunata, and all the way to Virginia Woolf) become figures for an exile's vision of a new Lady Philology.

But for all these fascinations with the past, I end with a vision of the future. The 1957 science fiction film *Forbidden Planet* becomes, in my purview, a fantastic allegory of the émigré academic. What better way to express the alienation of the scholar than to place him among aliens or even to transform him into something of an alien himself? The movie's Dr. Morbius (sole survivor or evil collaborator?) appears as a caricature of the European philologist: dark, brooding, goateed, and, in the word of that movie's contemporary novelization, "Oriental." This movie forms a perfect capstone to my study of the wanderings of scholars, the mistakes of literary and linguistic masters, the pitfalls of the paternalism that has controlled the academic life.

Taken in tandem, these studies script out an erratic history of my profession. They share a concern with all the things that have preoccupied me for the past two decades: etymology, memory, the sublime, identity (in particular, Jewish identity). The autobiographical quality of criticism possesses me, as it possessed the writers that I read here. But so, too, has the historical. My work has always seemed to focus on traditions on the cusp of change: shifts, say, from late antiquity to early medieval culture, from Anglo-Saxon to post-Conquest England, from medieval to Renaissance. So, too, these chapters stand as essays in transition, as encounters with the makings of professional modernity made through rhetoric and philology. When scholars wish to assert their modern status, when they wish to distance themselves from the past and look forward to a future, they do so through appeals to verbal discipline. They use the resources of historical philology to reinscribe themselves in the narratives of historical understanding, and they use rhetoric both to appeal to the antiquity of its undertaking and to define the task of future work. Each of my major scholars does so. They stand as the self-constructed modern figures for their time—or, by contrast, remain as unreconstructed archetypes of a receding past.

But my project is not wholly personal. It grows out of a larger recent turn to self-reflection in disciplinary scholarship. Histories of academic methodology and practice have come, more and more, to stand as the defining gestures of familiar fields seeking new places in a changing curricular terrain. But there is, in fact, little new here. Philology and rhetoric have been writing and rewriting their own histories since their inception. They are the original self-historicizing disciplines: forms of inquiry that take as their subject the origins and social value of their practice and the relationship of truth to felt opinion or expressive argument. No two disciplines have spent more time trying to determine just what they are—and just what their practitioners do—than philology and rhetoric, and I must give them their time now.

The status of philology has been debated ever since there were philologists; it is the question that defines the field. Conjuring a working definition of the field is the required move of virtually anyone who aspires to the title "philologist." F. A. Wolf may have been the first scholar to define himself as a philologist in modern times when he enrolled at the University of Göttingen in 1777 as "a student of philology."[2] But even Wolf did not define his course of study, save by contrast—he was a student of philology, as opposed to theology—and his claim raised more disciplinary questions than it answered. In fact, questioning and positing the nature of philology constitute the defining rhetorical move for philological discourse itself.

Philology apparently began almost as soon as there were writers to record it. Gregory Nagy suggests that a crisis in grammatical education was perceived as early as Herodotus.[3] The changing nature of the schoolroom, of the place of writing in society, and of the relationships between paternalistic teachers and their students made language and its institutions the subject of early Athenian debate; Herodotus, Plato, and Aristophanes are but the best-known writers who weighed in on the discussion.

For Nagy, the philological crisis of the fifth century B.C. hinged on the shifts from oral performance to written record. But the complexities of this development—complexities debated by a range of scholars on the early literacy of the Greeks—did not, in fact, bequeath the title *philologus* on anyone. That coinage had to wait until the Hellenistic period, the age of the scholiast and the librarian, the age long associated not with the composition but the copying of the Greek literary heritage. The first philologist, apparently, was Eratosthenes of Cyrene, the head of the library of Alexandria, and one of his successors, Aristarchus of Samothrace, came to be known not only as a philologue but as a *mantis*, a seer or prophet in his knowledge of poetry. Nagy notes that "in this concept of the seer we see again the nostalgia of philology for the Muses of inspired performance"—in other words, a scripting out of the disjunctions between oral and written modes of communication and the role of the philologist in somehow adjudicating among them (p. 47). But in this title I see, too, the iconography of the philologist: the sense of intellectual identity keyed to a vatic, charismatic personage, a sense of the philologist not as a dry-as-dust pedant but as a thrilling, pedagogical performer.

All histories of philology are possessed by what it means to study language in its literary, social, and philosophical contexts. Roberta Frank, in one of the most lively of a recent spate of philological apologias, recalls no less a scholar than Francis Bacon crying, in 1620: "down with antiquities and citations or supporting evidence from texts; . . . down with everything philological."[4] And she goes on to note that the modern history of the discipline has similarly been marked by such denigrations—yet denigrations only to be met by praises and revivals. It is as if philology is something always in a state of redefinition and resuscitation, a profession that inherently looks back to its great founders and laments its present decline. One of the earliest impulses of the German university philologists of the early nineteenth century was to write the history of their own discipline—or, perhaps it is better to say, their prehistory. An interest in the Greek and Roman theories of language (*Sprachwissenschaft, Sprachphilosophie*) gave rise to a spate of publications seeking to ground current practice in a deep historical inheritance. As early as 1808—barely a decade after Sir William Jones established the grammatical relationship of Sanskrit to the ancient European languages and, in consequence, sired the modern discipline of comparative philology—Friedrich Schlegel sought to legitimate this study as a science by associating it with earlier, institutionally sanctioned fields of inquiry. "The structure or comparative grammar of languages furnishes as certain a key of their genealogy as the study of comparative anatomy has done to the loftiest branch of natural science."[5] Three-quarters of a century later, the American William Dwight Whitney, professor of comparative philology and Sanskrit at Yale from 1853 until his death in 1894, echoed Schlegel in reminding his readers of how "comparative philology" is grounded, by analogy, in the established science of "comparative anatomy" (and would lead, he notes, to the study of "comparative mythology").[6] And he remarks, too, in an extended peroration to his major and most popular work, *The Life and Growth of Language* (1875), how reflection on the history of the field makes possible a larger conception of the science of language and how the relationships between the classical inheritance of Greek philosophy and the German inheritance of diachronic linguistics make possible the future (in particular, an American university future) for philology itself (pp. 317–19).

The writing of the history of philology is thus as much a part of the philological enterprise as is the history of language itself. Ferdinand de Saussure recognized as much when he began his *Course in General Linguistics* with a brief overview of the history of linguistics.[7] Beginning with grammar and then moving to philology, Saussure narrates a history of language study leading to the accomplishments nineteenth-century comparatists and, later, the Neogrammarians who were his teachers. Ending with a bow to Whitney, Saussure looks ahead to what he labels as the "fundamental problems of general linguistics, which still await a solution today" (p. 5). Roy Harris has perceived that this account contains a "hidden theoretical premise" of the *Course*: that the study of language is a discipline with "an identifiable history."[8] But what it also does is validate Saussure himself as a member of the discipline and, much like Whitney's closing gestures in *The Life and Growth of Language*, looks ahead to the sustaining of a practice fit for university professionals.

If philologists have always queried their profession, so, too, have rhetoricians. "What is rhetoric?" has been the question asked since antiquity. Ever since the Sophists appeared in Athens, debate has flourished on the nature and social function of eloquence. Is rhetoric a discipline, or is it a cover term, concealing a ruse for other things? As Socrates would lead the discussion in Plato's *Gorgias*, the answer to the question lies in whether we conceive of rhetoric as a true art or skill based on knowledge (*techne*), or whether we consider it a knack (*tribe*), a set of tricks acquired by experience (*empeira*).⁹ For Socrates, rhetoric seems a thing quite alien to the Athenian experience. Like writing (whose critique would be the subject matter of the *Phaedrus*), it comes from elsewhere—here, the Sophists are the outsiders. And yet, for all this debate, rhetoric was to form a central place in the *paedaeia* of Greek culture and its later Roman, medieval, and Renaissance inheritors. Just as philology has stood as a cynosure for histories of culture, so, too, rhetoric. George Kennedy, perhaps the leading historian of the discipline has averred: "a history of rhetoric might be thought of as a history of the values of a culture and how these were taught or imposed upon the society."¹⁰ Rhetoric, much like philology, is a self-reflexive and self-historicizing discipline. All its textbooks and discussions, from the *Gorgias*, through Aristotle's *Rhetoric*, through the *Rhetorica ad Herennium* and the works of Cicero, through the medieval *artes* and the Renaissance arts, begin with histories of the field. Such histories, of course, serve as a point of validation for the author. They impress upon the reader or the student the legitimacy of the writer: his alignment with a genealogy of teachers, his great reading, his awareness of the deep past of the discipline. But they also serve as points of validation for the discipline itself. To rephrase Kennedy, the history of rhetoric is something rhetoricians must rehearse in order to articulate the values of their culture and how they were taught or imposed on their own societies.

These self-historical narratives themselves become set pieces of rhetorical discourse. They are, as one recent critic has declared, "rhetorical iterations," fundamentally and inextricably enmeshed in the tropes and turns of the discourse they purport to study.¹¹ There is a pattern to their argument, a formal quality that makes them rhetorical exercises in the epidiectic. The history of rhetoric becomes a trope of rhetoric itself. More pointedly, we might say that when other disciplines engage in (or indulge in) telling their own histories, they reconstitute themselves as a subspecies of rhetoric, for they replay the central question of disciplinary definition: is what you do an art, or is it simply a knack? But they, like rhetoric itself, query the condition of the human as a verbal animal. They retell stories of disciplinary founding in order to remind an audience that they are precisely that: an audience, a community of listeners or readers, attentive to words, and thus members of a social group. Such is the myth of origins that opens Cicero's *De Inventione*, and such, too, is the myth that opens John Quincy Adams's Boylston lectures on rhetoric and oratory at Harvard in 1806. The question, as he puts it, of "whether eloquence is an art, worthy of the cultivation of a wise and virtuous man," is, in the end, really a question not about eloquence but about wisdom and virtue and manhood.[12]

But one may argue that the answers to these question are irrelevant. The construction of academic disciplines may not be keyed to an objective subject of study but to a subjective narrative of disciplinary maintenance. Rhetoric and philology become the paradigms for such self-reflective inquiry. Recounting the history of the field effectively justifies the field; anecdotalizing the experience of its experts is the means by which one makes oneself an expert.[13] One of the theses of my study is that academic culture—what Nietzsche called "the scholar's life [*die Lebensweise der Gelehrten*]"—is about the individual.[14] Histories of fields are told as histories of the self. Philological inquiries into the origins of words or the establishment of texts reveal the motives of the scholar. The rhetorical persuasions of an audience remain, when all is said, attempts at self-persuasion. Histories of disciplines are therefore histories of the disciplined, and it is no coincidence that memory is central to the fields of rhetoric and philology. *Memoria* was one of the key parts of rhetorical education, as it trained the orator or writer in the arts of organizing arguments and evidence. Mnemonotechnics—that elaborate system of constructing artificial aids to memorizing and displaying complex narratives—often hinged on coming up with what one might call parallel narratives: stories that could be used as templates for remembering information or a sequence of events.[15] But, as the rhetoricians knew, the best examples come from individual experience. The author of the *Rhetorica ad Herennium*, a textbook that would teach its students for over fifteen hundred years, put it this way: "When we see in everyday life things that are petty, ordinary, and banal, we generally fail to remember them, because the mind is not being stirred by anything novel or marvelous. But if we see or hear something exceptionally base, dishonorable, extraordinary, great, unbelievable, or laughable, that we are likely to remember for a long time. Accordingly, things immediate to our eye or ear we commonly forget; incidents of our childhood [*pueritia*] we often remember best."[16] Memory, I contend, is not just a subset of the verbal arts; it is its constitutive subject.

But what is it that we remember? During the past two decades, literary theorists have chosen to recall the practices of rhetoric and philology not simply to enhance an argument or to evoke a sense of erudition but to validate their study and themselves. They legitimate a professional practice, or, more precisely, they find ways of arguing that such a practice is, in fact, professional. Paul de Man, for example, in a clutch of highly influential essays, argued for "a return to philology" and a reinvigoration of rhetoric.[17] But his strategy, especially in the philology polemic, was not so much argumentative as it was memorial. What he remembers is the Harvard classroom of the 1950s, the distinguished teacher (Reuben Brower), the "personal experience." "I have," he wrote, "never known a course by which students were so transformed."[18] It is but a short step back from this appealing reminiscence to the philologist of Alexandria, that *mantis* of poetry. Recall again Gregory Nagy's comment: "in this concept of the seer we see again the nostalgia of philology for the Muses of inspired performance." De Man's vision of the return to philology is, in these terms, a return to a privileged past, a form of nostalgia that lies at the heart of the rhetoric of philology.

Perhaps the most startling of such acts of philological *memoria* I have come across is that by René Wellek in his contribution to a volume on the making of the field of comparative literature.[19] Born in Prague in 1905, he studied there and in Munich before seeking teaching positions in the States. Eventually, he settled at Yale, where he created the Department of Comparative Literature, wrote a highly influential series of books (most notably *The Theory of Literature*), supervised scores of dissertations, and died, virtually at his desk, in 1995. He was so much the defining figure in the field he could be parodied by David Lodge as Arthur Kingfisher in the book *Small World*—the Fisher King of literature, the King Arthur of comparison. When Wellek told his own story, it was not about power and control but about alienation and exile. Coming to the United States in the late 1920s to further his education and get some teaching experience, he showed up in Princeton and then got a job interview at Smith College.

> I wrote a letter to the chairman of the German Department at Smith, Mr. Heinrich Mensel, and was invited to present myself for an interview. I took the train to Northampton, which was then still a station stop. When I left the train Mr. Mensel saw me getting out and walked up to me with his hands stretched out and said (I swear that these were his first words): "I see you are not a Jew." He then

took me on a short tour of the college and finally to the office of the president, Mr. William Allan Neilson. There a contract was laid out for me to sign, which I did, of course, happy to have a job for the following year. If I had been a Jew, Mr. Mensel would have taken me on a tour of the campus but sent me back to New York or wherever without calling on President Neilson. (p. 3)

The powerful irony of this story is that this is precisely the problem not for Wellek but for the later generation of scholars. Indeed, one must consider whether Wellek's story is itself really a narrative of the profession as a whole. The statement "I see you are not a Jew" becomes the statement about literary study generally: in the sense not just that there are Jews and non-Jews but that the act of reading and interpretation is applied to both the person and the text. The young Wellek here emerges from the station as a readable text, and it is the responsibility of his interviewer to interpret what he sees. It is not even so much that, as Wellek says, "If I had been a Jew" but rather "if I had *appeared* to be a Jew."

Wellek's tale stands as a nodal point for much of what concerns me in this book: the idea of the socially defined other, what one might call the larger notion of the *juif errant*. For Erich Auerbach (whose Jewishness exiled him from Germany, first to Istanbul and then to America), tales of exile and return would not just characterize his own life but constitute the spine of his definitive work, *Mimesis*. This is a volume all about the ways in which we read accounts of exile and return: beginning with Odysseus's return to Ithaca at the close of the *Odyssey*, paired with the sacrifice of Isaac from Genesis, and ending with the enislement of the Ramsay family in Woolf's *To the Lighthouse*, paired with Proust's *Remembrance of Things Past*. Chapters with titles such as "The Interrupted Supper" make us ask how many suppers were interrupted, how many people forced to leave at a moment's notice. And in the final chapter, when Auerbach turns to Virginia Woolf, the first lines of the quoted passage read: "And even if it isn't fine tomorrow, . . . it will be another day."[20]

These are the stories of the exile, of the scholar enisled or away from home. As such, they are tales of error. Narratives of scholarship seem always to take error as their subject. They correct mistakes of others, but they also expose the ways in which the wrong, the errant, the displaced are central to the makings of professional identity. *Corrigere* in Latin means to draw a straight line. And so the inquiries of rhetoric and philology possess themselves of metaphors of straightness and deviation, of fixity and error. Rhetorical manuals since Cicero have exposed the etymology of "method" itself in these terms. The Greek *methodos* (literally, "about the way") became the Latin *via et ratio*, "the way and reason."[21] Rhetorical inquiry became an ordered way or method toward a proper goal, and later writers were not loath to moralize this idiom. The metaphor of geographical direction became a form of moral directive. The Latin term for what we think of as an academic discipline, *ars*, was defined over and over again as a set of rules offering a clear method and leading to truth. As Boethius would put it at the beginning of the sixth century, in his manual of dialectic *De Topicis differentiis*, the study of his discipline points the debater to the path of truth (*viam . . . veritatis*), to paths of discovery (*inveniendi vias*) (pp. 106–8).

There stands behind these idioms of error and correction, of rectitude and method, an overarching moral goal. One finds it everywhere. One opens Saussure's *Course in General Linguistics* to see the history of linguistics moving along similar *inveniendi vias*. "The science which has grown up around linguistic facts passed through three successive phases before coming to terms with its one and only true object of study [*son véritable et unique objet*]." The search for truth here is the search for the true object of linguistic study, for the truth of the discipline. Such a search moves along the byways of error and correction. Grammar begins the history of language study, and its sole aim is, as Saussure sees it, to provide "rules which distinguish between correct and incorrect forms [*à donner des règles pour distinguer les formes correctes des formes incorrectes*]." Next came philology, whose goal is to correct, or establish, interpret, and comment upon texts (*fixer, interpréter, commenter les texts*).[22] Then, third, there arose the practice of comparative philology, beginning with Sir William Jones's discovery of the grammatical relationships between Sanskrit and the European languages, moving through the systematic work of German scholars, and leading ultimately to the Neogrammarians. But Saussure's history here, as well, is a history of error: "The first mistake [*La première erreur*] made by the comparative philologists was one which contains the seeds of all their other mistakes. Their investigations, which were in any case limited to the Indo-European languages, show a failure to inquire into the significance of the linguistic comparisons they established and the connections they discovered" (p. 3; p. 16).

And he goes on: "An exclusively comparative approach of this kind brings with it a whole series of mistaken notions [*un ensemble de conceptions erronés*]" (p. 4; p. 17). Comparative philology, traditionally practiced, with its attentions to sound laws, its fascination with phonological correspondences, its preoccupation with reconstructing etymologies has, in the end, "no basis in reality." The Neogrammarians, Saussure concludes, went far in correcting these mistakes of emphasis, but, even for them, "At the same time there emerged a realization of the errors and inadequacies of the concepts associated with philology and comparative grammar [*Du même coup on comprit combien étaient erronés et insuffisantes les idées de la philologie et de la grammaire comparée*]" (p. 5; p. 19).

Saussure's story of the disciplines of language is a story of error and correction.[23] Reared in the Neogrammarian environment of the 1870s, he is acutely conscious of the limitations of his art and yet looks forward to a time when a "linguistic science" will emerge to resolve "the fundamental problems of general linguistics." For Friedrich Nietzsche, too, also working in the philologically heady 1870s, the discipline is a discipline of error—yet, for him, it is an error so deep as to be uncorrectable. The prototypical philologist, he states, is not the scientist of language but the proofreader.[24]

Nietzsche's own bitter history of philology finds itself scattered in the set of aphoristic fragments he assembled for his great, unwritten book *Wir Philologen*. This brilliant, wild, and at times clearly crazy collection of thoughts has long been both denigrated and invoked in academic wars about the academic life.[25] Trained as a classical philologist, granted a university professorship, publishing on the arcana of Greek texts, Nietzsche fell from philological grace after Ulrich von Willamowiz-Möllendorf savaged his *Birth of Tragedy* in a review that pinpointed every factual mistake. *Wir Philologen* bristles with condemnatory rebuttals. To the phenomenon of self-historizing in the discipline, Nietzsche retorts: "Nothing can be learned from talk about philology, when it comes from philologists. It is the purest rubbish" (5[125]). The history of the field is full of "the most nauseating erudition; slothful, passive indifferent; timid submission" (5[149]). "It is cripples of the intellect who found their hobbyhorse in verbal quibbling" (7[5]). A list of "Consequences of philology" ticks off the following: "Arrogant expectations; philistinism; superficiality; overrating of reading and writing; Alienation from the people and the needs of the people." It concludes: "Task of philology: to disappear" (5[145]).

Is there anything more here than rant? Certainly William Arrowsmith thought so, as he presented this collection of materials in English translation to reflect on his own quarrels with a modern philological profession. Arrowsmith makes an important point about the attack on Nietzsche, and he does so in a manner that reflects on my own interests in this book. His first point is that the *error philologicus* lies in the conviction that knowledge of linguistic detail or historical fact alone is enough both to make and criticize and argument. "A thesis like Nietzsche's—a large, intuitive, esthetic insight, addressed finally to esthetic experience—cannot be defeated by showing errors of fact in the argument."[26] What Arrowsmith calls the "*mis*application or *over*application of philological principles" leads only to pedantry. "There are," he avers, "after all, more important things than accuracy—there is life, for instance" (p. 9).

Mine is a book, then, about the relationships of accuracy to life: relationships between the aims of scholarship and the experiences of the scholar, between the poetics of error and the politics of institutional belonging. Some still hold that academic scholarship should be the search for truth and that our job should be to purge texts of corruptions and strip criticism of its errors. And yet, when we review the slips, errata, and defenses, when we read the tales of errant and estranged and see how disciplines of language seek, perhaps in vain, to represent the world we live in, we are left not with claims for truth but with admissions of mistake. The life of scholarship has, from its origins, been immured in the pains of penmanship and the *errori de la stampa*. Little rides, Nietzsche noted, on a correctly emended author (5[168]). It is the admission of error that stands as the mark of the professional. As Thomas Wyatt put it, in the chronicle of his defense against treason: "I dare warrante ye shall fynde mysreportinge and mysunderstandinge." We are always lost on the byways of the text, and any claims for an approach to truth or certitude must be left to misperceiving judges who claim correctness as the only virtue and find no lies in the proof sheets of our passion.

But then again, I could be wrong.

> *Agnosco, fateor.*
> —Guillaume Budé, letter to Erasmus, May 1, 1516

CHAPTER ONE

ERRATA:
MISTAKES AND MASTERS IN THE EARLY MODERN BOOK

Over twenty years ago, in a chapter of his *Renaissance Self-Fashioning*, Stephen Greenblatt addressed what he called "the word of God in an age of mechanical reproduction."[1] Alluding to the title of Walter Benjamin's famous essay, Greenblatt argued that the printing press made possible a new debate on scripture and power in early Renaissance England.[2] William Tyndale's New Testament in English had appeared in 1526, and his Old Testament in 1530.[3] Together with the many polemics these publications spawned—the responses of Thomas More, the ripostes of Tyndale, and the myriad royal proclamations seeking to control the printing, reading, and disseminating of books in the age of Henry VIII—these volumes contributed to what Greenblatt called "the magical power of the Word." The Tyndale Bible formed, at least in part, "a turning point in human history," not just through the availability of scripture in a printed English book (though that itself was a major accomplishment) but through Tyndale's exposing the *rhetorical* quality of holy writ: its power to persuade, its place in analysis and argument, in short, its new role in what Greenblatt calls "the seizure of power" by the movement of religious reform.[4]

So much since *Renaissance Self-Fashioning* has been written on the early printed book, and on the nexus of print, politics, and power in the English Renaissance, that it must seem temerity to add another chapter. For all its own reformist critical rhetoric, Greenblatt's book is as celebratory as Elizabeth Eisenstein's contemporary study, *The Printing Press as an Agent of Change*.[5] Both see the story of the book as a story of the text triumphant: the spread of literacy, the dissemination of knowledge for its own sake, the facilitation of empirical science, the spatialization of our habits of thought. But much has changed in the two decades since their publication. The celebratory model of the printing press has given way to a fragmented, materialist, and skeptical dismantling of the *grand récit*. The technodeterminist approach (that the very technology of printing effected social change) associated with the work of Eisenstein and her intellectual forbears is largely gone. Print is now understood to be not simply a technology but a form of social behavior located in encounters with the published word that define both a public life and a private subjectivity.[6] Those that have practiced what in France became known as *l'histoire du livre* stressed the reconstruction of distinctive moments in book history. The items of booksellers' inventories, the lists found in wills, and the acts of physically sitting down with books all have contributed to a larger, context-bound conception of the act of reading as more than the absorption of printed information.[7]

But in addition to locating the impact of the printed word, these researches have challenged just what "print" itself may mean. As Adrian Johns has put it, in his recent massive and revisionary *Nature of the Book*, we need to ask anew "just what printing *was*."[8] Rather than denoting a specific device or a definable social habit, "print" has been taken to have meaning only in relationship to something else. Printing is anything that differs from handwriting. It connotes any form of verbal reproduction, in Michael Warner's words, "relieved from the pressure of the hand."[9] Such a relational definition has deep historical importance. Early printed books were rarely distinguished from handmade documents. The typefaces of books made in the first half-century of printing were themselves modeled on manuscript hands.[10] If Johns compels us to ask what printing was, we may ask now just what a book *is*, when anyone can be a desktop publisher and when computer-generated fonts and laser printers can make any document look like anything from Gutenberg to Garamond. And, of course, we may ask whether all this preoccupation with the printed word remains simply a form of academic nostalgia at a time when more and more transmitted information is read off screens rather than pages. Is our interest in the history of the book conditioned by our sense of living at the end of that history?

This chapter seeks an answer to these questions in the history of error. Instead of moving, once again, to an account of print and progress, it argues for a story grounded in mistake. The history of the early book is fraught with error. Indeed, the story of the Tyndale Bible, Greenblatt's masterplot, is a tale of accusations of inaccuracy: failures of translation, faults uncaught at the press, errata that Tyndale himself sought to correct. Behind the list of "errours committed in the prynting" that closes the 1526 New Testament lies a hitherto unwritten history of the erratum. For the errata sheet, in the late fifteenth and early sixteenth centuries, records more than slips of typesetting; it details errors in doctrine, dialect, or usage. At its most complex and self-conscious, the errata sheet stands as the site of humanist erudition and early modern subjectivity. It is the place where the past is publicly brought into line with the present, where errors of all kinds could be confessed and corrected. To explore the early history of these sheets is to explore the loci of authority and action that make academic life both a performance and a defense. Together with a set of broader editorial and literary practices that I address here—humanist textual criticism, early lexicography, epistolary friendship, and the vernacular love-lyric—these early printed texts contribute to a new account of the self-fashioning sought by modern scholars of the Renaissance.

Though I attend, in part, to individual errors of the early printers and to the techniques of collation, comparison, and critical decision that went into the production of editions, I am primarily concerned here with the *rhetoric* of error and editorship and with the stories told through prefaces, errata sheets, and correspondence about the making— or mismaking—of books. The humanist account of error is invariably temporal: it situates the production of the book in a specific historical moment, charts its progress across time, and then invites the reader to locate it (and the reader's own act of reading) on a temporally defined continuum. The story of correction and the artifact of the errata sheet historicize the book, much as the humanist practice of philology historicized the text. For, by acknowledging the historical difference between text and reader, the humanist critic not only recognized linguistic change or corruption of copies but also understood that the completed work was not an autonomous object but a counter in the historical story of its making and reception. The early book is always a work in progress and in process, a text intruded upon for emendation, a text that invites the correction of the reader. There is nothing like an errata sheet to prompt the reader to seek out yet more errata—that is, nothing like the admission of *some* errors to provoke us to believe that the work is *full* of errors. Moreover, the need to narrativize the story of such errors—to offer up a personal history of detection and correction—makes the true subject of the early humanist book not so much its content but the complex relationships between textual and political fealty that write the history of its own production.[11]

The errata sheet stands not as a static marker of uncaught mistakes but as a placeholder in the ongoing narratives of bookmaking, and book reading, themselves. Like many of the paratexts of early print—the prefaces, notes, correspondence, and occasional handwritten comments in the margins of the book—errata sheets illustrate how an early printed book was used by the first ones to see it. Such sheets were often guides to reading itself. Several early books survive with handwritten corrections drawn from those sheets: illustrations of rereading, in which owner's pen corrected printer's faults.[12] But, more broadly, the study of the errata sheet and of the rhetoric of error also helps us understand the ways in which the disciplines of editorial review, legal judgment, political control, and religious devotion shared an idiom and imagery. In an age when the practice of confession came under close scrutiny (especially in early Reformation England), errata sheets and their accompanying paratexts became the places where the urge to confess could still find a voice and where the seeking of forgiveness found its listener not among the booths of the church but in the stalls of the bookseller.

Before beginning with the book, it is important to recall that the history of textual correction does not begin with print. Almost as soon as there were writers, fears of error motivated the control of textual dissemination. Roman authors, in particular, were acutely aware of the failings of scribes and the foibles of booksellers. Martial, quite specifically and at great length, could praise the careful scribe but could equally lament a careless one.[13] In later times, the copying of sacred scriptures often became the occasion for reflections on the scribal art and, as a consequence, the fear of error. Cassiodorus, in the sixth century, considered scribes the bearers of God's word, and he thought of writing (especially the copying of the Bible) as the highest of callings.[14] The twelfth-century poet Baudri of Bourgeuil, in a set of Latin poems clearly influenced by Martial, reflected on the need for accurate copies of his texts (and his invectives against faulty scribes are as vicious as anything by the earlier Roman poet).[15] Petrarch's letters, in the fourteenth century, are famous for their complaints of incorrect texts and unauthorized copies,[16] while, at the close of that century, Chaucer developed what may well be called a poetics of correction in his thematic attentions to the scribal culture of his day. All his work, he fears, is "subject to correction," not just because it may be erroneous in fact or doctrine but because it has been mangled by the hands of others. At the close of *Troilus and Criseyde*, he fears the mismetering and misspelling of his poetry by scribes of different dialect regions or different levels of ability. And in his famous "Words to Adam Scriveyn," he laments, almost godlike, the errancies of his aptly named and careless copyist, whom Chaucer curses unless he "wryte more trewe":

> So ofte adaye I mot thy werk renewe
> It to correcte and eke to rubbe and scrape.[17]

All this did not change overnight with print. Early printed books can be as much unique, individual artifacts as the manuscripts that had preceded them. Corrections in midpressrun, broken types, resettings and additions, changes in type and paper stock have textual-critical value, as they can reveal a book's relationship to the copy text or to the textual traditions of a different work. A close attention to such changes, too, throws into confusion traditional distinctions between such phenomena as error and variant. When is a printed book representative of an edition or an issue? And what role do errata sheets—and readerly engagement with them—play in the definition of just what we have when we hold an early printed book in our hands?[18]

Print enables publicly what was done privately before. It makes possible not the fixity of the text but the participation of the reading public in the act of correction. Though errata sheets enable readers to correct their personal copies, they also make readers active players in the game of textual confession. They serve to establish authorial authority through the acknowledgment of error. In the process, they refashion the relationship of author to reader along new templates of power. The writer stands as pleading witness to a knowing judge, as humble subject to a king or patron, as appellant student to a learned master. These are the metaphorical relationships of reading, and they govern both a rhetoric and a poetics of errata in the early modern period.

From the start, errata sheets recorded more than typos. The earliest account we have of one comes from the atelier of Sweynheim and Pannarz.[19] Library catalogs record, for their edition of Lactantius published on October 29, 1465, two concluding pages of the volume titled "Lactantii Firmiani errata quibus ipse deceptus est per fratrem Antonium Randesem theologicum collecta et exarata sunt" (The errata of Lactantius Firmianus, which he himself did not catch, have been gathered and written down by brother Antonio Randesi, theologian).[20] Other kinds of errors fill the sheets of early Italian printers. Francesco Bonaccorsi published an edition of the *Laude* of Jacopone da Todi in September 1490 that included not just a list of typographical mistakes but also those of dialect and historical idiom, in the words of Brian Richardson, an index that "had a threefold function as a glossary, an errata, and a kind of apparatus criticus."[21] Early editions of the works of Boccaccio, Sannazaro, Dante, and other Italian authors often contained, in addition to "errori de la stampa," those of dialect and usage,[22] while classical texts used the errata sheet as the occasion to review, reedit, and reprimand earlier editions or defective manuscripts. A Horace *Opera* printed by Antonio Miscomini in Florence in 1482 has on its last two pages the *errore* to be found in the edition and the commentary. Here, what is important is that these are not tipped-in extra sheets but an integral part of the foliation of the book. The errors noted are not printer's mistakes but instead substantive emendations to the text. Errata sheets become the place where textual criticism is done—not in the body of the poetry itself or in the commentary.[23]

Similarly, in the *Miscellanea* of Politian (1489), also published by Miscomini, the final pages of "Emendationes" offer up not only corrections to the printed text but also new readings based, apparently, on fresh consultation with the manuscripts of Politian's sources. Comments, for example, on the Greek text of Callimachus betray Politian's concern (voiced in his letters and in the later remarks to his readers at the close of this volume) with the proper accents in the Greek. His final, general remarks bear noting, too, as statements of the larger relationships of will and intention in the making of the book and the establishing of author-audience association:

> If any accents in the Greek words should be missing or wrongly written, let the well-educated restore or emend them according to their judgment. But if, reader, you find in addition to these errors, anything which escaped our hasty eyes, you will emend those also according to your judgment. Nor will you, whoever you are, consider that ours which is not quite right [i.e., don't think those things that are not right are ours]. Rather, you will ascribe all errors either to the printers or the editors [*curatoribus*]. For if you believe me to be responsible for any error herein, then I will believe you have nothing in your heart.[24]

Here, under the heading "Emendationes," are emended not just textual but personal relationships. The author offers up avowals of diligence and good faith and an invitation—or a threat—to readers for continued emendation *pro iudicio*.

By the beginning of the sixteenth century, errata sheets had become commonplace in European books. They are the stuff of scholarship in Latin volumes—Aldus Manutius's famous printing of the *Hypnerotomachia Poliphili* (1499), for example, has a full page of errata—and the markers of interpretation in vernacular ones as well. Paolo Trovato has detailed the ways in which errata sheets were used in Italian language books to correct differences in dialect or even to emend the text. They show up under titles such as "Errata corrige," "Errori de la Stampa," "Errori notabili fatti nel stampare," and the like. They stood, as Trovato illustrates, as invitations for the reader to correct the text. "Errori de la stampa" guided the corrections *con la penna*. Any other corrections could be made, in the language of one mid-sixteenth-century Italian book, *a la discrezione de lettore*, the equivalent of Poliziano's invitation three-quarters of a century earlier, for readers to emend *pro iudicio*.[25]

In England, the errata sheet becomes the stage for claiming authorial fidelity not just to text and type but to ruler and doctrine. There is evidence that, by the early 1520s, English printers were alert to the possibilities of typographical error. Of course, such sensitivities had been voiced half a century before by William Caxton, who had claimed that he himself had "dylygently ouerseen" (i.e., proofread) the text of the revised, new edition of the *Canterbury Tales* of 1484 and who had similarly invoked John Skelton as overseer of the *Eneydos* of 1490.[26] Yet, from Caxton's shop or from that of his successor, Wynkyn de Worde, there do not appear to be anything approaching the errata sheets or lists of emendations or corrections that were coming to be commonplace at Continental printers. Only with the next generation is something like this European attention to error voiced. John Constable's *Epigrammata*, printed by Berthelett in 1520, has a letter from the printer mentioning the possibility of errors being introduced.[27] By 1523 proofreading had become so central a part of the English press shop, that the printer Richard Pynson needed define its task in an indenture between himself and John Palsgrave.[28]

Perhaps the earliest sustained engagement with errata in the English book, however, lies with Thomas More and the printing of a range of doctrinal texts he published in the 1520s and 1530s. The *Responsio ad Lutherum* (*STC* 18089), printed by Pynson in 1523, has an errata sheet appended to the second issue of the work.[29] The *Supplication of Souls* of 1529 (*STC* 18092, 18093), printed by Rastell, had added errata sheets in both of its editions.[30] And the 1533 *Apology* (*STC* 18078), also printed by Rastell, offers an errata sheet, followed by another four pages of errata for the second part of the *Confutation of Tyndale* printed with it.[31] These texts have been explored in detail, most recently by the editors of the Yale edition of More's works, and there is some consensus that the role of More himself in their proofreading is debatable. The errata often list simple typographical errors. On occasion, there are substantive corrections made for sense or grammar. But what is significant, especially in the case of the *Supplication*, is the fact that the second edition of this work leaves uncorrected "dozens of . . . misprints" from the first edition. Are we dealing with the author reading proof or, in the case of the second text of the 1529 printing of the *Supplication*, what the Yale editors call "a careless compositor [who] hastily proofread to produce the brief and inadequate list of errata"?[32]

In the case of the *Dialogue Concerning Heresies*, however, it is clear that More himself was very much involved in reading proof and offering corrections to his work. In the editions of 1529 (STC 18084) and 1531 (STC 18085), substantive changes are made in the errata sheets, titled in both editions "The fawtys escaped in the pryntynge." Space does not permit an extensive engagement with the myriad alterations More made to his texts (indeed, the discussion of the textual condition of this work takes up nearly forty pages in the Yale edition).[33] But what should be pointed out, especially, is that More used the "fawtys" pages to correct what he perceived to be doctrinal error in his text. For example, the phrase, "nothing faut worthy / only to enface that" is corrected in the errata sheet to "nothing blame worthy / only to deface & enfame that." The phrase "pleasure and ellys" becomes "plesure / where wha[n] and wherfore god shal worke his myracles / and ellys."[34] The Yale editors point out, as well, that More made substantive corrections from the 1529 to the 1531 edition, and, furthermore, when corrections in both editions needed to be made, More had cancel slips inserted in the texts.[35] What is also significant is that the 1531 edition occasionally perpetuates some of the errors, typographical and doctrinal, of the 1529 edition—errors that were noted in the errata sheet to the 1529 edition. As the Yale editors put it, "The fact that the text of the 1531 perpetuates mistakes in passages like these which deal with important matters of doctrine raises the possibility that More did not proofread the entire second edition as carefully as he did the first, in which the errors were emended on the errata sheet" (p. 571).

These corrections do more than nuance an argument. They call attention to the authority of More's authorship itself, the need for the writer to oversee the publication of his work. But the main motive that prompted this scrupulous proofreading was the theological purpose of the *Dialogue*. Calibrated as a refutation of Protestant doctrine in the late 1520s, the *Dialogue* takes as its very theme the problem of error. In its central character, the Messenger, "More creates a composite picture of the layman who is tempted to break from the ancient oral traditions of the church and accept the Protestant idea that all doctrine and practices of the church must be based on the written word of the Bible" (p. 448). Protestant texts, he argues, are "maliciously" printed books, and his own text—submitted, as he states, to "the iudgement of other vertuouse & connynge men" before publication—seeks to avoid the problem of the wanton or corrupt book of Protestant belief. One of the central images, too, of the *Dialogue* is the issue of "ocular proof." Bad words blind the eyes, and the poor benighted Messenger of the book takes what he has heard rather than what he has read. In an argument against *sola scriptura* in Protestant doctrine (i.e., the notion that the reading of scripture alone is enough to establish doctrine), More makes a claim for the importance of getting words right. But the larger point is that More's Messenger is not so much a reader as a listener. Much of what he knows comes from what he has heard, and More defines this rough and unverifiable knowledge as "hearsay." What you hear is not always what is right. "For here may a man se that mysse vnderstandynge maketh mysse reportynge" (p. 449). Thus More advocates "ocular proof," a conception of understanding keyed to vision and, as such, correct reading. "Hearsay," then, embraces all the misinformation conveyed through the ear: rumor, false preaching, merry tales, popular belief, and jokes. It is, in short, the mark of "heresy." In the words of John Fisher, whose sermon of 1526 against Martin Luther has been seen as doctrinal kin to More's *Dialogue*, "Heresy . . . is . . . the blyndyng of our sight."[36]

The point of all this doctrinaire fine-tuning, it seems to me, is that More represents himself in the actual publication of his book as his own overseer and his own corrector. Self-correction in the print shop mimes self-correction in the court or church. It represents the public acknowledgment of error. Rhetorically, such an acknowledgment can only reinforce the power of a work such as More's *Dialogue*, itself concerned with problems of misrepresentation. Corrections of the press become a way of rectifying the relationship of word and deed, of sign and substance. It has long been noted that More often puns on the two terms of his argument, "heresy" and "hearsay," and what I suggest is that this wordplay works out, in a thematic way, the very notion of the printer's error that it is the purpose of the overseeing to correct (p. 449).[37] For if the logic of the *Dialogue* is ocular proof and careful reading, what better way to self-enact that logic than to offer up the author as his own best proofreader? And if the fear is that hearsay will lead to heresy, then what greater fear is there than that these two words might all too easily be shifted in the errors of the print shop? Correction is both moral and typographical.

Such multiple attentions to errata govern, too, the *Confutation of Tyndale*, first published in 1532. In the preface to the first part of the volume, More returns to the imagery of sight and blindness in the discussion of heresy. He hopes, throughout the course of his refutation, "to make euery chyld perceyue hys [i.e., Tyndale's] wyly folyes and false craftes . . . wherwyth he fayne wolde & weneth to blynde in such wyse the world." And then he states, reflecting on the great labor such correction needs: "I thynke that no man dowteth but that this worke both hath ben and wyll be some payne and labour to me / and of trouth so I fynde it. But as helpe me god I fynde all my laboure in the wrytynge not halfe so greuouse and paynefull to me, as the tedyouse redynge of theyr blasphemouse heresyes / that wolde god after all my labour done, so that the remembraunce of theyr pestylent errours were araced out of englysshe mennes hertes, and theyr abomynable bookes burned vppe." More then remarks that "deuelysshe heresyes" are so strong in his time that the heretical books are being read privately by people who believe them. But, he then goes on, "it were nede as me semeth that dyuerse wyse & well lerned men sholde set thyr pennys to the boke / whych though they shall not satysfye them that wyll nedes be nought, yet shall they do good to such as fall to these folke of ouersyghte, wenyng y^t theyr new wayes were well." I take this passage to imply that More imagines better readers coming to these heretical books and setting their pens to them—that is, correcting them personally—and that even though such corrections shall not satisfy those readers who believe the heresies, the act may be a good one for those "folke" (i.e., the good readers) who exercise their "ouersyghte" in correcting or emending the books.[38]

This is the language of press correction applied to doctrinal debate. It takes words such as "arace" and "ouersee" and applies them to the discussion of the dissemination of heretical volumes. It also refers to a common practice among early-sixteenth-century readers themselves: the act of personally setting the pen to the book to correct its errors. In the two copies of the *Confutation* I have seen in the Cambridge University Library, individual readers have corrected the text in pen, following the printed errata sheet at the end of the first part of the volume. But only one of these two volumes actually has the errata sheet still in it (H.3.42). In the other volume (Selden 3.135), only a stub of paper remains where the errata sheet has obviously been cut out. Clearly what has happened is that one reader read and corrected the book early, while it still was unbound. Going back and forth from text to errata sheet would have been a simple matter. But for the other reader, the book probably came already bound (or, more likely, the correcting reader of this copy was not its first owner). Flipping back and forth in a tightly bound volume would be difficult, and so the reader simply cut the sheet out, made the corrections from it (probably keeping it at hand), and then discarded it (the sheet being no longer necessary, the errata having been corrected). Such personal corrections are perfectly in keeping with recorded practice. Indeed, Pynson's own instructions (in an explanatory note at the end of the volume) in the second issue of the

Responsio ad Lutherum of 1523 ask the reader to "correct the errata which happened during the printing."[39] And, as Percy Simpson has noted in great detail, throughout the sixteenth and well into the seventeenth century, printers asked their readers to "correcte those faultes" that were itemized in the errata sheets.[40]

Self-correction, then, becomes the impulse for the author and the reader, and the textual phenomenon that stood behind many of More's protestations (and that prompted Greenblatt's analysis, with which I began this chapter) was the publication of the New Testament in William Tyndale's English translation. This signal moment in the history of English letters has not been without its chroniclers. From Edward Arber at the close of the nineteenth century to David Daniell at the end of the twentieth, scholars have sought to understand the making of this English Bible: the brilliance and endurance of its idiom; the complexities of its intellectual context; the details of its printing.[41] Only one complete copy of the 1526 New Testament, in fact, survives, though its text has been reprinted many times.[42] But what is lost in the reprinting is the set of errata at the end of the book; as far as I can tell, hardly anyone has noticed them.[43] Yet, in their form and detail, and their larger placement in the arc of Tyndale's volume and its critical reception, these errata locate Tyndale's work in the controlling rhetoric of scholarship for early modern England. For, like More's own corrections, they constitute a confession. But, unlike More's, they direct their attentions to the reader rather than the author, and they need to be reviewed in context to appreciate the larger force of Tyndale's project in its time.

Tyndale's errata sheets stand as the second of two closing gestures of the New Testament translation. The first is the address "To The Reader," that appears just at the end of the scriptural text (Sigs. Tt i v–Tt ii v). "Geve diligence Reder," it opens. Tyndale requests his reader to come to the scriptures with a "pure mynde" and a "syngle eye." At one level, it is a plea for moral rectitude. But at another level, it is an injunction to right reading. "Diligence" is the term that signals editorial attention to the printed word. "Con ogni diligenza" is the phrase invoked by the earliest Italian printers to announce their review of their texts and the correction of their errors.[44] The term enters English printing almost from the start; Caxton announces in his 1484 revision of the *Canterbury Tales* that he has "dylygently ouerseen" the text. By the 1520s, diligence is almost a cliché of authorship in print. Tyndale himself, in reviewing and revising his translation for its republication in 1534, noted how his text was "dyligentyly corrected," while the printer's colophon to that edition announced: "Here endeth the new Testament dylygentlye ouersene and correct and printed."[45]

"Diligence" signals a very special request of the reader, and Tyndale goes on in the 1526 "To the Reader" to enjoin: "Marke the playne and manyfest places of the scriptures." The reader is an annotator, coming to the book with pen in hand. To "mark" these places is not just to notice them but physically to mark them in the book—an idiom shared with one of this Testament's earliest critics, Robert Ridley, who would chronicle its many errors but lament that he did not have a copy of the book at hand "to marke them owt."[46] Tyndale's purported reader is a marker—in effect, the English version of those Italian *lettori* who would emend *con la penna*. The Testament requires reader input. The book does not, as he says, seem to have "his full shape, but as it were borne afore hys time." In time, "we will geve it his full shape, and putt out yf ought be added superfluusly; and adde to yff ought be oversene thorowe negligence." "Oversene" takes the reader back to "diligence," to the act of moral reading as an act of proofreading.

In this rhetorical environment, the errata sheets that follow "To the Reader" complete the confessional move. Titled "The errours committed in the prentynge," they are only superficially akin to More's errata. Notice, first, the very language of the headings. More's sheets are "faults" pages: lists of things that "escaped" in the printing. The word "faults" is clearly borrowed from the French, where "fautes" still means errata in typography.[47] But they are errata in that they are errant, escapees from the corral of the printer. More, as his own overseer, seeks to rein them in, to collect mistakes that escaped the eyes in the print shop. But for Tyndale, error resonates with moral failings chronicled in scripture itself. And like all sins, these errors are *committed*.[48] The author here is not some guardian of the escaped but rather an instructor in the arts of rectitude. Tyndale not only lists the errors; he must explain to his readers how to use this list. Unlike More, whose errata sheets are self-explanatory and who clearly relies on his readers' knowledge of their conventions in Continental books, Tyndale has to explain his abbreviations and his format: "F. with the nombre folowynge it / signyfiethe the leafe off the boke. sy / with the nombre before it / declareth the fyrst or the seconde syde of the leafe. ly. with the nomber before it noteth in what lyne the errour is / as here after apereth" (sig. Tt iii r). These are instructions for the lay reader. They are clarifications for those who may have never seen a printed book before, let alone an errata sheet, those for whom words like "folio" are new and need, in essence, a vernacular translation (thus while Tyndale uses "F." as his abbreviation, he translates it into the English word "leaf").[49] In short, More is concerned with protesting his own diligence; Tyndale concerns himself with educating his new readers in becoming diligent. Typography and moral purpose come together, as he effectively "translates" the idea of the errata sheet for a new English audience.[50]

Tyndale's closing gestures to the 1526 New Testament, then, do more than simply aver his humility or record lapses in typography. They invite readers to contribute and correct, and in the months that followed the book's publication, there was no lack of respondents. Robert Ridley, chaplain to the bishop of London, wrote a letter detailing the book's errors to his counterpart, Henry Gold (chaplain to the archbishop of Canterbury), in early 1527. This "common & vulgare translation," he states, manifests its heresy. "As for errors, if ye haue the first prent with annotationes in Mathew and Marcus, & the preface al is mere frenesy."[51] Tyndale's interpretations are a frenzy of mistake, an idea not unique to Ridley, for it was More himself who, in the *Confutations of Tyndale*, could ascribe the same level of wild folly to the translator: "Happy were Tindall, if he were as well recouered of his fransies."[52] For both More and Ridley, such frenzies include the highly charged translations of key Latin terms. Ridley notes that Tyndale's English version gets rid of a host of "christian wordes" central to the doctrinal vocabulary of the Catholic Church: penance, charity, confession, grace, priest, and church. Instead of this last word, Tyndale uses "congregation."[53] And More noted, specifically, that "charity" became "love," "priest" became "senior," and "confession" became "knowledge."[54] The core vocabulary of Christian ecclesiastical organization is being transformed into a vernacular. "Idolotria callith he worshyppyng of images," complains Ridley.[55] These are what More and Ridley considered the Lutheranisms of the Tyndale New Testament, and both men offer example after example of what More would call "what fautys were there in it" (p. 124).[56]

One might get the impression, reading Ridley's letter, that he had the book in front of him and that he had himself marked off all these offensive passages. But, apparently, he did not. "I have none of thies bowkes but only I remember such thynges I redde in the prefaces & annotationes." Later, he states to Gold: "I certefy you if ye look well, ye shal not look iij lynes withowt fawt in all the bowk, bot I have not the bowk to marke them owt, ye showd haue had lasure your selff to have doon it."[57]

Ridley's admission avers more than forgetfulness. It affirms precisely the whole point of his polemic: here is a book so bad, so vicious, and so full of error that it is no book at all. It is a book to be burned, a book to be effaced from the reading public. Ridley does not have the book because he *cannot* have the book. By claiming that he does not own a copy, Ridley erases the book from the language of his letter. He has, in effect, marked it out. But, by telling Gold to go through and record all its errors, he reproduces Tyndale's own language in the address "To the Reader" that closed the volume. "Marke the playne and manyfest places of the scriptures," Tyndale had enjoined. Now, Ridley asks his reader similarly to mark places in the book: but not, of course, those plain and manifest but those faulty.

Here is a book, in short, that is one great erratum. No enumeration of mistakes—either by the critic or by the author himself—can excuse it. Like More, Ridley develops a language of ocular proof, or moral proofreading, to justify his claims. The "fawtes & errores" of the translation should be plain to see, and Ridley adds, in what appears to be a postscript to his letter, the injunction: "Shew ye to the people that if any be of so prowde & stuburne stomac that he will beleve ther is no fawt ne error except it be declared to hym that he may se it, latt hym cum hither to my lordes which hath profowndly examined al & he shal heir & se errors except that he be blynde & have no eys" (p. 125). More and Ridley link acts of typographical overseeing with the larger imagery of sight and proof developed in doctrinal contexts. They take the idioms of the print shop and apply them to the ideologies of argument. Together with Tyndale's concluding "To the Reader" and his own errata sheets, these texts illustrate the ways in which the claims and counterclaims of error constitute the axes along which one read the word of God in the age of mechanical reproduction.

The acts of self-correction found in early errata offer, as I have suggested here, insight into the personal relationships of writers to their readers and, particularly in the cases of More and Tyndale, into the constructions of the author/translator as something of a self-correcting, and thus self-confessing, creature. Such acts, though, may be acts of public as well as private fealty. Perhaps the most elaborate, and most telling, of such public acts of overseeing are the "Corrections," that appear at the beginning of Thomas Elyot's *Dictionary* of 1538.[58] In the preface to the volume, Elyot notes that after the work was already at the printers, he became worried that he had neglected some aspects of its definitions. Henry VIII heard of Elyot's anxieties and placed before him the resources of the royal library. Elyot stopped the presses and revised the entries after *M*, those before *M* having already been printed. He then had to revise the first half of the alphabet, and he did so by noting the corrections in the first part of the volume but also by publishing a list of "Additions" at the volume's end. Here is his version of the story:

> But whyles it was in printyng, and uneth the half deale performed, your hyghnes being informed therof, by the reportes of gentyll maister Antony Denny, for his wysedome and diligence worthily callyd by your highnesse into your priuie Chamber, and of Wyllyam Tildisley, keper of your gracis Lybrarie, and after mooste specially by the recommendation of the most honourable lorde Crumwell, lorde priuie seale, fauourer of honestie, and next to your highnesse chiefe patron of vertue and cunnyng, conceyued of my labours a good expectation, and declaryng your moste noble and beneuolent nature, in *fauouryng* them that wyll be well occupied, your hyghnesse in the presence of dyuers your noble men, *commendynge* myne enterprise, *affirmed*, that if I wolde ernestely trauayle therin, your highnes, as well with your excellent *counsaile*, as with suche bokes as your grace had, and I lacked, wold therin ayde me: with the which wordes, I confesse, I receiued a newe spirite, as me semed; wherby I founde forthwith an augmentation of myn understandynge, in so moche, as I iuged all that, whiche I had writen, not worthy to come in your gracis presence, with out an addition. wherfore incontinent I caused the printer to cesse, and beginninge at the letter M, where I lefte, I passed forth to the last letter with a more diligent study. And that done, I eftesones returned to the fyrst letter, and with a semblable diligence performed the remenant.   (Aii v–Aiii r; emphases mine)

The story of the *Dictionary* is a story of intrusions and informancy: a story of royal power worked through minion service and Cromwellian intrigue. For Henry, the manipulations of the printed word extended through the 1530s in an arc of parliamentary acts and statutes. Writing, reading, and iconic presentation were the marks of fealty or treason. "Writyng ymprintinge [and] cypheringe" could all be seditious acts. The forging of the "kinges signe manuell signet and prevye seale" were treasonable, for which the punishment was death. And the control of the king's signs, and the inspections of his subject's texts, found itself relocated in the privy chamber.[59]

Stephen Merriam Foley has argued that the publication of Elyot's *Dictionary*, and a passage such as this one in particular, reifies these relationships between the royal body and the public word. "The king's body 'literally' stands between the two incomplete alphabets of the work. . . . [T]he king's intervention in the alphabetical order of the *Dictionary* demonstrates how the mechanical letters of the printing press and the human letters of the new learning could be reinscribed as the vehicles of a broadly nationalist and absolutist ideology."[60] But a close reading of the passage shows us that it is not so much the king's body as it is that of his surrogates that interrupts the progress of the *Dictionary* and provokes the correction of Elyot and his book.

First among such surrogates is Anthony Denny. Throughout the 1530s, Denny had risen in the king's bodily service. From a Gentleman of the Chamber, he worked his way up through diligence, intrigue, and patronage to Chief Gentleman of the Privy Chamber (installed in this position by Cromwell in the shake-up after the Boleyn affair), and he ended his royal service by being appointed, in October 1546, as Henry's last Groom of the Stool.[61] The roles Denny would have played would have embraced the range of diplomatic and political intrigue, bodily service, and even bawdry that had been filled by such predecessors as William Compton and Henry Norris. From wiping the royal bottom to securing mistresses for the king, the Gentlemen of the Chamber and the Stool were closest to the personality of power: in the words of David Starkey, "the mere word of a Gentleman of the Privy Chamber was sufficient evidence in itself for the king's will, without any other form of authentication whatever." Indeed, Starkey goes on, the Gentleman bore not just word and will but something of "the indefinable charisma of monarchy" itself.[62] Denny himself clearly bore something of this charismatic flair, so much so that John Leland wrote that "the whole court bore testimony to his 'gratia flagrans'"—what we might translate as his blazing repute with the king.[63]

What role, then, does Denny play in Elyot's story, and how does his placement introduce the string of intercessors and interrogators for the king? The *Dictionary* is the subject of inquiry, the object of intelligence gathering that filled the Henrician court in the late 1530s and has been amply chronicled by G. R. Elton in his tellingly titled *Policy and Police*. The word is out, as it were, and Denny comes first as the chief spy of court and privy chamber. From Denny and the chamber, we move to Tildisley and the library, and finally to Cromwell—here identified specifically as *lorde priuie seale*. It is as if Elyot himself is walking through the anterooms and private apartments of power, as if he has been granted a succession of audiences, each one of which leads him closer and closer to the body of the king. Cromwell appears here as the "fauourer of honestie, and next to your highnesse chiefe patron of vertue and cunnyng." Virtue and cunning are, indeed, the two poles of Henrician courtly life here, and the language Elyot uses is the language not so much of the scholar or the printer but the subject: "favoring," "commending," "affirming," "counsel." Elyot is himself on trial of a sort here, called before the king and his creatures to render account. The king's words of permission and encouragement do more than stimulate the mind; they provoke a confession: "With the which wordes, I confesse, I received a new spirite, as me semed: wherby I founde forthwith an augmentation of myn understandynge." This is the language of conversion, the accounting of a tale of turning from error to rectitude, from wandering to fealty found anew.

So just what was it that Sir Thomas Elyot felt in need of correcting? Here is his account: "And for as moche as by haste made in printyng, some letters may happen to lacke, some to be sette in wronge places, or the ortography nat to be truely obserued, I therfore haue put all those fautes in a table folowing this preface: wherby they may be easily corrected: and that done, I truste in god no manne shall fynde cause to reiect this boke" (Aiii v). Certainly, there are typos: haplographies, dittographies, and transposed letters. But occasionally there are mistakes of a different sort. Take, for example, *Qui*, where Elyot has felt the need to correct the translation of a Latin phrase offered in his definition. Here is the correction: "reade after the latine, wherfore was Epicurous more happy that he lyued in his owne countray, than Metrodorus whiche lyued at Athenes." To read such a correction is to feel the need to go back to the source, to reexamine the supposedly erroneous text itself.

Now, look at the actual entry for *Qui*, defined as "the whyche. Alsoo sometyme it sygnifyeth howe." What follows is a string of classical quotations (with translation) illustrating not just grammatical but social and political correctness (Vii v). The extracts tell a story of identity and power, of discovery and shame (I quote his English translations of the Latin excerpts).

> Doo what ye canne, howe or by whatte meanes thou mayste haue hyr.
> Howe arte thou callyd?
> . . .
> From whens is this suspycion happened vnto the?
> I pray god that a vengeaunce lyghte on hym.

And then we get to a remarkable self-reference: "For he spendethe his laboure in wrytynge of Prologues, not bycause he wyll telle the argumente, but for as moche as he wolde make answere to the yuell reportes of the olde envyouse Poete." And, finally, we get to the quotation that Elyot corrects (and the last one in the entry): "Wherefore was Epycure moore happye, that he *dydde dye* in his countrye, than Metrodorus *that he dyed* at Athenes" (emphases mine). In this correction lies, perhaps, an allegory of an Elyotic scholarly devotion, a miniature story that recaps the longer story of the preface. Happy is the man who lives in his own country, who needs not Athens—more tempting for the scholar—but who serves a king whose generosity extends to opening an Athens of the mind before him in the library. Elyot changes *die* to *live*, grants himself a reprieve after the intercessions of a king and his counselors. To read the entry *Qui*, now, is to see a story of the making of the man and book: a story about *which*, and *how, from whence, wolde to God, because, wherefore*. It is the single word that sums up the stories of the preface, an entry that, corrected in the "Corrections," invites the reader to understand the making of a lexicographical subject in a world of royal words and will.

Embedded in errata is the story of correction itself: correction more than typographical or even theological but human and political. The Finis of the *Dictionary* closes with another appeal to correction, now hearkening back to the old manuscript appeals for readerly correction. But, now, the corrections of these readers, their "honest labours," are described as "being benefyciall vnto this theyr countrey." This is a dictionary of English, the king's dictionary, the first text that, as Foley argues, "helped to establish the schoolroom as a new cultural field for instituting royal absolutism."[64] The story that this volume tells is, in the end, the story of a man publicly happy "in his owne countray." It is fitting, then, that at its close it should direct such nationalized ease to readers who, in finding fault, are offering not treason to a work published by Elyot the servant or Berthelett, *regius impressor*, but are, in fact, offering beneficence. The correction, as Elyot announced there, is "an exquisite tryall," whether performed by author or by reader, that affirms a shared participation in the trials of public service.

This image of the corrector on trial leads to a reconception of errata sheets and, indeed, of all pages of editorial avowal as legal transcripts: as account books in the judgments of political and scholarly loyalty (I recall in passing that the structure of More's *Dialogue* itself became a trial, with the author "defending the office of the priesthood and the divine right of the ecclesiastical courts to try heresy").[65] The text becomes a piece of evidence entered into the court of judgment. Erasmus recognized this judicial framework to the editorial condition in his letter to Thomas Ruthall of March 7, 1515, published as the preface to his edition of Seneca's *Lucubrationes* (Basel: Froben, August 1515). The product of his English sojourn, and addressed to one of the most powerful men in early Henrician England, the edition of Seneca begins with this epistolary meditation on the similarities between textual criticism and war. The letter begins, in fact, with an account of the Battle of Flodden Field (September 9, 1513) and moves through, by analogy, the "infinite army of corruptions" that Erasmus finds he must retake from the "enemy" in making his edition. "I had my pen for a sword," he states, and then goes on:

> Nor had I any outside help in all these difficulties except two ancient manuscripts, one of which was provided from his own library by the chief patron of my researches, that incomparable glory of our generation, William, archbishop of Canterbury [i.e., William Warham], and the other was sent to my assistance by King's College, Cambridge; but these were imperfect and even more full of error [*mendosiorum*] than the current copies, so that less confidence could be placed in one's auxiliary troops than in the enemy. One thing however helped me: they did not agree in error [*non consentiebant errata*], as is bound to happen in printed texts set up from the same printer's copy; and thus, just as it sometimes happens that an experienced and

attentive judge pieces together what really took place from the statements of many witnesses, none of whom is telling the truth, so I conjectured the true reading on the basis of their differing mistakes [*rem colligat, ita nos e diuersis mendis veram coniecimus lectionem*].⁶⁶

Erasmus's invocation of the trial judge, together with the military framing of his story, make editing an act shot through with the political and the forensic. At stake in his extended simile is a conception not just of the editorial but of the judicial: a recognition that no witness truly tells the truth, an appeal not to the authorities of history or text but to the judgment of conjecture.

And yet Erasmus appoints himself a judge not just of manuscripts and witnesses but of his author himself. Seneca's writings are not without controversy: "there are some things in him which I would gladly change myself." He is a bit long-winded, sometimes mean, at times "while making large claims for himself, he is sometimes an unfair judge of other men's talents." But, as Erasmus states, "what author was ever so perfect that no fault could be found in him at all?" And, further, "Not that I have failed [*Neque vero me fugit*] to notice that many errors still remain; but they are of a kind that without the aid of ancient codices could hardly be removed by Seneca himself."⁶⁷ Notice the Latin here: literally, not "not that I have failed" but really "It has not escaped me." Erasmus vivifies what would become the idiom of the errata sheet. The faults that would escape the printer are, now, those that escape even the most diligent of editors. Indeed, they would escape the author, Seneca himself, who would need all the help of ancient codices to restore his text.

The act of making books—for Erasmus, as well as for Elyot, and perhaps even for More and Tyndale—is thus a form of martial combat or judicial trial. Scholarship moves through wanderings and blots. Erasmus's primary word for textual mistake is *mendum*, meaning literally a blot, a smudge, a bad mark on the text, and clearly a holdover from its classical, Latin uses in the manuscript tradition.⁶⁸ Such blots are now, quite literally, marks on the reputation of the scholar, and Erasmus's reflections here would have great impact on how other scholars represent themselves as emenders of both a personal and a textual past. Lisa Jardine has made much of the rhetoric of this preface, and of the larger set of problems that Erasmus had with this edition: its misprints, poor layout, and garblings that, as Erasmus would aver in later editions, were the responsibility of his editorial assistants (his *castigatores*). Jardine retells the story of this edition's *fortunae* as a story of mistake and emendation, but she prefers to dwell on the later version of the Seneca that Erasmus would publish. My concern is with the language of this letter itself and how it stands as a fulcrum on which both the textual and the forensic could balance. The avowal of error makes the individual his own best judge and jury.

But what happens when one submits oneself to such a judge? Elyot sought approval from the king and his mediating minions—book production as an act of political allegiance. In the case of Erasmus's contemporary Guillaume Budé, the avowal of mistake becomes the entry point in an appeal to the master. The brilliant, long, and complex letter that Budé wrote to Erasmus in response to reading the 1515 edition of the *Lucubrationes* is a testimony to the ways in which the language of error contributes to the rhetoric of humanist identity.

On May 1, 1516, Guillaume Budé wrote in reply to a letter from Erasmus. That first letter, now lost, clearly praised Budé for his learning, and the recipient—so pleased to hear from someone whom he could address "O noster Erasme"—quickly replied with a remarkable missive, half in Latin, half in Greek, that inaugurated one of the great humanist correspondences of the early sixteenth century. Budé's letter writes a story of friendship as a tale of bibliography. From its opening ventriloquized exchange, through its accounts of scholarship and reading, to its detailed philological engagements with translation, this epistle charts a personal relationship through textual fidelity. Indeed, the very idioms of humanist philology—descent, affiliation, collation—find themselves transmuted here into the terms of personal life. Let us look closely at its language. The first text to appear is Erasmus's original letter itself: "When I got your letter and had read it two or three times, I decided then and there to take a holiday from business and devote my leisure entirely to you." Here, Budé locates the self in the texts, and the devotion to the man becomes the reading of his writing. No one, Budé remarks, could claim Erasmus "as his private property." And yet, he states, "I cannot express, I repeat, how wholly you have made me yours since I had your letter."[69] All the tropes of humanist friendship are in full display here. The language of devotion, of praise, and of personal humility come together to capture the attention, benevolence, and docility of the Erasmian reader.

The letter structures its exordium much like an old, forensic speech. But what is clear, too, is the way in which the individual becomes a property. A consequence of what Lisa Jardine had called "the construction of charisma in print" is the effective commodification of the charismatic writer himself. Not only is the book a thing to buy and sell, but any text the teacher generates can become property. No one can claim the man "as his private property," but one can certainly claim the written (or the printed) products of the man.

"You have made me yours": a new life is coming into being here, and a close look at Budé's Latin illustrates the subtle resonances of his language: "Verum, vt dixi, exprimere nequeo quam tuum me nuper feceris, posteaquam epistolam tuam accepi." Budé says that he cannot express. But *exprimere* means not only "to express" in words but, more precisely and more historically, to cast metal in a die or to hand shape a preliminary form in wax. Cicero had used it, throughout his rhetorical works, in a figurative sense: to develop the rhetor's skills through practice and example. At times, the verb refers to forms of imitation or translation; at times, it connotes his own practice of rendering Greek thought in Latin form.[70] In this context, the verb *feci* resonates with forms of making. It is not simply that Budé claims that Erasmus has "made me yours" but rather that Erasmus has fashioned Budé. He has shaped him into reader, student, devotee, and humanist. *Exprimere nequeo* now becomes the opposite of *me feceris*. I cannot shape, but you can; I cannot shape my words to give you praise, but you have shaped me. Budé phrases the nascent relationship with Erasmus in these precise terms of artistic creation: a self-fashioning, as it were, made over texts.

So, in order to please Erasmus, Budé will read Seneca. But as he is engaged with his own book, a new volume arrives. This is not a new text of the classical author but a new edition of the scriptures: Erasmus's bilingual *Novum instrumentum*, the first edition of his New Testament (printed by Froben in 1516). "Anyhow," Budé writes, "while I was poring over Seneca, lo and behold, news comes that the instrument of our salvation has arrived, Erasmus's edition, the bilingual text, that glorious work; . . . . The arrival of this book made me drop the Seneca that I already had in my hands."[71] Budé has limned a verbal portrait of the humanist reader, book in hand, that deeply resonates with the emerging tropes of visual portraiture that would define the scholarly and courtly subject for early-sixteenth-century readers. The scholar's hand is central to this iconography. In portraits of the time, the hand is the focal point of illustrating personal and professional identity. As Stephen Foley puts it, summarizing these developments in manual representation, the hands "clasped, grasping a collar, playing lightly over a book or clutching it, . . . provide a technical vocabulary for the representation of social codes and professional traits."[72] And as Jardine has shown in great detail, the paintings of Erasmus, More, Gilles, and many of the other merchants, scholars, and ambassadors of the early sixteenth century all define the character of their sitter in the hands.[73] The figure reading, writing, or manipulating the instruments of his profession sits, for many of these portraitists, absorbed in the manual dexterities of craft. Indeed, in the portrait of Budé himself by Jean Clouet, the humanist is shown with pen in hand, annotating an open book.[74]

Budé's letter, then, makes the humanist's hand the focus of attention, and perhaps the most arresting thing he can announce is the book dropping from the hands. But no less arresting than this action is the comparable action of a new hand producing a new book. François Deloynes—parliamentarian, scholar, friend, and dedicatee of Budé's earlier work—appears now, in this letter, as the go-between for reader and writer. He brings Budé evidence of Erasmus's own praise. He tells the writer of the letter that the reader is an admirer. Erasmus had praised Budé's translation of the Greek Gospel of St. Luke, for in the *Novum testamentum* Erasmus had relied on Budé's *Annotations on the Pandects* to clarify some problems in translating St. Luke's Greek. Erasmus used this scholarly reference as the occasion for a eulogy of Budé in the *Novum testamentum*, and it is this eulogy that Deloynes reads to Budé in the letter. "So now," Deloynes says, in Budé's letter to Erasmus "you have this same Erasmus not merely reading your works but heralding their virtues." And then Deloynes shows Budé the book. "He finished speaking and, while I was waiting in suspense, produced your book, still unbound and fresh from the printer, and showing me a passage in St. Luke, 'This Erasmus of yours,' he said, 'now there is a real friend, with very good taste.'"[75] One book has replaced another: the Seneca *Lucubrationes*, which Budé had been reading and which dropped from his hands, finds itself displaced by the *Novum instrumentum*. And Deloynes, in the drama of his bibliographical display, reveals a text. Indeed, it is a drama of revelation here in the etymological sense: *revelare*, to pull the covers off, to expose.

But if the book is being newly revealed, then so is the body. The details of Budé's Latin diction reveal something else, as well: a newborn volume, and a newborn friendship: "Promuit librum tuum solutum adhuc et recentem ab officina." *Recentem* can mean "fresh" or "young"; but it connotes, too, "whelped," or "newly foaled." The book is newly born, not even bound, or, more precisely, not yet severed from the cords of birth. *Solutum* means "freed," "loosened," "unattached." The idiom *partus solvere* means "to bear," "to bring forth," "to be delivered of offspring."[76] In other words, the book is being born here, much as the friendship of Erasmus and Budé is being born. And, in both cases, Deloynes functions as something of a midwife: the deliverer of newly printed books but also the effective helper in the making of a humanist friendship.

Budé thus draws on a range of idioms and images that announce the portent of a friendship and the import of the correspondence now beginning. And yet all is not joy at this birth. Budé captures Erasmus's attention by admitting not just success but mistake. In the course of the letter, he will find himself in error, and the force of this self-castigation is to reinforce that rhetoric of error I am exposing here: "Furthermore, I am most grateful to you, and gladly admit it, for your forgiveness in that matter of the word παρηκολουθηκοτι. You gave me the most gentle treatment on that point, leaving me as you did to detect and amend my own error. I was wrong, I admit; I cannot seek to avoid the blame, only the penalty and the disgrace, and it is normal to let a man off these if he owns up."[77] Such an admission is inseparable from the act of confession. Like More and Elyot, like Tyndale and Erasmus, Budé shows himself his own best corrector. Textual correction is a moral and, to some degree, a legal action. For in his discussion of his translation of the Greek word, παρηκολουθηκοτι, Budé states not only that he was wrong; he implies that the confession of that wrongdoing should generate a lenient response on the part of authorities. "It is normal to let a man off these if he owns up [*quae fatenti remitti solet*]." Budé asks to be let off, to be set free, to be, more pointedly, "remitted" from his crimes. And yet the very subject matter of his linguistic analysis is itself thematically concerned with issues of legality and witnessing: with acts that bear directly on the idioms of textual criticism in terms that both Budé and Erasmus had developed.

Budé's problem was that he had mistakenly translated a phrase in Luke's Greek as "a follower of the eye-witnesses," when it really should mean "arrived at" or "correctly understood." Budé looks at the Greek and Latin resonances of his terms and turns to Demosthenes for support. In his *De falsa legatione*, Demosthenes is quoted as saying, "that I, who know this man's misdeeds and have followed their whole course, may enjoy your full support as I accuse him." How, Budé says, "am I to understand this?" He goes on:

> Had Demosthenes uncovered all Aesthines' outrages and crimes and made careful enquiry into them and (as it were) followed up everything he said and did after the event, until in the end he fully understood them? Or was he present as a witness at all his misdemeanours, being his contemporary, a colleague in public life, and a member of the same foreign mission? In another place he says: "You, gentlemen of the jury, will follow (παρακολουθησετε) the whole story more easily"; nothing will escape you, but you will fully understand everything as I recount it. (3:279; 2:231)

Budé blends the subject matter of his own anxiety as translator with that of humanist textual criticism in the large. He seeks remittance, forgiveness in the court of Erasmian philological law. And so he focuses on a passage in Demosthenes that similarly raises problems of crime, guilt, and understanding. Demosthenes is something of a textual critic: following leads, looking for witnesses, measuring his own observation against that of others. In this role, he recalls that association of the scholar the judge made in Erasmus's preface to Seneca's *Lucubrationes*—the very text that Budé says he was reading at the beginning of the letter.

Read in tandem, then, Budé's and Erasmus's remarks inflect the act of textual criticism with the flavor of the law court. They make problems of witnessing—of seeing, attesting, telling the account—central to the ways in which both writers seek to legitimate themselves. For Erasmus, it is the establishment of himself as an editorial judge; for Budé, it is the modeling of himself on a classical legal scholar. "You, gentlemen of the jury, will follow the whole story more easily." These are Demosthenes' words, but they might as well be Budé's—or, for that matter, More's, Erasmus's, Elyot's, Tyndale's, or any humanist's. The reader is the jury, and the writer's job is to present the evidence (be it philological, bibliographical, or personal) in a manner that can be easily followed.

Budé's letter remains a brilliant essay in the tropes of humanism. It defines intellectual friendship as keyed to the exchange of texts. It makes the arts of *amicitia* the arts of reading, and it textures the language of those arts with terms brought from the law court and confessional. By working through a mistranslated passage, whose own subject is the status of eyewitnessing and the legal structures of review, Budé effectively responds to Erasmus's own legalistic idiom in the preface to his Seneca. The dialogue between Budé and Erasmus becomes a set of pleas, confessions, and self-witnessing avowals. And, in its dramas of bibliographical discovery and revelation—the book falling from the hands, the new text produced like a newborn creature—Budé invests in the narratives of textual presentation that would come to characterize courtly reading politics throughout the early sixteenth century.

All this contributes to what David Greetham has called, in an evocative phrase, "textual forensics."[78] The humanist becomes the master of his own mistake. Self-presentation as a reader and a writer works through avowals and corrections of errata. The language of the law becomes the rhetoric of scholarship. The case of Thomas Wyatt similarly interlards scholarly and legal idioms, but in precisely the opposite way. For if Budé and Erasmus would use legal discourse to make points of editorial control, Wyatt invokes the techniques of the editor to defend himself against accusations of treason. Soon after Cromwell's fall in 1540, Wyatt was accused of treason.[79] Dr. Edmund Bonner, in particular, claimed he had slandered Henry VIII, and one of the main accusations hinged on a crude recasting of a proverb. Wyatt was said to have announced "that he feared the King should be cast out of a cart's arse and that, by God's blood, if he were so, he were well served, and would he were so."[80] In his defense, Wyatt wrote two prose texts in 1541 that come to terms explicitly with these accusations but also review his ambassadorial service in the late 1530s: *A Declaration . . . of his Innocence . . .* and *Wyatt's Defence To the Iudges after the Indictment and the evidence.*[81] He goes to great lengths to affirm his habitual use of proverbs and to argue that Bonner, knowing of this habit, added one that Wyatt did not utter, in order to lend credence to a slanderous story about Wyatt himself. But at the heart of his defense is a concern with proper speaking, writing, and reading. The altering of a single syllable, Wyatt argues, "ether with penn or word," can change the entire meaning of an utterance, an argument he marshals to claim that his statement was heard and transcribed inaccurately. Though the *Declaration* and *Defence* range widely over many issues central to the early Tudor court, they bear directly on the forms, themes, and contexts of Wyatt's own poetry—in particular, what I would call their textual condition. Poem, book, and letter are all subject to the slippage of the pen, the intrusions of the interceptor, or the mistakes of the proof.

Much of the *Declaration* focuses on memory. Wyatt tries to recall, years later, "suche thynges as have passed me . . . by worde, wrytinge, communinge, or receauing."[82] This *Declaration* is not so much an appeal to innocence as a remembrance of letters—an accounting of all the documents that passed through his office while he was at the emperor's court.[83] "[L]ettres or wrytinges," he tries to recall, "came to my handys or thorow my handes vnopened" (p. 180). He never, he protests, knowingly communicated with a traitor. Some letters were, as he put it "ether so secretly handlede or yett not in couerture" that he could not see them (p. 181). Others never reached him (p. 183). The *Declaration* concludes, following Wyatt's signature, "This withowte correctinge, sendinge, or ouerseinge" (p. 184), and in the *Defence* that follows it Wyatt develops the activities of correcting, sending, and overseeing into an essay on the nature of reading and writing itself. Diplomacy becomes a form of editorship. The questions Wyatt asks about himself, and those that others asked of him, stand here as kin to Erasmus's inquiries into the status of a text. For much as any editor would collate or confer competing texts together, so Wyatt imagines such conferring as the centerpiece of political service.

> Intelligens concludethe a familiarite or *conferringe* of devyses to gyther, which may be by worde, message or wrytinge, which the lawe forbiddythe to be had with anye the kinges traytours or rebels, payne of the lyke. Reherse the lawe, declare, my lordes, I beseke you, the meaninge thereof. Am I a traytor by cawse I spake with the kinges traytor? No, not for that, for I may byd him "avaunte, traytor" or "defye hym, traytor." No man will tayke this for treasone; but where he is holpen, counceled, advertysed by my worde, there lyethe the treason, there lyethe the treason. In wrytinge yt is lyke. In message yt is lyke; for I may sende hym bothe lettre and message of chalinge or defyaunce. (p. 190; emphasis mine)

How can one defend oneself against words quoted, reported, and transcribed? "And what say my accusares in thes wordes? Do theie swere I spake them trayterously or maliciously? . . . Rede ther depositions, theie say not so. *Confer* ther depositions, yf theie agre worde for worde" (p. 196). The accusations against Wyatt become texts; the texts become subject to conferral, that is, comparison. Such documents are treated here as if they were the objects of an editor: compared, collated, and reviewed for accuracy. Wyatt goes on:

> Yf theie myseagre in wordis and not in substance, let vs here the woordes theie varie in. For in some lyttell thynge may apere the truthe which I dare saye you seke for your consciens sake. And besydys that, *yt is a smale thynge in alteringe of one syllable ether with penne or worde that may mayk in the conceavinge of the truthe myche matter or error.* For in thys thynge "I fere," or "I truste," semethe but one smale syllable chaynged, and yet it makethe a great dyfferaunce, and may be of an herer wronge conceaved and worse reported, and yet worste of all altered by an examyner. Agayne "fall owte" "caste owte," or "lefte owte" makethe dyfferaunce, yea and the setting of the wordes one in an others place may mayke greate dyfferaunce, tho the wordes were all one—as "a myll horse" and "a horse myll." I besyche you therfore examen the matter vnder this sorte. *Confere* theire severall sayinges togyther, *confer* th'examynations vpone the same matter and I dare warrante ye shall fynde mysreportinge and mysvnderstandinge. (p.197; emphases mine)

Wyatt claims that his words have been mistaken. His use of the proverb "I am lefte owte of the cartes ars" (p. 198) has been taken out of context, misheard, misreported, and mistranscribed into the environment of royal offense. Instead of saying what he has been accused of saying ("ye shall see the kinge our maister cast out at the carts tail"), what Wyatt claims he said was more like, "I fere for all these menes fayer promyses the kinge shalbe lefte owte of the cartes ars." He recalls that he may have very well said something like that and may well have invoked this proverbial sentiment on occasion. "But that I vsed it with Bonar or Haynes I neuer remember; and yf I euer dyd I am sure neuer as thei couche the tale" (p. 198).

Wyatt's appeal to memory and intention takes on the flavor of textual criticism. Comparison of manuscripts—signaled by the Latin verb *conferre* and its past participial form, *collatus*—was, of course, the hallmark of the humanist philological method, and Wyatt's words recall Erasmus's association of editorial and juridical judgment.[84] Just as the judge compares the testimony of witnesses, "none of whom," Erasmus slyly noted, "is telling the truth," so one conjectures a true reading out of the collation of accounts. But Erasmus is concerned with Latin texts, and his terms for editorship reach back to the classical and Continental contexts of analysis. Wyatt is writing English. In fact, he is more than simply writing English; he is seeking a vernacular expression for these learned terms. Much like Tyndale, who would translate for English readers European idioms of textual review, so Wyatt offers up an essay in translation. His two defense tracts (and especially the passages I quote at length here) now may be approached as studies in word meaning: attempts to define, precisely, just what may be meant by such terms as "intelligence" or "traitor" or what may be connoted by the idioms "fall out," "cast out," "left out." His is a project, too, akin to Thomas Elyot's—a cultural lexicography, as it were. And there are the recollections of Robert Ridley's phrasing as well. "Mark them owt" is the phrase he uses to define the act of critical reading.

What is emerging in the 1520s and 1530s is a growing use, in England, of the terms for printing, editing, proofreading, and the like, all applied in a more figurative sense to the act of verbal understanding. In the *OED*, the first attested use of the word "collation" in this textual sense comes from a book of profound national, literary import: the 1532 edition of Geoffrey Chaucer, edited by William Thynne. This is the first collected volume of Chaucer's works; indeed, it is the first single-volume publication of the whole work of any vernacular English writer. Much has been made of its importance, and we can see in the avowals of its preface (probably written by the courtier Brian Tuke) one of the earliest vernacular statements of editorial method in English: "as bokes of dyuers imprintes came unto my handes / I easely and without grete study / might and haue deprehended in them many errours / falsyties / and deprauacions / whiche euydently appered by the contrarietees and alteracions founde by *collacion* of the one with the other / wherby I was moued and styred to make dilygent sertch / where I might fynde or recouer any trewe copies or exemplaries of the sayd bookes" (emphasis mine).[85]

The collation of manuscripts helps what Tuke calls "the restauracion" of Chaucer's works in their authorized form, and this process, he avers, is not just a literary but a political "dewtie" growing out of his "very honesty and loue to my countrey" (Aiii r). Tuke's preface is a statement of national fealty, an appeal to King Henry VIII as patron to exercise his "discrecyon and iugement" and accept the volume as it has been printed.[86] If Wyatt's *Defence* reads as a statement of editorial principles, then Tuke's preface may stand as something of a defense of its own: a plea before a judging king for the authentic value of an author's works and, in turn, for a recognition of the editor's own searching out of falsity and error through the collation of texts.

In the making of an edition, the slightest slips can change the meaning of a line: "the settyng of the wordes one in an others place may mayke greate dyfferaunce." "I feare" or "I truste," Wyatt offers, differ only in "one smale syllable." But such a case is not a random call. "Fear" and "trust" are the two poles of Wyatt's poetic emotion. I have elsewhere adduced a wide range of Wyatt's uses of these terms, in the ballads, sonnets, and songs, where the two words scope out the literary and emotional anxieties of someone who seeks the "trust" of his beloved yet also queries "What may I do when my maister feareth, / But, in the felde, with him to lyve and dye?" (4.12–13).[87] "Fear" and "trust" play into the Petrarchan oxymora of love. In one poem, Wyatt distills the Italian lexicon of pain—sighing, hope, and desire—into a unique concatenation of his own: "An endles wynd doeth tere the sayll a pace / Of forced sightes and *trusty ferefulnes*" (28.7–8; emphases mine). And in another ballad, he expounds not just on the nature of his trust but on the very problems of transcription and substitution that are the subject of his *Defence*. Concluding the ballad, whose refrain line had been "Patiens, parforce, content thy self with wrong," he offers:

> I Burne and boyle withoute redres;
> I syegh, I wepe, and all in vayne.
> Now Hotte, now Cold, whoo can expresse
> The thowsaund parte of my great payne?
> But yf I myght her faver Atteigne,
> Then wold I trust to chaunge this song,
> With pety for paciens, and consciens for wrong.
>
> (121.15–21)

Wyatt performs an act of critical self-revision. He suggests changing words for words, locates the change in "trust," and posits a revisionary poetics that makes the language of the song subject always to rewriting, depending on the circumstances of performance.

"My word nor I shall not be variable" (11.13). In spite of this protest, Wyatt's words were variable. The very nature of the writing and transmitting of his poetry lies in the variations of the scribe, in the self-cancellations and revisions of the poet, and in the manipulations of the printer. It is a commonplace of Wyatt criticism to remark on the unstable quality of his verse line, on the idiosyncrasies of his spelling, and on the variations generated by competing manuscript and print editions. The practice of textual criticism runs up against the intractable wall of Wyatt's own texts. As Jonathan Crewe recognizes, modern editions of Wyatt's poetry (as of much early-sixteenth-century verse) are in themselves modernizations, recastings of his words and lines. "In quite a fundamental sense," Crewe notes, "to print Wyatt modernized is to censor his work."[88]

Let us examine an example of such censoring. The Penguin paperback edition of the poems of Sir Thomas Wyatt, edited by R. A. Rebholz, has, since its first publication over twenty years ago, become a standard text. It is the form in which most students, and most teachers, will encounter Wyatt (certainly most American students and teachers). Its prefatory explanations of the vexed problem of Wyatt's meters, the status of his work in manuscript, and the complex evidence and scholarly debates about the range of Wyatt's canon distill vast amounts of intricate material for modern readers. This is, admittedly, a modern spelling edition. Rebholz has brought orthography and punctuation into line with current practices, he argues, because "I became convinced that the sacrifices were eminently worthwhile because they make the poems genuinely available to modern readers when texts preserving old accidentals are frequently unintelligible."[89] He acknowledges that, on occasion, modernization may ruin a rhyme or metrical pattern and that added punctuation may fix syntax that, in Wyatt's time, would have been fluid enough to "create ambivalent meanings" (p. 14).

I have discussed in detail elsewhere some of the textual problems raised by this edition, especially in the long poem to John Poyntz, where Rebholz's choice of base text and his selective recording of variants suppresses the controlling verbal relationship of this poem to its deep Chaucerian subtext (especially Chaucer's ballad "Truth," itself a widely read text of the early Tudor period).[90] Here, I develop and correct an earlier engagement with one ballad in this edition that takes as its theme the problem of error and, in particular, locates that theme in the emergent print practices I have discussed above. "I see the change" (Rebholz 215) is a refrain ballad appearing only in the Devonshire Manuscript, a collection of Tudor verse. Here is the poem in the conservative, old-spelling edition of Kenneth Muir and Patricia Thompson.

> I se the change ffrom that that was
> And how thy ffayth hath tayn his ffflyt
> But I with pacyense let yt pase
> And with my pene thys do I wryt
> To show the playn by prowff off syght,
> I se the change.
>
> I se the change off weryd mynd
> And sleper hold hath quet my hyer;
> Lo! how by prowff in the I ffynd
> Abowrnyng ffath in changyng ffyer.
> Ffarwell my part, prowff ys no lyer!
> I se the change.
>
> I se the change off chance in loue;
> Delyt no lenger may abyd;
> What shold I sek ffurther to proue?
> No, no, my trust, ffor I haue tryd
> The ffolloyng of a ffallse gyd:
> I se the change.
>
> I se the change, as in thys case,
> Has mayd me ffre ffrom myn avoo,
> Ffor now another has my plase,
> And or I wist, I wot ner how,
> Yt hapnet thys as ye here now:
> I se the change.
>
> I se the change, seche ys my chance
> To sarue in dowt and hope in vayn;
> But sens my surty so doth glanse,

> Repentens now shal quyt thy payn,
> Neuer to trust the lyke agayn:
> I se the change. (195)

Aside from certain orthographical conventions—the double *ff*s, the early sixteenth-century spellings, the consistent use of *se* for *see*—the most important piece of verbal trickery in this text is the spelling of both the definite article and the second person pronoun as "the." Wyatt's poems are continually preoccupied with their own linguistic instability and with the inability of the poetic hand to transcribe the intentions of the heart. Even when the author's own text is presented as a proof, he recognizes that it may never suffice. The logic of the poem hinges on the instability of "the." Who is to say that, in the refrain lines (6, 12, 18, 24, 30), the speaker of the poem sees "the" change or sees "thee" change? Similarly, in the first lines of each successive stanza, the ambiguity is only barely resolved as the reader completes the sentence (e.g., lines 19 and 21: "I see the change" or I see "thee" change?). Following each refrain line, these first stanza lines create an unresolvable conundrum. Indeed, they reify the very problem of the text posed by the poetry itself: the act of proofreading. Proof is no liar, or, more pointedly, the proof of sight that shows the writing of the pen plainly. What should, the poem's speaker asks, I seek further to prove? And yet proofs always lie. For Wyatt, writing in the 1530s, the word "proof" must resonate with its new meaning in the realms of bibliography. The indenture between John Palsgrave and the printer Richard Pynson from 1523 sets out the responsibilities of author and printer, including proofreading: "farder more hyt ys agreed that the saide Richard schall vse good fayth in the printing off the saide worke and suffer the said Iohn Palsgraue or hys assignes to correct the proff."[91]

I have made much of this detail because, in Rebholz's edition, these ambivalences are completely effaced:

> I see the change from that that was
> And how thy faith hath ta'en his flight.
> But I with patience let it pass
> And with my pen this do I write
> To show thee plain by proof of sight
> I see the change.

I see the change of wearied mind
And slipper hold hath quit my hire.
Lo, how by proof in thee I find
A burning faith in changing fire.
Farewell, my part. Proof is no liar.
I see the change.

I see the change in chance in love.
Delight no longer may abide.
What should I seek further to prove?
No, no, my trust, for I have tried
The following of a false guide.
I see the change.

I see the change, as in this case,
Has made me free from mine avow;
For now another has my place
And ere I wist, I wot ne'er how,
It happened thus as ye hear now.
I see the change.

I see the change. Such is my chance
To serve in doubt and hope in vain.
But since my surety so doth glance,
Repentance now shall quit thy pain,
Never to trust the like again.
I see the change.

    Rebholz acknowledges, in his note in the back of the book, that lines 6, 12, 18, 24, and 30 offer a "pun on 'the/thee' in the refrain. The word 'thee' (l. 9) is spelled 'the' in the MS" (p. 522). But that is all he notes. The point is not just that there is a pun in the refrain nor that in one particular line "thee" is spelled "the." The point is that the poem as a whole presents one spelling throughout for these two words and that spelling is the key to the poem's theme. Indeed, spelling is the poem's theme—what you write with the pen is always subject to change; and when you read, you see the change.

In other poems, such as "Me list no more to sing," "Lament my loss," and "Who would have ever thought," relationships of text and reader, speaker and hearer, are similarly addressed. In the first of them, Wyatt laments—much as in his defense tracts—how his words have been mistaken: "For what I song or spake Men dede my songis mistake" (Muir and Thompson 210.4–5). "Marke well, I saye, this text," he commands in the middle of the poem (l. 29), and his marking takes us back to Ridley and to Tyndale, to a world of reading by censorious minds. Much like the translator or the polemicist, Wyatt avers his meaning in the face of readerly misapprehension.

> Yf this be undre miste,
> And not well playnlye wyste,
> Vndrestonde me who lyste;
> For I reke not a bene,
> I wott what I doo meane.   (210.40–44)

I know what I mean, even if no one else does.

If an impediment to understanding lies in foolish readers, then it lies, too, in bad writers. In "Lament my loss," error and correction are the purview of the errant pen. Taking the image of the quaking pen—one of the most familiar images of authorial excuse, from Chaucer through Lydgate—Wyatt develops a poetics of error itself.

> Yet well ye know yt will renue my smarte
> Thus to reherse the paynes that I have past;
> *My hand doth shake, my penn skant dothe his parte,*
> *My boddye quakes, my wyttis begynne to waste;*
> Twixt heate and colde in fere I fele my herte
> Panting for paine, and thus as all agaste
> *I do remayne skant wotting what I wryte:*
> Perdon me then rudelye tho I indyte.
>   (214.17–24; emphases mine)

What Wyatt, in the *Defence*, called "mysreportinge and mysvnderstandinge" resonates anew with the conventions of the envoy and the fears of the pen. In this ballad, however, the quaking pen has been transferred to the poet's whole body. The sequence of lines 19 to 21 is a veritable anatomy of a Chaucerian idiom: from hand, to pen, to body, to wits, to heart, the insecurities of writer move from the extremities of writing to the inner site of feeling and desire. By the time we get to the line "I do remayne skant wotting what I wryte," we can see that the narrator's self-ignorance grows from this fundamental separation of the writing hand from the feeling heart.[92] Notice the contrast between this line and the last line of "Me list no more to sing." I wot what I do mean, but I scarcely know what I write. To grant the writer our goodwill is not, therefore, simply to share in the topoi of modesty but to recognize that those texts inscribed with quaking pens are, quite simply, textually unreliable.

This question of the unreliable text is both a condition of Wyatt's textual transmission and a theme addressed throughout the poetry. When Wyatt concludes the short poem "Who would haue euer thought" with the lines "But note I wyll thys texte, To draw better the nexte" (191.17–18), what he implies is the possibility of endless rescription. The next poem will be better drawn; the scribal lessons of the previous will be incorporated in the next. But this will never happen. What we must see, as Wyatt's readers, is the constantly changing nature of his verse as it is always written and, in the process, that it exposes how both the poems and their scribes bring out the insecurities of manuscript transmission. From the standpoint of editorial practice, the sacrifices to modernity do not just misrepresent a historical artifact. They censor the controlling ambiguities in the poetry. Crewe's choice of words, then, is uncannily accurate, as Wyatt himself constructs, in the *Defence*, an argument for textual criticism grounded in the language of censorial politics. Repentance is a key word for both the poems I have looked at in detail here, as it is for More and Elyot in their respective meditations on error. The urge to confess remains; in "Lament my loss," so is the urge to pray.

And so, too, is the urge to prove. Pynson's indenture, in addition to offering what may be the earliest use of the word "proof" in textual terms in English (it predates the *OED* entries by nearly half a century), also deploys the rhetoric of good will, error, and correction, of responsibility and authorship, explored in all the texts I have discussed here. It reveals something of the habits of the print shop, and Percy Simpson uses this and other contemporary texts to show the ways in which the printer and his employees struggled with error and correction. In another document—a poem written in about 1530, describing the principles of selection in Robert Copland's printing house—the exchange between printer and an anonymous customer (called "Quidam") shows what is going on in language precisely equivalent to Wyatt's.[93] When Copland asks his customer if he has "any copy" of the work he wants, Quidam replies:

> I haue no boke, but yet I can you shewe
> The matter by herte, and that by wordes fewe.
> Take your penne, and wryte as I do say
> But yet of one thyng, hertely I you praye,
> Amende the englysh somwhat if ye can.
> And spel it true, for I shall tel the man
> By my soule ye prynters make such englysche
> So yll spelled, so yll poynted, and so peuyshe
> That scantly one can rede lynes tow
> But to fynde sentence, he hath ynought to do.

What is the nature of transcription; how can the pen transcribe what the heart knows; and how can printers accurately print those words? True spelling is as much at the core of Copland's craft as it is in Wyatt's imagination and the modern editor's responsibility. This versified exchange admonishes the modern editor much as it abashes the early Tudor printer: right down to the spelling of the word "the." "For I shall tel the man" really means "For I shall tell thee, man." Take your pen, says Quidam. "My pen, take payn a lytyll space," says Wyatt. But what happens when "My hand doth shake, my penn skant dothe his parte"?

In the end, it is faith both in heart and hand that leads the printer and the scholar to adjudicate the error. In 1560, summing up not just the personal but the historical situation of all authors, Jasper Heywood complained about the printing of his Seneca translations by no less a hand than that of Richard Tottel.

> For when to synge of Hande and Starre
>   I chaunced fyrst to come,
> To Printers hands I gaue the worke:
>   by whome I had suche wrong,
> That though my selfe perusde their prooues
>   the fyrst tyme, yet ere long
> When I was gone, they wolde agayne
>   the print therof renewe,

Corrupted all: in such a sorte,
    that scant a sentence trewe
Now flythe abroade as I it wrote.
    which thyng when I had tryde,
And fowrescore greater fautes then myne
    in fortie leaues espyde,
Small thanks (q; I) for such a woorke
    wolde Senec geue to me,
If he were yet a lyue, and shoulde
    perhapps it chaunce to see.[94]

Perhaps it is no accident that Tottel's sign should be the hand and star. When hands shake—be they the quaking bearer of the poet's pen or the of typesetter's letter—all is corrupted. How can we see the stars when we are fixed on the work of errant hands? If this is a complaint about the world of print, though, it recalls complaints about the world of scribes. Tottel plays Adam Scriveyn to Heywood's Chaucerian authority here: Chaucer's bad scribe was charged to "write more trewe," while the poet was faced with correcting the writing: "thy work renewe." But Heywood, too, is summarizing all the idioms of the erratic here. The faults that escape the printer (that tag line of the early English errata sheet) are vivified in the image of Heywood's sentences flying abroad—an image, too, that recalls Erasmus's lament that there still remain some errors in his Seneca that, literally, flew away from him (*Neque vero me fugit plurimum adhuc restitisse mendarum*). Heywood's enumerations of mistakes—greater than fourscore faults in forty leaves—recalls, too, Robert Ridley's moral accountancy of Tyndale's errors: "if ye look well, ye shal not look iij lynes without fawt." His overarching narrative of bookmaking resonates with the narratives of Thomas Elyot; his avowals of personal involvement in proofreading recall More. Proof and repentance, admission and control—these are the terms not just of excuse but identity. The admission of error and the public mark of self-correction stand as the identifying gestures of the humanist subject. In its typographical, political, and lyric forms, it represents the transformation of a voice into a text, a body into a book, an artifact into a narrative.

My forays into early printed books have led me to a rhetoric of error—to a chronicle of set pieces of admission and avowals of intention. Such examples could be multiplied, perhaps, almost endlessly. Scarcely a day goes by when I do not uncover yet another case of an errata sheet, an aphorism on erroneous behavior, or another idiom for botched lines and misplaced letters. It remains hard to keep them all in mind; in fact, keeping them all in mind is precisely the problem for the writers I survey here. All these stories are, like all rhetorical accounts, really tales of remembrance. Memory is the guardian of rhetoric, whose treasure-house (*thesaurus*) is invention. Certainly, Wyatt recalled this phrasing (familiar from as far back as the *Rhetorica ad Herennium*) when he noted, in "Me list no more to sing," "What vailith vndre kaye [i.e., key] / To kepe treasure alwaye?"[95] Wyatt is, in the end, a poet of great memory, and his defense tracts hinge, too, on just what was remembered (or misremembered) by accuser and accused. So, too, Robert Ridley remembers all the bad parts of the Tyndale New Testament, even though he has no book before him. And More, Erasmus, Budé, Elyot, and, finally, Jasper Heywood all tell stories of mistake and their correction as tales of remembrance. The temporality of bookmaking—that feature of the narratives of printing with which I began this chapter—is the temporality of all narrative. Errata sheets become the markers of our memories.

And so I return to the questions asked at the beginning of this chapter. As the age of mechanical reproduction segues into an age of digital transmission, is there any place for error? Spellcheckers and increasingly elaborate programs for grammatical and stylistic review may well make errata a thing of the past. If we are, in fact, coming to the end of (or at least to a turning point in) the history of the book, the study of errata reminds us of a time when proofreading was a labor, when skills at transcription were a valued style of scholarship, and when, in Lisa Jardine's arrestingly evocative phrasing, charisma could be constructed in print. Our memory of scholarship, in the end, is a memory of error, and our fascinations with the early printed book may grow out of a corresponding fascination with a material culture no longer ours.

> *We're ill by these Grammarians us'd.*
> —Abraham Cowley, "Life"

> *I had undergone*
> *something like illumination by philology.*
> —Seamus Heaney, *Beowulf: A New Translation*

SUBLIME PHILOLOGY:
AN ELEGY FOR ANGLO-SAXON STUDIES

Perhaps more than any other modern literary discipline, Old English studies has the reputation as a field of right and wrong. Its institutional idiom remains rigorously philological, a legacy of both the nineteenth-century German positivists, who developed the techniques of historical linguistics and stemmatic textual criticism, and early-twentieth-century British dons, who assembled texts and sources, variants and manuscripts, into an edifice of accuracy for their students. When I began to work in Anglo-Saxon literature in the early 1980s, this idiom was still in place, and leaders of the field could aver, in an almost Victorian progressivist vein, that "We are in a better position than our predecessors have ever been. . . . To our inherited philological base we have added a much improved technical understanding, encompassing advances in palaeography and in the study of sources and cultural background."[1] All the work I had watched in other fields—the claims of theory, the challenges to traditional editorial methods, the arc of cultural critique—appeared to be making but little impact. In the early 1990s, A. E. Housman could still be the source of an appeal to textual criticism as "the science of discovering error in texts and the art of removing it."[2]

The past two decades have seen many arguments about the history and direction of this field.[3] Attempts at bringing Anglo-Saxon studies into line with literary theory, cultural studies, or the broad analyses of the contemporary academy were often met with resistance.[4] Such approaches—with their privileging of the fragmentary over the *grand récit* and their gestures of exposing critical rhetoric as rhetoric—were perceived as powerful threats to the hegemony of traditional scholarship: its eulogistic emphasis, its genealogies of teaching, its praise of the past, its certitudes of bibliographical survey. It was not simply that pursuers of these projects (myself included) were wrong; they were destructive. Reviews from the mid-1980s through the 1990s of a clutch of theoretically adventurous books were filled with chronicles of local errors and global misunderstandings.[5] It was as if the literary scholar had been charged with Housman's challenge: as if Anglo-Saxon studies had itself become a science of discovering error (not just in text but in other critics) and trained its practitioners in the art of removing it.

The history of these conflicts has been told and retold, and I do not wish to recount it again. My purpose here is rather to explore the rhetoric of that history: to see how, behind the claims for accuracy and empiricism, or for signification and cultural critique, there lies a deep emotion and desire. For Old English is at heart a discipline not merely of detection and detail but of the sublime. The pursuit of the meaning of individual words, their etymologies, resonances, and afterlives, has always been the means by which the reader gained transcendent, emotional experience. The search for the authentic literary voice in Anglo-Saxon literature has been the search for illumination. Brilliant and glowing objects fill the pages of Old English scholars, and philology itself stands as the source of illumination for the poetry's readers from the seventeenth to the twenty-first century. Whether it lay in the antiquarian George Hickes's fascinations with the odic quality of verse, or with J. R. R. Tolkien's personal illuminations, or in Seamus Heaney's revelation that, in the course of translating *Beowulf*, he had "undergone something like illumination by philology," those who have studied Anglo-Saxon texts have found their uplift.

But mine is a historical as well as critical point. Old English scholarship begins with the sublime: with the late-seventeenth-century recovery of texts and contexts, with associations among elegies and odes, with claims for a personal and a political core to its canons. Fragments of brief and blinding brilliance were as central to the making of that canon as they were to the establishment of other literary histories in later centuries—and they are to us today. Philology, in short, is a sublime art. It centers on the close analyses of individuated passages, words, or etymons. Its practice reveals to its practitioners something about the literary text or social history. But it often also reveals something of the self.

This is a chapter, then, about the errant scholar in Old English, about figures who may find themselves marked by social upheaval or withdrawal and who quest for national, institutional, or individual salvation in the knowledge offered by the literature. The Anglo-Saxonist often seeks a literary and critical homecoming. Stories of heroic return intertwine with professional self-presentations of prodigality. For George Hickes, a fascination with Pindaric odistry led to a powerful conception of the early English literary canon. But his work went on during a time of riving social and political upheaval. His great *Thesaurus*—compiled in the last decades of the seventeenth century and published in three volumes from 1703–1705—remains a product of a world (in the words of one modern critic) "haunted by coercion and fear; rent by religion and politics; wary, in the aftermath of civil war, of the direction in which jealousies and fears might drive a commonweal."[6] Hickes looks for harmony in such discord. And perhaps, too, so did Tolkien. Best known among Old English scholars for his field-defining lecture of 1936, "*Beowulf*: The Monsters and the Critics," he was an immensely self-aware professional: one who (in this work as well as in other publications and in personal letters) made clear his need to rectify an error and align the errant self. Like Hickes, Tolkien concerns himself with defining a canon of Old English verse. And, again like Hickes, he seeks to draw aesthetic judgments out of philological analysis. But unlike the maker of the *Thesaurus*, whose work may be widely cited but is hardly read (and then largely denigrated for his textual mistakes), Tolkien is omnipresent. Can anything new be said of him? And, for that matter, can anything be added to the mass of recent readings of Heaney's *Beowulf* translation (a critical enterprise also shot through with Tolkien's inheritance)?

The answer is, of course, yes, for it lies in the framing of my narrative that I propose a future for Old English studies in the study of its past. By recognizing its rhetoric of sublimity and salvation, by seeking its debts to an Augustan canon, by finding in its modern claims or arguments a legacy of long debate, this chapter seeks a place for errant selves in scholarship. Old texts become new personal, political, or aesthetic experiences. Yet they still remain the marker of a memory and reminders of the genealogies of inquiry we may never escape.

If there is any single publication that marks the beginnings of modern Anglo-Saxon scholarship, it is George Hickes's *Linguarum Vett. Septentrionalium Thesaurus Grammatico-Criticus et Archaeologicus*, published at the Clarendon Press, Oxford, from 1703–1705.[7] Hickes (1642–1715) was one of the leading figures in the English antiquarian movement; a churchman fascinated with the linguistic, literary, and political origins of national institutions; and a scholar so prolific and enthusiastic that he could be dubbed, by one of his contemporaries, "Literaturae Anglo-Saxonicae Instauratori."[8] His three-volume *Thesaurus*, the culmination of his life's work, contains one of the earliest sets of scholarly editions of Old English vernacular documents. Its explication of the grammar of the early English language and its Germanic associates has been considered a remarkable accomplishment for its time. Its reports of coins, jewels, and the *disjecta membra* of pre-Conquest diplomatics are still valuable. And in its final volume, containing Humphrey Wanley's famous catalog of Anglo-Saxon manuscripts, the *Thesaurus* attained a status in the discipline unmatched until N. R. Ker's *Catalogue of Manuscripts Containing Anglo-Saxon*, published in 1957. J. A. W. Bennett ranked it "not far below the *New English Dictionary* itself" as a monument to scholarly learning and industry, and Hickes's own contemporaries—not least Jean Mabillon—welcomed the publication with enthusiasm.[9] Hickes himself considered the importance of his work not merely to reside in furthering the study of "antiquities" and what he called "ancient septentrionall learning" but (as he put it to one of his benefactors, the Reverend Dr. John Smith of Durham Cathedral) in maintaining "the honour of our English republick of letters."[10]

For someone writing at the close of the seventeenth century, that "republick of letters" has to resonate with the claims of Augustan criticism: with the stirrings of canon formation in the English critical tradition and with notions of the powerful relationships between political identity and literary form. Such claims infuse Hickes's understanding of Old English verse as well, and he emerges in the course of his *Thesaurus* not just as a grammarian, numismatist, and antiquarian but as an Augustan reader. He writes a history of early English poetry as one of ode and elegy, and his selection of texts, generic assessments, and critical judgments grow directly out of the late-seventeenth-century preoccupation with the legacy of Pindar and the example of Abraham Cowley. These two writers form the endpoints of the literary history that Hickes writes in chapter 23 of volume 1 of the *Thesaurus*. Titled "De Poetica Anglo-Saxonum," this chapter reflects on the style, the genres, and the literary impact of Old English verse. It offers one of the earliest printed compilations of that poetry (including the first publication of the famous *Finnsburh Fragment*), and it may well be the first sustained critical assessment of Old English literature ever written.[11]

Hickes is a fascinating figure in the history of scholarship. His own life exemplifies the profound political disjunctions that distinguish a late-seventeenth-century career as churchman and polemicist. An engaged and highly visible figure in the English ecclesiastical hierarchy—he was made dean of Worcester Cathedral in 1683—Hickes did not shy away from controversy. Wary of James II's Catholicism, deeply concerned with the rights of kingship and the order of dynastic succession, and engaged, as many of his antiquarian peers were, in using philological and historical study to explain or justify contemporary political behavior, Hickes found himself at the center of one of the greatest controversies of the later seventeenth century. Space does not permit a review of all the nuances of his positions, but the events of the late 1680s boil down to this: Hickes, while deeply suspicious of the emergent Catholicism of James II and his potential heirs, was nonetheless committed to the king's right to rule (he resolved this paradox under the concept of "passive obedience . . . as the appropriate Anglican establishment response to a Roman Catholic King").[12] Thus, when William and Mary were crowned in 1689, Hickes found himself unable to support their rule and take the oath of allegiance required of all members of the English Church. He was suspended in August 1689 and ultimately stripped of his position in April 1691. Hickes joined a group of what came to be known as the nonjurors (i.e., those who would not take the oath), and throughout the 1690s he lived as an outlaw, staying surreptitiously with friends, traveling in disguise, using false names. How he was able to complete the *Thesaurus* under these conditions is itself a marvel and is the story told in great detail and with substantial reference to Hickes's correspondence by Richard L. Harris and, as part of a larger narrative of antiquarian politics, Joseph Levine.[13]

It is no accident that Hickes should find in Anglo-Saxon verse a powerful reflection of both his political and literary times, and the Cowleyan Pindaric stood—for him, as well as for his contemporaries—as the unique site of that synthesis. Cowley's *Pindarique Odes* of 1656 have long been seen as central to the building of Augustan literary politics. At one level, Cowley's achievement was formal: to render Pindar's apparent freeness of metrical style in English and to evoke the wild digressiveness, bold inspiration, and inventive figurative diction of the odist in the new vernacular. Cowley drew heavily on Pindar's averrals of inspiration. "The Reader must not be chocqued," he wrote, "to hear him [the poet] speak so often of his own Muse; for that is a Liberty which this kind of Poetry can hardly live without."[14] Structurally, such inspiration often led to an apparent formlessness in individual poems—an emphasis, as Cowley himself noted, on digressions. Cowley explains the nature of one of his poems: "this ode is truly Pindarical, falling from one thing into another after [Pindar's] Enthusiastical manner." He refers to "figures unusual and bold even to Timeritie" in the verse, and he writes of the "violent course" of the diction, the narrative, and the invocation.[15] But, at another level, his impact was aesthetic and spiritual. He provided religious writers with a newly classicized conception of inspired, even prophetic, verse. Cowley himself associated Pindar with the "manner of the Prophet's writing," and later followers such as Samuel Woodford sought in Cowleyan Pindarism a precedent for an emotive, if not metrically unfettered, religious odistry.[16] So, too, John Dennis saw in these moves an aspiration to the highest strain of prophetic poetry.[17]

But, finally, Cowley's Pindar was the archetype for what late-seventeenth-century criticism saw as the telos of poetic expression itself. Beginning with Thomas Sprat's assessment in his *Life and Writings of Abraham Cowley* (printed in the posthumous complete works of the poet in 1668), English readers came to see in Pindar what Sprat called "the boldness of His Metaphors, and length of his Digression."[18] Pindar, and Cowley's versions of the Pindaric ode, were seen as pairing these narrative flights with great irregularity of meter, what Sprat called "irregularity of number." But such "loose and unconfin'd measure," he noted, "has all the Grace and Harmony of the most Confin'd." It "affects the mind with a more various delight." It is "large and free" (2:132). Within a decade of Cowley's death, these terms of description and praise had crystallized into an idiom of Augustan criticism.[19] By 1685 Dryden was developing the argument that the Pindaric ode represented the highest achievement of poetic form, and he considered Cowley's forays in the genre unmatched among contemporary poets. This kind of verse, he wrote in the preface to the *Sylvae*, "allows more latitude than any other" and, "As for the soul of it, which consists in the warmth and vigour of fancy, the masterly figures, and the copiousness of imagination, he has excelled all others in this kind."[20] The ode came to provide public poets with a model of encomiastic oratory and, in turn, with the permission to move beyond formal structure and control to express both nationalist subjects and private selves.[21] Rather than being hemmed in by Virgilian strictures or Horatian decorum, some poets and essayists sought a greater freedom of individual expression, and Pindar served as their model. The "Pindaric aesthetic at this stage," writes Penelope Wilson, "relates not to subject matter or even to the past, but to personality realized in style."[22]

Such personality often found its expression in the selective mining of antiquity for new and individual expressions. Cowley's ode "To Mr. Hobs" (described by Wilson as a "Pindaric manifesto of modernism" [p. 27]) offers this great charge:

> To walk in *Ruines*, like vain *Ghosts*, we love,
> And with fond *Divining Wands*
>   We search among the *Dead*
>   For Treasures *Buried*,
> While still the *Liberal Earth* does hold
> So many *Virgin Mines* of *undiscover'd Gold*.[23]

What Wilson calls "the pull of the past" in these lines lies not simply in the claims for ancient sources of inspiration but, more pointedly, in their precisely literate nature. "To Mr. Hobs" is a poem of what I would call vatic antiquarianism: a poem about finding the past ensconced in, and recoverable from, books.

>   Vast *Bodies* of *Philosophie*
> I oft have seen, and read,
> But all are *Bodies Dead*,
> Or *Bodies* by *Art fashioned*;
> I never yet the *Living Soul* could see,
>   But in thy *Books* and *Thee*.   (1.1–6, in Waller, 1:188)

This is a poem about reading, about the relationship of inspiration to erudition, and as such it forms a powerful segue to Hickes's own great scholarly project. The "Treasures Buried" of Cowley's fantasy becomes the etymon of the *Thesaurus*.[24] And the constant interspersals of the shards of Anglo-Saxon life and letters—be they the inscriptions, manuscripts, coins, artifacts, or the *fragmenta* of poetic quotations—make the project of his literary and linguistic history an assembly of such ruins.

All the issues raised by this tradition of Cowleyan Pindarism—poetic inspiration, generic redefinition, freedom of digressiveness, metrical complexity, audacious figures of expression, and the scholar's sensibility of digging up the literary and linguistic dead—come together in chapter 23 of Hickes's *Thesaurus*. Here he is on meter, moving quickly from a technical discussion of syllabics to an evocation of poetic power:

> Indeed, in several poems and several passages within poems, particularly those characterized by asyndeton, where the poet passionately aflame [*incalescens*] seems to rush through his speech, many tetrasyllables and pentasyllables are linked together continuously, with, every now and then, lines of more syllables interspersed among them here and there: as is generally the way with the [Old English] translation of the Meters of Boethius in the versions of the Cotton [Manuscript], and also, not infrequently, with Caedmon, p. 72 [of Junius's edition]. These examples will illustrate the way this works, placed below here disconnectedly [*disjunctim*], in the Pindaric way [*more Pindaricorum*], than which they are by no means dissimilar.[25]

One way of reading this passage is to apply the Pindaric manner to Hickes's own method itself. The ode's apparently disconnected quality may have inspired Hickes to offer up exemplary *fragmenta* of Old English verse. Dryden had written of the "hyperbata, or a disordered connection of discourse," central to the Cowlean, Pindaric sublime.[26] Is Hickes himself, one may ask, *incalescens* here, rushing through the collection and presentation of materials whose order may seem, to the reader, arbitrary, if not asynctic? The passages that follow, from the poems *Exodus* and *Judith*, from the *Meters of Boethius*, from the poetic passages of the *Anglo-Saxon Chronicle*, and elsewhere, pile up by accretion, becoming successively longer. It is as if, perhaps, Hickes is flipping through his books: here, a bit from Rawlinson's edition of Boethius; there, a page from Thwaites's *Judith*; and, now and then, a selection from Junius's Caedmonian biblical poetry.

But the phrase *more Pindaricorum* also evokes what Cowley and his heirs called "the Pindarique way," a quality not just of the presentation but of the poetry itself. The items Hickes offers here "are by no means dissimilar" to the Pindarics, and this comment suggests that there is a formal and generic association between Greek odes and Old English poetry. Just what those associations are appears in the very text Hickes quotes at this point, the depiction of the overwhelming of the Egyptian forces from the Old English *Exodus*.

> Folc wæs afæred. Flod egsa becwom.
> Gastas geomre. Geofon deaðe hweop.
> Wæron beorh hliðu. Blode bestemed.
> Holm healfre spaw. Hream wæs on ẏðum.
> Wæter weapna ful. Wæl-mist astah.[27]

[The people were terrified. The horror of the flood overwhelmed their sad spirits. The deep did them in. The mountains were spattered with blood, the sea spewed out gore, there was an outcry on the waves. The water was full of weapons. The mist of death rose up.]

This is as powerful and passionate a vision of the force of divine wrath as may be found anywhere in Old English poetry. And yet it is, as well, as powerful a passage as may be found in the canons of the Cowleyan Pindaric. Hickes had been building up to this quotation, offering a string of texts whose subjects are the storms and floods of an unregulated world. The chapter had opened with Metrum 3 from the *Meters of Boethius*, with its arresting imagery of the troubled soul beset by the "strongan stormas . . . weoruld bisgunga" (strong storms of worldly troubles). We then get a selection from Metrum 20, the translation of the great poem of Book 3.m9 of the *Consolation*, here a passage on the diurnal powers of the divine. Many other selections follow, most notably from Metra 4 and 6 of the *Meters*, with their evocations of the terror and beauty of the world in stormy conflict: from Metrum 4, the imagery of the black storm and the hateful wind (*swearta storm, laðran wind*); and, from Metrum 6, the powerful storms that sweep away the rose's beauty and the vision of the great sea beset by the northern blast.[28]

This imagery, of course, is central to a great deal of Old English verse and is indebted to the *Consolation of Philosophy* itself, where crazy weather undergirds the physical allegories of the soul in terror or of divine wrath. But, here, these selections stand as markers of the Pindaric. There is a kind of epistemological meteorology at work on Hickes's pages, a vision of the overflowing water, wind, and weather that cannot but recall Pindar's own "enthusiastic" flights and Horace's compelling imitation. Cowley's "Praise of Pindar," too, evokes the "swoln Flood from some steep Mountain," while "The Resurrection" (that most "truly Pindarical" of his poems) enthuses: "Not *Winds* to *Voyagers* at Sea, / Nor *Showers* to *Earth* more necessary be." The floodwaters of these Old English poems become, on Hickes's pages, the literalizations of Cowley's

> . . . impetuous *Dithyrambique Tide*,
> Which in no *Channel* deigns t'abide
> Which neither *Banks* nor *Dikes* controul.

So, too, becomes the vision of the Red Sea in the Old English *Exodus*, a poem now as much in *more Pindaricorum* as Cowley's own treatment of the very same subject in his "Plagues of Egypt."

> What tongue th'amazement and th'affright can tell
> Which on the *Chamian Army* fell,
> When on both sides they saw the roaring Main
> Broke loose from his *Invisible Chain*?
> They saw the *monstrous Death* and watry War
> Come rowling down loud Ruine from afar.
> (19.17–22, in Waller 1:230)

It may be no coincidence that Hickes should offer, too, on these first pages of the chapter, an Old English poem markedly in contrast to the "rowling" tides of *Exodus* or the *Meters of Boethius*, a poem that is precisely concerned with building channels, banks, and dikes, the poem we know now as *Durham*.

> Is ðeos burch breome. Geond breoten rice.
> Steopa gestaðolad. Stanas ymb utan.
> Wundrum gewæxen. Weor ymb eornað.

Ean yðum strong. And ðerinne wunað.
Fisca feola kinn. On floda gemong.²⁹

[This city is famous throughout Britain, steeply founded, the stones around it wondrously grown. The Wear runs around it, the river strong in waves, and there in it dwell many different kinds of fish in the movement of the water.]

The poem's theme lies in the institutional control of landscape.³⁰ Instead of Horace's swift mountain river running down its swollen banks, we have the river Wear, precisely circumscribing the monastery on a hill. The creatures that inhabit Horace's poetic riverbanks—and Cowley's, too, in his imitation—are here populating waters to support the monastery.³¹ And, indeed, what better contrast to this fish-filled river than the terrible impression of the Red Sea, rife with dead warriors and their weaponry?

As one reads on in chapter 23, poems and problems familiar to the modern Anglo-Saxonist emerge anew as exemplars of the Augustan Pindaric. In the discussion of word order and poetic figuration, Hickes notes that Anglo-Saxon verse often appears to separate words of agreement, nouns and verbs, adjectives and their nouns, and he goes on to remark on the elaborate figurative quality of the diction: "Secondly, I believe, in what I would call the Pindaric poems of the Anglo-Saxons, there is a daring (*audax*) and free (*libera*) transposition of words, a transposition quite different from the habit among orators, not only those using simple conversational style, but those who speak ornately. There would be no need for this transposition, it seems, unless some metrical law commanding that attention be paid to different rhythms and feet demanded it from the poets."³²

The words "*audax*" and "*libera*," together with the reference to the *lex* of metricality, recall explicitly the familiar idioms of Horace's ode on Pindar:

seu per audacis nova dithyrambos
verba devolvit numerisque fertur
lege solutis;³³

Pindaric prosody is freed from rule, or law, here, and something of that idiom is captured, too, in Hickes's Latin. He changes Horace's *lex soluta* to *lex requirens*: a law that demands violation of the laws, a metrical form that both expresses and embodies the audacity of inspiration. Such audacity resonates precisely with the claims of Cowley's Pindarism. The word "bold," in the English critical tradition, seems a precise translation of Horace's *audax*, and Hickes returns to it to give a new scholarly expression to a common judgment. So, too, the word *libera* connotes the freedom Cowley and his successors had found in Pindar. His was, Cowley had noted, a "free kind of poetry,"[34] and Sprat, recall, considered it a "loose, and unconfin'd measure . . . large and free."[35]

So, just what poems are these "Anglo-Saxon Pindarics," and what is *audax* about them? Hickes's examples, whatever their metrical exemplarity, do share a thematic interest. Great individual accomplishments and sacrifices are the subjects of these passages: the terror of Nero from the *Meters of Boethius*; the near-death of Isaac from *Genesis*; the fate of the fleeing Jews and the pursuing Egyptians from *Exodus*.[36] But it lies in his printings of the celebrations of the great heroic dead—the *Death of Edgar*, the *Battle of Brunanburh*, and, of course, the famous *Finnsburh Fragment*—that Hickes builds a canon of Old English verse designed to fit with his contemporary readers' tastes.

> Whether some brave young man's untimely fate
> In words worth *Dying for* he celebrate,
> Such *mournful*, and such *pleasing* words,
> As *joy* to'his *Mothers* and his *Mistress* grief affords:
> He bids him *Live* and *Grow* in fame,
> Among the *Stars* he sticks his *Name*.
> ("In Praise of Pindar," 3.5–10, in Waller, 1:179)

Cowley's refractions of Horace distill the public role of odic verse, and they provided the Augustan period with a template for the poet's calling. "The insistence," Howard Weinbrot summarizes, "on linking within terrestrial and divine communities" was central to the political impact of the Pindaric, and such a linkage controls the great elegies Hickes prints.[37] The *Battle of Brunanburh* (*Thesaurus*, 1:181–82) and the *Death of Edgar* (*Thesaurus* 1:185–86) become obvious examples of this encomiastic pressure. So, too, does the brief passage from *Judith*, centering on the beasts of battle (199–222, in *Thesaurus* 1:180). Hickes even goes so far as to suggest that he has been able to discern patterns of strophe, antistrophe, and epode in such texts, linking them by implication with the odic forms.[38]

And in *Finnsburh*, perhaps the most compelling and still the most enigmatic of these Anglo-Saxon tales of heroism and defeat, Hickes finds the shards of Pindar's verse itself.

> Swurd-leoma stod
> Swylce eal Finnsburuh. Fyrenu wære.[39]

"The sword-light stood out, as if all Finnsburh were aflame." This dazzling image leads Hickes, in a footnote, into an equally dazzling foray into the linguistic and literary resonances of the term *swurd-leoma*. "Splendor gladiorum," he translates, and yet it is the splendor of the poetry that compels him. He moves through Eddic parallels, Latin translations, scholarly treatments of the history of swords (Nicolaus Westman's *dissertatione philologica*), and, finally, to Pindar: "Simili figura, *aurum*, apud Pindarum, *ardenti igni* comparatur: Olymp. I.2, χρυσος, αιδομενου πυζ." In this reference to the opening of the very first of Pindar's odes, Hickes makes a clear association between the Greek and Old English panegyrics. For it is here that Pindar opens with the great allusion to the gold "like the fire flaming at night," which leads him to reflect on the nature and sources of praise poetry. His subject is the "famous song of praise that enfolds the thoughts of wise poets," and he enjoins: "Now take the Dorian lyre down from its resting place." He speaks of the "grace of song," and he announces that "I will tell you a tale far different from that of earlier bards." All these images will find their fuller exposition in Hickes's later arguments about the lyric and encomiastic quality of Anglo-Saxon verse. But, for now, they help the modern reader to imagine just what kind of poem Hickes thought *Finnsburh* was: a poem of heroic praise, whose subject matter reaches back to the deep past of a shared national and mythic history and which, like Pindar's, offers tales of "wonder" that not only "please" the listener but can make "even what is unbelievable to be, in fact, believed."[40]

Under the rubric of philology, Hickes offers literary criticism. As chapter 23 proceeds, the associations between Pindar and Old English become more and more precise. His definition of lyric poetry itself, richly keyed to the discussions of his contemporary English critics, makes the discussion of Old English and Pindaric poetry virtually congruent.

As for this kind of Pindaric or Lyric sort of poetry [*Pindaricum, Lyricumve genus carminis*], if Caedmon himself did not really discover it through the dictation of the divine, even, I say, divine dictation, he used that which had been discovered before by the ancient Skalds, as the fragment cited above clearly shows. I call the Lyric, therefore, a kind of poem suitable for the lyre and for the voice, which the inspired Poet is in the habit of singing according to the character and genius of the true poem, either his own poems or odes. Thus, to compose poems and to sing with an educating spirit were taught to be one and the same thing.[41]

"Begin the song and stroke the Living Lyre," invoked Cowley in his ode "The Resurrection," and the explicit association of Pindar with lyric performance—both generically and etymologically—goes back to Roman criticism. Quintilian had called Pindar "prince of lyric poets" ("principem Lyricorum Pindarum," *Institutio oratoriae*, 8.6.71), and the blend of lyric form and spiritual inspiration can be found throughout in the *Institutio*. What is at stake in Quintilian, as it would be for the later English seventeenth-century poets and critics, is the direct association of Pindar with lyric poetry (hence Hickes's virtual equivalence in his phrasing, "Pindarum, Lyricumve").[42] Dryden, in the preface to the *Sylvae*, establishes these associations in terms that explicitly echo Quintilian's formulation: "Since Pindar was the prince of lyric poets, let me have leave to say that, in imitating him, our numbers should for the most part, be lyrical: for variety, or rather where the majesty of thought requires it, they may be stretched to the English heroic of five feet, and to the French Alexandrine of six. But the ear must preside, and direct the judgment to the choice of numbers: without the nicety of this, the harmony of Pindaric verse can never be complete."[43] The harmony of the Pindaric, so central to Dryden's notion of the public, oratorical flavor of odic performance, comes into play in Hickes as well. Noting that Anglo-Saxon poetry frequently deploys alliteration, he attributes this prosodic feature not to anything inherent in Old English or Germanic versification but rather to a quality of all great poetry, stretching back to that of the Greeks and Romans. The repetition of initial sounds becomes a general feature of all poetry inspired by the muses, and Hickes then reels off a list of poets (complete with examples) who deploy it, beginning with Pindar and running through Homer, Hesiod, Dionysus, Ennius, Catullus, Lucretius, Virgil, the Scalds, Middle English lyrics, and then what he calls (in a nod, perhaps, to both Quintilian and Dryden) "nostrorum Principes Poetae": Langland, Chaucer, Spenser, Donne, Denham, Waller, Dryden, and, finally, Cowley.

This set of alliterative examples is precisely where the Anglo-Saxon and Augustan intersect. Hickes's selections come from the poets largely seen, by his contemporaries, as contributing to the development of "smooth numbers" in the verse line.[44] Such is the role, for example, that Waller had been seen to play: a kind of metrical way station between Donne and Dryden. As Jonathan Kramnick has discussed, summarizing a whole range of recent critical accounts, the Augustan concern with regularity in meter had both an aesthetic and a political purpose: first, in that it contributed to a controlling, ordered sense of literary unity, a creation of verbal artifacts; but, second, in that it led directly to an appreciation of the larger harmony of social purpose. "Poetry equals metered language. Meter should be regular. Regularity is the foundation of national culture."[45]

Such is the function of Hickes's compilation of alliterating poets, and such is the telos of his Anglo-Saxon literary Pindarism. For if we look at the content of Hickes's quotations, we see the narratives of strife and celebration central to his age. There are the disappointments of Donne's sixth elegy: "Then with new eyes I shall survey, and spy / Death in thy cheeks, and darkness in thine eye." Then, we read of the public conflicts in Denham's poem on the trial of the earl of Strafford, followed by a couplet from his poem on Cowley's death and burial. Two selections from Waller follow, the first from the widely read "Instructions to the painter" poem, followed by these memorable lines from the "Panegyric to Cromwell": "Illustrious acts high raptures do infuse / And every conqueror creates a muse." A selection from Dryden's *Absalom and Achitophel* follows (perhaps the most powerfully political poem of its time, and one that sparked a range of contemporary responses). Finally, we get to "The inundation of all liquid pain," in a selection from Cowley's poem to Dr. Scarborough.[46]

Taken together, these excerpts do more than illustrate a metrical device. They tell a story of political action keyed to their compiler's own experiences in the final decades of the seventeenth century. Read in sequence, these selections contribute to a narrative of service and betrayal, treason and great trial—a narrative fully in keeping with the stories told in Hickes's sermons and letters. They share a common vocabulary: hatred, pity, death, darkness, fate. "It is some comfort for me to think that I am a sufferer with the law," Hickes wrote to Edmund Gibson in 1691, announcing in that same letter, "I am an *exauctorat* man"—an amazing appellation, a word that conjures up the destruction of authority itself.[47] And, for a man so wracked by personal dissent, alliteration, too, could teach him something. Look at his sermon, preached in Worcester on May 29, 1684. Here, like Dryden, Hickes uses the story of Absalom and Achitophel to exemplify rebellion ("You see what Impostors Absalom and Achitophel were," Hickes avers). The sermon reflects on a man, a church, and a nation in a state of upheaval, and its description of the ejection of the bishops from the House of Lords must be read in conjunction with the Cowleyan Pindarics in the *Thesaurus*: "The Lords at first refused to consent to such a fundamental alteration, perceiving very well what might be the consequence thereof, upon which the people were brought down in Multitudes to the Parliament Doors, to cry against the bishops several days successively, till the Terrors of those Tumults did force them to Consent."[48] "The Terrors of those Tumults"—an alliterative half-line if ever there was one. Hickes uses alliteration here as he would describe it in the *Thesaurus*: as the mark of an inspired voice.[49]

Hickes, then, is well aware of the political and literary effects of the sonic. The harmonies of Anglo-Saxon verse, or of the smooth numbers of his Augustan canonical poets, contrast brilliantly with the deep political disjunctions of his time. The Worcester sermon—like so many other of his preacherly performances—shows something of a prophetic Hickes, and, in this, he is not out of line with literary critics of his time.[50] Like his close contemporary, John Dennis, he finds harmony to be central to the praise of God and the prophetic strain. Compare the quotations I have offered from Hickes's *Thesaurus* to the remarks of Dennis on Old Testament prophetic poetry: "Poetry was one of the Prophetick functions. . . . Praise God with songs of the Prophets composing, accompany'd with the Harp and other Instrumental Musick."[51] Indeed, Dennis's claims may well stand for Hickes's here: "There can certainly be no better way to reform the World, than the reading of those Writings which we believe to be divinely inspired" (1:372).

Harmony, lyric prowess, heroic encomium, and divine inspiration—all come together to reveal that Hickes's true concern, which he shared with his critical contemporaries, was the sublime. While Longinus had been known in English translation since 1652, it was not until the 1670s that *On the Sublime* began to be read and widely used, and, by the century's end, the Longinian sublime had, in Norman Maclean's words, "merged quickly" with the reception of Cowley to create a new concept of the odic form.[52] Dennis, in his 1701 essay "The Advancement and Reformation of Poetry," developed these associations in great detail, and he offers in the course of his discussion a string of poetic passages remarkably similar to Hickes's. His selections from Virgil, Dryden, and Milton are rich with scenes of weatherly terror, such as this one from Dryden's translation of Virgil.

> Oft have I seen a sudden Storm arise,
> From all the warring Winds that sweep the Skies.

Dryden's Virgil (a work, interestingly enough, that Hickes owned) becomes, in passages such as this one, Dennis's prime example.[53] But, he goes on to argue, "There is certainly no Subject so great as the Power of God,"[54] and it would seem that Hickes agreed. He transformed, through Latin translation, the exordial formulae of the Old English *Genesis* into the idioms of an Augustan critical aesthetic.

> Us is riht micel. Ðæt we rodera weard.
> Wereda wuldor cining. Wordum herigen.
> Modum lufien: He is mægna sped.
> Heafod ealra heah gesceafta. Frea ælmihtig:
>
> [Nostrum magnum est officium verbis laudare & animis amare coelorum custodem, exercituum (coelestium) gloriam. Ille enim est dominus omnipotens, virtus efficax, & sublime caput omnium creaturarum.][55]

God here becomes the sublime head of all creatures. To imagine the poet's responsibility (*officium*) as praising in words and loving in spirit the guardian of the heavens is to re-create the task of the inspired poet— and, in turn, to aver with Dennis "That Passion is more to be deriv'd from a Sacred Subject, than from a Prophane one."[56]

Hickes found that subject at the close of chapter 23 in the calendrical text known as the *Menologium*. As Hickes recognized, the list of festivals of the Anglo-Saxon church that makes up this poem segues, toward its close, into something else: clearly, a different poem but written in the same scribal hand as the *Menologium*. We know that something else as the separate, gnomic text now called *Maxims II*. For Hickes, it is clearly something special. He states, in a footnote: "At the end of this Calendar there is appended this poem, somewhat in dithyrambics [*quasi dithyrambicum*], whose first verse appears in written in red capitals. The poem concerns the mores of men, the condition of animate and inanimate natural things; additional subject matter includes the forms, habitations, ethics, and theology described in asyndetic gnomes and maxims, and with such elegance, splendor, and propriety that my Latin is incapable of presenting it."[57]

Here, at the close of chapter 23, are Anglo-Saxon dithyrambics unimpeded—and, in turn, a critical review of the Pindaric mode. The elegance (*elegantia*) of the *Maxims* recalls the elegant (*elegans*) quality Hickes had attributed to *Durham*; the *splendor* here recalls the *splendor gladiorum* of that shining light in *Finnsburh* (and, of course, its Pindaric association); and the reference to the asyndetic quality of the gnomes takes us back to Hickes's earliest reference to the Pindaric manner and the asyndeton of the poet *incalescens*. The flow of gnomic utterances is now incapable of translation, incapable, in other words, of being constrained by the Latin of the scholar. Modern critics have found this poem similarly "moving," in large part "because of the way its clear, precise images link up unexpectedly and suggestively."[58] Hickes is not far off in his assessment; indeed, he may be the first reader to define this kind of verse as "gnomic," and he certainly anticipates the legacy of critical response that has long tried to negotiate, in the words of T. A. Shippey, between this poetry's "barely imaginable purpose and [its] undeniable charm" (p. 12).[59]

Throughout "De Poetica Anglo-Saxonum," Hickes has sought to imagine both the purpose and, if not the charm, then certainly the power of Old English verse. In its assemblies of that verse may be discerned a chronicle of poetry divinely inspired, a form of critical assessment made, in Dryden's words, by the presiding ear. In his attentions to the sung, sounded, and heard qualities of poetry, his fascination with its "numbers" and its syllables, and his interest in alliteration, Hickes constructs for Old English verse a public, vocal, lyric quality—a quality of voice that, as he says of alliteration, is fundamentally celebratory. Like

Cowley, Hickes found in religious verse something akin to the Pindaric, and his broad associations between that tradition and the Anglo-Saxon offers us a captivating window into how Augustan readers read their literary past.

We thus may think of Hickes as playing a role in what Paul Fry called many years ago "the poet's calling in the English ode":[60] a way of defining the social and public quality of the poetic vocation in specifically generic terms. Hickes makes it possible for us to reimagine Anglo-Saxon poetry as part of an odic, rather than an epic, form. Instead of locating the Anglo-Saxon idiom in the Homeric, and instead of pursuing what Roberta Frank has dubbed "the search for the Anglo-Saxon oral poet" along the models of the epic singer,[61] Hickes seeks to make Old English verse participate in the odic nation building and bardic poet forming of his age. He offers a vision of the poet's calling, and he makes it possible to reconsider well-known poems in new, and not necessarily narrowly Augustan, ways. The *Finnsburh Fragment*, in his presentation, becomes something of an Anglo-Saxon *Olympian*: a mythological reflection on heroic death, framed in the conflagrations of a similarly heroic conflict. Might we then see the *Meters of Boethius* or Caedmon's *Hymn* as way stations in a line of vatic voices stretching from Pindar to Cowley? Could Caedmon's tale itself, as told in Bede's *Ecclesiastical History* and subsumed into the *Thesaurus*'s narrative, be understood as a seventeenth-, and not a seventh-, century account of what Fry calls "the ode from its first appearance [as] a vehicle of ontological and vocational doubt?"[62]

Such rhetorical questions may return us to Cowley. "We're ill by these Grammarians us'd," he claimed at the beginning of his ode "Life." Perhaps Hickes, too, had been ill used by those who followed him, though some of his contemporaries may have at least intuited what he was doing critically. The antiquarian and ecclesiast Edmund Gibson, in a 1695 letter to Arthur Charlett (a mutual friend of Hickes), seems to get the point of Hickes's work (though not of his unbridled enthusiasm) on Anglo-Saxon: "Dr H . . . s has given us a glorious character of their Poetry, and will hardly allow the Ancients to take place of them in that particular. I have read some of it formerly, but could never meet with any thing that relish'd half soe well as Homer or Virgil. It must be granted 'em, that their expressions are *full and Lofty, and carry in them something that's powerful enough*. But 'tis at least three years since I medl'd in that way; which has worn off the Little I knew of them."[63] Gibson is clearly in tune with the idioms of the Pindaric, recognizing in the "full and Lofty" quality of the Old English poetic expressions just what Hickes had wanted us to see: a power that could make the Anglo-Saxon stand with Homer and Virgil.

Hickes's reputation rests uneasily between the dithyrambs of the *poetae* and the scholarship of the *grammatici*. His linguistic and textual assemblies were widely praised and deeply influential, even as his critical perspective was apparently ignored by his followers. Wotton abridges this material clear out of existence, and Elizabeth Elstob (perhaps Hickes's best-known scholarly heir) clearly has no interest whatsoever in the Pindaric associations that frame "De Poetica Anglo-Saxonum."[64] By the time Old English verse became the purview of the analyses of nineteenth-century English, German, and Scandinavian philologists—and by the time *Beowulf* had asserted itself as the defining poem of the Anglo-Saxon canon—Hickes's rambling Latin and enthusiastic flights, together with his complete ignorance of that epic, may have put off all but the most diligent of readers.

But there is a compelling, critical afterlife to the *Thesaurus*, one not often explicitly acknowledged by his successors and, I think, one systematically effaced by modern critics of the discipline. True, many copies of the *Thesaurus* lay unsold at the time of Hickes's death, and Hickes himself lamented the apparent lack of enthusiasm for his work.[65] And yet its critical idioms percolated up through later-eighteenth-century reflection. The interest in the lofty and sublime character of Anglo-Saxon poetry, apparently in willful contradiction to just what those poems were about, is clearly due to Hickes's influence. Joseph Henley took up Hickes's claims explicitly in his 1726 *Introduction to an English Grammar*, when he noted that, in "the judgment of Dr. Hickes, . . . there is an Air of the Sublime in Caedmon . . . equal to that of the Greatest Masters, whether Greek or Latin."[66] John Campbell's *Rational Amusement* (1741) applied Hickes's association of Caedmonian verse with Pindar to define Welsh medieval poetry as "odes," controlled (much as Hickes's saw Old English verse controlled) with "wonderful Regularity, Elegance, and Harmony." Campbell even considered such verses "Pindaricks in Welch."[67]

Campbell has, most recently, been read bemusedly by Roberta Frank, who cannot quite understand how he could praise the "sublime sentiment," "furor poeticus," and "inspired, enthusiastic" outpourings of a poem such as *Durham*.⁶⁸ So, too, she finds it odd that Robert Henry, in his 1774 *History of Great Britain*, would locate "that strong propensity to the sublime and ardent strains" in Anglo-Saxon verse or that Thomas Warton, in his *History of English Poetry* of the same year, would praise that verse in similar terms, when, apparently, the only poems they really knew in detail were the *Battle of Brunanburh* and the *Death of Edgar*. But the point is not that these texts, as Frank states, "seemed to be written by clerics or monastic chroniclers" but that they were *printed* by Hickes (pp. 18–19). The reading of Old English verse in these later-eighteenth-century environments is shaped by Hickes's critical contextualizations. Just what *Durham*, or *Brunanburh*, or the *Death of Edgar* may historically have been is not as pressing as what they critically had been made: exemplars of the Anglo-Saxon Pindaric, poems of national celebration, heroic virtue, or—as, specifically, in the case of *Durham*—of the landscape controlled by a shaping hand and set in contrast to the roiling storms and uncontrolled waters of the Pindar-like poems of the *Meters of Boethius* or *Exodus*. In fact, Warton's opening dissertation "Of the origins of romantic fiction in Europe" is shot through with references to Hickes's *Thesaurus* and with an awareness of the Anglo-Saxon literary inheritance clearly shaped by his Pindarism: references to the "Runic odes" and to the "sublime and figurative craft of diction" in the northern poets and, in particular, an extended translation and discussion of the *Battle of Brunanburh* all bear the stamp of his close reading of Hickes.⁶⁹

Traditional accounts of Anglo-Saxon studies have considered the revival of interest in Old English poetry to have been a product of the later eighteenth century: the age of Gray's odes, of Johnson's *Dictionary*, of Warton's *History*, of the Society of Antiquaries, and, ultimately, of Thorkelin's and Grundtvig's rediscovery of *Beowulf*.⁷⁰ Indeed, such a constellation of phenomena has been seen, too, as constituting the discovery—or something of the invention—of literature as we have come to understand it: that is, of an autonomous category of aesthetic experience, human in theme, nationalist in purpose, and concerned with constructing the system of its canonical texts and authors.⁷¹ Hickes offers the possibility of an alternative early English literary history, one recognized by eighteenth-century enthusiasts but eventually effaced by the post-*Beowulf*ian tradition of epic analysis and philological historicism. And yet the fact remains that, for all his enthusiasm and excess, and for all his seeming wrong-headedness about the Pindaric quality of Anglo-Saxon poetry, Hickes does intuit many of the basic features now recognized as central to it by scholars: the centrality of alliteration; the encomiastic function of heroic narrative; the power of the gnomic.

I began my account by noting that the *Thesaurus* is the first modern work of Anglo-Saxon scholarship, and by that appellation I connote now more than just Hickes's uses of historical philology, textual criticism, and the resources of typographical innovation. The modernity of Hickes's project lies in its search for the philological sublime: in its recognition of Old English literature *as* literature; of the profound pastness of the English literary past; and in the isolation of distinctive idioms or verbal artifacts that offer up a tantalizing, and illuminating, bridge between that past and the modern reader.

If George Hickes seems modern, then what of Tolkien? Recently, he has been dubbed nothing less than the "author of the century," the writer who has most captivated twentieth-century readers and whose fantasies and scholarship have offered touchstones to debates on literature and language, childhood and maturity, politics and personal response.[72] He remains the best-known scholar of medieval English literature, and his work has been subjected to a range of finely nuanced studies, reading the criticism and the fantasy, his own and Anglo-Saxon poetry, together to reveal his appreciation of the power of philology. T. A. Shippey has defined that power in a benchmark critical account of such dual readings: "The regularity and rigour of its [i.e., philology's] observations can resurrect from the dead a society long since vanished of which no other trace remains than the nature of dialect forms in a few old manuscripts."[73] As Shippey argues (in his analysis of Tolkien's detailed, but today largely unread, scholarly article on verb forms in Middle English devotional prose), such rigor can resuscitate a dead, distinctively English society. The implication of his philological inquiries "was so clearly patriotic, that there had been an England beyond England even in the days when anyone who was anyone spoke French." Tolkien's philological patriotism, not unlike Hickes's, was, in part, due to a sentimental attachment to the provincial (for Tolkien, it was his ancestral Worcestershire; for Hickes, it was his childhood Yorkshire), where linguistic remnants of Old English still survived in dialect and where the churches, public buildings, and local customs still preserved something of older practices or artifacts. Tolkien's

Old English scribes, in Shippey's words, "are gentlemen, scholars, Englishmen too. Tolkien felt at home with them" (p. 32).

This criticism is but the tip of the great pedestal that has raised Tolkien to iconic status in Old English academic circles.[74] He is seen as the first original of scholarship: a figure who intuited the truly literary qualities of Anglo-Saxon poetry, especially of *Beowulf*; an English reader who could rescue an Old English literary heritage from interloping German *Philologen*; a mythologist who could draw on the archetypes of fairyland to script out moral fables for a postwar world. And yet in spite of—or, I venture, because of—his distinctive Englishness and intuition, Tolkien is a critic of the Anglo-Saxon sublime. Much like Hickes, he seeks a moment of almost divine illumination in the philological detail. Like Hickes, too, he seeks to recover not just the texts, forms, and idioms of Anglo-Saxon verse but to define its overarching genre, in this case, the elegy. And like Hickes's, Tolkien's is a critical aesthetic motivated by the literary politics of errancy.

Tolkien's Sir Israel Gollancz Memorial Lecture to the British Academy of 1936, "*Beowulf*: The Monsters and the Critics," sought to save the literary integrity of the poem from the hands of dismembering historians.[75] Responding to a half-century of philological and archaeological inquiries, "The Monsters and the Critics" redefined *Beowulf* as both an object of inquiry and a subject of professional discourse. The poem stands not as a repository of information but as an aesthetic whole. Powerful verse overshadows historical content; the thrill of the imagination overtakes our resistance to the improbable; deep themes replace superficial plots; the artifice of form effaces the artifacts of archaeology. Monsters are good, critics are bad; monsters are poets, critics are historians; monsters bring the poem to life, critics kill it.

This is the received version of Tolkien's account and its reception—an account that is as much a central myth of Anglo-Saxon studies as are, for example, stories of the saving of the poem's manuscript from the Cotton Library fire in 1731 or arguments about the superiority of Friedrich Klaeber's edition over all others.[76] Of course, that these are myths does not deny their occasion or their import. But that they *are* myths means that their retelling brings their tellers and their audiences into a shared bond of professional identity. They have been elevated as the great salvational moments in *Beowulf* scholarship. Rescue and restoration (what Shippey called philology's ability to "resurrect") are the centerpieces of Old English scholarly narrative. Nowhere is rhetoric of revival more vivid than in the opening of Tolkien's lecture. He begins by noting that the critical tradition of Old English studies has overwhelmed the original texts: "The original books are nearly buried." He goes on:

> Of none is this so true as of *The Beowulf,* as it used to be called. I have of course read *The Beowulf,* as have most (but not all) of those who have criticized it. But I fear that, unworthy successor and beneficiary of Joseph Bosworth, I have not been a man so diligent in my special walk as duly to read all that has been printed on, or touching on, this poem. But I have read enough, I think, to venture the opinion that *Beowulfiana* is, while rich in many departments, specially poor in one. It is poor in criticism, criticism that is directed to the understanding of a poem as a poem. It has been said of *Beowulf* itself that its weakness lies in placing the unimportant things at the centre and the important on the outer edges. (p. 3)

Tolkien begins by disinterring the dead. From a buried book and a deceased scholar, he conjures up a work of art. And he does so, first, by recovering the poem's proper name. Instead of calling it *The Beowulf,* "as it used to be called," he renames it simply *Beowulf.* He strips the poem of its classical patina (as we call Homer's works *The Iliad* and *The Odyssey* and Virgil's *The Aeneid*). He eponymizes its title (the poem and the hero now become interchangeable). And he encapsulates both its plot and its theme in such eponymy. It is a poem about "*man on earth*" (p. 23), a poem about its hero. Names and naming are a controlling strategy of Tolkien's argument. Not only do we now have a new poem, but we have the name of the originary figure of Old English studies, Joseph Bosworth, the first chaired professor in the field at Oxford. By contrast, we have only the anonymities of writing on the poem, the unnamed critics who, between Bosworth and Tolkien, are lumped together under the distancing epithet of *Beowulfiana*: "It has been said of *Beowulf...*," but we dare not ask who said it.

Tolkien, perhaps like St. Augustine, knows when he has read enough, and what he has read tells him that most writing on the poem has been marginal—or, to put it more precisely, that what has been said of the marginality of *Beowulf* is more accurately true of its criticism: "It has been said of *Beowulf* itself that its weakness lies in placing the unimportant things at the centre and the important on the outer edges. . . . I think it profoundly untrue of the poem, but strikingly true of the literature about it. *Beowulf* has been used as a quarry of fact and fancy, far more assiduously than it has been studied as a work of art" (pp. 3–4). What precisely Tolkien means by these terms—poem, art, criticism—will become clear by the lecture's end. In fact, the business of "The Monsters and the Critics" is as much to define these key terms as it is to appreciate the poem through them. Tolkien is interested in a poetry of power. At times, he says, the "poetry [is] so powerful, that this quite overshadows the historical content" (p. 5). Such power, though, is not an invitation to analysis but instead lies as an opening to appreciation. The legacy of W. P. Ker, for example, has led some to label *Beowulf* an "enigmatic poem," an appellation Tolkien clearly would resist. What, in the end, restores the poem's literary value is its sense of unity, its blend of form and content: "*Beowulf* is indeed the most successful Old English poem because in it the elements, language, metre, theme, structure, are all most nearly in harmony" (p. 31). This is high praise, but it is also high elegy, words spoken over what was labeled on the first page of the lecture a "buried" book. Compare this phrasing, and Tolkien's encomiastic idiom throughout, with that great eulogistic moment at the close of Shakespeare's *Julius Caesar*.

> This was the noblest Roman of them all.
> . . . .
> His life was gentle, and the elements
> So mixed in him that Nature might stand up
> And say to all the world, "This was a man."[77]

Mark Antony on Brutus is to Tolkien on the poem. It is not just that both speakers praise the heroic dead; not just that both invest in a language of manhood and deft control. Both make the object of the eulogy the emblem of a national identity. The poem *Beowulf* becomes the best of the Anglo-Saxon. *Beowulf*, Tolkien writes as he moves toward his close, "is not an 'epic,' not even a magnified 'lay.' No terms borrowed from Greek or other literatures exactly fit: there is no reason why they should. Though if we must have a term, we should choose rather 'elegy.' It is an heroic-elegiac poem; and in a sense all its first 3,136 lines are the prelude to a dirge" (p. 33). By refusing to affiliate the poem with the genres of the classics, Tolkien goes back to his opening critical feint: renaming the text without the classicizing definite article. No Swedish prince or treacherous friend defeats the hero—in other words, there is no tragic moment of martial interchange or deceit, the very stuff of both the classical and the Shakespearean stage. Beowulf does not fall with "et tu, Brute," on his lips. But all this Englishness is but a ruse. The word "elegy" itself is borrowed from the Greek, regardless of how native is the dragon that inspires it. Tolkien is searching now for something close to the sublime, something that he can only express in the terms of the classical tradition. For in his great appeal to *Beowulf*'s universality, Tolkien extends this paradox of criticism: a classic that is not a classic, an English poem that invites, perhaps at times unwittingly, discussion in the idioms of the classical and not the vernacular philologist. "At the beginning, and during its process, and most of all at the end, we look down as if from a visionary height upon the house of man in the valley of the world. A light starts—*lixte se leoma ofer landa fela*—and there is the sound of music; but the outer darkness and its hostile offspring lie ever in wait for the torches to fail and the voices to cease. Grendel is maddened by the sound of harps" (p. 35). And yet so, too, is Tolkien maddened by the sound of harps. Not for him the affiliations with the lyric, the Pindaric, the heroic Greek that would appeal so to George Hickes. But, like Hickes, Tolkien cannot resist the light. Recall, now, how Hickes found in the *Finnsburh Fragment* that splendid sword-light that illuminated both the drama of the poem and the meaning of his literary past. *Swurd-leoma*, for Hickes, led him to the great philological digression I mapped out earlier, and it led him to direct association with Pindar. For Tolkien, the light only *seems* to be vernacular. His discussion here is, in the end, as classical as anything in the *Thesaurus*. What he has done, in essence, is to rewrite the experience of *Beowulf* as a classical vision: Scipio Africanus looking down upon this little world, as he does in Macrobius's commentary on Cicero's *Dream of Scipio*; or, in a moment inspired by this late Roman text, the close of Chaucer's *Troilus and Criseyde*, when the dead hero looks down from his heaven on "this litel spot of erthe" and hears not the harps of men but the "hevenyssh melodie" of the "erratik sterres."[78] Tolkien's harmony is not the sound of harps or lyres but the music of Old English verse.

"The Monsters and the Critics" remains an amazing piece of literary criticism, even though it seems so anticritical. The transhistorical appreciation of a literary work outweighs whatever "enigmatic" theoretical agendas it invites or, for that matter, whatever narrowly historical conditions that fostered its creation and transmission. The purpose of its criticism is to define the poem's formal unity, to celebrate its quality as an aesthetic object, and—this, it seems to me, is the real legacy of Tolkien's lecture—to construct a way of writing about it. What "The Monsters and the Critics" does is to bequeath a rhetoric of *Beowulf* criticism: a notion not so much of what the poem is about as of the proper ways of writing about what it is about. The strategies of celebration and citation, of elegiac tone and eulogistic purpose, are all presented here for the first time, and they control the fundamental assumptions of Old English scholarship for the next fifty years.

These fundamental assumptions, however, are not those defining the position of a critic or the constructions of a method. They are, instead, those of a genealogy of critical *auctores*. There is a patrimony to the practice of Old English studies, traceable through the chaired professorships, dissertation directors, and textual critics who have constituted not just the instructive personnel of Anglo-Saxon but the living memory of its history. There was an anecdote in circulation in the early 1980s that before the publication of the *Bibliography of Publications on Old English Literature* by Stanley Greenfield and Fred Robinson the single most important piece of information on the history of Anglo-Saxon scholarship was Robinson's home phone number. Such a tale, which I myself heard on a panel at the Modern Language Association of America Convention, says much about the personalization of the field. Its reliance on oral lore and institutionalized figures led, as a consequence, to the construction of a coterie or club of those sharing in the vital social codes and currency of academic commerce. Old English studies re-created, in its academic practice, the *comitatus* it imagined for the heroic performers in and of its fictions.

Yet, even when the Greenfield-Robinson *Bibliography* was published, its editors maintained the inherited construction of the field *as* an inheritance. They offered this obeisance (complete with untranslated German) to define the scope of their project: "In deciding what constitutes Old English 'literature' as opposed to other types of writing in the vernacular, we have in general been guided by the formulation of Richard

Wülker in his *Grundriss* of 1885: 'Ausgeschlossen habe ich alle Denkmäler, welche man in einer Literaturgeschichte ausschliessen würde, weil sie kein selbstständiges Interesse haben' (p. vi)." What are the presuppositions behind this avowal? On the one hand, they purport to eschew self-conscious reflection on the definitions of the subject or the methodology of study in favor of intuition and common sense: a privileging of the "selbstständiges Interesse," those things of self-apparent interest. Literary works for Wülker, much as for Tolkien, are *Denkmäler*, monuments or memorials, with an aesthetic autonomy independent from cultural conditions or social production. But note that this is not a guide to understanding but a principle of exclusion, and Greenfield and Robinson announce that they have occasionally departed from its strictures. Their *Bibliography* includes entries on Aelfric's *Grammar*, "since it is a work by the leading literary figure of his age," as well as sections on Old English scientific writings and late Old English texts, "including a few which some scholars have preferred to call early Middle English (e.g., 'The Grave' and 'William the Conqueror'), but nothing that is generally regarded as Middle English has been included." Finally, they announce, again with an untranslated appeal to German authority, "The distinction between literary and historical scholarship is not always clear. . . . As Wülker ruefully remarked, 'Überhaupt liess sich die Grenze zwischen dem, was aufzunehmen, und dem, was wegzulassen war, nicht immer so scharf ziehen.'"[79]

Rhetorically, these statements from the Greenfield-Robinson *Bibliography* sustain the citational and patrimonial program of Tolkien. Wülker stands in relationship to the modern bibliographers as Bosworth stands for Tolkien, as the originary authority to whom one constructs appeals of control. Both Tolkien and Greenfield-Robinson hold to the fundamental, and therefore tacit, assumptions of the autonomy of the literary text. Indeed, it is that very autonomy that defines something as a literary text and thus enables one to demarcate the *Grenze* between it and the historical. In these terms, literature, as well as literary scholarship, is to be distinguished from history. But it can also be associated with certain social values or ethical positions. The tone of Tolkien, much like the tone of Greenfield and Robinson, is always recuperative. For the latter, Aelfric is recuperated as "the leading literary figure of his age," a named author in a world of anonymous scops. Similarly, certain texts such as "The Grave" and "William the Conqueror" are retrieved from that unsure midworld between Old and Middle English, though just who has "generally regarded [other works] as Middle English" is never made explicit.

Tolkien's criticism and Greenfield-Robinson's bibliographic scholarship are linked not just in their rhetoric or in their celebration but in their sense of an institutional purpose. They relocate the student in a sure landscape of historical and personal accounts: of scholars passing on endowed chairs, of publications savored in great libraries, of universities that stand in spite of social unrest or political change. Much has been made of Tolkien's role in all this and, in particular, of the creation of his academic and public career. But little has been said about those institutional documents, and I turn now to two texts that illustrate the errancies of Tolkien's scholarship and heroism and mark the Anglo-Saxonist as the returning hero.

Apart from "The Monsters and the Critics," Tolkien's best-known work of literary criticism is his 1953 essay "The Homecoming of Beorhtnoth Beorhthelm's Son."[80] Ostensibly a reading of the *Battle of Maldon*, the piece is largely taken up with Tolkien's own poetic fantasy on the return of Beorhtnoth's body to his homeland and, in turn, with a mediation on the *ofermod* (pride or reckless confidence) that led Beorhtnoth to give in to the Vikings and permit the defeat of the English and the loss of his own life. But Tolkien had voiced many of these thematic concerns over a quarter of a century before, in his letter of application for the Rawlinson and Bosworth Chair of Anglo-Saxon at Oxford.[81] The letter of application and the "Homecoming" lecture effectively bracket Tolkien's academic career. The first was written in 1925, when he was thirty-three and had barely published anything. The second was published in 1953, when he was sixty-one; *The Lord of the Rings* had just been finished, and the major philological work of his career had been completed. For all their differences in purpose and their distance in time, they are fundamentally the same.

The letter of application is a story of homecoming, an account of personal belonging shaped through scholarships, schools, and teachers. Tolkien begins by writing out his academic genealogy: Exeter College exhibitioner; classical moderations; first-class honors in English; the Lancashire Fusiliers; work on the *Oxford English Dictionary*; Dr. Bradley's assistant. Then, we get the five years at Leeds. "I began," he says, "with five hesitant pioneers out of a School . . . of about sixty members." The academic success story of philology at Leeds is a story of numbers. Tolkien claims to have increased the number of students in the area and to have filled classes in a spectrum of courses ranging from Old and Middle English through Icelandic and Welsh. But this is also a story of indoctrination: of domesticating the wilds of philology and making it a fit field for the young: "Philology, indeed, appears to have lost for these students its connotations of terror if not of mystery." It is impossible—at least for me—to read this letter without thinking of it as a professorial response to the coastguard's question of the hero in *Beowulf.* I have to know, he says, just who you are and where you come from. "Hwæt syndon ge?" he asks, and then: "ofost is selest / to gecyðanne hwanan eowre cyme syndon" (it is best to know soon where you come from and why [*Beowulf* 237, 256–57]). And Beowulf responds. He tells the coastguard of his birth, his father, his exploits, and his boasts (260–85). The litany of Leeds accomplishments for Tolkien fits rhetorically into this paradigm, as does the boast—it is now nothing less—for appointment. As Beowulf says,

> Ic þæs Hroðgar mæg
> þurh rumne sefan ræd gelæran,
> . . . .
> ond þa cear-wylmas colran wurðað.
>
> [Concerning this matter, I can show Hrothgar, in my great-heartedness, a plan . . . and how to calm his flood of cares.]
>
> (*Beowulf,* 277–82)

Like his hero, Tolkien has cleansed a place of mystery and terror. He has made philology safe for the young, sought out, too, diplomatic rapprochments between linguistics and literary study, two areas that had been fraught with confrontation: "An active discussion-class has been conducted, on lines more familiar in schools of literature than of language, which has borne fruit in friendly rivalry and open debate with the corresponding literary assembly." Tolkien plays the diplomat here. The linguists, he had stated earlier, are at Leeds "in no way isolated or cut off from the general life and work of the department." And such détente, if not collaboration, will be his goal in the Oxford chair: "If elected to the Rawlinson and Bosworth Chair I should endeavour to make productive use of the opportunities which it offers for research; to advance, to the best of my ability, the growing neighbourliness of linguistic and literary studies, which can never be enemies except by misunderstanding or without loss to both; and to continue in a wider and more fertile field the encouragement of philological *enthusiasm* among the young" (emphasis mine). These are the claims of academic politics. Tolkien's homecoming will bring a new peaceable kingdom to Oxford literature and language. Indeed, the conception of the enemy here is one of misunderstanding, a conception central, too, to his views of the political tensions both in *Beowulf* and *Maldon*. And, of course, there is enthusiasm. Tolkien's final claim returns the reader to the opening of his letter, where he notes that the chair would "afford such opportunity of expressing and communicating an instructed *enthusiasm* for Anglo-Saxon studies" (emphasis mine).

Just what is this "instructed enthusiasm"? Its odd, almost oxymoronic pairing of the controlled and the excitable seems, at first reading, but a symptom of the English academic rhetoric of the age. But behind it, I believe, lies the idiom of George Hickes and the legacy of a conception of Old English poetry and scholarship as precisely a form of instructed enthusiasm. Recall Hickes's discussion of Caedmon and the power of the lyric poet. "To compose poems and to sing with an educating spirit were taught to be one and the same thing." This notion of the educating spirit, of inspiration calibrated to a profound pedagogy, resonates with Tolkien's vision of a philological professor. His goal is to instruct in enthusiasm, not just to foster an appreciation of language or literature but to stimulate an appreciation for the voice of Anglo-Saxon verse.

More than a quarter of a century later, ensconced in his chair, Tolkien himself could give voice to that verse. "The Homecoming of Beorhtnoth Beorhthelm's Son" presents itself as an assay of *ofermod*. It seeks to understand the nature of heroic action in *The Battle of Maldon*, to define its hero, Beorhtnoth, in the light of other early English literary figures, and to characterize not just the literary but the cultural idiom of that fragmentary poem's narrator. Terms such as "uttermost endurance," "indomitable will," "richness," "chivalry," "heroism," "art," and "thought" pepper Tolkien's readings. By the end, "The Homecoming" has become as much a reflection on the elevating aesthetics of Anglo-Saxon literature as "The Monsters and the Critics" had been.

This essay, too, remains a statement of the professional as well as the literary life, and, in this claim, I see "The Homecoming" as answering the letter of application for the Oxford chair. Here, Tolkien's consideration of the philological persona finds its voice not in the prose analysis of the essay but in the long poetic conversation that lies at its heart. "The Homecoming" is, in fact, more the title of the poem than the subject of the essay, and its two characters, Torhthelm and Tidwald, present a vision of the two sides of Tolkien himself: the poet and philologist, the imagist and the empiricist.

The poem deals with the discovery and return of the fallen body of Beorhtnoth. Torhthelm and Tidwald survey the battle scene, express horror at the piles of fallen men, discover Beorhtnoth's body, and return it for a proper burial. But, in the process, they reveal two ways of looking at the world. Torhthelm is the imaginative poet: someone who always sees fantastic figures lurking behind everyday occurrences, who breaks into evocative verse at the slightest provocation, and who can rephrase the hard facts of war and sorrow in terms of the myths and metaphors of northern European narrative. In Tolkien's words of introduction, he is a youth, whose "head is full of old lays concerning the heroes of northern antiquity."[82] Tidwald is the hardheaded realist, an old farmer who constantly feels compelled to remind Torhthelm that the sounds of night are not the cries of the ghosts or wolf-men of a terrifying and mysterious past but rather just the hoots of owls in an ordinary present. He takes the omens and anxiety of his companion and recasts them as brute facts and actions.

Look, for example, at the opening discussion of the poem. Torhthelm reflects upon the weird experience of waiting among the dead.

> I've watched and waited, till the wind sighing
> was like words whispered by waking ghosts
> that in my ears muttered. (p. 3)[83]

For Tidwald, all this is just what his "eyes fancied." "My lad, you're crazed," he says.

> Your fancies and your fears make foes of nothing.
> Help me to heave 'em! . . . Think less, and talk less
> of ghosts. (p. 4)

One can imagine here not just the voice of the old Saxon but the voice of the professor himself. "Your fancies and your fears make foes of nothing." So, too, said Tolkien, in effect, to his Leeds students. To have removed the "terror if not [the] mystery" of philology had been his task there, and his imagined warrior now faces something of a similar challenge. Tidwald takes Torhthelm's fears and makes them everyday. Owls, to him, are not omens; they are only owls. Torhthelm is seeking something—Beorhtnoth's body but, in essence, really something more—but it is Tidwald who carries the lantern. They see the gruesome dead before them, but Torhthelm sees only what the poets tell him. As he states, in language rich with simile and metaphor:

> It's like the dim shadow
> of heathen hell, in the hopeless kingdom
> where the search is vain. We might seek for ever
> and yet miss the master in this mirk, Tida. (p. 4)

He looks for what, as he says, "the songs tell us." But Tidwald looks only for what is there.

> Curse this lamplight
> and my eyes' dimness! (p. 5)

So might the scholar say in his study, poring over strange texts with little light and fading vision. Tidwald sees these dead as just "dead and done-for." But Torhthelm sees vivid—if not vivified—horror in their faces.

> He's looking at me.
> I can't abide his eyes, bleak and evil
> as Grendel's in the moon. (p. 6)

When they find Beorhtnoth's body, this debate goes on. Torhthelm gives vent to a great dirge, an elegy to Beorhtnoth and to all fallen heroes, proffered in rhetoric so rich that we can only marvel at Tolkien's ability to imitate the language of his poetic inheritance. But Tidwald brushes all aside.

> Good words enough, gleeman Totta!
> You laboured long as you lay, I guess,
> in the watches of the night, while the wise slumbered.
> But I'd rather have rest, and my rueful thoughts.
> These are Christian days, though the cross is heavy;
> Beorhtnoth we bear not Beowulf here: (p. 7)

Tidwald must bring us back to earth. He must remind his companion, and Tolkien's readers, that the landscape of the battlefield is not the realm of poetry or the imagination but the purview of the modern world. In Christian days, it is the "monks [who] mourn him." Beorhtnoth—now like all modern dead—will be led home not with the kennings of the past but with the "learned Latin" of our modern rituals. "If you spent less in speech," Tidwald reprimands Torhthelm, "you would speed better."

But the poem is not over. Torhthelm thinks he hears more creatures. He imagines shades walking the battlefield, "Troll-shapes, I guess, / or hell-walkers." Tidwald will have none of these "nameless nightshades." Maybe they are other soldiers, friends or foes. Torhthelm attacks, kills one of them, but Tidwald remains unimpressed. To him, his hotheaded friend is but "my bogey-slayer." In the end, it turns out that these men are merely corpse strippers, and Tidwald strips away whatever mystery surrounds them by shedding real light on their trivial misery: "These are hungry folk / and masterless men, miserable skulkers" (pp. 8–9).

And so the two men lead their hero home. They review just what *ofermod* may be and how Beorhtnoth's pride or his moral stature may have led him to decide to let the Northmen cross. Torhthelm retells the story of the battle, rich with resonances of the *Maldon* poem, while Tidwald can only comment, "let the poets babble." "I'm tired of talk," he avers and says of his own speech, "It's only plain language" (p. 11). And, for all Torhthelm's rhetoric, Tidwald has the last words (in English) in the poem:

> Hey! Rattle and bump over rut and boulder!
> The roads are rough and rest is short
> for English men in Æthelred's day. (p. 12)

The roads are rough for English men in Tolkien's day, as well. Tidwald rephrases Torhthelm's verbal flourishes into the blunt vernacular of rattle and bump, and, in doing so, he poses the emergent question for this essay and, indeed, for Tolkien's philological career. For what *is* the place of the poetic in philological inquiry? What are the possible relationships between the Torhthelms and the Tidwalds of the world?

To answer such a question, Tolkien spends the final third of "The Homecoming" arguing for the poetic power of the idea of *ofermod*. Its meaning, he suggests, lies not so much in any exact translation of moral condition or martial action. Instead, we need to understand the term evocatively—as part of a larger history of heroic largesse stretching from *Beowulf* through *Gawain and the Green Knight*. Whatever character flaw Beorhtnoth may have had was formed by his "aristocratic nature" framed in poetry: "Why did Beorhtnoth do this? Owing to a defect in character, no doubt; but a character, we may surmise, not only formed by nature, but moulded also by 'aristocratic tradition', enshrined in tales and verse of poets now lost save for echoes" (p. 15). For Tolkien, Beorhtnoth's "folly" is, in the end, really more a literary trope than a moral failure. If he is "magnificent . . . but certainly wrong," the consequences of his error should be left to poets and not politicians (or perhaps, even, philologists):

> Beorhtnoth was wrong, and he died for his folly. But it was a noble error, or the error of a noble. It was not for his *heorðwerod* to blame him; probably many would not have felt him blameworthy, being themselves noble and chivalrous. But poets, as such, are above chivalry, or even heroism; and if they give any depth to their treatment of such themes, then, even in spite of themselves, these "moods" and the objects to which they are directed will be questioned. (p. 16)

Poets, Tolkien avers, are above chivalry, even if nobles are not—and this seems to me to be precisely the point of the entire "Homecoming" performance. For what Tolkien has done is to present both the poetic and the critical interpretation of the *Battle of Maldon*. For the latter, he explores the literary and linguistic resonances of *ofermod*; details the historical environment in which the battle happened; locates the poem on the continuum of literary history. But, for the former, he places himself above such matters and makes Beorhtnoth's homecoming—and even Tolkien's own—a matter of the personal sublime.

Torhthelm and Tidwald are the two sides of the problem and the two voices of Tolkien. He begins the essay, let us say, in Tidwald's voice, with a factual account of names and dates. But he ends in the voice of Torhthelm, with an appeal to the poetry and with the recognition that, just as in Torhthelm's youthful memory, the meaning of the poem as a whole lies in the "tales and verse of poets now lost save for echoes." But Tolkien's two characters embody the controlling conflict in Old English studies as a whole: debates between philology and literary criticism. In this, they go back to "The Monsters and the Critics" and to the letter of application for the Oxford chair. For, in the end, what are we meant to see in the text of *Beowulf* or on the battlefields of *Maldon*? Should we attend, like Torhthelm, to the monsters lurking just beneath the field of vision; or, like Tidwald, shall we ask only for the clear light of scholarship? Tolkien had figured himself forth as something of a slayer of those monsters in his application for the chair. He has removed from his Leeds students the air of "terror if not mystery" from philology and replaced it with "an active discussion-class . . . on lines more familiar in schools of literature than of language." The mysterious may find itself dispelled, and the more familiar territory of the classroom is revealed.

Tolkien's search for the philological sublime lies in maintaining, paradoxically, both sides of this story. The terror and the mystery are there, be they in the memories of Leeds undergraduates or in Torhthelm's imagination, but Tidwald always enters with his lantern. Tolkien recaptured this illumination once again in a 1958 letter to his son, Christopher. Himself a lecturer at Oxford, the son gave a paper entitled "Barbarians and Citizens" to a group at St. Anne's College. "I think it was a very excellent performance," father Tolkien opens and then goes on:

> It was enormously successful, and I realize now why you hold audiences. There was, of course, life and vividness in your phrases, but you are clear, generally unemphatic and let your stuff speak for itself by sheer placing and shaping. All the same, I suddenly realized that I am a *pure* philologist. I like history, and am moved by it, but its finest moments for me are those in which it throws light on words and names! Several people (and I agree) spoke to me of the art with which you made the beady-eyed Attila on his couch almost vividly present. Yet, oddly, I find the thing that really thrills my nerves is the one you mentioned casually: *atta, attila.* Without those syllables the whole great drama both of history and legend loses savour for me—or would.[84]

Once again, we have the image of illumination. Philology throws light on things, and the savor of both history and legend, its "great drama," lies in little syllables. And yet what syllables these are! The name Attila is, in fact, not Hunnish but Gothic, clearly a loan word from his Germanic-speaking minions. It comes from the Gothic word *atta*, the baby-talk term for father, and *attila* thus must mean little father (p. 447n). What thrills the nerves of Tolkien, then, is the encoding of the father-son relationship in such a little word. What his philology now makes "almost vividly present" is the vision of the father passing on the legacy of literary criticism to the son: of praising him for his Tidwald-like delivery ("clear, generally unemphatic") but, at the same time, recognizing his Torhthelm-like skill at vivid presentation. The father and the son—and, in turn, the whole genealogical quality of Anglo-Saxon scholarship—find themselves now illuminated in the philological sublime.

Tolkien here may, in some sense, pass the torch to Christopher, and (in language resonant of the encomium to Beorhtnoth) he ends his letter calling the paper "of vast nobility and importance." He was, he wrote, able to "retire to bed really happy." And maybe, too, could Tidwald and Torhthelm. For their recovery of Beorhtnoth's body reflects on the nature of Old English scholarship itself. The rescuing of literary texts from the pedantries of philology or the excesses of a critical theory is, as I announced at the beginning of this chapter, the defining narrative of Anglo-Saxon studies. Beorhtnoth's body is the corpus of that work, the body of materials marked, mutilated, and beheaded and yet nonetheless enshrined in the institutions of the learned. Like *Maldon* itself, a scarred, headless fragment of a text, his body is the object of a loving recovery by those assigned to do it. Whether we read it, and all literature, like Tidwald or Torhthelm, is, of course, the lesson of "The Homecoming." But, at the very least, we can, like Tolkien after his son's lecture, retire to bed happy knowing that that corpus lies safely enshrined among the learned.

For many critics of my generation, such a celebration of the literary corpus—let alone bedtime complacencies about its canonicity—would be alien. The hierarchies valorized by Tolkien and his heirs were those of inheritance, of genealogy and social ritual, that placed the literary and academic body where it was thought to belong. Of course, much late-twentieth-century theory has challenged these verities. From deconstruction's often playful reversal of familiar polarities through the New Historicism's supposition that the culturally marginal is the symbolically central, academic discourse has, in essence, seemed to answer Tolkien's opening critical feint. "It has been said of *Beowulf* itself that its weakness lies in placing the unimportant things at the centre and the important on the outer edges. . . . I think it profoundly untrue of the poem, but strikingly true of the literature about it." So some had said of theoretically minded readings of Old English verse—and yet some of those very theorists explicitly set out to find the marginal at the center.

Few things in *Beowulf* have captivated critics of my stripe as much as the sword hilt that the hero recovers from Grendel's mere. Midway through the poem, after Grendel has been killed, his mother has avenged his death, and Beowulf sets out to kill this second monster. The hero travels down beneath the bloody lake that, legends say, holds her home. Beowulf finds his evil quarry, fights her hand to hand, and sees the great sword Hrunting (a gift from the once skeptical but now sympathetic Unferth) fail upon her form. He spies another giant sword lying there. He lifts this sword, cuts off Grendel's mother's head, and then a light appears and the water clears. Then, he cuts Grendel's head off, and, in the monster's blood, the blade melts. Beowulf thus returns to the surface, and to Hrothgar's court, with two souvenirs: the head and the hilt. When Hrothgar accepts the hilt, back in Heorot, he examines it and finds it engraved (the poem's word is "*writen*") with a story about a great clash of giants, a flood, and the retributions of the Lord. And written on the hilt, apparently in runes (*þurh run-stafas rihte gemearcod*), is the name of its first owner (*Beowulf,* 1687–98).

I shared with many critics a preoccupation with this object.[85] It stood as a figure for the poem itself. It reminded me of that moment in the *Iliad,* when Bellerophon bears the enigmatic inscription—the *semata lugra,* or baleful signs—that will eventually kill him. Both these objects functioned as unique written texts in poems of an oral origin (or, at the very least, poems that similarly were concerned with representing their own oral texture in repeated scenes of bardic performance). The hilt provides the opportunity for Hrothgar, then, to function as a kind of reader, and his so-called sermon that follows this scene in the poem reflects on the social function of literature and the nature of performance. There is a tension in the alliterative pairings of the words "*run*" and "*raed*" (writing and speech, or secret and open counsel), one that appears throughout

Germanic poetry and that suggests something of a hermeneutic impulse in craft-literate societies.

The sword hilt stands as the nexus of theory and philology. As the only piece of writing in *Beowulf*—however obliquely envisioned—its very entry into the narrative replaces the primacy of speech with the originality of writing. It challenges the authoritative presence of performance by the authorial stance of the incised text. When the hilt becomes the object of critical analysis, it stands as a metonymy for the poem as a whole, the center of the story. One might consider it an ideal place to locate the textualization of Anglo-Saxon culture, the place to link the inheritances of the Germanic and the ministrations of the Christian, and the place to begin a substantial query of the oral-formulaic quality of early English verse (and, in turn, the embrace of that theory by professional Old English scholars). And yet the modern theoretical fascination with the hilt ironically reenacted the very narrative of Anglo-Saxon scholarship itself. By making it the center of the poem, the critic replaced a performance with an artifact. As the recovered object from the mere, the hilt embodied that controlling myth of scholarly recovery that has so dominated discourse in the field. For, by miming Beowulf's own act of retrieval and Hrothgar's own act of interpretation, the modern critic projects a heroic hermeneutic all his or her own. The true act of recovery here, the true act of salvation, is the act of critically interpreting the poem.

I once had argued vigorously for this position.[86] I had claimed that, by representing a textual self-consciousness within the poem, the hilt may be recovered as the object of a theoretical inquiry concerned with the self-referentiality of texts. By enabling the mimetic replication of recovery and restitution, the critical valorization of the hilt could illustrate what Paul de Man saw as the inherent tension at the heart of theory (the ironization of the language and the metalanguage) or what New Historicism came to see as the paradox of the master's tools (in the words of Aram Veeser, "that every act of unmasking, critique, and opposition uses the tools it condemns and risks falling prey to the practice it exposes").[87] Finally, I suggested that by seeking to replace the traditional centers of *Beowulf* criticism with an object relegated to its margins, the theoretically minded reading of the hilt invites critiques of traditional Old English scholarship—a scholarship that found its rhetoric and ideology in Tolkien's original gesture of replacement.

Reviewing these responses, I see now that this episode in *Beowulf* stands as but a way station on the search for the sublime. The critic's journey mimes the hero's, and the sword hilt becomes the place where the modern, textually minded reader seeks to find the written artifact in what has long been seen as but the legacy of oral performance. The hilt emerges from the mere as damaged: as headless, enigmatic, and seemingly useless as the battered body of Beorhtnoth in Tolkien's poem. And my fascination with the hilt may also link me with another Tolkienian moment. In listening to his son's lecture, Tolkien notices something seemingly ancillary to the talk that nonetheless illuminates the subject—and, more importantly, himself. The hilt is the illuminating moment, the *swurd-leoma* akin to *Finnsburh*'s fragmentary light that so inspired Hickes. *Lixte se leoma, leoht inne stod.* When Beowulf cuts off Grendel's mother's head, the light appears, and the place brightens up (*Beowulf*, 1570). The sword blade melts away, and all that is left is the runic hilt. But this Old English formulaic phrase reminds us of that moment earlier in the poem, when Beowulf and his men first see Heorot from their ship: *lixte se leoma ofer landa fela* (its light shone over many lands [*Beowulf*, 311]). This is the line that Tolkien quotes when he imagines Grendel coming. It is the light of the literary sublime, the light that maddens the monster almost as much as the sound of harps does. For all the claims of theory, we are still searching for the light.

And so is Seamus Heaney. Perhaps the most touted rescue of Old English poetry in recent years has been his translation of *Beowulf*.[88] Doled out, in tantalizing bits, throughout the 1980s and 1990s, the translation was spurred on by the editors of *The Norton Anthology of English Literature*, and it now stands as the first major literary text that students will encounter in the volume.[89] Heaney's *Beowulf* is thus already instantly canonical (in a way that few translations ever get to be), and yet it carries with it something of a double imprimatur. For in addition to its placement in *The Norton Anthology*, it comes from the hand of *our* canonical poet: the Nobel prize–winning Irishman, whose lyrics have chronicled the growth of an expressive literary and political self-consciousness. Heaney has always had a taste for the linguistically archaic—for the sound of early speech, for the etymological resonances in both English and Irish, for the exquisite play of history and language.[90]

Come back past
philology and kennings,
re-enter memory
where the bone's lair

is a love-nest
in the grass.   ("Bone Dreams")

But in his *Beowulf*, Heaney's philology was greeted with some skepticism by professional Anglo-Saxonists. The translation of the first word, "Hwæt," as "So," in what Heaney states is a glib impersonation of the "Scullion speak" of his own family retainers, was an obvious point of ingress for those, like T. A. Shippey, who would find in this translation "two folk narratives: a personal one and an academic one."[91] For Nicholas Howe, "'So' sounds too understated, too domestic for the start of a poem such as *Beowulf*." The deep, epic past seems flattened out; the "tight, compressed style" of the poem finds itself colloquial, almost, at times, too "folksy" in this version. But, of course, it is a folksiness of an embattled folk. As Howe points out, this is a translation come out of an imaginary "Whitby-sur-Moyla," a place half Anglo-Saxon and half northern Irish, joined by an improbable French preposition that, ironically and historically, links both.[92] Heaney's *Beowulf* is thus an event, akin to Hickes's or Tolkien's confrontations with Old English poetry: an evocation of the philological sublime, an attempt to place the poetry in a tradition of a European literary history, and an engagement with the errors—literal as well as metaphorical—of the text.

From the start, this translation stands as an act of personal redemption. Like Tolkien, whom he cites approvingly, Heaney begins his introduction by naming. To call something by a name is to gain power over it, a theme obsessively striped through his own early verse, and Heaney here begins: "The poem called *Beowulf*. . . ." Called by whom? By the poem itself? Surely not. By critics? Well, we see none but Tolkien. Calling will be the theme of Heaney's introduction, for the question really lies in just what this text is. There is something delightfully strange about the poem, he admits. "Readers coming to the poem for the first time are likely to be as delighted as they are discomfited by the strangeness of the names and the immediate lack of known reference points." He goes on.

> An English speaker new to *The Iliad* or *The Odyssey* or *The Aeneid* will probably at least have heard of Troy and Helen, or of Penelope and the Cyclops, or of Dido and the golden bough. These epics may be in Greek and Latin, yet the classical heritage has entered the cultural memory enshrined in English so thoroughly that their worlds are more familiar than that of the first native epic, even though it was composed centuries after them. . . . First-time readers of *Beowulf* very quickly rediscover the meaning of the term "the dark ages," and it is in the hope of dispelling some of the puzzlement they are bound to feel that I have added the marginal glosses which appear in the following pages. (pp. xi–xii)

Notice the vocabulary here: "enshrined," "native epic," "the dark ages," "dispel." There is the contrast not just between the classical and the vernacular but between the sacred and the profane, the elevated and the native, the lucent and the dark. Part of Heaney's job is thus to *illuminate* in the root sense of that word, to bring a light unto the darkness. Such imagery will be familiar to readers of Heaney's earlier poetry: "All I know," he announces in "The Forge," "is a door into the dark." To *dispel*, in his introduction, is to demystify, to scatter whatever spells may have been cast by the poetry's dark magic. So when Grendel appears "as a kind of dog-breath in the dark" (p. xviii), he carries with him the smell not just of the fearful monsters of the distant past but of the still familiar creatures who inhabit Heaney's literary barnyards: the drowned feral cats of "The Early Purges"; the rogue bull of "The Outlaw"; or the weird "turnip-man's lopped head" at Halloween that

> Blazes at us through split bottle glass
> And fumes and swims up like a wrecker's lantern.
>
> Death mask of harvest, mocker at All Souls
> With scorching smells, red dog's eyes in the night—
> We ring and stare into unhallowed light.
> ("No Sanctuary")

Such poetry rings with an almost uncanny familiarity for anyone accustomed to the shape of Grendel's habitation—here rendered in the voice of Heaney's Hrothgar.

> A few miles from here
> a frost-stiffened wood waits and keeps watch
> above a mere; the overhanging bank
> is a maze of tree-roots mirrored in its surface.
> at night there, something uncanny happens:
> the water burns. (1361–66)

These creatures live in an "unhallowed light."

So, to dispel the poem's puzzlement, Heaney relies on some critical verities. He stresses the poem's "mythic potency," alludes to Yeats, and calls up archetypes of phantasms, agons, and deep imagery. The poem's use of gold—"gleaming solidly in underground vaults, on the breasts of queen or the arms and regalia of warriors on the mead benches"—becomes, in Heaney's vision, something like the glories of that earlier Irish poet's Byzantium, "persisting underground as an affirmation of a people's glorious past and an elegy for it" (p. xvii). The transience of earthly wealth finds its survival in the language of the poet. *Beowulf* is not so much an elegy for a past age as the occasion for an elegiac reading. It reflects on the ways in which poetic language can, paradoxically, both inhume the past and bring it back imaginatively to life. Writing of the poem's monsters, Heaney observes that the poem needs them "as figures who call up and show off Beowulf's physical might and his superb gifts as a warrior" (p. xviii). But surely what he means is that the poem needs them as figures who call up and show off the *poet's* imaginative might and his superb gifts as a storyteller—for which we may read, as well, Heaney's own recognition that they pose a challenge to his own gifts as a translator.

Translating *Beowulf* is Heaney's own self-represented agon: his response to the call from the editors of Norton, his rise to the occasion of monstrous representation. It is his Herculean labor. Indeed, in the poem "Hercules and Antaeus," he notes how all the prowess of the hero will be "bequeathed . . . to elegists."

> Balor will die
> and Byrthnoth and Sitting Bull.

And, with each death, there comes not just the keening of a person but the lament of a people. Politics—not Swedish wars or English dynastic disturbance but modern, everyday conflict—is never far from this *Beowulf*. Episodes such as the well-known "Father's lament" rise, he avers, "like emanations from some fissure in the bedrock of the human capacity to endure."

> Such passages mark an ultimate stage in poetic attainment. . . . At these moments of lyric intensity, the keel of the poetry is deeply set in the element of sensation, while the mind's lookout sways metrically and far-sightedly in the element of pure comprehension. . . . And nowhere is this more obviously and memorably the case than in the account of the hero's funeral with which the poem ends. Here the inexorable and the elegiac combine in a description of the funeral pyre being got ready, the body being burnt, and the barrow being constructed—a scene at once immemorial and oddly contemporary. The Geat woman who cries out in dread as the flames consume the body of her dead lord could come straight from a late-twentieth-century news report, from Rwanda or Kosovo; her keen is a nightmare glimpse into the minds of people who have survived traumatic, even monstrous events and who are now being exposed to a comfortless future. We immediately recognize her predicament and the pitch of her grief and find ourselves the better for having them expressed with such adequacy and dignity and unforgiving truth. (pp. xx–xxi)

This great extended reading offers up a vision of the postcolonial sublime. Like all sublime experiences, it trades in fragments, in the burst of "lyric intensity" (a phrase that could come right out of an Augustan or a Romantic reader of Longinus). The brilliant metaphor—"the keel of the poetry"—takes us back to the stormy seas not just of *Beowulf* but of the Cowleyan Pindaric. And where that keel is set is in the "element of pure comprehension," a phrase that recalls, as well, Tolkien's grand praise of the poem's "elements . . . all most nearly in harmony." The light of fire rises as it does throughout so many of the texts I have surveyed here, and the political resonances of these passages in *Beowulf* come for Heaney (as all sublime experiences must come) in immediate recognition. And, if that recognition helps us "find ourselves the better," it may be a betterment as much aesthetic or spiritual as political, a betterment akin to Longinus's own sense of *hupselon*, elevation. The soul "takes a proud flight, and is filled with joy and vaunting, as though it itself had produced what it had heard."[93]

And yet it is Heaney himself who is producing what we hear. His own translation stands, in this discussion, as the vehicle of, as well as testimony to, the sublime experience. And such translation is the agon of his age. If Norton's invitation opened up a door into the dark—if this is, to recall the phrasing of the early section of his introduction, Heaney's encounter with a dark age of poetry—then it is philology that turns on the light. Reviewing his experience of early English language in school, in the university, in the shards of the words that still survive in local dialect, Heaney remarks how he discovered the true meaning of the Old English verb "*þolian*." It means "to suffer," but it survives, too, in British, Irish, and American dialects: "What I was experiencing as I kept meeting up with *thole* on its multicultural odyssey was the feeling which Osip Mandelstam once defined as a 'nostalgia for world culture.' And this was a nostalgia I didn't even know I suffered until I experienced its fulfillment in this little epiphany. It was as if, on the analogy of baptism by desire, I had undergone something like illumination by philology" (p. xxvi).

Much like Tolkien listening, in old age, to his son's presentation, Heaney undergoes illumination by philology. The study of the word reveals not just a history of culture but a history of the self. While Tolkien's fascination with *atta, attila,* placed him in the role of little father to his newborn academic son, Heaney's obsession with *þolian* makes him now the rightful son and heir to generations of "my father's people." "I realized," he writes, that he wanted *Beowulf* to sound as if it were "speakable by one of those relatives" (p. xxvii). But if this is a philological move, it is also a rhetorical one. Not only does it jar his reader into recognition; not only does it move us into the sharing of Heaney's brilliant "epiphany." It recalls, too, the clear directives of rhetorical theory—the very principles of argument laid out in the *Rhetorica ad Herennium* for schoolboys of a millennium and a half. I have already quoted this passage in my introduction, but it bears repeating now as it affirms the tropes of Heaney's turnings:

> When we see in everyday life things that are petty, ordinary, and banal, we generally fail to remember them, because the mind is not being stirred by anything novel or marvelous. But if we see or hear something exceptionally base, dishonorable, extraordinary, great,

unbelievable, or laughable, that we are likely to remember for a long time. Accordingly, things immediate to our eye or ear we commonly forget; incidents of our childhood we often remember best.[94]

Translating *Beowulf* becomes a return to the past, an encounter with the philological sublime that takes us back to the poet's childhood, to the overarching concerns of paternity and inheritance that mark the discipline of Anglo-Saxon studies. The Scullions function, rhetorically, as Bosworth does for Tolkien, or Wülker for Stanley Greenfield and Fred Robinson, or Tolkien himself for legions of Old English critics, as the invocation of a paternalistic authority, as the source of philological knowledge and literary judgment. Even when Heaney admits he is wrong, he has the family, in essence, to back him up. *The Norton Anthology*'s appointed scholarly chaperone was Alfred David, and, as Heaney notes in a concluding acknowledgement: "Al's responses were informed by scholarship and by a lifetime's experience of teaching the poem, so they were invaluable. Nevertheless, I was often reluctant to follow his advice and persisted many times in what we both knew were erroneous ways." Heaney persists in his errors, I think, much as Beorhtnoth persisted—at least, in Tolkien's interpretation—in his. Both follow a higher calling, one not really moral but literary, and the arbiter of error in both cases must remain not the philologist but the poet. Heaney's authority, even when he really is wrong, lies in rhetoric of the inheritance he has established in his introduction: the sure voice of the Scullions, the unimpeachable rectitude of the political experience that he, as his kin, have undergone. If Alfred David brings to *Beowulf* a "lifetime's experience of teaching the poem," Heaney brings a lifetime's experience of having lived it.

But, in the end, for all the politics of Heaney's verse, and for all the politicizing gestures of his introduction to the *Beowulf* translation, I find him more poetic than political. And, in sum, I think this true of Anglo-Saxon studies in the large. I have called this chapter an elegy, and I mean this appellation in a clutch of interlocking ways. For I have focused on the elegiac quality of Anglo-Saxon scholarship itself: its fascinations with the past, with a nostalgic re-creation of events, with the genres of ode and elegy, and with the controlling interest in its own disciplinary inheritance. But I have also called my work an elegy because I seek to praise the as-yet-inhumed body of its discipline. Rather than dismissal, drudgery, and darkness, I find in its history illumination. And, if there remains a future for Old English, it may lie less with the ministrations of philology (new or old) or with the polemics of theory than it does with a return to the poetry itself. Anglo-Saxon studies has continuously recapitulated the controlling idioms of its subject: journeys of exile and return; moments of enlightenment; recoveries of powerful, inscrutable objects. I have traced such a rhetoric of scholarship not just to call attention to its feints or fallacies but to work through it—to pass in and out of philological inquiry in order to return to literature. "We search among the Dead," wrote Cowley, "for Treasures Buried." "The original books," lamented Tolkien, "are nearly buried." Shall we be Tidwald or Torhthelm in bringing back for ritual interral the decapitated corpus of our hero? Shall we find written texts in Beowulf's heroic dive? And, if we do, we may find light in Grendel's *dygel lond.*

Here we have some of the keys to mythology, but the manner of handling them can only be learnt from comparative philology.
—Max Müller, "Comparative Philology"

CHAPTER THREE

MY CASAUBON:
THE NOVEL OF SCHOLARSHIP AND
VICTORIAN PHILOLOGY

After he died, I lost all interest in the novel. The picture of his pedantry—his self-absorption, self-importance, and self-pity—seemed to me the icon of the academic I had feared myself to be. Throughout the book's first chapters, I found aphorisms of my calling that I could not leave alone. His first word in the novel, responding to Mr. Brooke's question as to whether he knows Southey, is a simple "No,"[1] and, for all his claims for scholarship and inquiry, he appears throughout more a figure of negation than control. His bad eyes force him to defer the literary for the documentary; his project, perhaps much like his mind, is organized in pigeonholes; and he is ever living in the barely lit rooms of his libraries. He is a confined creature, akin to those metaphorical pigeons. By chapter 20, Dorothea comes to realize, "with a stifling depression, that the large vistas and wide fresh air which she had dreamed of finding in her husband's mind were replaced by ante-rooms and winding passages which seemed to lead nowhither" (p. 186). And again, just two pages later in that chapter: "Poor Mr. Casaubon himself was lost among small closets and winding stairs, and in an agitated dimness about the Cabeiri, or in an exposure of other mythologists' ill-considered parallels, easily lost sight of any purpose which had prompted him to these labours. With his taper stuck before him he forgot the absence of windows, and in bitter manuscript remarks on other men's notions about the solar deities, he had become indifferent to the sunlight" (p. 188). For Will Ladislaw, Casaubon's failures similarly find their form in spatial displacement, as if, left outside for but a moment, he would lose himself, "groping about in the woods with a pocket-compass" (chap. 21, p. 198). Casaubon remains a failed traveler, a failed carpenter of the imagination, for even in his own enhoused world, the furniture of his mind remains without repair. "Do you not see," Will reminds Dorothea in chapter 22, "that it is no use now to be crawling a little way after men of the last century—men like Bryant—and correcting their mistakes?—living in a lumber-room and furbishing up broken-legged theories about Chus and Mizraim" (p. 211).

Throughout these and many other passages (and I use that word to connote both strings of words and winding hallways), Casaubon emerges as the image of an intractable textuality that breeds only inwardness. He comes off as not so much a parody of Eliot's contemporary academics—for the rigors of nineteenth-century German positivist philology had largely banished such amateurish curiosities as Casaubon—as a picture of an earlier dilettante. He struck me, on first reading, as someone like Horne Tooke, locked away in his country house and conjuring, almost like a magician, arcane etymologies out of the dross of modern spellings.[2] I soon learned I was not alone in seeking sources. Eliot's own readers speculated widely on her model for him. Mark Pattison, the famously learned rector of Lincoln College and a friend of Eliot and her partner, George Henry Lewes, was an early candidate.[3] So, too, was Robert William Mackay, whose expansive *Progress of the Intellect, as Exemplified in the Religious Development of the Greeks and Hebrews* Eliot reviewed for the *Westminster Review* in 1851 (in terms that would come back to texture *Middlemarch*'s idiom two decades later).[4] And there was Dr. Robert Herbert Brabant, who, in 1843, at the age of sixty-two, took the fourteen-year-old Mary Ann Evans off to Devizes and ensconced her in his library and who was himself engaged in a project of such daunting scholarship that, in the words of Eliot's contemporary, Eliza Lynn Linton, "he never got farther than the introductory chapter of a book which he intended to be epoch-making."[5]

But for all the speculation on Casaubon's historical model, the best-known anecdote centers on Eliot herself. In an obituary essay from the

Century Magazine in 1881, the tale is told that a young friend asks the author directly: "But from whom, then, did you draw Casaubon?" George Eliot, "with a humorous solemnity, which was quite in earnest, nevertheless, pointed to her own heart."[6] Not only, as we know now, was Eliot herself engaged in a deep program of reading in the philological and mythographic (far outstripping, in fact, her fictional Casaubon in German learning and orientalism), but she was calling attention to the problem of authorship itself.[7] The Key to All Mythologies remains an exercise in failed authorial control. In chapter 10, Casaubon finds himself "condemned to loneliness . . . [and] despair . . . while toiling in the morass of authorship" (p. 80). By chapter 20, he is a "desponding author" (p. 191); by chapter 28, he has a "wavering trust in his own authorship" (p. 267); by chapter 42, we get a taste of the "autumnal unripeness of his authorship" (p. 398). But *Middlemarch* is full of writers: authors, editors, publishers, annotators. Mr. Brooke himself—with his almost manic flitting from unpursued idea to idea—had made a whole career out of a kind of negative authorship. So, too, Will Ladislaw finds himself in a form of authorship: first, as the writer/editor of the *Pioneer* and then as a political orator and parliamentary rhetorician. Dorothea, moved from taking notes for her husband, eventually seeks something of an authorial control over the pagelike properties of her estates, hoping to drain lands and improve the plight of tenant poor. And, throughout, there are letters, wills, drawings, and paintings by the novel's many hands.[8]

Though many try their hands in *Middlemarch* (the word "hand" seems almost everywhere, beginning with the second word of the novel's second sentence), and many fail, Casaubon remains the most pointed challenge to any author, Eliot or me. He is the ultimate in failed writing: someone incapable of anything other than marginal comment; someone who, as he is assisted by his Dorothea, abandons writing altogether and relies on his amanuensis to mark up texts read aloud to him, to sort what would be left as posthumous fragments of an unwritten book. We might call him a figure of unwriting, whose initial "No" to Mr. Brooke denies the possibility of authorial power altogether. "I have little leisure for such literature just now," he says, in an almost tongue-twistingly alliterative denial (chap. 2, p. 13). His great project, as Dorothea realizes in chapter 20, remains unwritten (as the novel's narrator again reminds us in chapter 29, p. 267). His is a world of illegible characters, of specks and blots, of (as the narrator finally puts it bluntly) "nothing" (chap. 42, p. 398).[9]

Casaubon embodies error in all senses of the word, and he embodies, too (and, at times negates), all those activities that I have addressed throughout this book: the expression of the scholar's authorial identity; the production and editing of texts; the location of the academic self in the disciplinary histories of philology and rhetoric; and, finally, scholarship itself as the pursuit of the sublime.[10] With his dim tapers and his lack of light, Casaubon is a source not of illumination but of darkness, not of elevation but of earth-bound drear. In a passage that seems written almost with Longinus in mind, Eliot presents Casaubon as negating all the classic features of sublimity: "never to be fully possessed by the glory we behold, never to have our consciousness rapturously transformed into the vividness of thought, the ardour of a passion, the energy of an action, but always to be scholarly and uninspired, ambitious and timid, scrupulous and dim-sighted" (chap. 29, p. 267). There was, we finally and bluntly read in chapter 42, "nothing to strike others as sublime about Mr. Casaubon" (p. 403). For all his winding stairways, he remains firmly seated in a chair. And that is how he dies, benched on a divergent pathway in the garden (chap. 48, pp. 458–59).

So much has been made of all these images and idioms, so much historical scholarship and so much recent literary criticism has explored their resonances and their sources, that my own attempt at saying something new about this novel must seem as futile as Casaubon's own project. The massive researches of Gordon Haight have been augmented by editions of the journals and by detailed, textual accounts of the drafting, rewriting, publication, and reception of Eliot's novels, *Middlemarch*, in particular.[11] Critics of the novel have long recognized its imagery. A quarter of a century ago, J. Hillis Miller brilliantly revealed the optic and the semiotic, the place of history in narrative, and, most generally, the ways in which the metaphors of web, key, room, light, mirror, and flowing water (among many others) figuratively represent the "generalizing, rationalizing, order-finding activity of the narrator throughout the book."[12] For Neil Hertz, building on Miller's insights, *Middlemarch* becomes a novel of interpretation, and the relationship between Casaubon and Dorothea scripts itself in the language of the "unintelligible," the "illegible," the blotted. There is, as Hertz avers, a "dark sublimity" in Dorothea and a governing impression that the novel as a whole seeks to confront the problems of the sublime in recognizing Casaubon—not just in the book, but in ourselves.[13]

Yet, throughout these accounts—and the many others that I have reviewed—there is also a pervasive, if at times unsettling, autobiographical cast to the critical engagement. Gordon Haight's "Poor Mr. Casaubon" begins with the avowal that "Every teacher of *Middlemarch* has encountered the disgust that undergraduates feel at the marriage of the nineteen-year-old Dorothea Brooke to 'loathsome old Edward Casaubon.'"[14] Hertz opens "Recognizing Casaubon" by reminding us of just what "teacher-critics have always admired in *Middlemarch*," while, toward its close, he breaks the flow of his analysis of Dorothea's powerful experience of the sublime with this bracketed aside: "I have enough of Casaubon in me to take an intense, bleak pleasure in interrupting a passionate moment with a scholarly gloss."[15] And other critics, often focusing on the long-standing response of Eliot's readers to her book, frequently reflect on just who they are as readers, teachers, or scholars. Catherine Maxwell, for example, in one of the most recent reviews of Dorothea, Casaubon, and intellectual desire in the novel, begins: "Anyone who reads much critical writing on George Eliot . . . ." Certainly, her announcement becomes more than just a trope of criticism; it stands as the opening avowal of a critical professionalism, of a scholarly identity shaped precisely through the experience, if not the business, of reading "much critical writing on George Eliot."[16] There remains something about *Middlemarch* that makes its invitations to the autobiographical—or, at the very least, the autocritical—irresistible.[17]

This chapter rises to that bait. Casaubon's mythography stands as a *philological* activity, one keyed to the intellectual milieu of English scholarship both at the moment of the novel's fictional setting (1829–1830) and at the time of its writing and early reception (the 1870s and 1880s). But my account of Casaubon's—and Eliot's—inquiries, and of the history of nineteenth-century philology that they embrace, proffers not another analytical and linear account of this material. What I propose is something of a Casaubon-like project of my own: not so much a writing as an unwriting of the history of philology, a fractured lexicon of intellectual inquiry. My chapter reproduces as its method an alphabetical assembly of "erratic fragments" central to the Key to All Mythologies (chap. 3, p. 20). But my chapter also reproduces an assembly of fragments central to what may well be the one truly successful labor of Victorian erudition. For if

Casaubon's project echoes the attempts of such assemblies as Tooke's *Diversions of Purley*, Brabant's unwritten tome, Mackay's *Progress of the Intellect*, or the myriad projects of such mythographers as Henry Sumner Maine or Friedrich Creuzer, it finds its answer in the *Oxford English Dictionary*. Lexicography and novelistic authorship have powerful associations in this period, and my chapter hopes not just to expose their mutual resonances but also to enact them.

The story of the *Oxford English Dictionary* has been written many times.[18] We now know a great deal about just who provided slips of entries for the definitions; how the books were chosen; how Murray himself and his assistants conceived—philosophically, politically, and even aesthetically—of their mission; and how, most generally, the canons of Victorian literary, editorial, and social behavior shaped the principles of its selection, publishing, and presentation. This philological enterprise had a vast impact on its contemporary literary culture.[19] To read *Middlemarch* and the *OED*, Casaubon and Murray, side by side is to appreciate their mutual contributions to ideas of authorship. It is to juxtapose the individual against the group, the scholar against the amanuensis, the reader against the user. It is to see both works as forms of serialized publication: as exemplars of and challenges to the technologies of printing, trade in books, and habits of review that defined the acts of reading for the later nineteenth century. The *OED* was built, collaboratively, out of Victorian habits of reading. The *Dictionary* began with calls for readers to write down the usages of words found in their books and send them in. The vast collection of material assembled offered up, for its editors, not only a history of language but a history of reading taste, a record of the ways in which the scope of English prose and poetry was understood. The *OED* embodies, then, conceptions about authorship and authority, notions of canonicity, and a controlling vision of the history of English literature. Philology and lexicography become the lenses through which that literature is read. The *OED*, as Arnold Bennet put it, was "the longest sensational serial ever written."[20] Its main characters are not just words themselves but the readers and editors who wrote it. A close reading of its entries can reveal embedded narratives of philological inquiry. On occasion, it relies on writings by its editors themselves (notably Murray) to illustrate the uses of a term. On occasion, too, it may deploy quotations to illuminate a seemingly neutral word in ways that reflect the scholarly ideology of its compilers. Much as its compilers and editors would read a novel for its language, I propose reading this *Dictionary* as a novel.

And the novel that, I think, bears closest contact to its project is *Middlemarch*. Published serially—in a unique eight-section, four-volume serial that stretched from December 1871 to December 1872—the book appeared as Eliot was writing it. Lewes had arranged with Blackwood an agreement on format and royalties that, for the modern scholar, makes the novel's publication a defining episode in the history of authorship itself. But *Middlemarch*, too, is thematically concerned with problems of publication, and Casaubon's great unwritten Key to All Mythologies is the fulcrum on which the technologies, the perils, the ideals, and the motives of authorship balance.

For both *Middlemarch* and the *OED*, in the end, are stories about reading. The vast collaborative effort of the *Dictionary* yielded huge amounts of paper—slips set in pigeonholes much like those of Casaubon's world—but it also helped change the ways that people read. Now every reader could become an annotator, every man or woman his or her own Dorothea. As the call for contributors, published in the *Academy* on May 10, 1879, put it, in terms richly resonant with any study of philology and fiction:

> This is work in which anyone can join. Even the most indolent novel-reader will find it little trouble to put a pencil-mark against any word or phrase that strikes him, and he can afterwards copy out the context at his leisure. In this way many words and references can be registered that may prove of the highest value.[21]

Such a request cannot but recall Casaubon's injunction to his wife:

> "You will oblige me my dear," he said, seating himself, "if instead of other reading this evening, you will go through this aloud, pencil in hand, and at each point where I say 'mark,' will make a cross with your pencil. This is the first step in a sifting process which I have long had in view, and as we go on I shall be able to indicate to you certain principles of selection whereby you will, I trust, have an intelligent participation in my purpose." (chap. 48, p. 453)

What does it mean to read in these ways: to confront the book not as the sequence of a story but as some repository of detail? Perhaps it is to move away from being "indolent"? The word originally meant "painless" but connoted, by the eighteenth-century, "averse to toil or exertion, slothful, lazy, idle" (*OED*, s.v. "indolent"). Mr. Brooke, on meeting Will, advises that "You clever young men must guard against indolence. I was too indolent, you know: else I might have been anywhere at one time" (chap. 9, p. 75). Let us not read, then, as the indolent, directionless Mr. Brooke but as the active and directed . . . who? Casaubon? How can this way of reading not recall Casaubon's initial "No" to Mr. Brooke and his remark that he has "little leisure for such literature just now"? Perhaps our literary criticism makes us all pencil markers of our texts and convinces us that, far from being indolent, we bristle with intelligent participation in a purpose. The explosion of my own critical narrative into the fragments of what follows may thus be—now armed with computer concordances, online texts and dictionaries, and fast search engines—both a very modern and, paradoxically, very historical way of engaging with Eliot's novel and its contexts.[22]

But there is one last story that I cannot resist retelling. One of Lewes's letters reports that, in Dublin, a certain Judge Fitzgerald reported that "at the opening of the Dublin Exhibition he was struck with the attention of the Archbishop [Richard Chenevix Trench, formerly the editor of the *OED*] to the interior of his hat which at first he took for devout listening to the speeches, but on close examination saw he was reading something, and as this was so intent he was prompted to look also into the hat, and found the Archbishop had *Middlemarch* there laid open—what a much better way of listening to 'opening speeches'!"[23] The founder of the *Oxford English Dictionary*, the author of polemics on lexicography and philology, reads *Middlemarch* secreted in his hat. Perhaps no better image caps this study of my Casaubon and introduces my imaginary lexicon of novels and philology.

Author, Authorship

The etymology of "author" lies in the Latin word "*augere*," meaning to grow, increase, or propagate (itself, the source of our word "augment").[24] Though the word could refer to the writer of a document or the composer of a book as early as the fourteenth century, its connotation of increase or propagation survived well into the nineteenth. The *Oxford English Dictionary*, clearly in this case not a disinterested record, documents a range of modern uses of the word that look back to its etymology. Authorship becomes a matter of increase. Under the word "voluminous," it offers this quotation from Scott's *Nigel*: "It is some consolation to reflect, that the best authors in all countries have been the most voluminous" (1822). And no doubt its compilers found remarkable this quotation culled from an anonymous review of the now-forgotten book *Marjory*, which appeared in the *Saturday Review* of 1880: "What size will the author's writings attain when she gets beyond her studies?"

But look up "author" in the *OED*, and you will find not tales of writers but accounts of power. Its quotations center on progeniture, development, and control. Of all the possible opportunities for offering nineteenth-century examples of the word used in its literary sense, the *Dictionary* presents only two: Byron's satiric jibe from 1818 ("One hates an author that is all author, fellows In foolscap uniforms turned up with ink. So very anxious, clever, fine, and jealous") and then the *Saturday Review* remark from 1880. It is as if the editors are offering an exercise in literary criticism as much as lexicography. The entries under "authorship" are similarly thin: a few quotations to illuminate "occupation or career as a writer of books" or "literary origin or origination (of a writing)." Literary authority must be sought in places other than the obvious entries.

One place to locate that authority can be in the aggregate quotations used to illustrate the *Dictionary*'s words.[25] That Shakespeare is the single most cited author in the first edition of the *Dictionary* may come as no surprise. But that Sir Walter Scott is second only to Shakespeare might, at least to a modern reader.[26] Scott's overwhelming presence, especially in key quotations dealing with things literary, testifies to his impact on nineteenth-century conceptions of the novel and on reading taste itself. He was perhaps the most prolific and commercially successful of the English novelists, embodying what would become the Victorian idiom of massive productivity and the commodification of intellectual activity. But, in addition, Scott's books offered a compendium of rare phrases, old words, dialect usages, and great gobs of detail about, in Thomas Carlyle's words, "phraseology, fashion of arms, of dress and life, belonging to one age."[27] They were, in some sense, philological assemblies of their own, peppered with odd or archaic verbiage that their narrators paused, often, to explain. Scott is a model of authorial identity for the *Dictionary*, and it is no accident that his remark on the relationship of quality and quantity stands as a signal statement for the century: "the best authors . . . have been the most voluminous." Other defining statements would be the quotations the *Dictionary* used to illustrate "author-craft" and "authorial." For the former, we find Scott's phrase, "the mysteries of Author-craft," implying not the economics of production but the inspirations of the writer. For the second, we get "I am a total stranger to authorial vanity," an avowal that, however sincere it may be, sustains its author's reputation as a kind of noble, hero-writer—as the worshipful figure that George Eliot would come to find him.

The history of authorship encoded in the *OED* provides a context in which *Middlemarch* may be examined as a novel of authorial identity.[28] Eliot herself was clearly vexed by the vocation of the writer. On the one hand, it motivated themes for many of her novels, notably *Middlemarch*; but, on the other, it provoked her to distinguish between that vocation and ambition. "How or on what principle," she wrote in the essay "Authorship," "are we to find a check for that troublesome disposition to authorship arising from the spread of what is called Education, which turns a growing rush of vanity and ambition into this current?"[29] Recall here Scott's claim, "I am a total stranger to authorial vanity." By decrying the vanity of modern authorship and the ambition of its new practitioners, Eliot seeks a personal legitimization in the earlier writer's example.

Casaubon stands, in the first third of the nineteenth century, as someone on the cusp of change in intellectual vocation and ambition. Cleric and writer, he holds no active position either in the church or university (though he has ties to both). A country-house mythographer, an amateur in the root meaning of that word, his scholarly project grants him identity. He thinks of himself as "the author of a 'Key to All Mythologies,'" (chap. 10, p. 80), an appellation as defining as, say, being "the author of *Waverley*." No doubt Casaubon imagines himself imprinted on such title pages, known not by his name but by his book. And, no doubt, Eliot imagines him, too, as a victim of the vanity of authorship. The German painter Naumann dismisses him in Rome: "Nothing like these starchy doctors for vanity!" (chap. 22, p. 207).

But, for all his ambition, Casaubon remains "a desponding author" (chap. 20, p. 191). As Dorothea calls attention to his notes, his "rows of volumes," his "vast knowledge," he sinks deeper into resentment. In Eliot's words, Dorothea observes "abundant pen scratches and amplitude of paper" (pp. 190–91). Casaubon's authorship has now become the realization of its etymology: all mass, all size, all growing things. For Eliot, too, the massive undertaking of *Middlemarch* led to Casaubon-like moments of despondency. To Harriet Beecher Stowe, she writes using that very word and wishing that Stowe "could have a momentary glimpse of the discouragement, nay, paralyzing despondency in which many days of my writing life have been past." To Alexander Main, she wrote of her "oft-recurring hours of despondency."[30] But if she shares something of Casaubon's emotional condition, she sees the novel itself as taking on the unmanageable bulk of his great book. On March 19, 1871, having written 236 pages of the book, she complains that she may have "too much matter, too many 'momenti.'"[31] "It was clear," writes Gordon Haight, "that so many complex strands could not be woven into the compass of an ordinary three-volume novel."[32] Size, length, scope, and range of social understanding would mark *Middlemarch* as something different from just about anything that had preceded it. For a time, it seemed that it would stand for Eliot as an exemplar of her distaste for "excessive literary production." "I am haunted," she wrote as she was finishing the novel, "by the fear that I am only saying again what I have already said in better fashion. . . . Every one who contributes to the 'too much' of literature is doing grave social injury."[33] Eliot's authorship taxes the very nature of the term; "*augere*" is the verb of operation here.

Middlemarch is a novel of authorship not just in the vocational but in the etymological sense. Casaubon's growing notes in need of sifting by his Dorothea match the growing volume of the book itself (Lewes wrote to Blackwood, Eliot's publisher, that the book "will require 4 volumes for her story, not 3").[34] The very word "volume" here takes on the connotation—emerging in the nineteenth century—of mass, space filled, something occupying an existence. Such a sense inheres in the initial characterization of Casaubon's work itself. "His notes," Eliot writes early in chapter 3, "already made a formidable range of volumes, but the crowning task would be to condense these voluminous still-accumulating results and bring them, like the earlier vintage of Hippocratic books, to fit a little shelf" (pp. 20–21). The burgeoning volume of materials that should become the Key to All

Mythologies reads curiously like *Middlemarch* itself in Lewes's calculating correspondence. How can, he seems to ask, one fit a formidable range of volumes on a little shelf? And Casaubon himself, a creature more of texts than feelings, becomes a veritable volume of materials. His memory "was a volume where a *vide supra* could serve instead of repetitions" (p. 23). How fitting for a man who seemed to dream, in Mrs. Cadwallader's words, only of footnotes.

Casaubon's authorship becomes a paradox: volumes of unused work, a book whose final writing becomes less and less a prospect as the notes accumulate. Authorship for him is a "morass" (chap. 10, p. 80)—quite literally a swampy tract or bogland and, in figurative terms, precisely akin to the mazy wood in which Will Ladislaw would later find him lost without his pocket compass. Casaubon's morass, too, places him on the windy landscapes of Sir Walter Scott. "The slightest aberration," Scott wrote in *The Surgeon's Daughter*, in the quotation used to illustrate that word in the *OED*, "would plunge him into a morass, or throw him over a precipice" (s.v. "aberration," def. 1). "The precarious track through the morass," wrote Scott in *The Highland Widow*, "the dizzy path along the precipice" (*OED*, s.v. "precarious," def. 4). And, in *The Lady of the Lake*, Scott paints a picture of such vividness, that the *OED* editors would use it twice, to illustrate the words "bog" and "springing": "With short and springing footsteps pass the trembling bog and false morass." Scott offers up a lexicon of being lost, as central to the *OED* as to *Middlemarch*.

For it is Walter Scott who stands at the center of Eliot's understanding of authorship.[35] She had come to read him early in her life. During her father's last years, as she wrote to Alexander Main in August 1871, she "was able to make the evenings cheerful for him . . . by reading aloud to him Scott's novels. No other writer would serve as a substitute for Scott, and my life at that time would have been much more difficult without him."[36] And Scott stands at the center of the novel. Haight notes that "Scott first introduced her to the writing of fiction" when, in 1827, a neighbor lent her a copy of *Waverley*. She had not the time to finish it before returning the book, and "in her distress she began to write the story out herself."[37] As a girl, she sought to visit the locales of the Waverley novels; she and Lewes read the novels together (and, memorably, read Lockhart's *Life of Scott* aloud); for New Year's 1860, Lewes had given Eliot a forty-eight-volume set of Scott's collected works. And when *The Mill on the Floss* appeared in July 1860, it was such a great success that Blackwood himself wrote to Eliot, claiming that the sales had not been equaled since the Waverley novels.[38]

The theme of authorship in *Middlemarch* grows out of Scott's defining impact on Eliot. Even that small aside about Casaubon's "morass of authorship" associates, for an attentive reader of his novels, the writing of great books with the example of the author of *Waverley*. In fact, there are moments in *Middlemarch* when Scott rears up as the alternative author of the story: that is, when we are offered to imagine *his* treatments of its material. In chapter 39, Mr. Brooke goes off on one of his characteristic reports of a local encounter: "Well, now, Flavell in his shabby black gaiters, pleading that he thought the Lord had sent him and his wife a good dinner, and he had aright to knock it down, though not a mighty hunter before the Lord, as Nimrod was—I assure you it was rather comic: Fielding would have made something of it—or Scott, now—Scott might have worked it up" (p. 375). Scott replaces Fielding, and Eliot's reportage of his monologue brilliantly captures the eruptions of Brooke's mind. Scott interrupts, coming between the dashes, effectively displacing, if not effacing, the writers who had gone before. What would Scott have done with this story? Mr. Brooke asks, and I think so must we. Scott stands as something of the shadow novelist for Eliot, the author always in the back of her mind. So, too, the idyll of her childhood reading of that author is evoked, not only in the epigraph to chapter 57 but in its opening scene.

> He [Christy Garth] was lying on the ground now by his mother's chair, with his straw-hat laid flat over his eyes, while Jim on the other side was reading from that beloved writer who has made a chief part in the happiness of many young lives. The volume was *Ivanhoe*, and Jim was in the great archery scene at the tournament, but suffered much interruption from Ben, who had fetched his own old bow and arrows, and was making himself dreadfully disagreeable, Letty thought, by begging all present to observe his random shots, which no one wished to do except Brownie, the active-minded but probably shallow mongrel, while the grizzled Newfoundland lying in the sun looked on with the dull-eyed neutrality of extreme old age.
>
> (chap. 57, p. 543)

That Scott was "the chief part in the happiness" of Marianne Evans's own young life is well attested, and this comment here is nothing less than unadulterated autobiography. But what occurs in this scene is fiction or, to put it more precisely, the realities of an Eliotic fiction intruding on Scott's great story. Just as in Mr. Brooke's earlier scene, this is a story of interruption. Real life—the silliness of children, the quotidian of dogs—irrupts into the fantasy of *Ivanhoe*. Here, it is Scott who is effaced by Eliot. The realistic nuances of *Middlemarch* brush the historical sweep of *Ivanhoe* aside.

It is as if Scott threatens to intrude on Eliot, as if his writings must be pushed away, made childlike, or evoked only to be erased before the burgeoning talent of Eliot the author. Earlier in the novel, it is left to Dr. Lydgate to perform that literary resection. In chapter 27, young Ned Plymdale tries to engage the doctor in a discussion of books and writing. Rosamond is playfully dismayed at her husband—"I think I shall turn round on you and accuse you of being a Goth"—for not knowing of the latest writers.

> "But Sir Walter Scott—I suppose Mr. Lydgate knows him," said young Plymdale, a little cheered by this advantage.
>
> "O, I read no literature now," said Lydgate, shutting the book, and pushing it away. "I read so much when I was a lad, that I suppose it will last me all my life. I used to know Scott's poems by heart." (p. 257)

At one level, Lydgate's denial recalls Casaubon's in chapter 2. To Mr. Brooke's question if Casaubon knows Southey, he replied, "No, . . . I have little leisure for such literature just now" (chap. 2, p. 13). But, at another level, Lydgate's answer is profoundly different. Rather than simply revealing the character to be a boor or pedant, it reveals the author of *Middlemarch* as a literary competitor. Lydgate denies the very presence of Scott. He locates him in his childish past and, in shutting the book and pushing it away, gets Scott out of this novel's present.

The characters in *Middlemarch*, then, find themselves presented as readers—or antireaders—of literature. They outline themselves against books they read, or do not read, and scenes of reading heighten the novel's figurations of its plot. But *Middlemarch* is both a novel of reading and one of writing, and the fate of its characters is determined by their own status as authors. Casaubon is, of course, the failed authorial figure, and there are also Brooke and Ladislaw. But, at the close of *Middlemarch*, Eliot resolves the future of her characters by making them *all* authors.

Fred Vincy, for example, "surprised his neighbours," among other ways, by writing a book on the "Cultivation of Green Crops and the Economy of Cattle-Feeding." "In Middlemarch admiration was more reserved: most persons were inclined to believe that the merit of Fred's authorship was due to his wife, since they had never expected Fred Vincy to write on turnips and mangel-wurzel" ("Finale," p. 793). But when Mary Vincy turns her hand to authorship, "a little book for her boys, called 'Stories of Great Men, taken from Plutarch,' and had it printed and published by Gripp & Co., Middlemarch, every one in the town was willing to give the credit of this work to Fred, observing that he had been to the University 'where the ancients were studied,' and might have been a clergyman if he had chosen" ("Finale," pp. 793–94). Even Dr. Lydgate becomes an author at the novel's end. His practice came eventually to extend to Continental spas, "having written a treatise on Gout, a disease which has a good deal of wealth on its side" ("Finale," p. 795). Whatever the merits of the book, it paid him money—something that Dorothea forfeits along with her own status as author. Casaubon's Key to All Mythologies remains unpublished; Will becomes a public speaker and reform parliamentarian. She gives birth to a son. But there is no memorial, no book, no signature. The novel ends with anonymities. "Her full nature, like that river of which Cyrus broke the strength spent itself in channels which had no great name on the earth." And the novel's final words find Dorothea's influence to center on her "unhistoric acts"; the good of a society rests in the works of those like her who "rest in unvisited tombs" ("Finale," p. 799). Dorothea stands as something of an antiauthor, one without name or signature. Her tomb stands as a symbol of that anonymity that faces the failed author—that faces, in fact, the posthumous authorial condition of Casaubon. "He willingly imagined," Eliot writes in chapter 50, after he is dead, Dorothea "toiling under the fetters of a promise to erect a tomb with his name upon it. (Not that Mr. Casaubon called the future volumes a tomb: he called them the 'Key to all Mythologies.')" (p. 470). If the book is a tomb, then the tomb is a book, and Dorothea's great unwritten project is, in essence, that whole lifetime of reform that she has set herself to author.

And what of Casaubon? Is he really an author, or is he little more than a compiler? Is he someone like that described in the words of *Scribbleomania* of 1815 (quoted by the *OED* to illustrate "compiler"): "The pond'rous compiler, with nought that is new"? Indeed, the *OED* defines the word as "in modern use often opposed to an original author." The entry ends with "compilership," called a nonce word and attested in this single illustrative quotation, drawn from the *Spectator*, December 14, 1867: "The authorship or compilership of a dictionary . . . is indeed, a question like that of the identity of the darned and redarned stockings with the original pair."

By associating authorship and compilership, the quotation implies that a dictionary can well have an author—that there can be, in the words that define "authorship" in the *OED*, an "occupation or career" of lexicographer; that dictionaries can have "literary origin"; that there can be a "dignity or personality of an author." But such a question, for the author of this *Spectator* remark, remains a matter not of origins but copies. Dictionaries become likened to darned stockings, rewoven articles of clothing—texts that retain their textile form. Such a remark must resonate with the impression of the *OED* as that great web of words, in Murray's granddaughter's evocative phrasing, and with *Middlemarch*, too, as this particular web, "woven and interwoven" in a way that Eliot could claim her goal as "unraveling certain human lots" (chap. 15, p. 133). But this quotation has a source, and, by returning to its larger context, we may, too, unravel the web of associations that link *Middlemarch* and lexicography.

The contribution from the *Spectator* is an unsigned review of *A Dictionary of General Biography*, edited by W. L. R. Cates, and it begins precisely with the issues of voluminosity and naming central to the history of authorship.

> A large octavo volume of 1,300 pages, turns out to be a new edition of our old friend Maunder. The editor would perhaps have acted more wisely, and certainly protected himself from possible unpleasant comments, had he avowed this on the title page, instead of letting the book go forth as a new work. In the preface, however, he does tell us that, though "based on the thirteenth edition of the well known *Treasury of Biography*, which, as reconstructed, revised, and very greatly enlarged by myself, was substantially a new work, it is

nevertheless far from being a mere reprint." (Is it accident or design that even here he avoids all mention of Maunder's name?)[39]

This essay on a book of names reflects on the very problem of authorial attribution and the nature of the appellation. The review begins by recalling the suppressed name. What does it mean to make a new edition of a work? How are works of scholarship or reference granted an identity—if not an authority—by their named compilers? Such are the questions, too, for dictionaries. The history of lexicography is the history of names. Bailey, Johnson, Richardson, Webster—all stand as the antecedents of the *OED*, and all their works can be referred to simply by their names. Discerning just what different lexicographers contributed to dictionaries was a preliminary task for the initiators of the *OED*. Liddell and Scott, who put together the definitive modern lexicon of ancient Greek, were themselves indebted to the work of Franz Passow. Herbert Coleridge, the first editor of what would become the *OED*, defined his project with specific reference to Passow's work: "'every word should be made to tell its own story'—the story of its birth and life, and in many cases of its death, and even occasionally of its resuscitation."[40]

So, too, the reviewer for the *Spectator* acknowledges the example of Liddell and Scott, and he does so, now, with the statement that the *OED* would place—albeit truncated—in its definition of compiler: "The authorship or compilership of a dictionary which has gone through numerous editions is, indeed, a question like that of the identity of the darned and redarned stockings with the original pair, and Mr. Cates is probably as fully justified in now treating the work as his own as Messrs. Liddell and Scott were in regarding their *Greek Lexicon* as their own work, *based* on that of Passow."

First, let us compare the original quotation with its version in the *OED*. The ellipses there denote that a portion has been excised. The phrase, "which has gone through numerous editions," is precisely the key point of the original quotation. Someone has left this out, and it is a telling omission. For the fact is that this dictionary is, at least in its inception, the *New* English dictionary: it explicitly is not a revision of an earlier work but something new in origin and execution. Still, it borrowed much from the techniques of Passow; it owed its historical framework to Richardson; it relied on many definitions from Johnson; and, for a time, its editors viewed it in competition with the *Century Dictionary* being published in America under the direction of the Yale philologist William Dwight Whitney.[41] Was it, in fact, a new web of words or just a redarned stocking?

The *Spectator* review goes on: quibbles with selections, omissions and challenges of emphases, quarrels with what the experts might find. "A diligent search might no doubt discover some inaccuracies and omissions which could hardly be avoided." And, in words smartly resonant of Ladislaw's critique of Casaubon's shortcomings, the reviewer notes: "for however incorrect it may be found by the deeper studies of modern Orientalists, it must always have a literary value and a certain fascination for readers of all classes." Literary value contrasts scholarly exactitude. Diligence apposes fascination. In the end, the reviewer concludes, "Living persons are excluded."

The *Dictionary of General Biography* is a book of the dead. The tome becomes a tomb, and, as such, it returns us to the close of *Middlemarch* and to the tombs, both real and literary, that fill that book. The living author is a paradox, one constantly assessing his—or her—achievement against past exemplars, be they Scott or Maunder. And, for all of Casaubon's attempts to kill off (figuratively speaking) Carp at Brasenose, he does not live to see it. Herbert Coleridge, Richard Chenevix Trench, and Franz Passow all recognized that dictionaries all tell stories. A dictionary should present "die Lebensgeschichte jedes einzelnene Wortes," the life history of every individual word. The biographical impulse of lexicography that emerges from this idiom informs a novel as concerned with scholarly and novelistic authorship as *Middlemarch*. In his remarks on the *Deficiencies in our English Dictionaries* (first published in 1858, reprinted in 1860), Trench argued that a dictionary should be "an historical monument." How different would such a monument be from the pedantic quibbles of a Casaubon? "[His] pamphlets—or 'Parerga' as he called them—by which he tested his public and deposited small monumental records of his march, were far from having been seen in all their significance" (chap. 29, p. 266). "These minor monumental productions were always exciting to Mr. Casaubon" (p. 268). And, when Casaubon is dead, and Dorothea gazes on his "rows of note-books" ranged like stones, what she sees is "the mute memorial of a forgotten faith" (chap. 54, pp. 510–11).

For Casaubon, lost in the morass of his authorship, whose ways are mazy, overgrown, and truly erroneous, his failure should be measured against the far more productive *errores* of the history of words themselves: a history that would be chronicled in the great dictionary Trench imagines. "And the wrong ways in to which a language has wandered, or been disposed to wander, may be nearly as instructive as the right ones in which it has traveled."[42]

And what of Eliot herself? Her authorship outlasts that of her failed Casaubon: indeed, it becomes the centerpiece of the reviews of *Middlemarch* as it appeared. The *Spectator*'s four reviews of the novel as its sections appeared are really essays in Eliot's attainment of a kind of sublime authorship. [43] She emerges, in these reviews, as "a really great author" and a "fine author."[44] She is, by the third review, an "authoress with an excessive, almost morbid intellectual ability."[45] "Every page in the book," the reviewer admits, even when finding fault, "is written as no author in the world could have written it." George Eliot "is incapable of pedantry"—a vivid contrast to what would be, in the fourth and final *Spectator* review, the dismissive characterization of Casaubon as "the would-be author of 'The Key to all Mythologies.'" Eliot possesses "the creative power of the author," and the greatness of the book, in conclusion, lies in its writing by "the greatest of English authors, but also . . . by far the greatest of English authoresses." And the reviewer goes on: "and though it would be too much to say that the latter [i.e., authoresses] ranks next to the former [i.e., authors] in our literature, even with a whole firmament of power between, it is not too much to say that George Eliot will take her stand amongst the stars of the second magnitude, with the cluster that contains Scott and Fielding."[46] Now, the authoress can stand as author against Scott and Fielding—the two authorial models who have been consistently evoked in *Middlemarch* and, just as consistently, dismissed or bettered.

Henry James, in his unsigned review of *Middlemarch* in the *Galaxy* (March 1873), similarly used the novel's own authorial paradigms to assess it. His objections, he begins, "may seem shallow and pedantic," a review by a Casaubon of literature (whom James refers to, just a page away, as "an arid pedant"). And yet, at the close of his review, he writes:

> George Eliot seems to us among English romancers to stand alone. Fielding approaches her, but to our mind, she surpasses Fielding. Fielding was didactic—the author of "Middlemarch" is really philosophic. These great qualities imply corresponding perils. The

first is the loss of simplicity. George Eliot lost hers some time since: it lies buried (in a splendid mausoleum) in "Romola." Many of the discursive portions of "Middlemarch" are, as we may say, too clever by half. The author wishes to say too many things, and to say them too well.[47]

When measured against Fielding, Eliot becomes "the author of 'Middlemarch.'" But when fault is found, she reemerges with her own name. Now, her earlier artistry (her "simplicity") lies buried in a mausoleum—not one of the "unvisited tombs" of a Dorothea Brooke but in a volume to which, clearly, we are meant to return. And, like the reviewer in the *Spectator*, like Eliot herself, and like the readers for the *Oxford English Dictionary*, James voices the just barely hidden etymology of authorship: the need to increase, to say too many things.

We have here moved away from Scott's claim that the best authors are the most voluminous. We have moved closer to the heart of Eliot's own struggles with authorial control. And, in what stands for me as one last capstone to this essay on authorship, James's own review becomes the primary authority for the *OED*'s entry for "*repoussoir*," defined as "an object in the foreground of a painting serving to emphasize the principal figure or scene": "Mr. Casaubon is an excellent invention: as a dusky *repoussoir* to the luminous figure of his wife he could not have been better imagined" (p. 427). So, in the end, if James's review pointedly picks up on the idioms of *Middlemarch* itself—the brush at Fielding, the concerns with overwhelming volume or detail, the anxieties of cleverness, the affectations of the artist, the desire to be an author—it may well be because, quite frankly, he is writing not as a Casaubon-like pedant but as the authorial equal he intuited himself to be.

Casaubon

"Mrs. Lewes calls it Casaubon, i.e., Ca-saw-bon, with the accent on the second syllable. But she says a good many people of that name in England call themselves Cas-au-bon, with the accent on the first syllable." So wrote the American John Fiske after spending a Sunday in November 1873 with Eliot and Lewes. It is an odd detail in a letter otherwise unconcerned with any of her writings. Fiske spends most of his time describing Eliot. "She is not a 'fright' by any means"; "She is *much* better looking than George Sand"; "There is nothing a bit masculine about her"; "She thinks just like a man"; "Spencer thinks she is the greatest woman that has lived on the earth—the female Shakespeare, so to speak; and I imagine he is not *far* from right."[48] By the early 1870s, Eliot had become an icon of English authorship. Many came to pay her court, and Fiske's letter remains but one of a host of personal accounts that testified to her charisma. Against this powerful and public figure—always described as warm, intelligent, well read, unaffected—Casaubon enters this letter almost as an afterthought. In spite of all the chatter about whom she modeled him on, Fiske's letter reports a discussion about pronunciation.

But what else could they have discussed? What better way to handle Casaubon than in his own pedantic philological terms? "But Mr. Casaubon's theory of the elements . . . floated among flexible conjectures no more solid than those etymologies which seemed strong because of likeness in sound, until it was shown that likeness in sound made them impossible" (chap. 48, p. 455). George Eliot, faced with a young admirer, performs a Casaubon-like gloss on her own character's name. For this brief anecdote is nothing other than a study of "likeness in sound." The meaning of Casaubon lies, in this account, not in his similarity to scholars living, or dead, but in the pronunciation of his name. To understand him is to understand just where to put the accent, and yet, as Fiske reports, there are many in England who call themselves Casaubon with the accent elsewhere. Such a discussion recalls Mary Garth's lesson to her son Ben in *Middlemarch*, where the young boy obstreperously hates his grammar lessons and finds in the regional pronunciations of old Job something "funnier" than correct speech. "These things belong only to pronunciation, which is the least part of grammar," replies Mary (chap. 24, p. 231). But it was a central part of lexicography. The founders of the *Oxford English Dictionary* debated what role pronunciation should play in their entries, and the varieties of sounds—and the alternative graphemic ways of representing them—led James A. H. Murray to recognize, in his 1879 address to the Philological Society, that "Englishmen do not take their pronunciation from dictionaries and spelling books" and that "the most different pronunciations may coexist, without those who use them having any suspicion of the fact."[49] In the end, though, the *OED* would aver that "the pronunciation is the actual living form of a word, that is the word itself. . . . [T]he living word is sound recognizable by the ear."[50]

Fiske's anecdote stands as an allegory of the search for Casaubon. Almost from the novel's first publication, readers have debated who he is. Sources have been proposed, only to be dismissed; historical resonances with the Renaissance Isaac and Meric of that last name have been proffered; Eliot, in a famous incident, associated him with herself; and Lewes, we are told, in moments of high humor, sometimes went around proclaiming himself the author of the Key to All Mythologies.[51] For the first generation of reviewers, he remained one of *Middlemarch*'s most finely drawn, if most transparent, characters. For modern critics, he becomes the node of thematic and structural discussion, the heart of a novel of interpretation read by a new class of professional interpreters. And, for any reader in the academic life, he stands as a chastening antitype of ourselves: in Henry James's words, a figure of "hollow pretentiousness and mouldy egotism," just the kind of character that would inhabit university departments in his time—and our own.

Casaubon's intellectual forbears have long been known.[52] Jacob Bryant—the man with whom Will Ladislaw explicitly associates Casaubon's failed project—had published his *New System; or, An Analysis of Ancient Mythology* in 1774–1776. Like many of its peer publications, Bryant's work sought to consider Christianity in the light of the history of world religions (as they were becoming known during the eighteenth century). Mythography looked to the symbols of religious ritual, to natural imagery, to what we now would call the archetypes of social rite and organization. Such mythographic projects were not so much cultural as philological enterprises. They looked in particular to the origin of language as keyed to the origin of belief. They inquired into the Adamic tongue; proffered etymologies more metaphysical, or metaphorical, than historical; and keyed their inquiries to Hebrew roots and Biblical names.

Eliot had read widely in the mythographic traditions, and she read widely, too, in the traditions of historical (especially Germanic) philology that would supplant them.[53] Her review of Mackay's *Progress of the Intellect* in the *Westminster Review* illustrates her awareness of the Indo-Europeanists of the first half of the nineteenth century.[54] Ottfried Müller's *Prolegomena to a Scientific Mythology* (published in 1825 and referenced in her review of Mackay) must, it has been conjectured, be one of the many German works of which Casaubon remains unaware.[55] But, more generally, the Mackay review brims over with a Casaubonian vocabulary. She writes of "the grand means of expelling error," of arguments that serve as the "pioneer" in research, of "erudition," "intellect," and "inspiration." She announces, almost in anticipation of her Will, that "England has been slow to use or to emulate the immense labours of Germany in the departments of mythology and biblical criticism." And, in a similar prolepsis for her Casaubon, she writes about "the master key to this revelation" and imagines "the introduction of a truly philosophic spirit into the study of mythology."

But there remains something more about Casaubon that entices readers to discern just who he is, as if such a creature could not be a purely fictional invention, or as if we want to displace his identity on to someone, anyone, else and not have him stick to us. The first attempts to identify him came within a decade of the novel's publication. Mrs. Oliphant recorded in her autobiography that she met Mark Pattison, the learned classicist and rector of Lincoln College, Oxford, in 1879, noting that he "is supposed to be the Casaubon of Middlemarch." In Pattison's obituary in the *Academy* (August 9, 1885), Henry Nettleship denied this association. "There was, however, nothing in common between the serious scholar at Lincoln and the mere pedant frittering way his life in useless trivialities." The claim was revived by Mrs. Pattison's second husband, Sir Charles Dilke, and, in recent times, by John Sparrow in his study of Pattison. Central to this century of associations is the personal acquaintance of George Eliot and Pattison; some superficial similarities between the Pattison's marriage and that of Dorothea and Casaubon; and the fact that Pattison, a few years after *Middlemarch* appeared, published his study of Isaac Casaubon. But beyond these concatenations, what drives the association of Casaubon and Pattison is the need to find a topical, historical anchor for Eliot's social fiction. So much of the novel had been grounded in political and cultural events that it must seem, to some, exceptional for such a character as Casaubon not to be anchored in reality.[56] At stake is not who is or is not Casaubon but why so many readers have so much invested in identifying him. Gordon Haight spends many pages on proposed (or purportedly remembered) sources from the Eliot circle. His venom and his vigilance (at one point, he calls the affiliation with Pattison a "canard," and, in his "Poor Mr. Casaubon," he calls John Sparrow's version of the hypothesis "absurd") have more to do with his critical imagination of Eliot the novelist than with any archival fidelity to fact.⁵⁷ For Haight, Eliot's personal experience feeds into her development as a writer. Intellectual friendships abound, all contributing to the creation and expression of "George Eliot" as *the* novelist of the late nineteenth century. Youthful experiences fertilize that creation, and Haight often pauses to reflect on how the terms of Marian Evans's life—relationships with men, habits of reading, favorite literary themes—were set at early age. Haight's Casaubon must lie in the recesses of her childhood, not in the public world of her maturity, and so his candidate is Dr. R. H. Brabant.⁵⁸

Robert Herbert Brabant was, in 1843, a sixty-two-year-old doctor living in Devizes whose daughter, Elizabeth Rebecca, had become acquainted with Mary Ann Evans. The girls apparently became quite close; they read books and studied German together, and eventually Mary Ann served as a bridesmaid to Elizabeth (who had been nicknamed Rufa, for her red hair, by no less a family friend than Samuel Taylor Coleridge). After Rufa's marriage, Dr. Brabant brought Mary Ann back to Devizes, ensconced her in his vast library, and invited her to read to him. Young Mary Ann was something of a pet for Brabant. Mrs. Brabant, old and blind, knew, in Haight's words "quite well what was going on."⁵⁹ And Rufa wrote to John Chapman nearly a decade later that Mary Ann, out of "simplicity" and "ignorance," gave Dr. Brabant "the utmost attention; they became very intimate." For Rufa, her father exhibited "unmanliness in the affair." For Haight, he was simply "contemptible." Eliza Lynn Linton—who would eventually become one of the most formidable women of letters in late Victorian England and, perhaps significantly in this matter, one of the most virulently antifeminist—also visited Brabant in 1847. Her description in her posthumously published *My Literary Life* has been taken as an outline of the raw material behind Eliot's fictional character:

> My first introduction to Bath and Walter Savage Landor was through Dr. Brabant, a learned man who used up his literary energies in thought and desire to do rather than in actual doing, and whose fastidiousness made his work something like Penelope's web. Ever writing and rewriting, correcting and destroying, he never got farther than the introductory chapter of a book which he intended to be epoch-making, and the final destroyer of superstition and theological dogma.⁶⁰

But what, precisely, is the context of this portrait, and just what is Linton—and Gordon Haight—doing? Linton's description of Dr. Brabant, in fact, comes at the opening of her reminiscences of Walter Savage Landor. Brabant had introduced young Eliza to Landor, and she contrasts the two older men—the doctor vacuous and self-involved, the poet generous and brilliant—as two father figures for a young girl. Nowhere in *My Literary Life* does Linton mention Casaubon or *Middlemarch*. And yet Haight takes it as gospel. Only in Haight's earliest foray into this material, his *George Eliot and John Chapman*, published in 1940, does the barest of footnotes point to a source: George Soames Layton's *Mrs. Lynn Linton*.[61] Layton repeats the description of Brabant, and then, in a footnote of his own, he states: "My friend Mr. H. A. Acworth tells me that Mrs. Linton assured him that Dr. Brabant was the original of Casaubon in *Middlemarch*. This is interesting in view of the fact that Casaubon has generally been identified with Mark Pattison."[62] Hearsay and personal, undocumented information feeds virtually unacknowledged into Haight's elaborately developed (and thrice-repeated) theory of Brabant and Casaubon.

But there is more than a whiff of Casaubon in my own critical discovery. Is this investigation little more than, in Will Ladislaw's words, "crawling a little way after men of the last century . . . and correcting their mistakes"? The inquiry into the origins of Casaubon leads any reader into the pedantic trap that Eliot herself sets, and I think this is precisely the problem. For it is not that Eliot had one, unique model for her creation, someone we are left to discover. Rather, it is that she has placed so much of her wide reading, personal experience, and growing private iconography in Casaubon that she has made him into a sign to be interpreted. Casaubon is not just a figure for the scholar; he becomes the goad to scholarship itself. And anyone who would claim, as Haight triumphantly does, a "key" to his identity will be as subject to correction and complaint as Casaubon himself would be.

So what is left? It is Casaubon's afterlife rather than his forbears that shape his literary meaning. Let us return to Linton's reminiscence. Writing, at the close of her life, of memories of more than half a century before, Linton must surely be recalling Brabant through her reading of Casaubon. Her very words—"used up," "fastidious," "web," "correcting"—are those of *Middlemarch*, and her remarks may constitute as much a critical analysis of the fictional scholar as they present a portrait of the historical one.⁶³ Such were the images, as well, that caught the eyes of Casaubon's first readers. The reviews in the *Spectator* call him, at various points, "dry and formal," "cobwebby," "a dried-up formalist," a "pedant."⁶⁴ The reviewer of book 1 in the *Athenaeum* similarly calls him "a dry, old pedant," adding—to complete the physical debasement of the character—"a lump of horribly disappointing negations."⁶⁵ The weblike world of Casaubon's researches, "cobwebby" in the *Spectator*'s phrasing, is "labyrinthine" for the *Athenaeum*. "We close 'Miss Brooke' with only the ends in our hands of the tangled skein" (p. 714). The *Academy* found him "empty," while Henry James described him as an "arid pedant" in his *Galaxy* review.⁶⁶

All this may seem just obvious. But what is not is how these shards of Casaubon survive into the novel's philological afterlife. James's remark—that "as a dusky *repoussoir* to the luminous figure of his wife he could not have been better imagined"—finds its way into the *OED* as the first illustration of the word "*repoussoir*."⁶⁷ And the passage singled out for commentary by the *Athenaeum*—"the poor girl 'looks deep into the ungauged reservoir' of the pedant's mind"—is also cited in the *OED* to illustrate a usage of the word "ungauged."⁶⁸ Later, F. R. Leavis would define him as "an intellectual *manqué*," phrasing that would also find its way into the *OED* (the second edition) to illustrate that final word.⁶⁹ Casaubon survives in the great tomes of philology as the exemplar of new words: dictionary language for the dictionary minded.

And so he tempts all scholars. Look at Neil Hertz, who simply cannot resist falling into Eliot's trap. Building to a complex, almost sublime, reading of the sublime in Dorothea's encounter with Rome, Hertz has to interrupt his exposition to call attention to his own, intrusive presence as a reader: "I have quoted this passage at length both in order to recall its intensity and to draw attention to its organization. . . . I mention this not simply to identify a literary tradition—though I have enough of Casaubon in me to take an intense, bleak pleasure in interrupting a passionate moment with a scholarly gloss—but because to recognize the rhythm of the sublime in these sentences is to anticipate where the text might go from here, what one might expect to follow after that abrupt shock."⁷⁰ Hertz is the least Casaubon-like of Eliot's readers. But it is still a pose that he, rhetorically, must take. This moment of anxiety—have I quoted too much? am I being bleakly pedantic?—is set precisely against Henry James's rhetorical pose of refusing to quote too much, of denying his own pedantry ("we have marked innumerable passages for quotation and comment: but we lack space").⁷¹ Both Hertz and James confront the problem of just how to read a novel that so prominently represents a bad implied reader.

By cataloging Casaubon's wrongs we right ourselves. To correct—Latin *corrigere*—is to draw a straight line. Correction of the earlier scholar places us on the straight path, not along the crooked byways of the wood of error or the mazy stairs that Casaubon must tread. Hertz brilliantly transforms Casaubon's *errores* from those physical labyrinths to syntactic ones. In the passage I have quoted here, Hertz mimes the wanderings of Casaubon with mazy wanderings of his own. He implies—by syntax, rhetoric, and narratorial stance—what Eliot avowed when she pointed to herself when asked just who Casaubon was. "Casaubon, c'est moi," she might as well have said, in echo of Flaubert's famous retort about the origins of Emma Bovary. And so, too, might we all.

Error

Middlemarch is a book of errors. From Casaubon's misguided project, through myriad mistakes of marriage made by its key characters, to the overarching imagery of wandering and loss, the novel chronicles the wrongs and wrong-headedness of intellectual aspiration. But *Middlemarch* itself was also found in error. For Henry James, "the error in 'Middlemarch'" lies in its accumulation of detail at the expense of the whole. What remains wrong, for James, is this amassing of material, the sacrificing of "organized, moulded, balanced composition, gratifying the reader with a sense of design and construction" (p. 425) to what he sees as "a mere chain of episodes, broken into accidental lengths and unconscious of the influence of a plan" (p. 426). James looks for a plan, only to find "diffuseness." There is much, though, that James likes in the book. Casaubon, in particular, comes off well, as do many of the secondary characters (though Ladislaw "on the whole . . . seems to us a failure. It is the only eminent failure in the book"). In spite of its "faults . . . it remains a very splendid performance" (p. 428).

The pointing out of error is both theme and practice for the critical review.⁷² The *Spectator*'s account of part 2 of the novel (February 3, 1872) quotes prominently this remark from *Middlemarch*, as if it were a kind of monitory maxim for the reader: "To point out other people's errors was a duty that Mr. Bulstrode rarely shrank from, but Mr. Vincy was not equally prepared to be patient" (p. 148). A comparable point is not lost on the reviewer (signed as "H. Lawrenny" but identified by W. J. Harvey as Edith Simcox) for the *Academy*, writing in a review of the whole novel (January 1, 1873): "All critics are not like Mr. Borthrop Trumbull, who 'was an admirer by nature, and would have liked to have the universe under his hammer, feeling that it would go at a higher figure for his recommendation.'"[73] Are we to read like Bulstrode or Vincy, like Trumbull or, for that matter, like Casaubon himself? Eliot raises such questions throughout the novel's narrative. But she also enacts their answers in her own responses to its editing and publication. The *errores* of *Middlemarch* are many, and my book of errors highlights them to illustrate the intersections of historical scholarship, textual criticism, and literary response.

At a certain level, everyone is wrong. Dorothea, early in the novel, responds to her sister's criticisms in silence, "too much jarred to recover her temper and behave so as to show that she admitted any error in herself" (chap. 3, p. 33). In spite of everything, by the end of the novel, she still has an "errant will" (chap. 80, p. 751)—a statement not just about her inner state but, punningly, about her husband. Will Ladislaw, for all his critiques of Casaubon, is throughout a creature of the errant: moving constantly from place to place; from poetry, to painting, to politics; from journalism in the *Pioneer* to, finally, Parliament. Lydgate, too, mires himself in the wrong. The medical profession of his time is rife with error: "For it must be remembered that this was a dark period; and in spite of venerable colleges which used great efforts to secure purity of knowledge by making it scarce, and to exclude error by a rigid exclusiveness in relation to fees and appointments, it happened that very ignorant young gentlemen were promoted in town" (chap. 30, p. 273). Those ignorant young men grow up into erratic older doctors. "Great statesmen err, and why not small medical men?" (chap. 26, p. 246).

But it is Casaubon who remains in the wood of error. From the novel's start, his project is defined precisely in this term. He "had undertaken to show . . . that all the mythical systems or erratic mythical fragments in the world were corruptions of a tradition originally revealed" (chap. 3, p. 20). And Dorothea, in the narrator's ventriloquism, imagines that he may well be on to something: "wrong reasoning sometimes lands poor mortals in right conclusions: starting a long way off the true point, and proceeding by loops and zigzags, we now and then arrive just where we ought to be" (pp. 21–22)—a statement not just about scholarship or love but about the progress of this vast novel Eliot had set herself to write. But, in the end, nothing can redeem the author of the unwritten Key to All Mythologies. Even though "a vigorous error vigorously pursued has kept the embryos of truth a-breathing," Casaubon's search, as Dorothea comes to recognize, is little more than "questionable riddle-guessing" (chap. 48, pp. 455–56).

Casaubon's *errores* are all encompassing. Throughout the novel, words for winding, mazes, loops and zigzags, pathways that go nowhere, and a veritable architecture of intricacy come together to place Casaubon in his "morass" of authorship. And yet Dorothea finds, initially, in this deeply errant man a kindred spirit. She sees her own qualities reflected in him, "in vague labyrinthine extension" (chap. 3, p. 20). To her, social life "seemed nothing but a labyrinth of petty courses, a walled-in maze of small paths that led no whither" (p. 24)—an impression that, in chapter 20, would come back to haunt her when she realizes the same about Casaubon's mind.

This constellation of images has long been seen as central to the broader imagery of webs and weaving that articulates Eliot's notion of her realistic fiction.[74] But these images also reflect Eliot's larger concern with the progress of study and the intellectual trajectory of her life. Her notebooks and diaries are filled with tales of travel, not only her own great peregrinations but fictive, if not allegorical ones, too. There is the story of the Buddhist pilgrim, copied into her notebook from Max Müller's *Chips from a German Workshop*, that narrates a journey to enlightenment beset by difficulties.[75] She copied out selections from Milton's *Areopagitica* rich with the idioms of indirection (p. 100). Her many quotations from Dante, too, testify to her fascination with the pilgrimage motif (pp. 42–49, 169–74), as does her summary of Chaucer's *Canterbury Tales* (pp. 188–91, 210–11). And, from Jacob Grimm's *Deutsche Grammatik*, she copied out this quotation, in German: "Die geschichte der mahlerei, poesie und sprache lehret viele abwege eiden, denn sie zeigt uns, dass jederzeit die wahrheit denen erscheinen ist, welche auf die spur der natur, fern von menschlicher schulweisheit getreten sind" (The history of painting, poetry, and language teaches us to avoid many byways, because it shows us that truth is always revealed to those who follow the trail of nature, far from ordinary human schoolroom teaching; pp. 134, 219 n. 3).[76] This passage distills the double sense of error that controls the idiom of *Middlemarch*—and, too, the idiom of my own study. Truth is revealed to those who follow the trail of nature: literally, the spur, or spoor, the track or droppings left by hunted animals. Ordinary human schoolroom teaching can only get us so far, and this statement poses a challenge to the academic reader.

And yet it challenges Eliot as well, revealing tensions between the course of writing and of editing. Eliot, in the proofreading of her own work, reveals herself to be as prepossessed by error as any scholar: as much a creature of *menschlicher schulweisheit* as any of the learned characters of her novels. Correction, accuracy, and review are central to her work. Writing to John Blackwood on September 25, 1861, she commented on the travails of preparing a new edition of her first four books.

> I have read carefully all through "Adam Bede" and "The Mill" and have marked all the *errata* I have discovered. I hope the new editions will be carefully printed after these corrected copies, which I shall presently send. I have also marked in the "Clerical Scenes" some corrections which Mr. Lewes noted when he last read them. But I cannot read these and "Silas Marner" through, as I have done the other two books—I find this reading excite [*sic*] me too much and carry me away from the present. I am very glad, however, that I have given the needful time to "Adam" and "The Mill," for there were several mistakes which affected the sense in an important manner.[77]

The act of marking passages, of making corrections, of finding mistakes—all this is central to Casaubon's relationship to Dorothea. Casaubon seeks to correct the mistakes of predecessors, and yet he is the one most vigorously in error. Dorothea marks selected passages, not for correction but for inclusion in the imagined Key to All Mythologies. Throughout, she is a reader of the characters of Casaubon, be they in the handwriting he at times trembles to produce or in the letters of the ancient languages he has her read aloud. The blots and margins, the illegibilities of hands and texts, are the marks that intrude into acts of reading in the novel. Casaubon, J. Hillis Miller notes and Neil Hertz agrees, "is a text, a collection of signs which Dorothea misreads, according to that universal propensity for misinterpretation which infects all the characters of *Middlemarch*."[78]

I would go one step further. That propensity for misinterpretation—and the urge to read, note, and correct—infects the character of Eliot herself. Her role as author finds one of its public forms in the location and correction of errata, and the many stages of the text of *Middlemarch* that survive have provided editors with ample proof of her attentions. There is the author's manuscript; the proof of the first, serialized edition; that first edition itself; the proofs of the second, so-called cheap edition; and that second edition of 1874; finally, there is the three-volume Cabinet edition, published as part of a series of Eliot's collected works in 1878. Eliot had to reread her works many times, and she made literally thousands of corrections to her texts. She wrote to Alexander Main (who had noticed several errors throughout the serialization of *Middlemarch*), "I shall note the error which you have kindly pointed out. There are doubtless many others either of pen or type, and I have a great longing to make the text as correct as I can."[79] Her pleasure in the reprinting lies (as she wrote John Blackwood, on another occasion, in italics), "*that I can see the proof-sheets and make corrections.*"[80] (Ironically, in a fascinating aside in the obituary that ran in *Blackwood's Magazine* [February 1881], it is said that Eliot "had rarely much to correct in her proof-sheets.")[81]

Eliot establishes herself as an establisher of texts. She writes consistently about her need to ferret out the errors of the earlier editions, and she does so in strikingly emotional terms. Her "great longing" expressed to Alexander Main is for textual accuracy, a brilliant phrasing that recalls the longing of love and intellectual pursuit that had brought Dorothea to her Casaubon and later to Will Ladislaw (see chap. 54, p. 511: "through it all there was always the deep longing which had really determined her to come to Lowick. The longing was to see Will Ladislaw"). Or think of the excitement that prevents Eliot from reading further in her own books and compare it with the "excited feeling" that possesses Dorothea when she realizes that she could have learned German or, by contrast, just a few pages later in the novel, when she starts to cry after Casaubon's blunt reproaching: "You are excited, my dear" (chap. 21, pp. 198, 200). Textual criticism lies in the purview not of the disinterested scholar but of the feeling author. It is cause for longing and excitement.

Eliot's intense engagement with the technical details of publishing is exemplified both by and in the revisions she made to the close of

Middlemarch. She reworked the penultimate paragraph greatly in its passage from manuscript, to first serialized edition, and finally to the 1874 cheap edition, and here are its transformations.[82]

> Certainly those determining acts of her life were not ideally beautiful. They were the mixed result of young and noble impulse struggling with imperfect conditions. Among the many criticisms which passed on her first marriage nobody remarked that it could not have happened if she had not been born into a society which smiled on propositions of marriage from a sickly man to a girl less than half his own age, and, in general, encouraged the view that to renounce an advantage to oneself which might be got from the folly or ignorance of others is a sign of mental weakness. While this tone of opinion is part of the social medium in which young creatures begin to breathe, there will be collisions such as those in Dorothea's life, where great feelings will take the aspect of error, and great faith the aspect of illusion. For there is no creature whose inward being is so strong that it is not greatly determined by what lies outside it. It is not likely that a new Theresa will have the opportunity of reforming a conventual life. (manuscript)

> Certainly those determining acts of her life were not ideally beautiful. They were the mixed result of young and noble impulse struggling under prosaic conditions. Among the many remarks passed on her mistakes, it was never said in the neighbourhood of Middlemarch that such mistakes could not have happened if the society into which she was born had not smiled on propositions of marriage from a sickly man to a girl less than half his own age—on modes of education which make a woman's knowledge another name for motley ignorance—on rules of conduct which are in flat contradiction with its own loudly-asserted beliefs. While this is the social air in which mortals begin to breathe, there will be collisions such as those in Dorothea's life, where great feelings will take the aspect of error, and great faith the aspect of illusion. For there is no creature whose inward being is so strong that it is not greatly determined by what lies outside it. A new Theresa will hardly have the opportunity of reforming a conventual life. (first edition)

Certainly those determining acts of her life were not ideally beautiful. They were the mixed result of young and noble impulse struggling amidst the conditions of an imperfect social state, in which great feelings will often take the aspect of error, and great faith the aspect of illusion. For there is no creature whose inward being is so strong that it is not greatly determined by what lies outside it. A new Theresa will hardly have the opportunity of reforming a conventual life. (1874 edition)

We can see how Eliot pared down her reflections from the start, moving from explicit statements in the narrator's voice to a more general, almost aphoristic tone. But if these versions record changes in the narrator's position, they also record changes in the book's own textual thematics. The manuscript considers the determining acts of Dorothea's life to be the "mixed result of young and noble impulse struggling with imperfect conditions." The first edition changes that phrasing to "struggling under prosaic conditions." The change from "imperfect" to "prosaic" signals a shift in just where the narrator locates Dorothea's life. For it is not simply that her impulses would fail when set against the everyday experiences of living; it is that Dorothea becomes a poetic creature trapped in prose. This is the very problem of the novel: how to capture character in prose? And, more to the point, just how "prosaic" is the business of the novel's making? The first edition makes the word "mistakes" central to Dorothea's life. Such mistakes are, in essence, the conditions of prosaic life. As Eliot wrote to Blackwood, concerning the printing of the second edition of the novel, "I am not fond of reading proofs, but I am anxious to correct the sheets of this edition, both in relation to mistakes already standing, and to prevent the accumulation of others in the reprinting."[83]

The act of revising involves the locating of mistakes, and Eliot writes into her revision of the novel's close the climate of errata hunting that emerged as the book was being printed. Alexander Main was catching errors as it came out in serialized form, and the revisions to these last sections—made after the first parts had already appeared in print—may very well ventriloquize "the many remarks passed on her mistakes."[84] In this context, the reflections on error—"great feelings will take the aspect of error," in both manuscript and first edition—take on a different tone in the revised edition. Unlike in the manuscript version, Dorothea's predicament in the first edition appears as a collection of mistakes building to error. But, in the 1874 revision, those mistakes are left unsaid. Here, it is the "social state" that is imperfect, not the more general "conditions" of the manuscript. The long reflection on the first marriage, on the problems of education and ignorance, on the social expectations of female behavior, are gone in the 1874 text, and we get a shorter, single-sentence structure in which "an imperfect social state" is the venue for "great feelings" taking on "the aspect of error."

Eliot's revisions expose her struggle with the idea of error in the novel. From "criticisms," to "mistakes," to "error," these versions circle around this theme. The difference between mistake and error is between a local wrong and a more global sense of errancy: the difficulties of writing and reading, the blots and illegibilities of the many texts that pass among its characters, the inability of Casaubon to bring his big book to fruition, the judgments passed on other novelists throughout the story. The sense of resignation at the novel's close mimes, too, Eliot's own sense of resignation to the state of her writings. "But the book is stereotyped, and I fear that I cannot well make corrections for the next edition," she wrote to Main.[85] Once the plates of the book are set in stereotype—that is, once they are set as pages rather than as lines of movable type—she fears that whatever emendations she would wish to make would involve resetting new plates rather than simply new lines. "But I am afraid of looking at it [i.e., the book], until I can be free from the sense that every correction demands a new plate."

Nonetheless, Eliot was able to make changes, even when her books were set in plates, as the extensive revisions to the 1874 edition attest.[86] But one change she kept from the first edition was the novel's final sentence. With its own tone of resignation—and its resonant last words, "unvisited tombs"—this last sentence seems so perfect, so epitomizing of the novel's idiom, that it is hard to imagine it in any other way. But, as the manuscript reveals, it had been:[87]

> But the effect of her being on those around her was incalculably diffusive; for the growing *life* of the world is *after all chiefly dependent* on unhistoric acts, and that things are not so ill with you and me as they might have been is owing to *many of those* who sleep in unvisited tombs, having lived a hidden life nobly.
>
> (MS; emphases mine)

But the effect of her being on those around her was incalculably diffusive: for the growing *good* of the world is *partly dependent* on unhistoric acts; and that things are not so ill with you and me as they might have been is *half* owing to *the number* who lived faithfully a hidden life, and rest in unvisited tombs.

(first edition; emphases mine)

The difference lies in the rhetoric of reckoning in these two versions. The manuscript expresses fullness and completion: "after all chiefly dependent," "many of those." The first edition seems to hedge: "partly dependent," "half owing," "the number." It is as if this first edition's ending is sustaining the accountancy of that edition's earlier paragraph: the noting of the many remarks passed on Dorothea's mistakes and the list of reasons for them. Eliot cut that material from the 1874 edition, but the numeracy of the final sentence still remains. I suggest that we see this final sentence as part of the first edition's changes: a need to catalog things, reckon up individual mistakes, create, in essence, an errata sheet of life itself. And as we tote up all those things, we find ourselves left with the tomb. So, too, Dorothea looked upon the "rows of note-books" as a "mute memorial" (chap. 51, p. 510).

And just whose *acts* are we left to consider? Look at the way this word is used, in this same scene in chapter 51, when Dorothea consigns Casaubon's work to oblivion: "One little act of hers may perhaps be smiled at as superstitious. The *Synoptical Tabulation for the use of Mrs. Casaubon*, she carefully enclosed and sealed, writing within the envelope, '*I could not use it. Do you not see now that I could not submit my soul to yours, by working hopelessly at what I have no belief in?—Dorothea.*' Then she deposited the paper in her own desk" (p. 511). By closing *Middlemarch* with the word "tomb," Eliot returns her readers to scenes such as this one. The association between Casaubon's work and the tomb now textures an association between Dorothea and the—female—author of *Middlemarch*. The act of writing and depositing the envelope stands as a formal burial of Casaubon's unwritten book. The Key to All Mythologies becomes, irrevocably, an unvisited tomb. And yet *Middlemarch* itself will be returned to again and again, not just by others but by Eliot herself.

The revisions to the novel's final paragraphs feed into a thematics of revision itself. They comment on the author's own rereading of her text, correction of her mistakes, and review of the errata of life as well as books. *Middlemarch*, if it is a novel of mistakes, is also a textual testimony to authorial correction. When Mrs. Cadwallader chides Dorothea, after Casaubon's death, we may find in her remarks, then, a reflection of the novelist's own anxiousness about the uses of mistake, about the "great longing" to make things as correct as one can, about the daily work of proofs: "But I suppose you have found out your mistake, my dear, and that is proof of sanity" (chap. 54, p. 509).

Etymology

What would the young Casaubon have known of the practice of etymology? In the last decades of the eighteenth century, it concerned itself not simply with the origins of words but with word elements. There was an assumption that certain individual sounds, or their combinations, quite simply meant something—not just in one but in all languages. This doctrine of the *cognatio literarum*—what Hans Aarsleff explains as the "phonological correspondence of sounds"—became a norm in linguistic inquiry.[88] Perhaps the most influential English beneficiary of this etymological tradition was John Horne Tooke's *Diversions of Purley*.[89] Published in two parts, in 1798 and 1805, and reprinted frequently thereafter (an edition appeared in 1829, the same year in which *Middlemarch* opens), the *Diversions* argued that human thought depended on language. It keyed the study of sense impressions to the study of linguistic forms. As a methodological consequence, the etymologies of individual words offered keys to the roots of intellection. All words had, at their core, a basic meaning. There are no abstract ideas but only names of things. Words that we think have abstract or active connotations—prepositions, for example—all descend from proper nouns or, if not from nouns, then from the imperative form of verbs. In the words of Tooke's interlocutor in *Diversions*, "You mean to say that the errors of Grammarians have arisen from supposing all words to be immediately either the signs of things or the signs of ideas: whereas in fact many words are merely abbreviations employed for dispatch, and are the figures of other words" (1:26–27). This is the heart of Tooke's theory of representation and the core of his etymological method. The little words of language—particles, conjunctions, prepositions, words like "that," "if," "from," "but," and so on—became the nodes of etymology. Thus "if," for example, really comes from a verb, the imperative of the Gothic and Anglo-Saxon "*Gifan.*" "Our corrupted if has always the signification of the English Imperative Give; and no other." "If" is an abbreviation for "give that" (1:102–3). As Aarsleff summarizes this procedure: "All these etymological explanations rest on the assumption that a word which originally followed the participle or the adjective has since disappeared and must now be understood or supplied to complete the construction before the right etymology will emerge."[90]

Tooke's work had an immense impact on nineteenth-century English thought (in her notebook, Eliot lists "Horne Tooke, d. 1812," under the heading "Remarkable Persons"), and I think it is his legacy that Eliot dismisses along with Casaubon's "theory of the elements" based in "likeness in sound."[91] For English scholars of the 1820s, though, such conjectures were the bread and butter of linguistic inquiry. Likeness in sound *was* the presiding principle of etymology, and the associations between "Gog and Magog" that Eliot's narrator ridicules some lines later in *Middlemarch* would have filled the studies of mythographers.

For it is only to a reader of the Germans that Casaubon's work seems foolish. Ladislaw intimates as much when he derides him, to Dorothea, for not knowing German and for not being a true "Orientalist." After the pioneering work of Sir William Jones at the end of the eighteenth century—with his recognition that the grammar and vocabulary of Sanskrit bear close resemblances to Greek and Latin and thus, by implication, the languages must in some sense be related—Rasmus Rask, Franz Bopp, and the Grimm Brothers came to synthesize a new Indo-European linguistic inheritance.[92] The study of language, in their terms, would proceed by historical inquiry. Living languages descended from earlier ones; different dialects or language groups branched off from others; and the sounds of those languages were related according to fixed, and thus recoverable, principles or laws. Philology became comparative. Its method was to discern phonological and morphological relationships among extant languages in order to reconstruct earlier forms. The system of inflections was the real key to recovering linguistic relationships. As Holger Pedersen put it in *Linguistic Science in the Nineteenth Century* (in terms that resonate with Casaubon's own scholarly morass), "It was the establishment of this fundamental principle in method which pulled etymological scholarship out of the bog where it had stuck fast since classical times, and rendered the existence of comparative linguistics possible."[93]

Pedersen's figurative phrasing, however, is not without precedent in the philologists he praises. Bopp himself develops a highly organicist vocabulary for linguistic study: word *roots*, language *stocks*, and *anatomical* investigations control his sense of relations and descent.[94] "For what is more important," he wrote in the preface to *Vergleichende Grammatik* (in the Victorian English translation), "or can be more earnestly desired by the cultivator of the classical languages, than their comparison with our mother tongue in her oldest and most perfect form" (p. viii). And the organic metaphors continue: "I am rather at giving a physiology of them [i.e., the Indo-European languages] than an introduction to their practical use . . . ; and I have gained thereby more space for the discussion of matters more important, and more intimately incorporated with the vital spirit of the language" (p. ix). "Cultivate," "physiology," "vital spirit"—all come together to inflect the rhetoric of comparative philology with the idioms of biology. The goal of etymology is thus the establishment of true relationships. The legacy of Grimm's work lay in "the discovery of new affinities, or the more precise definition of those discovered, and to catch with greater truth, at every step of grammatical progress, the monitory voices of the Asiatic as well as the European sisterhood. It was necessary, also, to set aside many false appearances of affinity" (pp. ix–x). Comparative philology, in these terms, reads like an investigation into family relationships—an investigation not to be misled by false appearances.

Linguistic science by the last third of the nineteenth century seemed to have come a long way from the speculations of Horne Tooke and the associations of a Casaubon. But there were still those who, in Eliot's time, might pursue them. James A. H. Murray, in 1879, mocked the foolishness of what he ironically quoted as the "well-considered etymologies" provided by contributors: "Thus one eminent philologist has 'always had an impression that *abide* is from the Hebrew *beth* a house, which is in Persian *abad*.' He is 'not sure whether *body* is from the same root, but the Ags. synonym *banhus* supplies strong supporting evidence.' Another eminent orientalist derives *able* from an Ethiopic word, which is picturesquely given in Ethiopic characters, meaning *artful*."[95] Surely, the word "eminent" here drips with sarcasm. No true orientalist would make such claims.

George Eliot was following a good deal of this progress in philology. And yet in spite of—or perhaps even because of—her wide knowledge of the new philology, *Middlemarch* is a novel full of etymologies grounded in likeness in sound. The novel's names display, at times, an almost Dickensian wordplay. Casaubon settles himself at Lowick: the low wick that barely lights the pathways of his life. Will Ladislaw appears preeminently as a creature of the will, and the play on his name and on Casaubon's own will—both his desires and his legal document limiting Dorothea's remarriage—reflect the essences of both men. Other names resonate with historical sounds and sources. Dr. Lydgate, for all his advances in the field of medicine, bears the name of the fifteenth-century poet whom Eliot's contemporaries would have seen as one of the most slavish of Chaucer's imitators.[96] The list can go on: Bulstrode, Freshitt, Brooke, Raffles, Wrench, Featherstone. And Casaubon himself. "His very name," the narrator avers when he is introduced, "carried an impressiveness hardly to be measured without a precise chronology of scholarship" (chap. 1, p. 11).

That chronology may take us back to the Renaissance figures Isaac Casaubon and his son, Meric, scholars far more adventurous and prolific than this modern namesake. But it also returns us to the etymological pressure of *Middlemarch* itself: its concern with the origin of things, with tracing out historical lineages, with genealogies of words and people. Like many of its Victorian compeers, *Middlemarch* draws into its plot a story of inheritance and descent. Ladislaw's mother married badly; Bulstrode's fortune really belongs to Ladislaw; Casaubon's will tries to limit lines of future wealth; Dorothea's son inherits Mr. Brooke's estate; Fred Vincy seeks a bequest from Featherstone. But what distinguishes these plotlines from those of so many other nineteenth-century novels is this association between etymology and genealogy. It reifies the central metaphors of language study governing that first generation of Indo-European linguistics: affiliation, family, descent. The families of languages were grouped together; lines of historical descent were drawn; branches emerged (August Schleicher's famous *Stammbaum*, or family tree, of languages, posited in the 1860s, became a central image for historical linguistics).[97] Eliot took copious notes on Indo-European language families. "The modern languages of India . . . bear the relation of daughters to Sanskrit, not that of sisters."[98] Or, on another occasion, she noted: "The results of [Rasmus] Rask's labour, as presented by himself were: 1. That Zend is a brother of Sanskrit" (p. 131).

Such idioms recall Bopp's familial and organic language. Eliot filled her notebooks with etymologies, lists of alphabets, digests of Grimm's Law and Max Müller's speculations, and groupings of ancient and modern languages. Her entries bear eloquent testimony to the association of etymology and genealogy. And so does *Middlemarch*. The very word "likeness" associates the familial with the linguistic (recall the etymology of German comparative philology: *vergleichende Philologie*, a philology of likenesses). Beholding Casaubon's portrait gallery, Dorothea comments on the dissimilarities between the pictures of Casaubon's mother and her sister: "There is not even a family likeness between her and your mother" (chap. 9, p. 71). Likeness becomes the fulcrum on which recognition, naming, and identity balance when Raffles reminisces—with the maximum amount of imposed discomfort—with Bulstrode: "Some said you had a handsome family likeness to old Nick, but that was your mother's fault, calling you Nicholas" (chap. 53, p. 502). Will Ladislaw responds to Dorothea's offer of the picture of his grandmother, culled from Casaubon's things: "It is not very consoling to have one's own likeness" (p. 516). And when Raffles meets Will at the Larcher estate auction in chapter 60, he exclaims: "It was at Boulogne I saw your father—a most uncommon likeness you are of him, by Jove!" (p. 581).

Raffles becomes at moments such as these a mock genealogist: a reader of faces and names, a noticer of "likeness," a Bopp-like discerner of "false appearances of affinity." As if in some gross parody of Casaubon's etymological fancies, his attentions to likeness lead to real relationships, productive inheritances, and narrative resolution. In one more great mockery of likeness in sound, Mr. Trumbull auctions off, at the Larcher sale, "a book of riddles" that stands as comic foil to Casaubon's huge and unwritten book.

> "This I have in my hand is an ingenious contrivance—a sort of practical rebus I may call it; here, you see, it looks like an elegant heart-shaped box, portable—for the pocket; there, again, it becomes like a splendid double flower—and ornament for the table; and now"— Mr. Trumbull allowed the flower to fall alarmingly into strings of heart-shaped leaves—"a book of riddles! No less than five hundred printed in a beautiful red. . . . What can promote innocent mirth, and I may say virtue, more than a good riddle. . . . Here is a sample: 'How must you spell honey to make it catch lady-birds? Answer—

money.' You hear?—lady-birds—honey—money. This is an amusement to sharpen the intellect; it has a sting—it has what we call satire, and wit without indecency. Four-and-sixpence—five shillings." (chap. 60, p. 577)

The search for the Key to All Mythologies had been the attempt to solve a great puzzle. Unlike this little book, which can fit easily into the pocket, Casaubon's notebooks spill over shelves and tabletops. His search for likenesses in sound now becomes the joke of the auctioneer. "You hear?" he asks. Do *we* hear the likeness in sound? "Honey," "money." This is the heart of family life, for in a novel of inheritances, Trumbull's joke stands as something of a comic etymology. Dorothea has given up the money for the honey—forfeited her legacy from Casaubon to marry Will—and, in that act, gives all the etymologists a sting.

Germans

Even before the Indo-Europeanists had codified their methods, classical philology had established itself as the mainstay of a German university education. By the late eighteenth century, philology had become the defining academic discipline for German-speaking universities, and, by the late 1820s, academic life began to move, throughout Europe, along German lines. In England, university identity began to shift from clergyman to don.[99] The Oxford fellow of the early nineteenth century—in holy orders, often out of college in his living as a parson—was gradually disappearing, and, by the time *Middlemarch* was published, this figure had almost completely vanished. Government commissions from the 1850s to the 1870s had provoked changes in college and university statutes. The teaching of undergraduates and the publication of research emerged as the professor's primary callings. By the last quarter of the nineteenth century, the concept of the university professional had arrived. German scholarship stood as the benchmark against which to measure the accomplishments, or failures, of other nations, and it was philology that epitomized that scholarship: "die Erkenntniss des Erkannten."[100]

English philology, however, had taken a different direction. But so, too, had English educational institutions. The college fellows of the late eighteenth and early nineteenth centuries were often chosen not for merit but for being what a mid-eighteenth-century Oxford reformer called "men of Family and Fortune"—though even this critic refused to acknowledge that the job of fellows was to teach (he simply lamented that fellowships were being awarded to men rich enough to do without them).[101] By the first decade of the nineteenth century, critics of the universities, especially of Oxford, were complaining of the overwhelming focus on the classics. And here, in the opening salvo of the century's debate on university reform, there is the opposition of the English and the European (especially the German). Look closely at the imagery of this complaint from the *Edinburgh Review* of 1809: "Though this learned Body [i.e., Oxford's Clarendon Press] have occasionally availed themselves of the sagacity and erudition of Rhunken, Wyttenbach, Heyné and other *foreign* professors, they have, of late, added nothing of their own, except what they derived from the superior skill of British manufacturers, and the superior wealth of their establishment; namely, whiter paper, blacker ink, and neater types."[102] The English books are better made than European ones. They are more legible, and in this imagery of British printmanship lies a delicious resonance with Casaubon's failed publication. His texts are all blots and pen scratches. Even when he commits something to print—those little pamphlets or "Parerga"—his products remain either unread or uncritiqued. "The difficulty of making his Key to all Mythologies unimpeachable weighed like lead upon his mind" (chap. 29, p. 266)—as if the raw materials of "British manufacturers," the lead of the type itself, oppresses him.

By Casaubon's time, the dilettantes were losing ground. University reformers sought to have specialists in fields tutor the students, rather than have tutors teach all subjects, regardless of their expertise. Such a project would lead directly to the advancement of knowledge, and Sir William Hamilton published two essays in the *Edinburgh Review* in 1831 that suggested, among other things, that Oxford follow the German model in this matter.[103] Oxford was quick to reply. Vaughn Thomas, one of Oxford's city clergymen, mocked this attention to the German. The writer for the *Edinburgh Review*, he wrote, seemed to come "just fresh from the classroom of a Dr Birchschneider or a Dr Wagschneider, or some other Teutonic Gamaliel, with a name as unutterable as his blasphemies."[104]

In 1837 another writer took up the cause of reform, arguing explicitly for academic reconfigurations along German lines. His comments, voiced in "Reform of the University of Oxford," published in the *Eclectic Review*, could have been voiced by Ladislaw himself.

> [In Oxford] philology itself, in which one would expect Oxford to excell, is not known as the science which it has become in the hands of the inquisitive Germans. . . . Once she [Oxford] stood on a par with the most celebrated foreign universities. Even more recently her Professors were of leading rank in oriental studies. Now we hear of Paris, Copenhagen, and Petersburg as the center of numberless publications in the languages of the East and North; but of Oxford, nothing of the kind. She seems to have been living on German classics and on French and Cambridge mathematics. The Germans have so outstripped her in Greek, Latin, Arabic, and Hebrew criticism, in Philology at large, in Biblical antiquities, in Ecclesiastical and other ancient history, that for a length of time she will have nothing to do but translate from German authors.[105]

The Germans are inquisitive, scientific, industrious. They are, along with their European contemporaries, the true orientalists.

"Young Mr. Ladislaw was not at all deep himself in German writers," but he is—as a budding political journalist and reformer—deep in the public discourse of his time. His comments to Dorothea reflect an awareness of the popular debates on scholarship and education in the first third of the nineteenth century. But Dorothea's responses, too, mime these kinds of reactions. "How I wish I had learned German when I was at Lausanne!" she laments. "There were plenty of German teachers. But now I can be of no use" (chap. 21, p. 198). She would play Oxford to her Casaubon, lamenting that, in fact, she would *not* "have nothing to do but translate from German authors."

George Eliot's own career began with translating from German authors, and she always had "a word for the Germans." Her 1865 essay of that title provides another set of links between the trope of German scholarly superiority and *Middlemarch*'s idiom.[106] The essay's strategy is to affirm and then dismantle national stereotypes. The British, she avers, have certain images about the French, Italians, and Germans. But, while all nationalities can be subjected to caricature, for "a caricature to be good, [it] must come from close observation" (p. 390). And so she observes the Germans closely. Like many of her predecessors, she finds in the German mind a characteristic "largeness of theoretic conception, and thoroughness in the investigation of facts" (p. 389). Such habits may well fit the kind of work done in, say, Indo-European studies or philosophy, but they chime, too, with the Dorothea's characterization early on in *Middlemarch*. "Her mind was theoretic" (chap. 1, p. 4), her nature "altogether ardent, theoretic, and intellectually consequent" (chap. 3, p. 24).[107] There is a sense in which this key term of the German intellectual identity becomes the template for the novel's ideals. Dorothea's grand ideas, whether they be for the improvement of the tenants or the success of Casaubon's Key to All Mythologies, are, perhaps, almost too German for her world. "Your German," Eliot continues in her essay, "can not write about the drama without going back to the Egyptian mysteries; he sees that everything is related to everything else, and is determined to exhaust you and the subject; his doctrine is all-embracing, and so is his detail" (p. 389). How like, and unlike, Casaubon. In spite of his apparent ignorance of German, he remains in pursuit of a key to everything. All seems to be related in his work, and he has even authored a "tractate on the Egyptian Mysteries" (chap. 37, p. 353).

These German ideas also stand as foil for Lydgate. "No man is more likely to be contemptuous towards desultory labours which are not *wissenschaftlich*," Eliot wrote, using that very German word for the Germans themselves (p. 389). And Lydgate seems, at the very least, to aspire to a *wissenschaftlich* goal. "If he is an experimentor [*sic*], he will be thorough in his experiments" (p. 389). Certainly Lydgate is the most thorough of experimenters: "That evening when he went home, he looked at his phials to see how a process of maceration was going on, with undisturbed interest; and he wrote out his daily notes with as much precision as usual" (chap. 27, p. 258). He is the very model of a European-trained empiricist who would find meaning in a drop of fluid. So it remains a source of brilliant humor to find Mrs. Cadwallader the operator of a social microscope on Casaubon. "Somebody put a drop" of his blood "under a magnifying glass, and it was all semicolons and parentheses" (chap. 8, p. 66). And she goes on: "Oh, he dreams footnotes." And yet, as we can imagine, those footnotes could not be in German. "[T]he footnotes of every good French or English book that appears, whether in scholarship, history, or natural science, are filled with references to German authors" (p. 389). If *Middlemarch*'s characters fail, they fail against these German models. Dorothea's theoretic impulse yields to simple love; Lydgate, for all his *wissenschaftlich* and experimental ambitions, dies early as a doctor at a wealthy spa; and Casaubon fails in his own inquiry into mysteries.

If Casaubon does succeed, it is, in a weird way, as a kind of anti-German: one who lives through not the goals of German science but the byways of their rhetoric. "The German is never in a hurry: for him, art is long, and life, expanded by the absence of adventitious needs, is not so short as for Englishmen making haste to be rich. His writing will sometimes seem to be all stairs and landing-places without any floors" (p. 390). Casaubon is a creature of such places, "lost among small closets and winding stairs," a writer, perhaps, full of the turns and tropes of pedantry yet without any of the substance of the German *wissenschaft*.

Orientalist

The word "orientalist" once conjured an impression of great learning and arcane knowledge. In this matter, though, the *OED* is little help. The word is sparsely attested under its heading. Only in definition 3 does it present, "One versed in oriental languages and literature," illustrating the definition with but two quotations, both, in a sense, self-referential: the first, from Samuel Johnson's *Lives of the Poets* (1779–1781, "The great Orientalist, Dr. Pocock"); the second, from Murray's own 1879 *Address to the Philological Society* (though, here, it is unattributed to him by name; the phrase quoted is "The Congress of Orientalists at Florence"). "Orientalist," for the *OED*, is purely a dictionary word, confined to the discourses of lexicographers describing others of their ilk. Curiously, there is another reference to "orientalist" embedded in the *Dictionary*, under the word "curious" (def. 3a). "It is to be desired that some curious orientalist may think the subject worthy of attentive enquiry." This quotation, from Singer's *History of Playing Cards* of 1816, at least attests the word's currency in the early nineteenth century. But for a term that would be so central to Indo-European studies—that would distill the great historical discovery of the affiliations of the European languages to those of India and Persia, that would grant a deep history to those languages going back to Sanskrit—the *OED* remains curiously quiet.

The history of orientalism in the nineteenth century *is* the history of linguistics.[108] It begins with Sir William Jones, who, in his lectures and reports, recognized the grammatical affiliations between Sanskrit and the European languages. Jones was, in some sense, the original orientalist, imagining an "Oriental Renaissance" as the result of his studies, and those who followed in his wake similarly looked east for their inspiration.[109] Bopp's phrasing (in the Victorian English translation) is telling:

> Who could have dreamed a century ago that a language would be brought to us from the far East, which should accompany, *pari passu*, nay, sometimes surpass, the Greek in all those perfections of form which have been hitherto considered the exclusive property of the latter, and be adapted throughout to adjust the perennial strife between the Greek dialects, by enabling us to determine where each of them has preserved the purest and oldest forms?[110]

Bopp's own researches had been published first in 1816 and were translated soon afterwards as "Analytical Comparison of the Sanskrit, Greek, Latin and Teutonic Languages" in the *Annals of Oriental Literature*, published in London in 1820 (p. vii).

The orientalist temptations of this new philology were great, and Max Müller is perhaps best known as its popularizer in the study of language, myth, and culture.[111] He is a perfect foil for Casaubon, and his 1856 essay "Comparative Mythology" encapsulates his method—and, at times, his vivid metaphorics—in ways that chime with the Casaubonian failed project.[112] It is a long and rambling performance, but its central thesis is that it is possible "to account in a more intelligible manner for the creation of myths" (p. 311) by practicing comparative philology. The etymologies of key words in the Indo-European languages point back to shared concepts, from which it is possible to extract the main plotlines, characters, and themes of ancient mythology. The study of mythology becomes the study of language, but the study of language leads to the study of thematic archetypes and idioms that motivate what Müller comes to see as literature itself. There are poets, he finds, "who still think and feel in language," who can "use it as a spell to call forth real things, full of light and colour" (p. 361). Among such writers who enliven words with personal expression ("life and blood") is Wordsworth. In a series of carefully chosen excerpts, Wordsworth becomes, in Müller's handling, a mythic poet—not because he trades in ancient mythic stories but because his very language vivifies abstraction with the presence of feeling, because Wordsworth's nature is an animated, almost personified, thing. "There are some poems of this modern ancient which are all mythology" (p. 363), and here is one:

> Hail, orient Conqueror of gloomy Night!
> Thou that canst shed the bliss of gratitude
> On hearts, howe'er insensible or rude;
> Whether they punctual visitations smite
> The haughty powers where monarchs dwell,
> Or thou, impartial Sun, with presence bright
> Cheer'st the low threshold of the peasant's cell!

And on, and on (pp. 363–64). Müller quotes from "Ode: Morning of the Day Appointed for a General Thanksgiving, January 18, 1816," and his text clearly has less to do with Wordsworth or the historical moment of this poem's composition than it does with Müller's own autoallegories of research.[113] The "orient Conqueror of gloomy Night" is, here, philology itself—the new philology, with its awareness of the languages of India and Persia, with its illuminating method of historical etymology, with its scientific dedication to things "punctual" and "impartial." Philology is like a sun in that it makes language visible. It reveals the importance of language of social development, and it illustrates how language itself can be the object of a scientific study. "Language," Müller argued in one of his public lectures, "remained unnoticed" in all the inquiries of humankind. "Like a veil that hung too close over the eye of the human mind, it was hardly perceived."[114]

The oriental is the source of light, and Müller's work—in particular, his quotation of Wordsworth—exposes the illuminating etymology of "orient" itself: from the Latin "*oriens*," "rising," and thus the direction of the rising sun. Wordsworth's own lines, too, play on something of that etymon, redolent as they are of Milton's opening to book 3 of *Paradise Lost* ("Hail, holy Light, offspring of Heav'n first-born"). And they are redolent of Casaubon as well. For Eliot herself, steeped in the oriental studies of the German scholars, the eastern texts remained a source of illumination.[115] Representative is her excerpt on Buddha's cave from Müller's *Chips from a German Workshop*.[116] This selection tells the story of a traveler who finds a cave in which the Buddha had supposedly converted a dragon "& had promised his new pupil to leave him in the shadow, in order that, whenever the evil passions of his dragon-nature should revive, the aspect of his master's shadowy features might remind him of his former vows." The traveler eventually finds a guide to take him to the cave; he undergoes a series of difficulties on the journey; he is beset by robbers, whom he converts; and he finds the cave, where "All was dark." After much prayer and devotion, and the apprehension of a few dim lights, he eventually sees the cave "suddenly bathed in light." "A dazzling splendour lighted up the features of the divine countenance." The account ends with a moral Müller culls from another source: "Though one does see something, it is only a feeble & doubtful resemblance. If a man prays with sincere faith, & if he has received from above a hidden impression, he sees the shadow clearly, but he cannot enjoy the sight for any length of time."

This excerpt fits precisely into Eliot's notebook, and into her palette of images, in ways that anticipate the central idioms of *Middlemarch*.[117] The language of the journey, of the byways of experience, of illumination, and of mythic narrative as something of a key to understanding—these are the stuff of Casaubon's researches. And, in the language of resemblance and impression, Eliot would have found imagistic kin to the controlling idioms of those researches and, more generally, of the novel's plot: the search for likeness in sound that motivates Casaubon's misguided etymologies; the search for family resemblances among the many intertwining relatives of *Middlemarch*; the centrality of impression in guiding both the fates and fears of many of its characters. Compare the accounts of Will and Casaubon in Rome, whose meeting Eliot describes in ways that almost make the two into mythic creatures out of Müller's solar pantheon:

> The first impression on seeing Will was one of sunny brightness, which added to the uncertainty of his changing expression. Surely, his very features changed their form; his jaw looked sometimes large and sometimes small; and the little ripple in his nose was a preparation for metamorphosis. When he turned his head quickly his hair seemed to shake out light, and some persons thought they saw decided genius in this coruscation. Mr. Casaubon, on the contrary, stood rayless. (chap. 21, p. 199).

Will's changing visage mirrors the changing vision of the Buddha, sometimes appearing bright, sometimes a shadow. Indeed, he comes off here as something almost godlike, as if light halos his head. By contrast, rayless Casaubon stands like a creature of the cave, without illumination, either in the literal or metaphorical senses.

To say that Casaubon is not an orientalist is—now, in the richness of its etymology—to say he has no sense of sun. Lost in the darkness of his hallways, with his dim taper, "he forgot the absence of sunlight." As Müller put it in defining the etymological method: "Here we have some of the keys to mythology, but the manner of handling them can only be learnt from comparative philology" (p. 379). Casaubon's Key, without that philological learning, is useless. And so, too, is the problem with his lack of oriental knowledge. His is not simply a failure to know a language or a philological tradition but a failure to face dawning light itself, a refusal to acknowledge the sun rising and, in turn, to find himself not "punctual" or "impartial" (in Wordsworth's words), but stiflingly polemical and always late.

Pigeonhole

"But now, how do you arrange your documents?"

"In pigeon-holes partly," said Mr. Casaubon, with rather a startled air of effort.

"Ah, pigeon-holes will not do. I have tried pigeon-holes, but everything gets mixed in pigeon-holes: I never know whether a paper is in A or Z." (chap. 2, p. 15)

In this early exchange between Mr. Brooke and Casaubon, we see the central problem of the documentary life. Brooke finds himself beset by "documents." He has used the word four times in the lament just preceding this discussion, as if his repetition verbally enacts their piling up before him. "Arranging" is his problem, and not even the apparently simple system of alphabetical pigeonholes will work. Brooke cannot keep his A and Z from mixing with each other, and, when Dorothea interjects that she would gladly help her uncle "sort" his papers ("I would letter them all, and then make a list of subjects under each letter"), Brooke disapproves: "No, no, . . . I cannot let young ladies meddle with my documents. Young ladies are too flighty" (p. 16). Of course, the joke there is that few are more flighty than Mr. Brooke himself, and

Casaubon had noticed that he has "an excellent secretary at hand" on the basis of this evidence.

This passage, and the discussion that surrounds it, says as much about the novelist herself as it does about her characters. The young Mary Ann Evans's early letters fill themselves with lists of interests and activities that she tries (at times, almost hopelessly) to wrestle into order. The amount of learning the young girl acquired and, later in life, the amount of material the author would collect for her novels posed a challenge. Early letters chronicle the disorganization of her pastimes and responsibilities: in one, she laments that her mind, "never of the most highly organized genus, is more than usually chaotic" and then goes on to list, almost randomly it seems, all the different things she reads and remembers, "an assemblage of disjoined specimens."[118] Later work similarly seeks to find a pattern to such specimens. Her writer's notebook is prefaced by an index in which she attempts to organize alphabetically the quotations, asides, and fragmentary comments assembled in the book over twenty-five years. And that book is filled with lists of its own: a "synopsis of languages"; a table of Grimm's Law; the chronology of English translations of the Bible; the order of Chaucer's *Canterbury Tales*; the Hebrew alphabet; the phonemes of English; a book-by-book summary of the *Iliad*.[119]

Arranging, organizing, finding, and selecting—these are personal concerns for Eliot, controlling themes for *Middlemarch*, and methodological hurdles for philology. In these contexts, the history of "pigeonhole" recorded in the *OED* presents more than the story of a word; it writes, in miniature, a cultural history of Victorian literary values. The entry for the word begins historically, with quotations illustrating aviculture, prison maintenance, children's games, the history of printing, and the theater (defs. 1–6). Only at definition 7a do we find the meaning we associate with organizing knowledge: "One of a series of compartments or cells, in a cabinet, writing-table, or range of shelves, open in front, and used for the keeping (with ready accessibility) of documents or papers of any kind, also of wares in a shop." And, in the first edition of the *Dictionary*, definition 7a concludes with this quotation: "1879 J. A. H. Murray *Addr. Philol. Soc.* 8: This has been fitted with blocks of pigeon-holes, 1029 in number, for the reception of the alphabetically arranged slips."[120]

The endpoint of this section is the making of the *OED* itself. The keeping of documents, with ready accessibility, remained the primary challenge of the *Dictionary*'s original editors. K. M. Elisabeth Murray recounts that Herbert Coleridge—the first editor, who died prematurely in 1861—had "a set of fifty-four pigeon-holes made which would hold 100,000 slips," and she notes that these holes are still preserved by the Oxford University Press.[121] When Murray set out to revive the project, he adapted Coleridge's model and had, in the words of his 1879 address, "commenced the erection of an iron building" fitted with those pigeon-holes.[122] Now, at a basic level, Murray's arrangement for organizing the slips of definitions and illustrative quotations that would come in from the *Dictionary*'s readers seems a fair one. Many materials had been lost in the shuffle of the previous decade; there were bits and pieces sitting in Furnivall's care ("some ton and three-quarters of materials which had accumulated under his roof," Murray states); some slips had been lost; books and entries from America had never come back; "old materials," he states, still remained "in the hands of sub-editors" (p. 569 n. 1).

But, at another level, Murray's language in the address speaks to a much larger project than the simple organization of words and extracts. The arrangement of the *Dictionary*'s raw materials is nothing less than that of the creation itself. It makes order out of chaos; it imposes the lexicographer's great will on the things he finds.

> I have been engaged ... in turning out, examining, sorting, and bestowing these materials. Only within the last few days have I succeeded in gaining some general idea of what materials exist, and of the state in which they exist, and in sending to our Secretary a sort of inventory of what we have in hand. With gladness I say that one or two of the letters, and sections of letters, are in excellent order, and really sub-edited, in a true sense of the word. This refers especially to F, K, parts of C and R; in a less degree to A, E, N, parts of O and U; of others of the letters ... I have to report that they are in primitive chaos. (p. 569)

Murray well knows of what he speaks; the "primitive chaos" evokes a world as yet unformed. A word such as "bestowing" grants an almost divine power to the editor; his "gladness" as he surveys what has been done is a frank acknowledgment of seeing what is good; and in the "last few days" we see the editor reflecting that the task before him is not six mere days of creation but a lifetime of examination, without time for rest.

Unlike a god, however, Murray invites visitors to see the handiwork in process, and, in 1882, an article in *Fraser's Magazine* recorded just what could be seen. The writer of the article—Miss Jennett Humphreys, an author of children's books and an early and prolific contributor of quotations to the *Dictionary*—remarks on the plainness of the Scriptorium. Everything is "plain deal" and "white wood."[123]

> Then the plain deal is plain deal pigeon-hole. It is pigeon-hole, at any rate, along this wall and along that (barring, only, that intermission across there of a square yard, about, of flat, bare side-window). It is pigeon-hole higher than the arm can reach; going down so low there is need to stoop. It is pigeon-hole, all up and down, and anglewise, of this plain deal screen that shuts off the door, that keeps the inner side—where all is pigeon-hole again—snug and weather-tight for settled sitting. For the remainder, it is only just that much different from plain deal pigeon-hole that it is plain deal shelf; that it is sweeps of shelf; and shelf erected above shelf; and upright divisions of shelf; and sloping shelf, with beaded stop-edge running all along, that books and papers can lie there open, escaping the danger of sliding off to the floor. Utilitarianism it shows again, pure and simple.
>
> (p. 447)

The word "pigeon-hole" repeats itself six times; "plain deal" echoes five times; then we get "shelf" upon "shelf" (also five times), before the sentence splays itself, like its books and papers, on the floor. The brilliance of this reportage mimes not only the very structure of the *Dictionary*'s architecture (with its repeating rows of holes and shelves), but the language of *Middlemarch*'s Mr. Brooke. Compare his obsessive iterations just before he turns to Casaubon: "But I have documents. I began a long while ago to collect documents. They want arranging, but when a question has struck me, I have written to somebody and got an answer. I have documents at my back. But now, how do you arrange your documents?" (chap. 2, p. 15). The very problem of arranging is the problem of repetition. The image of the pigeonhole, in the discourses of the *OED* as well as in *Middlemarch*, now comes to be revealed as the emblem not of difference but of sameness. Brooke cannot keep his *A*s and *Z*s separate, implying that, in fact, there probably is little difference between the items beginning with either letter. And, for all Murray's attempt to distinguish words and letters, meanings and their histories, the visitor to the Scriptorium at Mill Hill only sees the row on row of iterated sections. No differences at all.

And Murray himself, in Humphreys's report, seems dead set on eliminating difference, too. His goal is uniformity.

> "The pigeon-holes," he begins—since he sees these are getting lively noting—"I saw at once that we must furnish ourselves with them; that, in fact, they were indispensable. They number more than 1,100 now, though we shall want to add to them even yet, as the work goes on; and they hold the quotations, or the slips, as our word is, for them. These are all—see—on uniform sheets of paper, of notepaper size, and they are all now being reduced to a uniform plan.... [T]he original method differed little from mine, in the position of the catch-words, book-titles, and other details; and now the time has come when differences must no longer be." (pp. 447–48)

Again, the rhetoric of godhood: let there be no difference. For, as Murray himself would note in the address of 1879, the great fear here is a primitive chaos. As Humphreys interjects, had there not been such uniformity, "There would be chaos, manifestly" (p. 448).

What are the pigeonholes creating, then? Look at the *Dictionary's* quotations for definition 7b (the figurative uses). From Kemble, 1847: "People whose minds are parcelled out into distinct divisions—pigeon-holes, as it were." From Leslie Stephen, 1902: "He was incapable of arranging his thoughts in orderly symmetrical pigeon holes." From an article in the *Academy* of 1899: "Mr. Saintsbury has the pigeon-hole form of mind . . . collecting any quality of conclusions and facts, and after tying them up and labelling them, putting them away for future use in the pigeon-holes of memory." And from the illustrative quotations for the verb *pigeon-hole*, one finds again a set of quotations describing habits of mind. There is, too, a quotation from Murray's own 1879 address, "I had proposed to pigeon-hole the walls of the drawing-room for the reception of the dictionary material." But there is also, as the final quotation, a remark of George Meredith, dated 1904: "Most women have a special talent for pigeon-holing."

Do they? Certainly, Murray's project is a man's. Though he occasionally enlisted his wife and daughters in the *Dictionary*'s making, and though many of the volunteer contributors were women (including Humphreys herself), the overwhelming impression one gets from the accounts, and notably the photographs, of Murray's world is of a great man and his male staff (Humphreys remarks that, in the Scriptorium, there are "two ladies, at their simpler work" [p. 447]). But Meredith's remark must take us back to *Middlemarch* and to the habits of the woman reader of the later nineteenth century.

Dorothea is, in many ways, the ideal pigeonholer. From her initial offer to her uncle to sort out his papers, letter by letter, to her later work for Casaubon, she is the soul of organized—and, in particular, alphabetical—reading. Her first work is learning characters, the very letters of the alien alphabets in which Casaubon works. Thus she imagines Casaubon teaching her to read aloud Latin and Greek. Even if she cannot understand the words, she could "copy the Greek character" (chap. 7, pp. 58–59). Later in the novel, when "Dorothea had learned to read the signs of her husband's mood" (chap. 29, p. 268), she notices him so disturbed that his trembling hand writes in what appears to be "an unknown character" (p. 269). And yet, when she writes, copying the quotations that she had been given, she "felt that she was forming her letters beautifully" (p. 270). On the penultimate day of her husband's life, she takes his instruction in marking "with a cross" those passages that Casaubon selects. Finally, after his death, Dorothea finds herself charged with the burden of preparing the *Synoptical Tabulation* of his work (chap. 54, p. 511).

Dorothea's labor resonates with the process of quotation gathering proposed by the founders of the *OED*. "Even the most indolent novel-reader will find it little trouble to put a pencil-mark against any word or phrase that strikes him, and he can afterwards copy out the context at his leisure."[124] But the gender of the pronoun here belies the fact not only that many of the contributors were women but also that the habit of reading in this way had long been associated with the feminine. Eliot's own "Silly Novels by Lady Novelists," published in 1857, ridicules those women who mark up their books, noting "moral comments," saws, and aphorisms: "There is, doubtless, a class of readers to whom these remarks appear peculiarly pointed and pungent; for *we often find them doubly and trebly scored with the pencil, and delicate hands giving in their determined adhesion to these hardy novelties by a distinct très vrai, emphasized by many notes of exclamation.*"[125] Thackeray, too, mocked all the "little pencil-marks" that filled books owned by women.[126] Dickens made sport of women who read novels as if they were scholars, disputing each others' marginal comments "like commentators in a more extensive way."[127] And, writing in 1900, Andrew Lang saw in the marginalia of young girls something of a parody of his own kind of masculine scholarship: "Mrs. Radcliffe has been read diligently, and copiously annotated."[128]

This history of reading has a double edge that cuts both at the fictional representations of the scholar's life in *Middlemarch* and at the historical representations of that life surrounding, and within, the *OED*. For, as a female reader, Dorothea finds herself charged with precisely the condition of the woman reader of the nineteenth century: to underline, to mark, to cull for usage. Even when she does not fully understand what she is reading, she is left to trace out characters (in precisely the opposite way that Eliot herself would copy out the Hebrew alphabet in her notebook, as she could, in fact, read the language—well enough, at some point, to tutor Lewes in it). But what the editors of the *OED* are asking, in effect, is that all readers become women with a pencil in hand. The very phrase "indolent novel-reader" reeks of the antifeminist; it conjures up the imagery from Eliot's own silly novelists through Thackeray and Dickens. And yet it does so through a paradox. Indolent reading finds itself pressed into the service of a great enterprise. This is the philological telos of what Leah Price has called the tension between "masculine scholarship" and "female novel-read[ing]."[129] It is, in essence, the admission that, as Meredith attested, "Most women have a special talent for pigeon-holing."

The pigeonhole stands at the nexus of the literary and the lexicographical, the male and the female, the indolent and the productive. Its appearance in *Middlemarch* highlights the ways in which the alphabet becomes only the facade of an organizing principle. It shows up the contrasts between the massive inutility of Casaubon's collections and the organizing impulses of Dorothea. Masculine scholarship and female annotation blur here, as they do in the discourses of the *OED*. And it may well be left to Jennett Humphreys—breathless Dorothea to the *Dictionary*'s Casaubon—to comment on the workings of great men and the great structures that support their pigeonholes.

Pioneer

The *Oxford English Dictionary* defines a pioneer as, first, "one of a body of foot-soldiers who march with or in advance of an army or regiment, having spades, pickaxes, etc. to dig trenches, repair roads, and perform other labours in clearing and preparing the way for the main body." It then goes on to record other, figurative senses, including "One who goes before to prepare or open up the way for others to follow . . . ; an original investigator, explorer, or worker, in any department of knowledge or activity."

Middlemarch is a novel of pioneers—and their opposites. In Lydgate, it presents a new man of the medical vocation, striking boldly in directions of diagnosis and management. His plans for hospital improvement, though controversial, are central to the reformist spirit of the late 1820s and early 1830s, while his particular instruments of investigation—most notably, the stethoscope—have for his contemporaries the look of something new (see chap. 30, p. 273). But Lydgate is a pioneer precisely in the terms of exploration and geography that were emerging as the word's primary connotation in the nineteenth century: "[W]e are apt to think it the finest era of the world when America was beginning to be discovered, when a bold sailor, even if he were wrecked, might alight on new kingdom; and about 1829 the dark territories of pathology were a fine America for a spirited young adventurer" (chap. 15, p. 139). Central to this passage is a set of images that cluster around pioneering in the novel and in later-nineteenth-century intellectual parlance: the vision of the journey of discovery; the opening of territories dark or foreboding; the sense of adventure; and, in all, the social politics of intellectual inquiry.

In these terms, Will and his kind are the true, explicit pioneers of *Middlemarch*. His comments, early in the novel, on those German scholars, who "laugh at results which are got by groping about in the woods with a pocket-compass while they have made good roads" (chap. 21, p. 198) resonates with the word history of "pioneer" itself. His phrasing here exposes the metaphor inherent in the word and resonates with the opinion of Eliot herself, voiced twenty years before, in her review of Mackay's *Progress of the Intellect*: "Now, though the teaching of positive truth is the grand means of expelling error, the process will be very much quickened if the negative argument serve as its pioneer; if, by a survey of the past, it can be shown how each age and race has had a faith and symbolism suited to its need and its stage of development" (p. 29). Eliot's words still carry with them the topographies of politics and power that stand behind "pioneer" and its associations: "survey," here, still connotes the surveying of a landscape, and the "expelling" of error suggests the removal of an undergrowth or settlement or populace inimical to progress. And so it is no accident that the newspaper Will Ladislaw edits and Mr. Brooke backs is the *Middlemarch Pioneer*, "purchased to clear the pathway for a new candidate" (chap. 30, p. 279).

But if the *Pioneer* sets out to clear new ways, its editing will only follow old, familiar paths. Will's life with Mr. Brooke is little more than a mad, at times manic, replay of Casaubon's life with Dorothea. Both older men become the pedagogues of textual interpretation; both make assignments keyed to the production and dissemination of great texts; and, of course, both fail. The Key to All Mythologies remains unwritten, while the *Pioneer* will ultimately fold. As Dorothea explains it to Casaubon, her uncle has asked "Mr. Ladislaw to stay in this neighbourhood and conduct the paper for him" (chap. 37, p. 353). Conducting paper is, of course, Dorothea's own job, as she sifts the slips and scribbles of her husband. And it is Casaubon who will reject Will as a textual adventurer. Sir James Chettam remarks how he finds that Will "is in everybody's mouth in Middlemarch as the editor of the *Pioneer.* There are stories going about him as a quill-driving alien, a foreign emissary, and what not." The rector replies: "Casaubon won't like that" (chap. 38, p. 362).

But there are, in spite of Casaubon's dislike, great similarities between the *Pioneer* and his great project. Both have about them the patina of the philological, and the *Pioneer* sets out, at least on one occasion, to teach its readers a new word. Look at the exchange among Brooke, the rector, and Cadwallader in chapter 38.

"Here is the *Trumpet* accusing you of lagging behind—did you see?"

"Eh? no," said Mr. Brooke, dropping his gloves into his hat and hastily adjusting his eye-glass. But Mr. Cadwallader kept the paper in his hand, saying, with a smile in his eyes—

"Look here! All this is about a landlord not a hundred miles from Middlemarch, who receives his own rents. They say he is the most retrogressive man in the country. I think you must have taught them that word in the *Pioneer*."

"Oh, that is Keck—an illiterate fellow, you know. Retrogressive, now! Come, that's capital. He thinks it means destructive: they want to make me out a destructive, you know," said Mr. Brooke, with that cheerfulness which is usually sustained by an adversary's ignorance.

"I think he knows the meaning of the word. Here is a sharp stroke or two. If we had to describe a man who is retrogressive in the most evil sense of the word—we should say, he is one who would dub himself a reformer of our constitution, while every interest for which he is immediately responsible is going to decay: . . . But we all know the wag's definition of a philanthropist: a man whose charity increases directly as the square of the distance. . . ."

(chap. 38, pp. 365–66)

And it goes on. Think of this episode as an education in the arts of lexicography, a bit of country-house political philology. At the most basic level, the word "pioneer" contrasts dramatically with "retrogressive"; they remain, in fact, polar opposites. For the newspaper of that name to be the teacher of that other word remains a great, and perhaps obvious, irony. But Keck, the writer in the *Trumpet*, is dismissed as an illiterate, and, with this word, Mr. Brooke conjures up all the images of reading and intelligibility that motivate his niece's chores with Casaubon. And so the rector reads aloud from the text of the *Trumpet*, offering not only proof of how the word was used but showing himself master of the verbal explication. This scene presents a parody of Casaubon-style reading. It vivifies close textual analysis. But it also makes vivid the importance of the very physicality of paper in this world. Cadwallader "kept the paper in his hand," while the rector, upon finishing his long quotation, ends by "throwing down the paper, and clasping his hands at the back of his head." Mr. Brooke then, in desperation, tries to respond, "taking up the paper," and recalling some quotation from another one, the *Edinburgh*.

But are these fellows right? Look up "retrogressive" in the *OED*, and the first definitions come, in fact, from writers of Brooke and his generation. The earliest citation, under the definition "retrograde; tending to return to an inferior state; going back to a worse condition," (def. 3) comes from 1802. The first definition, meaning "working back in investigation or reasoning," comes from Coleridge from 1817, and the second, "moving or directed backwards," comes from 1830. The *Middlemarch* debate on "retrogressive" fits precisely with the historical contexts for the word's emergence. It develops, in parodic form, the debate on word definition, on historical lexicography, so central to the scholarly milieu of both the moment of the novel's fiction and the period of its writing. And, finally, this episode as a whole expands on the thematic associations of progress and reform, scholarship and understanding, clearing pathways and direction, reading and enlightening, that lie at the novel's, as well as Casaubon's, beating heart.

The *Pioneer* appears throughout the rest of *Middlemarch* as the place to comment on the lexicography of social reform. Brooke's injunctions to Ladislaw stand more and more like Casaubon's to Dorothea. Compare the relationship between the latter two to this exchange between former in chapter 46. "That is fine, Ladislaw: that is the way to put it. Write that down, now. We must begin to get documents about the feeling of the country, as well as the machine-breaking and general distress" (chap. 46, p. 437). And when Will and Brooke part company—nothing less than a divorce, now—they return to the etymologies of the newspaper's name to restore just what they have done. Mr. Brooke begins:

> "I must pull up. Poor Casaubon was a warning, you know. I've made some heavy advances, but I've dug a channel. It's rather coarse work—this electioneering, eh, Ladislaw? I daresay you are tired of it. However we have dug a channel with the *Pioneer*—put things on track and so on."
>
> "Do you wish me to give it up?" said Will, the quick color coming in his face, as he rose from the writing-table, . . .
>
> (chap. 51, pp. 484–85)

Will rising from his writing table, with his color up, recalls Casaubon's response to Dorothea's queries, in chapter 20, about when he will "begin to write the book." As if in similar response to questions of the writing life, Casaubon's "face had a quick angry flush upon it" (pp. 190–91). And, in a more striking parallel, this scene—this journalistic divorce—recalls the argument between Rosamond and Lydgate, when the young girl reports that her father is not pleased with the engagement and will come to the doctor to "say it must be given up." "Will you give it up?" said Lydgate, with quick energy—almost angrily (chap. 36, p. 334). And the hands that motivated so much work in *Middlemarch*—the writing, folding, sorting, piano-playing, diagnosing hands that fill the book—now come back as Brooke tells Will that the men "on our side . . . are inclined to take it into their hands." Will has always been, as Brooke says, "a right hand" (chap. 51, p. 485).

The work of hands becomes the center of a history of "pioneer." It is the handiwork of men with spades and axes, clearing roads, digging channels, putting things on track—words used by Mr. Brooke that could make up a dictionary definition of the word. It comes to be associated with the work of writing, or, to put it more precisely, it would seem that spades and axes find themselves replaced by pens and pencils. Writing becomes a form of labor throughout *Middlemarch* precisely because it finds its associations with the act of pioneering. And, in its use of the *Pioneer* to center a discussion of word meaning and word usage, the novel makes explicit an association between lexicography and social reform, philology and politics, that lies at the center of the nineteenth-century's romance with language.

Such a romance is the subject matter of the *OED* itself. The quotations that illustrate "pioneer," garnered from readers throughout England and America, write out a history of intellectual pursuit in terms of land and power. We may read its illustrative quotations as a narrative of pioneering scholarship: as something of a gloss, in essence, on the project of the *OED* itself and, in turn, as a context for appreciating the late-nineteenth-century reception of *Middlemarch*.

> 1605 Bacon *Adv. Learn.* II. vii. 1 To make two professions or occupations of Naturall Philosophers, some to bee Pionners, and some Smythes. 1627 Hakewill *Apol.* 22 The other pioner, . . . which by secret undermining makes way for this opinion of the Worlds decay, is an excessive admiration of Antiquitie. 1700 Blackmore *Paraphr. Isa.* xl. 33 Ye Pioneers of Heav'n, prepare a Road. 1768–74 Tucker *Lt. Nat.* (1834) I. 541 Come then, . . . Philology, pioneer of the abstruser sciences, to prepare the way for their passage. 1836 W. Irving *Astoria* III. 262 As one wave of emigration after another rolls into the vast regions of the west, . . . the eager eyes of our pioneers will pry beyond. 1856 Kane *Arct. Expl.* I. xxiii. 300 The great pioneer of Arctic travel, Sir Edward Parry. 1866 Duke of Argyll *Reign Law* ii. (ed. 4) 111 The great pioneers in new paths of discovery. 1890 "R. Bol-

drewood" *Col. Reformer* (1891) 147 He made the acquaintance of more than one silver-haired pioneer.

"Pioneer" stands at the nexus of the intellectual and the imperial. To read these quotations in sequence is to find a narrative of late-nineteenth-century inquiry pressed into the service of political control. Such an association is no accident, for it lies at the heart of the imperial enterprise behind the *Dictionary* itself. In his president's address to the Philological Society in 1884, Murray called himself and his assistants "simply pioneers, pushing our way experimentally through an untrodden forest, where no white man's axe has been before us" (p. 509).[130] Murray and his men now stand as the soldiers in advance of not a martial but a philological army. They have explicitly taken up the white man's burden, and the forest of words they must explore now resonates not really with the wood of error but with the jungles of Africa. They are the kin of Eliot's Lydgate, clearing out "dark territories" of a discipline. And they answer, too, Casaubon's brusque dismissal of Ladislaw: "he said he should prefer not to know the sources of the Nile, and that there should be some unknown regions preserved as hunting grounds for the poetic imagination" (chap. 9, p. 76).

But Murray's words stand at the center of a jungle of a sentence all his own. His claims for his pioneering come in the course of subordinating clauses, parentheses, asides set out in dashes, all shaped through the anaphoras of introduction. "Notwithstanding all the dictionaries already made . . . notwithstanding their number . . . notwithstanding also the expressly etymological work of [others]"—and then the axe falls, and the sentence ends. This jungle finds its own, material life, on the floor of Murray's own study.

> Only those who have made the experiment, know the bewilderment with which editor or subeditor, after he has apportioned the quotations for such a word as *above, against, account, allow, and, art, as, assize*, or *at* among 20, or 30, or 40 groups, and furnished each of them with a provisional definition, spreads them out on a table or on the floor, where he can obtain a general survey of the whole, and spends hour after hour in shifting them about like the pieces on a chessboard, striving to find in the fragmentary evidence of an incomplete

historical record, such a sequence of meanings as may form a logical chain of development. (pp. 509–10)

Spread out on Murray's floor, these slips of definitions now stand like unencumbered countries on a map, in need of "general survey"—a brace of words one would have found in the very first quotation for *survey*, def. 5a, in the *OED*: "The process (or art) of surveying a tract of ground." The 1610 quotation from W. Folkingham reads "Suruey in generall is an Art wherby the view and trutinate intimation of a subiect, from Center to Circumference, is rectified. The Suruey of Possessions . . . is the Art by which their Graphicall Description is particularized." Such is Murray's survey of his possessions, again like a colonist controlling his dark continent. His "provisional definitions" are nothing less than a provisional government—an idiom recorded in the *OED* as early as 1803, from, significantly, an American context: "Look at the power given to the President by the provisional government of Louisiana" (s.v. "provisional"). Murray mimes the colonial administrator's great dilemma, faced with seemingly unclassifiable groups, where historical records of affiliation or legitimacy remain fragmentary, where logic can barely hold sway.

But Murray's words, for all their political resonances, have a literary idiom as well. His bewilderment recalls scenes of pioneering, only now, instead of clearing pathways in the woods, the editor is lost in them. "Bewilderment" in the *OED* means "confusion arising from losing one's way" and "a tangled or labyrinthine condition of objects." It is the condition of literally being lost in the wilderness, and the quotations that illustrate the *OED*'s entry attend precisely to this etymology. Significant among them is a line from Eliot herself, a passage from the beginning of *Silas Marner*, which in full reads: "Thought was arrested by utter bewilderment, now its old narrow pathway was closed, and affection seemed to have died under the bruise that had fallen on its keenest nerve."[131] What better epigraph for Murray's own despair? Or, for that matter, what better epigraph for Eliot's *Middlemarch* than Murray's own phrase: "striving to find in the fragmentary evidence of an incomplete historical record, such a sequence of meanings as may form a logical chain of development." The central language of the novel chimes in Murray's claim: the "striving" Dorothea attributes to Casaubon; the "historical inquiries" for which Will praises the Germans; the "chains of discovery" that Lydgate seeks to make in science; the "fragments of a tradition" that Dorothea imagines herself sorting out.

"Sometimes," Murray laments, "the quest seems hopeless" (p. 510). A pioneer in lexicography, he invests, much like Eliot herself, in idioms of conquest or knight errantry. "The quest of gold," the narrator of *Middlemarch* wrote, reflecting on Dorothea's task for Casaubon, is "at the same time a questioning of substances. . . . But Mr. Casaubon's theory of the elements which made the seed of all tradition was not likely to bruise itself unawares against discoveries." The word "bruise" in this passage takes us back to that passage from *Silas Marner* and compels us to see Casaubon as an antipioneer. Instead of clearing pathways, he is lost in woods; instead of making progress, he is retrograde; instead of standing up, he is, in Will's words, "crawling a little way." And, in his bogus etymologies—resonant of the "men of the last century" (again, in Will's words)—Casaubon stands as the antitype to the new philological inquiries behind *The Oxford English Dictionary*. His is, in Eliot's words, "a vigorous error vigorously pursued" (chap. 48, p. 455), a futile quest, unlike that of Murray, who would no doubt have found in Samuel Tucker's invocation in the *Light of Nature* (in the quotation that stands at the dead center of the *Dictionary*'s entry for "pioneer") cause for great hope along the quest: "Come then, Philology, pioneer of the abstruser sciences, to prepare the way for their passage."

Sublime

Casaubon is no creature of the sublime. His movements through dark halls and his refusal to see sunlight mark him throughout the novel as the antitype of the illuminated philologist. And the idea of elevation, so central to the classical and neoclassical conceptions of sublimity, is similarly outside his ken. The very locus of his life, Lowick, conjures up an image of the antisublime. It is the place of sputtering candles, the site of that "small taper of learned theory" that explores "the tossed ruins of the world" (chap. 10, p. 78). *Middlemarch* explores the sublime and its contradictions, from the classic moment in which Dorothea sets foot in Rome to the static evenings of her time in Lowick after Casaubon is dead. But there remains much more to see. There is sublimity in error—in the wanderings of the scholar and the sting of being wrong. Philology is a sublime pursuit, and to trace the word in the discourses of the novel and the *OED* is to feel, once again, the emotions of scholarship.

The trajectory of the sublime in *Middlemarch* follows the arc of reading. Chapter 5 begins with Casaubon's letter of proposal and goes on to develop a sublimity of errors: constant mistakes, misreadings, and bad moves that lead to certain recognitions of the self. All utterances seem to fail. Casaubon scrapes his spoon; he blinks; his rhetoric, though "frigid . . . was as sincere as the bark of a dog or the cawing of an amorous rook" (pp. 43–45). We are enmired, here, in a nonverbal world, where communication works, or does not work, through utterances awful in the hearing. Even Casaubon's own words seem to fail, and Dorothea must supply their meaning. "Dorothea's faith supplied all that Mr. Casaubon's words seemed to leave unsaid: what believer sees a disturbing omission or infelicity? The text, whether of prophet or of poet, expands for whatever we can put into it, and even his bad grammar is sublime" (p. 45). What is sublime about bad grammar? At one level, Eliot is arguing that one may find, in anyone to whom we attribute prophecy or poetry, an elevation of our own imagining. But, at another level, she is pointing toward a notion of the sublimity of error. Just how sublime—how wonderful, how elevating, how brilliantly funny—is this following scene of "bad grammar" later in the novel!

Mrs. Garth is teaching her young Ben, and "like more celebrated educators," she has "her favourite ancient paths" (chap. 24, p. 231). Her intransigent son can only blurt: "I hate grammar. What's the use of it," and she replies:

> "To teach you to speak and write correctly, so that you can be understood," said Mrs. Garth, with severe precision. "Should you like to speak as old Job does?"
>
> "Yes," said Ben, stoutly; "it's funnier. He says, 'Yo goo'—that's just as good as 'You go.'"

This episode stands as a brilliant parody of Casaubon's ideals of learning. His conversations with Dorothea often hinge on problems of correctness, as if his goal is to teach his new wife "to speak and write correctly." But the power of this scene lies in its dialect. Mispronunciation leads not—at least, in Ben's eyes—to misunderstanding but to pleasure. The world of the Garths in this chapter is a world of sounds, not quite real language: of the music of a mispronunciation or, more generally, of the working rather than the learning world. Consider Caleb Garth: "The echoes of the great hammer where roof or keel were a-making, the signal-shouts of the workmen, the roar of the furnace, the thunder and plash of the engine, were a sublime music to him. . . . His early ambition had been to have as effective a share as possible in this sublime labour." What is sublime here is not just the sound of labor in full force but the words that Eliot deploys to echo it. A locution like "a-making" has the reek of the rural or the archaic about it, as if what she is ventriloquizing is the language of Caleb's own boyhood. And the "plash" of the engine is clearly, from the evidence assembled by the *OED*, a word that enters English through the North—a word from Gavin Douglas's Scots translation of the *Aeneid*, a word from Walter Scott (cited three times in the *OED* entry), and a word, too, that Eliot herself clearly enjoyed (the *Dictionary* cites her use of it in *Felix Holt* and, in the entry for the verb "plash," from *Adam Bede*; it appears three times in *Middlemarch*). The sublime here lies not in scholarship or literature but in the diction of a rural world. As the narrator says of Caleb Garth: "all these sights of his youth had acted on him as poetry without the aid of the poets, had made a philosophy for him without the aid of philosophers, a religion without the aid of theology" (chap. 24, 237).

The Garths posit a different vision of sublimity from Casaubon, specifically, in the sounds and words of childhood. Turn to young Lydgate for another vision of its revelations. As a boy, he would come home from play and find a book to read. *Rasselas, Gulliver,* Bailey's *Dictionary,* the Bible, and others consume his interest, "but no spark had yet kindled in him an intellectual passion" (chap. 15, p. 135). And then he comes upon "the volumes of an old Cyclopaedia. . . . [T]hey were on the highest shelf, and he stood on a chair to get them down." But when he opens up the volume, and his eyes light on the entry for anatomy, he finds his vocation: "He was not much acquainted with valves of any sort, but he knew that *valvae* were folding doors, and through this crevice came a sudden light startling him with his first vivid notion of finely-adjusted mechanism in the human frame" (p. 136). Here, it is the mechanism of the human frame, rather than the engines of the workmen, that inspires him. But his experience, and Caleb Garth's, are of a piece. Here, too, the language of the passage reflects on the nature of the sublime, but in a different and more pointedly philological sense. Just what is that "old Cyclopaedia" he pulls down? I think it would have been none other than Chambers's *Cyclopaedia*, published in 1728 and contemporary with the other books in Lydgate's family library.[132] Whatever its account of anatomy, its account of the sublime is equally relevant—and clearly still of interest in the later nineteenth century. It contributes to the *OED*'s definition of the word (def. 6, "Of language, style, or a writer. Expressing lofty ideas in a grand and elevated manner"). From the *Cyclopaedia*, the *OED* quotes: "The sublime Style necessarily requires big and magnificent Words; but the Sublime may be found in a single Thought, a single Figure, a single Turn of Words."

No better definition could fit Eliot's own sense of these sublime moments in her novel. Single words, turns of phrase, or thoughts—be they mispronunciations of a rustic or the plash of work—are moments of illumination. And, for Tertius Lydgate, that single word is here the very etymological heart of "sublime" itself. Standing on the chair, up on the highest shelf, Lydgate knows that *valvae* are folding doors. The etymology of "sublime" hinges on the door. From the Latin, *sub* plus *limen*: that is, up to the top of the doorway or the lintel. Lydgate's childhood moment of illumination literalizes the etymology of the sublime. It takes him up to the top, to open doorways through which sudden light may enter.

Against these visions, "there was nothing to strike others as sublime about Mr. Casaubon," (chap. 42, p. 403), even though, as that same paragraph would query, "are there many situations more sublimely tragic than the struggle of the soul with the demand to renounce a work which has been all the significance of its life . . . ?" Casaubon fails even as a tragic figure. Lydgate may speak for us in his "contempt" for his "futile scholarship." And yet what could be more sublime than the successful scholarship of Eliot's contemporary lexicographers? Within a decade of the publication of *Middlemarch*, the *OED* was in full production. As Jennett Humphreys put it, in her article for *Fraser's Magazine* of October 1882, every leaf of old books "is yielding some line, some distich, wherein words shine out with their author's signification, wherein words will never cease to shine out with their author's signification whilst words endure."[133] Humphreys's account of the Philological Society's *Dictionary* and her visit to Dr. Murray stands as an essay in the sublime pursuits of philology: an exfoliation, as it were, of the *Cyclopaedia*'s location of the sublime in a single turn of words.

Humphreys is moved to the point of rhetorical exuberance by the project of the *Dictionary*. She calls it, following the lead of Trench and Herbert Coleridge, a "biography" of English, and she reviews the original proposals, false starts, and eventual successes of its making. Coleridge and Murray stand here as ideals of scholarship, flip sides of the Casaubonian obsession. Compare Coleridge's words from the late 1850s, quoted by Humphreys, with Casaubon's claims to Dorothea when she asks about publishing his great work:

> "It is well," he said, "not to be forced into print with undue precipitation by the impatience of individuals; and this maxim, which is true of all literary composition, claims more especial attention in the case of a book which is to serve as a general interpreter and a standard of the noblest and most copious language now spoken by man." (Humphreys, p. 440)

> [I]t is ever the trial of the scrupulous explorer to be saluted with the impatient scorn of chatterers who attempt only the smallest achievements, being indeed equipped for no other. And it were well if all such could be admonished to discriminate judgments of which the true subject-matter lies entire beyond their reach, from those of which the elements may be compassed by a narrow and superficial survey. (chap. 20, p. 191)

We laugh at Casaubon's self-importance but are meant to admire Coleridge. And, similarly, when Casaubon faces death, his great project nowhere complete, we find him simply pathetic: "Nay, are there many situations more sublimely tragic than the struggle of the soul with the demand to renounce a work which has been all the significance of its life—a significance which is to vanish as the waters which come and go where no man has need of them?" (chap. 42, p. 403). But Herbert Coleridge is, in Humphreys's overwrought prose, sublimely tragic.

> Oppressed with the unhelpfulness of unhelpful helpers, constrained by it, and by his own enthusiasm, to exertions more than he had strength to bear, Herbert Coleridge fell ill. Suffering, he still hoped for the two years to pass; and so they did. But they brought no recovery to him; and as they waned away he was gone. "All through his illness

he worked for our proposed dictionary," said Mr. Furnivall. . . . It was because of all this devotion, it was because of all this winning ardour, that his death came as such a heavy blow. In beautiful compensation, it was because of all of it, also, that his death did not bring his work to a thorough end. (p. 440)

Humphreys's rhetorical repetitions, her asides, her language of beatitude and beauty all contribute to a sense of the sublime here. Read on: "In 1865, though, all this brave light begins to flicker. There is some growing feeling manifest that the work is a very uphill battle" (p. 441). Now, read on in *Middlemarch*, and see Casaubon brought even lower: "To Mr. Casaubon now, it was as if he suddenly found himself on the dark riverbrink and heard the plash of the oncoming oar. . . . And Mr. Casaubon's immediate desire was not for divine communion and light divested of earthly conditions; his passionate longings, poor man, clung low and mist-like in very shady places" (chap. 42, p. 405). There is that word "plash," again, as if to contrast the antisublime quality of Casaubon's sad longings with the elevating reminiscences of Caleb Garth. And there is that overwhelming pressure of the low and dark, the very etymology of Lowick splayed out in these final days.

But, for Humphreys, the making of the *Dictionary* is a constant, even if at times interrupted, passage to illumination. Dr. Murray appears here as a kind of savior, clearing away tons of books and papers, blazing straight paths through the mazes of material. "He was aware, in other words, that, notwithstanding all this bewildering labyrinth of treasure, he had only yet two-thirds (about) of what his purpose demanded" (p. 445). Unlike Casaubon, trapped in his own labyrinths, Murray will forge a way. And he will forge a way, too, through the barely legible slips and scraps of definitions that come in. When good quotations come in, Murray says; "these quotations are to be valued immensely. They are lovely" (p. 451). But others are not so; some are barely readable; some not English at all; some rife with errors in citation. In all this mess, "It is no wonder that when excellent legibility and purpose are received, they should be gratefully welcomed, and thought as worthy of a tender adjective as light after darkness, or flowers found in bloom refreshingly, in an unexpected spot" (p. 451). And, in the end, when Humphreys finishes her survey of the vastness of the project, when she recounts all the books and parcels coming in, the manuscripts and proof sheets, she announces: "There is every item of the working paraphernalia that the business of postage enforces, that literature, on the grand and marvellous scale of this grand piece of nineteenth century literature, is compelled to gather about it in close possession, so that its purpose may be successfully attained" (pp. 455–56).

Humphreys reports the making of the *Dictionary* as a work of sublime energy, of light and power, of great setbacks and great progress, of moments of profoundly unexpected beauty. But it is, too, a work of business, of distinctively Victorian mechanical progress. Her essay's subject really is "the immense forces philology has placed at this scholar's [i.e., Murray's] command, the immense machinery by which this eminent philologist directs and regulates these forces" (p. 443). With its corrugated iron framing and its vast pigeonholed interior, Murray's Scriptorium becomes, in Humphreys's phrasing, a "Word Factory" (p. 445). Compare now her imagination of the *Dictionary* as a project of great labor with the reminiscences of Caleb Garth: "The philological raw material, spread abundantly and heterogeneously, could be ground out by division and subdivision, mechanically, and afterward with reason" (p. 445). This is the philological equivalent of Garth's remembrance of "the indispensable might of that myriad-headed, myriad-handed labour," of that "great hammer where the roof and keel were a-making," of the "sublime labour, which was peculiarly dignified by him with the name of 'business'" (chap. 24, p. 237). So, too, the making of the *Dictionary* is a business, and the expressive masculinity of scholarship—of Murray's command of these immense forces and machinery—contrasts profoundly here with the sad pedantry and dried-up self-absorption (even impotence) of Eliot's Casaubon.

Writing at the beginning of her literary career, Eliot gave voice to an ideal of scholarship that would, eventually, find itself refracted through the dim lens of her Casaubon and, later, in the ministrations of the *OED*. "It would," she wrote in her *Westminster Review* essay on Mackay's *Progress of the Intellect*, "be a very serious mistake to suppose that the study of the past and the labours of criticism have no important practical bearing on the present." And yet that study seems to stand in opposition to the human need for nature. Should we look up, behold the heavens, and admire or look down upon the books of ancient times? "[B]etter to look with 'awful eye' at the starry heavens, and, under the teaching of Newton and Herschel, feel the immensity, the order, the sublimity of the universe, and feel the forces by which it subsists, than to pore over the grotesque symbols, whereby the Assyrian or Egyptian shadowed forth his own more vague impressions of the same great facts" (p. 28). Pure Casaubon, or so it seems: a condemnation of a man who would pore over his collection of vague symbols rather than see the stars. But what Eliot's review suggests—and what *Middlemarch* may imagine, and the *OED* may realize—is the possibility of a sublime scholarship and the apprehension of the immensity and order of philology.

Supplement: American

"English readers may fancy they enjoy the 'atmosphere' of 'Middlemarch'; but we maintain that to relish its inner essence we must—for reasons too numerous to detail—be an American. The author has commissioned herself to be real, her native tendency being that of an idealist, and the intellectual result is a very fertilizing mixture."[134] What does it mean to read *Middlemarch* as an American? Perhaps, as James implies, it is to read not for the local color or the topical allusions but instead for the idealism of the novel. It is to read, perhaps, too, like James's own American, the Christopher Newman of the novel of that title that James would publish in 1876. But it may also be to read for the American in *Middlemarch* and, for that matter, in the *OED*: that is, to read the history of philology and, more generally, the academic life as an American. America stands as the image of the untamed discipline. "We are apt to think it the finest era of the world when America was beginning to be discovered, . . . and about 1829 the dark territories of Pathology were a fine America for a spirited young adventurer" (chap. 15, p. 139). For all Lydgate's European training and for all his aspirations to a scientific, rational pursuit, he stands, here, like some great pioneer on the American shores. Eliot's lines chime with the image of that pioneering James Murray, who would clear pathways through an "untrodden forest where no white man's axe had been before." Is the American of James's critical imagination this ideal reader—and is *Middlemarch*, then, something of a "fertilizing mixture" for a new literary criticism to take root on our shores?

To read as an American, as my following chapter argues, is to read rhetorically as well as philologically. It is to pay attention to the tropes and turns, the estrangements of language from the real. Such are the classic, modern American readings of *Middlemarch*—those of Miller and Hertz, who, for all their feints to European deconstruction, are profoundly American in their attentions to rhetorical devices, public stances, and the search for what James would call an "inner essence." To read as an American, too, is to recognize our double debt to both the English and the German models of research and education—for the former, the tradition of the belletristic critical review; for the latter, the example of empirical scholarship and historical research. Adams Sherman Hill, the Boylston Professor of Rhetoric and Oratory at Harvard from 1876 to 1904, could used *Middlemarch* (as well as a host of other recent novels) as examples of good style. His *Principles of Rhetoric* extracts selections from George Eliot which, read in sequence, reveal a rhetorical approach to reading fiction.[135] And William Dwight Whitney, the Yale professor of comparative philology who was acknowledged in his time as "the foremost philologian that this country has ever produced,"[136] argued for a distinctively American approach to historical linguistics. The world, he noted, has been "accustomed . . . to look to Germany for guidance in all matters philological." But, as he and his Johns Hopkins contemporary Basil Lanneau Gildersleeve argued, the world will look now to America.[137]

American philologists remain great rhetoricians. Not only are their writings filled with turns of phrase and gestures calculated to persuade a reader, they are themselves rhetorical readers of others—most famously, in Whitney's reading of Max Müller. Whitney sees Müller as passing off rhetoric passing as philology. Worthy of praise are "the manner and the style" of Müller's work, but "we are hardly disposed to recognize him as the founder and promulgator of a new science."[138] Müller, in Whitney's reading, is a great metaphor maker,[139] and his many "erroneous views" stem not from simple lapses of fact but from a much larger confusion about the nature of language and scientific research itself (p. 277). What Whitney recognizes is that Müller's work "is not science but literature. Taken as literature, it is of high rank." Müller is, Whitney states, "a born *littérateur.*"[140]

For all Whitney's philological acumen—indeed, because of it—he reads Müller rhetorically. And so have I. My critical analyses throughout this chapter bear upon my project of a rhetoric of scholarship: a study of the tropes and idioms of academic expression, an inquiry into the literary narratives behind philology and, in turn, into the philological and rhetorical bent of literature. My next chapter writes a history of the rhetorical philology defining the American academic condition. All the themes of my book—the relationships of word and world, the utility of etymology, the shaping of the academic self, the national frameworks for a humanistic learning—take on a distinctively American cast. Rhetoric fights with philology for disciplinary pride of place from the late eighteenth to the late twentieth century. Their various practitioners argue for accuracy but, too, find themselves in errancy and error, and American philological life becomes, to take a cliché now imbued with a new intellectual significance, an errand into the wilderness.

*It is better to be a doorkeeper in the house of philology,
than to dwell in the tents of the rhetoricians.*
—Basil Lanneau Gildersleeve, *Hellas and Hesperia*

ARDENT ETYMOLOGIES: AMERICAN RHETORICAL PHILOLOGY, FROM ADAMS TO DE MAN

"The American," wrote H. L. Mencken, "from the beginning, has been the most ardent of recorded rhetoricians. His politics bristles with pungent epithets; his whole history has been bedizened with tall talk; his fundamental institutions rest far more upon brilliant phrases than upon logical ideas."[1] Mencken's rhetorical American remains, like most myths of the culture, an uneasy fixture in the popular and pedagogic landscape. In *The American Language*, he stands at the intersection of the many features Mencken sought to classify as the "hallmarks of American." Mencken is first and foremost concerned with the growth of the American vocabulary: with the burgeoning of coinages, loanwords, and creative expressions that, like the example "rubberneck" he gives, form *in nuce* "almost a complete treatise on American psychology." But if Mencken is fascinated with the new words of the language, he is also concerned with defining rhetoric itself. Its province here is largely public oratory and tale telling: persuasion and celebration; the art of convincing people that they need to vote for, believe in, or buy something; the rites of bringing people into ceremonies of occasion. But whether they be public addresses or private gatherings, speeches before great halls or tales around campfires,

American rhetorical performances remain just that: performances that display both the national and individual character.

The American rhetorical tradition has long been understood as a form of public language that reveals a private self. Writing half a century after the fourth, and final, edition of Mencken's book, Jay Fliegelman considers what he calls the "culture of performance" that shaped Jeffersonian democracy as concerned precisely with the public and the private.[2] His survey of Enlightenment rhetorical traditions and their impact on American discourses hinges on reactions against older Ciceronian and Aristotelian practices that came to be considered as unnatural or artificial. The oratorical ideal of the late eighteenth century was one of natural theatricalism, where the personal could be effectively expressed through language handled well. Questions of authorship and individual identity, national belonging, individual sincerity, and public authenticity were all considered to be subspecies of rhetorical theory. Self-presentation was not to be shadowed by the artifice of learned expression; rather, such learning was to be pressed into the service of revealing, not concealing, the person behind the persona. As Parson Weems had put it, in a passage that stands at the heart of Fliegelman's embedded history of American rhetoric, "Private life is always *real* life."[3] Self-presentation through the forms of rhetorical staging is not, as Fliegelman argues, "merely a strategy of concealment. Rather, it represents a particular moral and social conception of identity."[4]

This moral and social conception of identity stands, too, at the heart of American philology—a practice that, I argue in this chapter, is a fundamentally rhetorical enterprise. American philology and rhetoric preoccupy themselves with estrangement and displacement: with the separation of words from things, with the fluidity of meanings, with the pursuit of political argument through scholarly inquiry. These are the projects of the errant and the erroneous, projects that look back to the first claims for linguistic study in the new nation. Addressing the Americans of 1793 in his *Cadmus*, William Thornton avers: "You have corrected the dangerous doctrines of European powers, correct now the languages you have imported, for the oppressed of various nations knock at your gates, and desire to be received as your brethren. As you admit them facilitate your intercourse, and you will mutually enjoy the benefits.—The AMERICAN LANGUAGE will thus be as distinct as the government, free from all the follies of unphilosophical fashion, and resting upon truth as its only regulator."[5] Language is something to be righted. To "correct" is—for this Cadmus or my Casaubon—to draw a straight line, to be placed on roads not errant but exact. The true method of analysis gave rise to idioms of straightness, of correction, and of rectitude in all its forms in both rhetorical and philological instruction. The American will vivify these metaphors. To wander in the woods, to find a clear path through the forest, to err along pathways ill advised or ill marked—all these dead clichés take on a new life in a landscape rife with being lost.

Such imagery was always central to American writers on language. John Quincy Adams saw ours as a land of tropes and figures: of place names estranged from their points of origin, of forests filled not with the hydras of a classical mythology but with the rattlesnakes of local fears. "An error," he notes, "was a wandering of the feet"—an etymology designed to make us ask not just where we shall wander but on what our feet will step.[6] And for Henry Tuckerman, writing in the mid-nineteenth century about the importance of Horne Tooke and his theories of etymology, the figurations of familiar imagery become uniquely ours: "He certainly opened many new vistas in the dense and tangled forest of words."[7] Philology becomes the servant of expansion; linguistic history is manifest destiny.[8]

Philologists and rhetoricians have both made claims for the unique importance of their subject in America, and, at times, their polemics may seem indistinguishable from each other. "There is a sense," wrote the modern historian of rhetoric George Kennedy in 1994, in a revivalist vein, "in which a history of rhetoric might be thought of as a history of the values of a culture and how these were taught or imposed upon the society."[9] How different is this statement, really, from the claims for the philologist made by Albert S. Cook a century before?

> The function of the philologist . . . is the endeavor to relive the life of the past; to enter by the imagination into the spiritual experiences of all the historic protagonists of civilization in a given period and area of culture; to think the thoughts, feel the emotions, to partake the aspirations, recorded in literature; to become one with humanity in the struggles of a given nation or race to perceive and attain the ideal of existence; and then to judge rightly these various disclosures of the human spirit, and to reveal to the world their true significance and relative importance.[10]

The history of American philology and rhetoric is part and parcel of that struggle of a given nation, whether it be the "free republic" that John Quincy Adams said "bestows importance upon the powers of eloquence" or the distinctive "cosmopolitan blend" that makes America, for Basil Gildersleeve, the ideal place for the "ready assimilation of whatever makes for life in the philological world."[11] This chapter offers, then, a double history of American rhetoric and philology. It looks at the *errores* of academic life, not simply in the wanderings of scholars or the mistakes that they made but as part of a larger claim about the wanderings of meanings. For in this *telos* lies a further claim. The recent moves in literary theory for returns to rhetoric and philology resonate with the history of those disciplines in this country. The legacy of Paul de Man—the habits of etymologizing the names of rhetorical tropes, the fascination with irony—lies, for all its apparent European patina, squarely in the inheritance of American rhetorical philology. To read as an American is to make tropes of words and, in the process, to replay in linguistic terms the patterns of emigration and estrangement that have made us who we are.

But if this is a chapter about disciplines, it is a chapter, too, about feelings. Ardor lies at the very heart of argument. For Cicero—whose writings form the spine of the American rhetorical tradition and, in turn, my chapter's exposition—the orator must seem as much to burn (*ardere*) with passion as the audience he would convince.[12] Each of my scholarly characters is, if not an ardent rhetorician of Mencken's imagination, then an ardent etymologist of my own: zealous, emotionally charged, at times aflame with philological desire (recall George Hickes and his vision of the poet, and, by implication, the philologist, *incalescens*). But they are ardent, too, in that they all confront the very problem that this word exemplifies: a challenging historical relationship between the literal and metaphorical. From Samuel Johnson onward, such words provoked the philological imagination. "The original sense of words is often driven out of use by their metaphorical acceptations, yet must be inserted for the sake of regular origination. Thus I know not whether *ardour* is used for *material* heat, or whether *flagrant*, in *English*, ever signifies the same with *burning*."[13] Should we privilege the older, literal sense or the newer, metaphorical meaning? My etymologists all ground their scholarship in a notion of origination, not just of the word but of the nation.

For John Quincy Adams and his academic heirs, for William Dwight Whitney, for Basil Lanneau Gildersleeve, for the Cornell rhetoricians at the beginning of the twentieth century, and for the deconstructionists at its close—for all, the pursuit of etymology is the pursuit of national identity. Their writings reveal scholarly personae that enable a new understanding of the American academic self, one shaped by an ardent attention the errancies of a career or the slippages of signifying.

I begin with John Quincy Adams, the first Boylston Professor of Rhetoric and Oratory at Harvard, whose *Lectures on Rhetoric and Oratory* (delivered in 1806–1809 and published in 1810), for all their civic Ciceronianism, give voice to a metaphysical philology rooted in the tradition of Horne Tooke. In his emphasis on figurative language and his obsessive etymologies, his political analysis and historical reflections, Adams writes a philological rhetoric: an argument for the word histories of tropes themselves, a claim for the devices of poetic expression and the politics of literary purpose.[14] Take, for example, his inaugural oration. Its historical sweep, long periodic sentences, appeals to authority, paired oppositions, and practical philosophy are reminiscent of such texts as the opening of Cicero's *Tusculan Disputations*, while its distinctive blend of patrician Harvard and republican America work out, almost as a contemporary allegory, the appropriative and political relationship that Cicero had voiced both toward his Greek predecessors and his Roman contemporaries.[15]

> [T]he arts and sciences, at the hour of their highest exaltation, have been often reproached and insulted by those, on whom they had bestowed their choicest favors, and most cruelly assaulted by the weapons, which themselves had conferred. At the zenith of modern civilization the palm of unanswered eloquence was awarded to the writer, who maintained, that the sciences had always promoted rather the misery, than the happiness of mankind; and in the age and nation, which heard the voice of Demosthenes, Socrates has been represented as triumphantly demonstrating, that rhetoric cannot be dignified with the name of an art; that it is but a pernicious practice . . . the mere counterfeit of justice. This opinion has had its followers from the days of Socrates to our own; and it still remains an inquiry among men, as in the age of Plato, and in that of Cicero,

whether eloquence is an art, worthy of cultivation of a wise and virtuous man. To assist us in bringing the mind to a satisfactory result of this inquiry, it is proper to consider the art, as well in its nature, as in its effects; to derive our inferences, not merely from the uses which have been made of it, but from the purposes, to which it ought to be applied, and the end, which it is destined to answer.[16]

Note the appositions here: art versus science; Demosthenes and Socrates; Plato and Cicero. Note, too, the yoking together of metaphors from science ("zenith") and social competition ("palm"), and the evocatively oxymoronic "unanswered eloquence." Like Cicero, Adams offers a syncretic view of rhetorical history. He goes back to the central question of the discipline—whether rhetoric is truly an art or simply a knack—and invokes not just Cicero's name but the very terms of his own historical surveys. The image of the "wise and virtuous man" translates Cicero's *magnus vir et sapiens*.[17] The question of whether the sciences promote misery or happiness echoes the opening feints of *De Inventione*, where Cicero reflects on whether societies "have received more good or evil from oratory" (1.1.1, pp. 2–3). Adams's subsequent history of the origins of human reason and the emergence of the man of eloquence mime the continued story of *De Inventione*, where the making of social community hinges on the unification of *ratio* and *oratio* in the man who would unite "wild savages into a kind a gentle folk" (1.1.2, pp. 6–7).

If Adams seeks a Ciceronian argument to his opening polemic, he is most decisively American in the metaphors that express it. His first lecture on the nature of rhetoric and oratory distinguishes these two disciplines in an idiom uniquely keyed to both the time and place of their expression. He begins by defining terms, noting that "our language offers a facility, which neither the Greek nor the Latin possessed," to distinguish the art from the theory (1:41). *Rhetoric* and *rhetor* are inadequate, he claims. "Some attempts were made to put into circulation the term oratoria, but they were resisted by their philological critics, and it is expressly censured and rejected by Quinctilian [*sic*], as irreconcileable with their etymological analogies" (1:42). The many titles of Cicero's works, Adams claims, bear witness to this terminological deficiency in the classical languages, but "[t]he English language however has been less scrupulous in its adherence to the niceties of etymology. It has admitted the term oratory, which the Romans fastidiously excluded, and annexes to it a modification of the idea, distinct from that of the Grecian term, which has also been made English by adoption. Thus accumulating our riches from the united funds of Grecian genius and Roman industry, we call rhetoric the science, and oratory the art of speaking well" (1:42). Adams's inquiry is more than quibbling. It rephrases the whole problem of rhetorical terminology into a central set of cultural metaphors and, in the process, makes the meaning of those terms not their referents in an antique past but their idioms in a political present.

For this *is* a philological disquisition. It seeks the origins of national identity in the histories of individual words. It uses etymology as argument, associating the history of languages with the history of a people. In essence, it proposes something of political lexicography, and, like many of his compeers, Adams got his philology from Horne Tooke. Tooke's intellectual preoccupation with the metaphysical linguistics of French theorists (Condillac, De Brozes, Turgot) melded with his political claims for the rights of individuals in an age of revolution. But Tooke also shared in the late-eighteenth-century English recovery of Anglo-Saxon, and he argued vigorously for the origins of English in the pre-Conquest forms of the language. He honed his techniques of speculative etymology to argue not just for the histories of individual words but for the power of those histories to reveal truths philosophical and cultural. The study of "the meaning of words," he wrote, should matter "not only (as has been too lightly supposed) to Metaphysicians and School-men, but to the rights and happiness of mankind in their dearest concerns."[18] Here, many readers (both British and American) found an argument for democracy over monarchy, and well they should have. "To the ears of man," Tooke began part 2 of *The Diversions of Purley*, "what music sweeter than the Rights of man" (2:2). And it is in the pursuit of those rights that "we [must] always be seeking after the meaning of words. Of important words we must, if we wish to avoid important error. The meaning of these words especially is of the greatest consequence to mankind" (2:4). Tooke's interlocutor accuses him of being a Democrat, and he responds that he has always held beliefs that "confirm my democracy" (2:12): "I revere the Constitution and constitutional LAWS of England; because they are in conformity with the LAWS of God and nature: and upon these are founded the rational RIGHTS of Englishmen" (2:14). No wonder the conservative reviewer of the *Monthly Anthology* wrote, in 1808: "The real object of Horne

Tooke's writings on language is believed by many intelligent persons to have been, merely to obtain a medium through which he might defame his government and his country."[19]

For Tooke's American readers, however, etymology and Saxon origin, sensation theory and political dissent, contributed not to the defamation but the celebration of a new government and country.[20] As early as 1788 (only two years after volume 1 of *The Diversions* appeared), Tooke's banner had been raised, quite literally, by Noah Webster at the celebrations for the Constitution on July 23 of that year. Bearing the standard of the newly founded Philological Society, Webster marched in the parade in New York on that date, in the words of the *New York Packet*, "carrying Mr. Horne Tooke's treatise on language; as a mark of respect for the book which contains a new discovery, and a mark of respect for the author, whose zeal for the American cause, during the late war, subjected him to a prosecution."[21] Webster himself relied on Tooke's principles throughout his writings. His *Dissertations on the English Language* (1798) drew on many of the metaphysical etymologies of *The Diversions*, deriving conjunctions from verbs and finding in the pronunciations of his everyday Americans an afterlife of Anglo-Saxon verbal origins.[22] Those origins were of great importance to Webster, too—in particular, the notion (really a myth) of the early English yeoman. Such notions fed into Webster's ideas of an early English yeomanry, a kind of natural identity that would resist a foreign domination and that, in its American form, could stand as an ideal of linguistic (and, of course, political) independence.[23] To Tooke, Webster owed his arguments on spelling reform, his attempts at local etymology, and, most broadly, his apparent populism. In essence, Webster writes a national genealogy through etymology; he does politics through philology.

And so does John Quincy Adams. When he remarks how English has "admitted" the term oratory and "annexes" it to another term, he is acutely aware of these words' etymologies and sensitive to connotations in contemporary usage. Language is akin to statehood. We are admitting words much as the fledgling country had admitted states, and "annex" would have had a specifically political connotation for Adams and his readers. *The Oxford English Dictionary* cites Wellington's remark of 1800 on early colonial acquisition: "The whole country is permanently annexed to the British Empire" (s.v. "annex," vb. 3). The word "adoption" similarly carried with it both a linguistic and a political metaphorics. For the late-eighteenth-century American polemicists, "adoption" stood as symbol for the new national family created after the irrevocable break with a paternalistic England. It was a highly charged term in the fiction and the public writings of a period that figured stories of belonging as adoptive tales of immigration and acceptance.[24] But it is also a term of lexicography, apparently coined by Samuel Johnson, in this usage, to refer to borrowing new words without changing their form. Such direct loanwords, Johnson wrote in the preface to his *Dictionary*, "must depend for their adoption on the suffrage of futurity" (cited in the *OED* as the sole reference, s.v. "adoption," defs. b, c). And, finally, the idiom of accumulating riches from a united fund makes the rhetorical inheritance a kind of national bank (or, for that matter, national debt). The word "funds" takes on a uniquely fiscal sense in the eighteenth century (for example, R. Langford, cited in the *OED*, "Funds is a general term for money lent to government, and which constitutes the national debt"), as does the word "accumulate" (witness J. Mores, in *American Geography* 1 [1796]: 417, cited in the *OED*: "These funds . . . are fast accumulating by interest"). Writing a decade after Adams, John Marshall used the phrasing figuratively in a way that resonates with Adams's own sense of Grecian genius and Roman industry as funds: "Industry, talent and integrity constitute a fund which is as confidently trusted as property itself" (*OED*, s.v. "fund," sb. 5a, dated 1819).

The gestures that shape Adams's exordia form the core of his own rhetorical practice. He is an etymologist of the imagination. Whenever a new word, a technical term, or a point of history appears, he goes back to its roots. The history of words scripts out a history of disciplines—a history that matters, to appropriate Tooke's phrasing, not just to schoolmen but to the rights and happiness of mankind. Look, for example, at how Adams handles "invention": "originally compounded from the two Latin words, *in venire*, to come in, to enter." He continues: "By the natural progress of all languages from the literal to the metaphorical meaning, it came in process of time to signify discovery" (1:164). Thus rhetorical invention is the finding of topics. Mechanical invention signals "a higher degree of ingenuity." Poetic invention involves not only finding words but "the glory of creating." Poetical invention, Adams states, "disdains the boundaries of space and time," and he illustrates the brilliance of such invention with a quotation from Shakespeare.[25]

> The poet's eye, in a fine frenzy rolling,
> Doth glance from heaven to earth, from earth to heaven;
> And, as imagination bodies forth
> The forms of things unknown, the poet's pen
> Turns them to shape, and gives to airy nothing
> A local habitation and a name.
>
> (1:166)

The etymology of "invention," then, traces the history of the human arts and sciences. *Inventio* encapsulates a journey of the mind and body—a journey of discovery charted in America. For it is with this language of discovery, this sense of searching and finding, that *inventio* becomes the practice of Americanization itself. As Shakespeare puts it, in Adams's quotation, the poet "gives to airy nothing / A local habitation and a name." So, too, does the explorer or the colonizer. Adams's political philology shapes a distinctively American landscape.

Look at his other etymologies for confirmation. Words such as "elegance," "composition," and "dignity," when traced to their etymologies, reflect a similar concern. "A retrospect . . . upon their etymology will immediately show, that they are descended from one common stock, and are of close affinity" (2:146–47). "Elegance" comes from Latin "*eligo*," to choose, and even though contemporary English appears to have "deviated" from this root, Adams can find that etymological meaning in Milton. For when Adam says to Eve, upon their eating of the apple, "I see thou art exact of taste, / And *elegant*," he is, as Adams notes, playing upon this older meaning. And yet so is Adams, for it is here that the new world of Milton's poem (quoted with an almost obsessive frequency throughout these *Lectures*) takes on its moral flavor. Is our new world one of paradise or taint? What have we chosen? "Composition," Adams notes, like "elegance," "signifies only putting together" (2:147). But "dignity" "embraces the whole theory of figurative language" (2:148).

The etymologies of words expose hidden narratives: miniature tales of travel and displacement, finding and discovering, ordering and building. The parts of rhetoric contribute to the making of a civilized state. What Adams calls "the progress of civilization and refinement" hinges on "the necessities of articulate speech" (2:189). The ordering of words, whether in simple sentences or in complex orations, depends on "principles" (a word Adams iterates throughout the lecture on order). The rule by law and precept orders "volatile particles" (1:187)—a phrase as redolent of political overtones as it is of the experimental chemistry to which it owes its origin. The reader is enjoined to see in etymologies—phrased here in terms of "common stock," "close affinity," and "rules and principles"—political and social arguments about the making of American identity.

And so, too, with "extend" and "influence," Adams writes a history of nation building through word history. Quoting Samuel Johnson's tract "Taxation no Tyranny," which states that "The legislature of a colony . . . can extend no influence beyond its own district," Adams reflects:

> To extend is to stretch out; influence is flowing in. Unless you discard entirely this figurative meaning, you see how absurd the connexion between them would be. But the writer is speaking of an abstracted operation of political power. There is a literal meaning annexed to his word, which none of his readers will mistake. He may therefore extend his influence freely, without needing a floodgate to be opened for its extention [*sic*]; and he may extend the influence of a legislature, without being bound to invest it with all the other properties of matter. (2:282–83)

There is that word "annex" again, and there, again, in the word "invest," is an allusion to the funds and riches of that inaugural lecture. Johnson the lexicographer morphs into Johnson the social commentator. Adams the rhetorician segues into Adams the politician. The lectures stand as object lessons in the arts of government as much as the arts of speaking.

Those arts, throughout these lectures, are distinctively American. But America stands not just as a fount of easy example or topical allusion. America *is* figurality and fits precisely into Adams's larger argument that figures are the rule (rather than the exception) in human discourse. "Nothing is more common than figurative language" (2:250), Adams announces, and he goes on to observe that all ancient societies used "symbols, . . . hieroglyphics . . . [and] allegories."

> Among the savages of this continent the same figurative character is found in their modes of communicating thought. It is among the most unlettered classes of civilized society, that figurative discourse principally predominates. The disposition so generally observed in men of every trade and profession to supply the technical terms, with which they are most familiar, bears the same indication. They all use figuratively the words, with which they are acquainted, instead of the proper terms, of which they are ignorant. So figurative speech, instead of being a departure from the ordinary mode, is the general practice, from which the words, rigorously confined to their proper sense, are rare exceptions. The use of figures must indeed have preceded metaphysical reasoning. They communicate ideas not by abstractions, but by images. They speak always to the senses, and only through them to the intellect. They give thought a shape. They are therefore the mother tongue, not only of reflection, but of the imagination and the passions. (2:250–51)

Adams locates the essence of the figurative in primitive America. The "savages" here stand not as the representatives of some lost Eden or of an ideal of civic virtue (as they came to be represented early on in Roger Williams and then, later, in James Fennimore Cooper)[26] but as the first speakers in a curiously nativist rewriting of Cicero's history of civilization (Adams invokes Cicero immediately after this passage, to aver his agreement with the Roman that "figures were in the first instance used from necessity, and afterwards were multiplied on account of their beauty" [2:251]). But this is, too, a Tookean account of language. One of the most politically charged of Tooke's arguments was that the languages of the uncultivated—the "savage," "primitive," or "barbaric"—were just as much languages as those of the civilized. Language does not, he argued, change according to the level of the speaker's civilization. Every language relies on abbreviation, on figures to take the nouns and verbs that constitute its elements and transmute them into the particles that make up grammatical sentences. "Savage languages are upon an equal footing with the languages (as they are called) of art, except that the former are less corrupted."[27] Adams's reflections on the "savages" has more to do with a theory of language than it does with the experience of American life.

And so, too, does his claim for human understanding. Like Tooke, Adams appears to dismiss abstractions as linguistic categories. As he stated a few sentences preceding this quotation, "It is equally clear that language, the purpose of which is to communicate our ideas, must be composed of words, first drawn from ideas of sensation" (2:250). Compare this claim with Tooke: "The business of the mind, as far as it concerns Language, appears to me to be very simple. It extends no farther than to receive Impressions, that is to have Sensations or Feelings."[28] Adams's conception of the mother tongue and his reflections on the passions are central to the kind of philological philosophizing long associated with *The Diversions*. In fact, when Adams reaches his conclusion—that "every word in every language . . . is a trope" (2.254)—he backs it up with an explicit appeal to Tooke's authority: "The author of the Diversions of Purley contends at least with great plausibility, that those subsidiary parts of speech, called articles, prepositions, and conjunctions, are all abbreviations from words, which were originally verbs or nouns; and if so they are, as now used, all tropes" (2.254–55). This is Tooke in a nutshell, a recognition of the most important and most radical claim in *The Diversions* and testimony to its impact on American readers.[29]

But Adams takes it one step further. He defines the American condition as "all tropes." The "propensity to affix old words to new ideas" may be old, he writes, but "[t]here is no part of the world, where this disposition more generally predominates, than on our own continent." "Look over," he enjoins, "a map of the American hemisphere," and you will see the names of familiar kingdoms, states, mountains, lakes, and so on "but scarcely a new name." The natural objects of the landscape have the names borrowed from the languages of Native Americans. "But the whole new creation," by which Adams means the European settlements and the political entities comprising the United States, "has received names already familiar to those, by whom they were adopted, and significant of different objects." Once again, Adams invokes the idea of adoption to refer both to linguistic and political change. He argues, in effect, that naming American settlements after English and European ones is a kind of transferal of signification: an act of figurative language use—in essence, a metaphor. "In this sense," he concludes, "perhaps nine tenths of the words in all languages consist of tropes" (2:255), for what else is a trope but the application of a familiar term to a new signification. America is the country of tropes, a map of metaphors. The etymological resonances of the opening lecture now take on full force, as Adams indulges in a speculative essay on the figuralism of etymology itself.

America becomes the most effective means of talking about figurative language. In lecture 32, Adams responds to Burke and Johnson on the increase of the American population. Central to the difference between the two men is their use of figures. Burke's speech on conciliation seeks to move the audience by reference to the children of American families. Johnson's, by contrast, seeks to antagonize them by evoking an America not familial and familiar but unique and feral. Americans, says Johnson, "multiply with the fecundity of their own rattlesnakes" (2:299). This phrase is the node of Adams's explication. What is at stake is not merely the obvious: that, to "instill ideas of disgust and abhorrence against the Americans," Johnson associates their brood with "the most odious and most venomous of reptiles" (2:300–301). Rather, it is that Johnson has transformed a classical allusion into a contemporary one—he has troped on a trope. The obvious association would have been to the Hydra. The classical allusion here would have effectively associated American procreation with the very symbol of monstrous and unchecked multiplicity, and Johnson, in fact, concludes the remarks Adams quotes by noting that America will "shoot up like the hydra," and we must, he argues, therefore remember "how the hydra was destroyed" (2:300). Embedded in this play of allusions is the classical myth; yet, it remains embedded. Johnson, says Adams, "seems however ashamed of disclosing it in all its nakedness"—that is, he does not wish to make explicit the association of the story of the Hydra and its Herculean destruction with the task of England in America. For Adams, Johnson's figuration leaves the implications of his story "under the veil of a general and indistinct allusion" (2:301).

By deploying the figure of metonymy, by having the rattlesnake stand for the American experience itself, and by displacing classical allusion with contemporary reference, Adams makes America itself the site of figural discourse. For the American to read the British—for Adams to read Burke and Johnson—remains an act of troping, an exposing of the metaphorical implications of what appear to be straightforward arguments. To read as an American is to read rhetorically, and the goal of Adams's lectures lies not simply in the verbal education of the privileged undergraduate but in the public education of America itself. America embodies the rhetorical. When Adams concludes, therefore, by remarking how "masters of language, in oratorical works, make their imagery coincide with the sentiments which they entertain, and which they wish to communicate" (2:302), he is doing more than simply telling us that orators choose their words well. He is rephrasing the tradition of classical rhetoric into contemporary terms, making the discipline of speech the venue for epistemology.

And, at the close of Adams's lectures, the rhetorician thematizes his own physical removal as an instance of the trope of *translatio*. Removed to Russia, leaving the position of pedagogue for the role of ambassador, Adams becomes the bearer of American identity across the sea. Yet, at the close of the lectures, the students should be well prepared to see their teacher's departure not just as a mere movement from the scholarly to the political life but rather as a figure, in itself, for the condition of American rhetoric and the shape of oratorical life. It is, perhaps, no accident that Adams's lectures conclude with disquisitions (in order) on allegory, metonymy and synecdoche, memory, and delivery. For what we have here, at the close, is a progression of figures themselves: a story of the lecturer who asks his students to consider the inherently figurative quality of their own condition; who has consistently used metonyms to make his points; who asks them, in his farewell, to remember the sound of his voice. His final pages recall the story of two lovers, separated by time and distance, agreeing to "turn their eyes towards one of the great luminaries of heaven; and each of them, in looking to the sky, felt a sensation of pleasure at the thought, that the eyes of the other at the same moment were directed towards the same object" (2:399). This little allegory constitutes the final gesture of the rhetorician. "Let me cherish the hope, that between you and me there will be some occasional, nay frequent remembrance, reciprocated by analogical objects in the world of mind" (2:399–400). It is an allegory of remembrance but, as well, an allegory of reading—a story of two sets of eyes fixed on the same interpretable object. And the goal of that direction is, of course, illumination. These "luminaries of the moral heavens" (2:400) are as much aflame as Adams's memory of a "celestial colloquy sublime." And, hence, his ardent wishes: "To open the avenues to science is the duty of the teacher. To explore them must be the labor of the scholar himself. . . . Of my ardent wishes, that your success in this and every other laudable pursuit may answer every expectation of your friends, and every hope of your country" (2.392). Here, again, lie embedded etymologies of argument: the burning stars that are the cosmic equivalents of ardent feeling; the opening avenues, the explorations that recall the many journeys—or errors, those "wandering[s] of the feet"—that opened up the country.

Was Adams wrong? Were his errors not just "wanderings of the feet" but misguided attempts to relocate American political identity along linguistic lines? Or were his claims for rhetoric simply the last gasp of an eighteenth-century Ciceronianism that would lose out to college belletristics? Certainly, his first readers seemed to think so. Only three reviews of the *Lectures* appeared in Adams's lifetime, and but one—in the *Port Folio* (1810)—paid much attention to his arguments.[30] Indeed, for this reviewer, Adams's *Lectures* are an anthology of errors. Page after page of mistakes are recorded; words found "superfluous" stand out, in italics, from Adams's quoted prose; sentences that ramble to the point of unintelligibility are held up to ridicule. "Errors, that on the most deliberate revision, would not have been corrected or acknowledged, are certainly fair objects of notice. Such as illegitimate words, or words which the fathers of our language would disown" (pp. 123–24).

Language has a genealogy, and the *Port Folio* reviewer labels Adams's language not just erroneous or, as he puts it elsewhere, "garish" but illegitimate. The very bastardy of his vocabulary undermines the *Lectures*' own claims for "adoption": for that gradual acceptance of new words, for language growth as kin to kin itself. The reviewer refuses to acknowledge Adams's claim. "Language," he writes, "is indefinitely improvable. . . . But it is improvable only by rejection, not adoption. As to words, this is true. But philologists need not complain. They will find work enough in their hands in this business of negative improvement" (p. 133). Rather than see the language as a welcome home to newly coined or fresh imported words, he sees it carefully excluding the unwelcome outsider. Is there a philological xenophobia to this reviewer? Is there a claim in his remark, "what necessity is there for new words in the English language," akin to claims for countrymen (what necessity is there for new people in America)? Language, not unlike nationhood, defines itself by inheritance, here—for, if the fathers of our language would disown the bastard word, just whom would the fathers of our country disavow?

This *Port Folio* review rejects Adams because his rhetoric is un-American; his language garish, verbose, full of superfluities; his fascination with metaphor overwhelming (p. 124); his theories of language counterintuitive. For this final point, the reviewer recognizes Adams's claim that "words by familiar use are made to deviate widely from their primitive meaning" (p. 130). The argument goes back to Johnson, and it stands at the heart of Adams's fascination with the metaphorical and figurative—the sense that all words, ultimately, become tropes. And it inflects, too, Adams's predilections for the metaphysical etymologies of Horne Tooke, the sense that there is something essential about a word and its history. But this account cannot please the plain-speaking Philadelphian of the *Port-Folio*. "Is it not agreed, that there is no possible, natural connexion between signs and things signified? Can any reason under heaven be assigned, but use, why one word should denote one thing more than another?" (p. 131).

The *Port Folio* reviewer is more canny than he has appeared. He recognizes that these *Lectures on Rhetoric* are approaches to philology, and he responds in kind. They raise questions fundamental to an understanding of the nature of linguistic utterance; to relationships between the literal and metaphorical; to the argumentative association of a people and their words, a nation's genealogies and etymologies. "But philologists," he noted, "need not complain." The proper reader of these *Lectures*, then, is the philologist, and that fact, it seems to me, is why they disappeared from nineteenth-century American rhetorical discourse. They just are not rhetoric.

And this is the point. Throughout the nineteenth century, rhetorical instruction had become so estranged from the philological that there was no need, it seemed, to take account of recent historical studies or the comparative method. Rhetoric, in effect, ceded its interest in linguistic speculation, becoming the basis not for inquiry into the nature of expression but for training practical professionals. Such was the goal of the succession of Boylston Professors that followed Adams. Ministers, antiquarians, and journalists would hold the chair to reflect on aspects of writing and composition, pulpit oratory, and English and European literature. Emphasis shifted from the social implications of a rhetorical ideal to the pedagogical concerns of writing and speaking well. Eloquence became a means of emotional persuasion, and the orator was taught less how to organize his speeches in precise Ciceronian form than to find strategies for affecting his audience.[31]

For Adams Sherman Hill, who held the Boylston Professorship from 1876 to 1904, philology arises only to be brushed away.[32] His *Principles of Rhetoric*, published soon after he ascended to the chair in 1878 and revised and republished in 1895, defined rhetoric as an "art, not a science."³³ Linguistic usage lies not in mere "fastidiousness" of correctness or in the pedantries of the classroom. Instead, it resides in the shared experience of educated speech and writing, exemplified by the best authors. Hill sets the stage for a rhetorical anthology of English literature: a collection of passages designed to represent words, grammar, idioms, strategies, and, most generally, an overall ideal of style. His preference, too, is for recent authors, as they show the English language being used, and modern usage is, for Hill, always the best guide to correctness. The grounds for usage are not found in early precedent or in the etymologies of English words. "In the English of to-day, one word is not preferred to another because it is derived from this or from that source; the present meaning of a word is not fixed by its etymology, nor its inflection by the inflection of other words with which it may, for some purposes, be classed" (p. 2). After reviewing a collection of such words—mocking those who would claim that new or imported are not as good as native English ones and those who would find in recent historical changes in the language (the form "its," for example) only oddity—Hill uses Walter Savage Landor to beat down the ghosts of eighteenth-century etymological argument.

> "There is," says Landor, "a fastidiousness in the use of language that indicates an atrophy of mind. We must take words as the world presents them to us, without looking at the root. If we grubbed under this and laid it bare, we should leave no room for our thoughts to lie evenly, and every expression would be constrained and crampt. We should scarcely find a metaphor in the purest author that is not false or imperfect, nor could we imagine one ourselves that would not be stiff and frigid. Take now, for instance, a phrase in common use. *You are rather late.* Can anything seem plainer? Yet *rather*, as you know, meant originally *earlier*, being the comparative of *rathe*; The "rathe primrose" of the poet recalls it. We cannot say, *You are sooner late*; But who is so troublesome and silly as to question the propriety of saying, *You are rather late?*" (p. 3)

Go to the bottom of the page, and Hill's footnote, in addition to citing the source of this passage ("Landor's Conversations, Third Series"), offers the apparently gratuitous "Johnson and Horne (Tooke)." Surely, what Hill is doing here is referencing the very tradition that Landor mocks. Indeed, this is the kind of argument that John Quincy Adams would have used in his own Boylston Lectures. The etymological prestidigitation he would display in exposing the hidden meaning of a phrase such as "error and capital punishment"—where error is a "wandering of the feet" and capital refers to taking off the head—is ridiculed here. Landor's joke is Adams's high seriousness.

If Hill appears to have little patience with the etymologists, he has even less with the Anglo-Saxonists. In fact, he lumps them both together, calling those who would prefer Old English words over those from French or Latin subscribers to an "etymological theory" of diction. One should choose "words, not because they came from this or that source, but because they served the purpose in view" (p. 96). True, there are differences. Hill recognizes the effectiveness of pairing short words from Old English with long words from Latin (pp. 97–98). But, in the end, adherence to an "etymological standard" (p. 99) leads only to pedantry. New words are always coming in; old words are changing; ours is "now a composite language, in which every part has its function, every word in good use its reason for existence" (p. 100).

And yet Hill himself is not above a bit of philological play. When he dismisses the etymologists, he does so by exposing their own rhetorical fissures. "[T]he words of some of the most ardent champions of the Anglo-Saxon abound in words form the Latin" (p. 96). What better way of undermining your opponents than by showing them in contradiction? But Hill's own language mimes the diction of that contradiction. "Ardent champions"—words from the Latin and the French used to modify "Anglo-Saxon," a philological joke played on the philologists. Hill relishes such verbal oppositions. "Our associations with words of Anglo-Saxon origin often differ widely from those called up by words form the Latin" (p. 98). And, again, he quotes Landor at length (and, again, offers a footnote to Johnson and Horne Tooke) on enriching the language—that even though "the Saxon [is] always the ground-work," words from a range of languages have come into English (p. 100). Argument from etymology makes difficult the acceptance of such words: "bloody" and "sanguine," for example, "mean" the same thing yet connote far different values (p. 99). "[T]o give prominence to the etymological fact is to substitute an obscure for an obvious ground of preference" (p. 102). Hill's quarrel is not with the old legacy of Platonic dichotomy—is rhetoric a true skill or is it merely a knack?—but rather with contemporary academic claims. Rhetoric, as he announces, is "an art, not a science: for it neither observes, nor discovers, nor classifies . . . it uses knowledge, not as knowledge, but as power" (p. v). By the end of the nineteenth century, the science that observed, discovered, and classified was philology.

Philology *was* the science of language—that *wissenschaft* whose historical principles had been taught to at least three generations by the time Hill's lectures first saw print. The very phrase "science of language" had become a code for the disciplinary foundation of language study: a foundation that associated comparative philology with comparative anatomy or comparative biology. In Departments of English, in particular, conflicts between philologists and rhetoricians played out the larger conflicts of an academic selfhood. Hill's comments on etymology and Anglo-Saxon must be seen in this context: in part, perhaps, a jibe at his all-too-philological predecessor in the Boylston chair, Francis Child; in part, too, a turf claim for his field against those who, much like James Morgan Hart, would deny to rhetoric the aegis for a literary study. In 1884 Hart (then a professor at the University of Cincinnati but soon to move to Cornell) wrote in *PMLA*:

> There are still only too many persons of influence and culture who persist in looking upon the instructor of English literature as necessarily the instructor of rhetoric. I am unable to share this opinion. To me rhetoric is a purely formal drill, having no more connection with the literature of England than it has with the literature of Greece, Rome, France, Germany, or Arabia. The canons of the art were laid down two thousand years ago by Aristotle, and quite one thousand years before there was an English literature in any sense.

"Rhetoric," Hart went on, "always savors to me of the school-bench. It is, if we look into it scrutinizingly, little more than verbal jugglery."[34] And for Albert S. Cook, who would address the Modern Language Association in 1898 under the title "The Province of English Philology," the philologist (as I quoted at this chapter's opening) "endeavor[s] to relive the life of the past; to enter by the imagination into the spiritual experiences of all the historic protagonists of civilization in a given period and area of culture; . . . to judge rightly these various disclosures of the human spirit, and to reveal to the world their true significance and relative importance."³⁵ Philology seems quite like rhetoric itself here, a province of what Hill would call things "of the imagination." Cook's phrasing makes philology seem very much like rhetoric in the classical tradition: not just the art of speaking well but the rubric under which the emotions and the sensibilities were studied. Just who, then, has priority over the life of the past: the rhetorician or philologist? Just who should be charged with the study and the teaching of its literature and language? And just who should stand in the academy as model of professional identity?

For William Dwight Whitney (1827–1894) and Basil Lanneau Gildersleeve (1831–1924), the answer to these questions was themselves. German trained, research oriented, empirical in idiom, indomitable in work habits, they embodied an ideal of academic professionalism in sharp contrast to the rhetoricians and belletrists who had inhabited the older colleges.³⁶ Their science was philology; their subject of research, the languages and literatures of classical antiquity (which, for Whitney, included Sanskrit); their venues, the professional journals. But they were also great popularizer of their fields: Whitney, through his public lectures, dictionary editing, and summaries in such volumes as *The Life and Growth of Language*; Gildersleeve, though his addresses and magazine pieces, many of which were brought together into widely read collections of his work. Both had distinguished and distinctive careers, and both differed markedly in regional origin and public politics (Whitney, the scion of two old New England families who spent his whole career at Yale; Gildersleeve, the Virginian who fought for the Confederacy, taught at Virginia and Johns Hopkins, and never quite gave up his elegaics for the Old South). But what they shared was a commitment to philology as a discipline. For all their own rhetorical poses and ploys, they were at pains to distinguish what they did from rhetoric. And, in the process, they made philology the defining field for academic cultural identity in their America.

Though esteemed in his own time as the leading American scholar of Sanskrit and as a great exponent of the comparative method in the study of historical philology, Whitney is largely known today for his anticipation (what one critic has called his "clairvoyant glimpse") of the semiotics we have come to associate with Saussure.³⁷ The classic paradigms of Saussurian theory—the arbitrariness and conventionality of the sign, the conviction that language is a form of social behavior, the recognition of the independence of historical sound change from any essential bearer of meaning—have all been recognized as central to Whitney's approach to language. Whitney labored hard to stress the point about the fundamental arbitrariness of words, and etymology had to be pressed into that service. Time and again, he argues against what he called "the old helter-skelter method of etymologizing,"[38] the search for essential meanings in word elements or the comparison of unrelated languages in order to make claims for broad linguistic universals. We do not study etymology in order to recover hidden meanings; nor do we pay attention to the histories of words in order to select effectively the vocabulary that we use.[39] The history of language, too, is not self-consciously concerned with etymology. As Whitney puts it, "The internal development of a vocabulary, too, would be greatly checked and hampered by a too intrusive etymological consciousness." (*LSL*, p. 132). He goes on, "Those, then, are greatly in error who would designate by the name 'linguistic sense' (*sprachsinn*) a disposition to retain in memory the original *status* and value of formative elements, and the primary significance of transferred terms" (*LSL*, p. 132).

But, on occasion, etymological attentions could have a powerful rhetorical effect: "As we rise, too, in the scale of linguistic use, from that which is straightforward and unreflective to that which is elaborate, pregnant, artistic, etymological considerations in many cases rise in value. . . . A pregnant implication of etymological meaning often adds strikingly to the force and impressiveness of an expression" (*LSL*, p. 133). Whitney, then, wishes to distinguish the pursuit of etymology as a philological concern from its rhetorical implications. He narrowly circumscribes the range of acceptable etymological inquiries, ruling out older metaphysical speculations, on the one hand, and mythological or cultural associations, on the other. In the process, he defines not just the proper uses of etymology but the discipline of philology itself. The error of those who would claim a *sprachsinn* for the elements of words becomes an error not just of a local misinterpretation but of a conceptual misunderstanding. And the philologist most guilty of that error, and a host of others, was none other than Max Müller.

No one worked a metaphor as much as Müller, and his penchant for figurative expressions and analogies led him, ultimately, to argue for an inherently figurative aspect to language itself. His many etymologies fed into a linguistic mythology. Each word was something of a fossil history of culture. The meaning of a word lay not so much in its present as its past. "Thought was bred of words," wrote his obituarist, E. W. Hopkins, "not words of thought," a conviction that led Müller to believe, at his most extreme, in their almost magical power. As Hopkins put it: "As Müller advanced, he appears to have fallen a victim to the very factor in his mental furnishing which made his books so interesting to beginners, even an imaginative, fanciful way of looking at facts. He seems to have regarded words as endowed with some mysterious potency, and thus was drawn to the peculiar view which he upheld in his mythological studies and later in his 'Science of Thought.'"[40]

It was precisely this imaginative fancy that struck Whitney. Müller had the tendency, he noted, "to substitute figurative and rhetorical phrases for close thought and clear statement." His was a language rich with "the graces and the ornaments of style," an asset all too often taken to extremes.[41] "In some instances, however, we think that he has been led too far in this direction—has given too loose a rein to poetic fancy, and talked in tropes and pictures when more exact scientific statement had been preferable" (p. 95). Yes, we may be "charmed by [his] eloquence,"[42] but that should not prevent the reader, Whitney claims, from ignoring the controlling error of his work: the confusion of language with thought (p. 249). Müller emerges from these pages a mythologist and not a linguist, a rhetorician setting out to persuade, move, or dazzle his audience. "To express by a figure something which is only half-understood or wholly obscure, then to dwell upon the figurative expression as if it were a true definition, and let it hide from sight the thing meant to be expressed, is a good process in mythology, though not in science."[43] In the end, Müller's "science of language" is not science at all, but literature. "Taken as literature, it is of high rank, as the admiration of the public sufficiently testifies. Its author has a special gift for interesting statement and illustration, for lending a charm to the subjects he discusses; and he carries captive the judgments of his hearers and many of his readers. He is a born *littérateur*."[44]

But what of Whitney's own "special gift for interesting statement and illustration," what of his own rhetorical strategies? What should we make of this remark, offered in closing *Max Müller and the Science of Language*?

> It is questionable whether I should myself ever have written a work on the general subject of language if I had not been driven to it by

what seemed to me the necessity of counteracting, as far as possible, the influence of such erroneous views [as Müller's]. . . . To one living in such an atmosphere of adulation as has been his environment for the past thirty years . . . , and who has established so tyrannical a sway in British public opinion that even those most opposed to him hardly dare to raise avoice in public against him, it may well enough have seemed that I was playing Mordecai to his Haman.

(p. 78)

Or, for that matter, what should we make of the extended description of his own New England dialect in his "Elements of English Pronunciation"; or his brutal criticisms of the now-forgotten Henry Alford's *Plea for the Queen's English*, which Whitney held up to ridicule, both for its "violent ebullition of spite against [my] native country" and its ignorance of basic philological detail?[45] Or again, in his essay "How Shall We Spell," what should we make of his witty obeisances to "that unscrupulous radical" Noah Webster, who, in spite of his "false etymologies and defective definitions," nonetheless remained "one of the best-abused men of his generation"?[46]

What we should make of all these statements is a claim for American identity. His critique of Müller remains not just a philological but a profoundly rhetorical act—a declaration of American scholarly independence. By placing himself in line with the great and greatly misunderstood (Webster, in particular), by giving us a personal self-portrait in his vowel sounds, by appealing to American readers against a silly British schoolmaster, Whitney gives us what Fliegelman would call, now going back to his encapsulated ideal of early republican rhetoric, "a particular moral and social conception of identity." Whitney's work is as much performance as Müller's. The etymologist, he had said elsewhere, must, in his inquiries, be both an advocate and "play the part of the opposing counsel" (*LSL*, p. 239). Whitney puts Müller himself on trial. In doing so, he takes on not just the correction but the intellectual effacement of the highest ideal of an Anglo-German philological authority. Words such as "tyrannical sway" must resonate with a republican ideal, with the old Websterian critique of the king's aegis and his English. In fact, much of the rhetoric of Whitney's blast at Müller could be traced back to attacks on Samuel Johnson by Webster and his contemporaries. For, much like Müller, Johnson had the "sway in British public opinion."

Like Müller, Johnson was condemned for his elaborate idiom—in Webster's terms, he only seeks to dazzle with "a glare of ornament."[47] Archibald Campbell, one of Johnson's British critics, shared with Webster a distaste for gaudiness, and he associated this decadence of English style with the decline of Rome, "when their licentious republick had degenerated into a most despotick tyranny."[48]

And finally, perhaps, Whitney's own dialect description takes us back to Webster and the ideals of American linguistic purity. His deceptively titled "Elements of English Pronunciation" is, in fact, "an analysis and description of the elements of *my own native* pronunciation of English.... For aught that I know, my speech may be taken as a fair specimen of the ordinarily educated New Englander from the interior; a region where . . . the proper distinction of *shall* and *will* was as strictly maintained, and a slip in the use of the one for the other as rare, and as immediately noticeable and offensive (unfortunately, that is the case no longer), as in the best society of London."[49] For Whitney of Northampton—"a shire-town of long standing, which in my youth had not lost its ancient and well-established reputation as a home of 'old families,' and a scene of special culture and high-bred society"—English pronunciation *is* his own native pronunciation. A philologist's appeal to etymology now becomes a rhetorician's appeal to genealogy. And yet both go back to Webster, whose characterized ideal English speech as "the common unadulterated pronunciation of the New England gentlemen, [which] is almost uniformly the pronunciation which prevailed in England, anterior to Sheridan's time, and which, I am answered by English gentlemen, is still the pronunciation of the body of the British nation."[50] By looking back to Webster, by locating his inheritance in New England speech, by invoking the buzzwords of an eighteenth-century linguistic battle, Whitney articulates his declaration of independence. He claims a philology as "native" as his vowels or (to go back to the language of William Thornton's *Cadmus*) an American philology "as distinct as the government, free from all the follies of unphilosophical fashion, and resting upon truth as its only regulator."

Truth may be the great regulator, but, for Basil Gildersleeve, "Grammar is a regulative art." Its province is "correctness," though its practice should not be left to the pedants.[51] Instead, the true masters of grammatical or philological analysis should be the literary critics, and the goal of their study should be aesthetic evaluation. "So sharply objective is the character of the dominant school of philology," Gildersleeve noted, "that the very mention of the word 'aesthetics' is almost enough to send the utterer into the camp of the *littérateur* and the essayist" (*ES*, p. 106). An exile to that camp was just what Whitney had in mind for Müller—that "born *littérateur*"—and Gildersleeve, too, would dismiss the belletrism or elaborate figurative diction of "fine substantives, superfine adjectives, . . . or sympathetic phrase-mongery" (*ES*, p. 133). And yet Gildersleeve wants to make the case for literary artistry. Phonetic analysis—the study of "the sensuous effect of sound"—need not be the domain of the phonologist but may instead, along with syntactic description, lead to "literary criticism [and] aesthetic appreciation" (*ES*, p. 506). For, unlike Whitney, Gildersleeve is an aesthetician of philology. He recognizes that in the traditions of rhetorical analysis we may recover "an *organon* of aesthetic appreciation" (*ES*, p. 145).

What is American about this philological aesthetics? Gildersleeve shares with Whitney a desire to declare an independence from the European academic. The history and literature of the ancient world, he argued, could be best read in the light of the American experience. Americans should draw on the unique resources of their character, what he called our "practicality,"[52] and our "unequalled adaptability, our quick perception, our straightforwardness of intellectual motion" (*ES*, p. 93). For, while he acknowledges a profound debt to European teaching—"To Germany and the Germans I am indebted for everything professionally"—Gildersleeve argued vigorously for an independence of American scholarship:

> An audacious, inventive, ready-witted people, Americans often comprehend the audacious, inventive, ready-witted Greek *à demi-mot*. . . . No nation is quicker than ours to take in the point of a situation, and there is no reason discernible why Americans should not excel in the solution of the most subtle problem of antique manners and politics.
>
> (ES, p. 105)

These polemics have more about them than a mere appeal to native know-how or a plea for a naive comparatism of contemporary and classical life. They powerfully exemplify rhetorical philology: a suasive argument deployed to praise or justify a calling. Use Gildersleeve's own categories of analysis on this text. By mirroring his statements on the present and the past, by using parallel constructions, he sonically, syntactically, and substantively equates the American and Greek. Such an equation is impossible for European scholars: "the German professor phrases, and the English 'don' rubs his eyes, and the French *savant* appreciates the wrong half" (*ES*, p. 105). Professor, "don," *savant*: a rapidly descending hierarchy of mock callings, from the mere title, to the sniffily dismissed nickname in scare quotes, to the untranslated and italicized pose.

But Gildersleeve's rhetoric, too, returns us to the central idioms of academic inquiry: the crooked and the straight, the errant and the correct. Embedded in the very idea of "straightforwardness of intellectual motion" is a criticism of that perceived European, particularly German, circularity. Recall George Eliot's "Word for the Germans," where she characterizes their scholarship as full of "involved sentences, like coiled serpents, showing neither head nor tail."[53] Not so Gildersleeve's American, who can quicker than any other "take the point of a situation." Like James A. H. Murray—whose *Dictionary*'s progress Gildersleeve had clearly followed closely (*HH*, p. 55)—philologists may be pioneers, hewing straight paths through uncharted lands. The "scientific study of syntax," for example, has produced "[a] few pioneers [who] have opened avenues here and there, and monographs on isolated points or separate authors are appearing in greater and greater numbers in Germany" (*ES*, p. 107). But there is still "ample room" for work. "Here, then, is a province which has not been so occupied that American philologians may not find in it abundant room for the native sagacity, the unresting energy, which have distinguished our people in other departments of science. It is, indeed, a noble province" (*ES*, pp. 107–8). Though Germans may have opened up the way, it is the Americans who will effectively take over, occupying the province much as an army occupies a land. But even "an able explorer may be an indifferent teacher; a good teacher may not have the spirit of initiative which leads to successful investigation; but the two faculties, though not always in perfect balance, are seldom wholly divorced, and a university professor should possess both" (*ES*, p. 91).

Gildersleeve revels in the paths of inquiry, in part, to participate in the old tropes of scholarship but also, in part, to engage with rhetoric itself. For rhetoric remains the domain of the ornate and elaborate (*ES*, p. 141). Rhetoric, of course, may be pressed into scholarship's service, and Gildersleeve has much to praise in the ancient rhetoricians, whose discipline could embrace the study of both language and culture in the large.

But there remains much that is mere ornament: "I believe in rhetoric, but it must be rhetoric in the service of truth; not jingle, but tocsin. The fair facade must be the growth of the living rooms" (*HH*, p. 25). When the "professional philologians push their studies into the domain of the Greek and Roman rhetoricians," even they "are apt to become impatient with what must seem at first to be fanciful detail" (*ES*, p. 144). For, in the end, as he put it in his *Hellas and Hesperia*, "It is better to be a doorkeeper in the house of philology than to dwell in the tents of the rhetoricians" (p. 45).

Much like Whitney, Gildersleeve finds in rhetoric only the byways of an argument, and like Whitney, too, he is suspicious of the rhetorical uses of etymology. "The study of origins, of etymology, has very little, if anything, to do with the practice of speaking and writing. . . . The study of etymology may help a scholar here and there to a happier use of language, but over-consciousness is fatal to supreme excellence in composition, and the best etymologists, the best grammarians, are not the best stylists" (*HH*, p. 56). In these discussions, etymology is not a category of linguistic history but a trope of rhetoric: a device for enhancing an argument, for coloring a claim. And so, too, Gildersleeve relies on it. "We have to deal not with the roots but with the foliage of language" (*HH*, p. 57). Words from Greek and Latin are that foliage, he claims, and thus they constitute an ornament to English. "Root" from the Old English; "foliage" from the Latin, by way of the French. Translate, then, Gildersleeve's claim philologically. We have to deal not with the Anglo-Saxon origins of words but with the Latin, Greek, or other words that leaf it out, that give it color, shade, and fullness. It is as if Gildersleeve himself is now appropriating foreign words and naturalizing them: performing not just a linguistic but, of course, a political act, one whose idiom goes back to the terms of William Thornton and John Quincy Adams. "Admit" words as one admits peoples, Thornton claimed; "annex" and "adopt" new words, wrote Adams.

But there is a world of difference between the politics of language in the nation at the turn of the nineteenth century and at the turn of the twentieth. And there is a world of difference between the politics of revolutionary men and those of Gildersleeve's age. For what Gildersleeve is really talking about is the restoration of a country after civil war. The politics of verbal meaning, here—the ardent quality of his philology—comes from an enduring personal memory of the Old South: of the lost cause, of the atrocities that Gildersleeve saw perpetrated on his home.[54] Born and raised in Charleston, South Carolina, attending Princeton, teaching at the University of Virginia, serving in the Confederate Army, Gildersleeve was unabashedly a scion of the aristocratic South. "I have shared the fortunes of the land in which my lot was cast, and in my time have shared its prejudices and its defiant attitude."[55] He joined up in 1861, saw action in the battles of the Shenandoah Valley and at Wyer's Cave, followed from his sick bed Sherman's march to the sea, and prided himself on his membership in a "heroic generation." And when he neared death, at age ninety-three, he asked to be buried back in Charlottesville.[56]

This Southern background shaped both the aesthetics and the politics of Gildersleeve's rhetorical philology. His *Creed of the Old South* (a collection of magazine articles originally published in 1892 and revised and reissued in book form in 1915) argued for a distinctive humanist and literary Southern culture—an ideal of gentlemanly ethics, where young soldiers' "talk fell on Goethe and on Faust," where Princeton college roommates and Virginia students could die with the classics on their lips.[57] In his other autobiographical reflections, Gildersleeve could look back on a Charleston childhood rich with *littérateurs*, poets, and artists. One of those writers was Paul Hamilton Hayne, who averred that his contemporaries "looked upon literature as the choice recreation of gentlemen, as something fair and good, to be courted in a dainty, amateur fashion, and illustrated by *apropos* quotations from Lucretius, Virgil, or Horace."[58]

At the University of Virginia, where Gildersleeve taught from 1856 until he left for the newly created Johns Hopkins University twenty years later, this belletristic Southern culture was enhanced by a distinctive vision of philology as similarly keyed to geographical inheritance. For, if the young man could quote Lucretius, or Virgil, or Horace, he should, too, be able to see his life refracted in the heroisms of *The Battle of Maldon* or *Beowulf*. The Southern Anglo-Saxonists had taken their philology explicitly in response to the Civil War and Reconstruction. Maximillian Schele De Vere, Gildersleeve's contemporary professor of modern languages at Virginia, noted that the survival of Anglo-Saxon after the Norman Conquest could be likened to the survival of Southern culture after the Civil War. As defenders of individual liberty, as speakers of a language rich with heroic poetry, as figures of defeat, the Anglo-Saxons came to stand, in the last decades of the nineteenth century, as models for the Southern self. Indeed, some philologists came increasingly to believe that the Southern dialect preserved the forms and sounds of early English. The defeat in war, then, meant defeat not just for a society or cause but for the history of the language itself.[59]

Such sentiments were made explicit in an essay published in the second volume of the *Sewanee Review* in 1894 by J. B. Henneman. "The Study of English in the South" reviewed the previous half-century of education to chart the curricular shifts from rhetoric to philology.[60] Students were reading Blair and Campbell still in the mid-nineteenth century, while "English" very much meant "rhetoric": instruction in "the old-time orations and methods of essay writing," with "classes in 'rhetoric and belles-lettres'" taught by the professor of metaphysics (p. 181). Even though the old "graces of the Southern orator" survived in the classroom (and clearly survived in Gildersleeve's essays), German-trained philologists were coming to the colleges to teach philology. The interest in the history of the English language, though, Henneman stresses, "was a movement essentially of native growth, and nowhere of foreign importation or imitation" (p. 189). Robert E. Lee, the president of Washington College (later, Washington and Lee University), marked his administration by a "sympathy" for the historical study of English. Such study "was a product answering to local needs, as those needs had become intensified through the interruptions and derangements of the War" (p. 189). Henneman goes on, in a vein perfectly parallel to Gildersleeve: "A knowledge of the early forms of English was demanded, not as philology pure and simple, constituting an end in itself, but as a means for acquiring a true, appreciative knowledge of the mother tongue" (p. 189). *Beowulf* ("this stirring Germanic epic" [p. 195]), the heroic poems, and what Henneman calls *The Fight at Maldon*, were read and translated at the Southern universities by the 1880s (p. 194). And even though the founding of Johns Hopkins made historical philology, both English and classical, part of the accepted university curriculum, the Southern schools were well ahead of the curve.

> We cannot too strongly emphasize the fact of this native growth, this development from the needs of the country just after the interruptions and distractions occasioned by the War. Nor should we forget that it was an offshoot from the study of the classic tongues, especially Greek—the love of the grandest of ancient literatures nat-

urally giving birth to a desire for a closer knowledge of the spirit of our own, a literature which so many of us would place in the forefront of all modern expressions of life. (p. 195)

Philology became a means of regional identity, a way of locating the Southern self against an old, heroic literary figuration. Indeed, the South—with all these claims for a historical link to Anglo-Saxon, the associations between Civil War defeat and classic battles, the identification of gentlemanly action with antique heroism—in these discourses becomes some purer version of America itself, perhaps in answer to the claims from Webster to Whitney for a New England purity of diction and historical inheritance.

In this environment of Southern scholarship, Gildersleeve emerges as "an ardent lover of literature" (*ES*, p. 506). And in his 1878 address as president of the American Philological Association, he announced: "While special research has, it is true, the drawback that it tends to make the course of instruction symmetrical, what is lost in the rounded completeness of form is more than made up by the kindling of life that goes forth from every one who is engaged in the ardent quest of truth; and so thoroughly correlated is all knowledge, that there are subtle lines of connexion between the most remote regions of scientific study which vitalize them and method through the whole intervening space."[61] The ardent quest of truth itself is flaming here, lit by the "kindling of life." What connections may we find between this passage and the "most remote regions" of Gildersleeve's own thoughts? For how can we not think of that great conflagration so fixed in his memory that, half a century after the Civil War, he could still call it up?

> Those who suffered in Sherman's March to the Sea . . . were not, are not so philosophic. . . . Nor was I so philosophical when I followed the raiders of 1863, nor when I saw the fires that lighted up the Valley of Virginia in 1864. . . . "When our army," says Merritt (Battles and Leaders 4, 512), "commenced its return march, the cavalry was deployed across the Valley, burning, destroying or taking nearly everything of value, or likely to be of value to the enemy." . . . In a vivid sketch of Sherman's March, Prof. Henry E. Shepherd . . . winds up by saying that the portrayal of it "baffles all the resources of literary art and the affluence even of our English speech."[62]

The rhetoric of scholarship becomes the elegiacs of the war. The pioneers, the provinces, the tracks, the fires—all the artistry of word and will cannot express what he had seen. Go back, now, to the language of the philological pioneer: not just in James A. H. Murray but in Gildersleeve and, again, in Whitney—Whitney, who could write of Bournouf as "essentially a pioneer and pathmaker" or who could claim "the labors of the etymologist must precede and prepare the way for everything that is to follow."[63] The etymology of "pioneer," of which I made so much in my previous chapter—a soldier who goes first, to blaze a pathway for an army—now, in these reminiscences of war, takes on an elegiac edge. What good is etymology? "The only good compound evolved during the Civil War," Gildersleeve tossed off in *Hellas and Hesperia*, "is 'gripsack'" (p. 63).

But, surely, what that war gave to Gildersleeve was more. Philology becomes a vast amnesty project for Southern resistance. Etymology takes on a profound importance as it leads us back through personal reflection to American identity. Even an old cliché such as "sweetness and light" refracts itself through Gildersleeve's memory. "Sweetness" recalls how hard it was for the Confederate soldier to get his sugar, and this recollection then leads to a discourse on honey, the sweetener of the ancient world. Attic honey was a special treat. "The Peleponnesians would not have been soldiers if they had not robbed every beehive on the march." The old war recalls an even older one, and both recall a personal experience. "Attic honey has the ring of New Orleans molasses; 'those molassesses,' as the article was often called, with an admiring plural of majesty" (*Creed*, pp. 99–101). Grammatical analysis is never far away, even from this string of an old man's free associations.

And, of course, there was the light. "A Confederate student," he wrote, "could more readily renounce sweetness than light, and light soon became a serious matter." He goes on: "The American demands a flood of light, and wonders at the English don who pursues his investigations by the glimmer of two candles. It was hard to go back to primitive tallow dips. Lard might have served, but it was too precious to be used in lamps. . . . Many preferred the old way, and read by flickering pine-knots, which cost many an old reader his eyes" (*Creed*, p. 101). Recall, now, *Middlemarch* and Casaubon's dim tapers; recall Henry James's avowal that to read that novel well one must read as an American; recall Seamus Heaney, who, in his meditations on the Old English word "*þo-lian*" (to suffer), had "undergone something like illumination by philology." So, too, I think has Gildersleeve. His arguments and reminiscences have vivified the etymology of "ardent." Everything remains aflame, the lights are burning, and the rhetoric of his accounts is like the old way of illumination by pine knots.

By the close of the nineteenth century, rhetoric had lost out to philology as the venue for a nationalist academic discipline. Though the rhetorical approach had inflected philological inquiry, and though the teaching of rhetoric had remained a mainstay of the undergraduate curriculum, its syllabi had ossified into instruction in good taste, good writing, and good oratory. James Morgan Hart's dismissal of rhetoric in the 1884 *PMLA* as "a purely formal drill," without relevance to literary study, spoke for one side of the curricular debate. As he put it, in a pungent rhetorical analogy of his own: "Rhetorical exercises are, of course, useful. So are the parallel bars and dumb-bells of a gymnasium. Need I push the comparison farther?"[64]

Yet there were those, especially at the new universities in the Midwest, who would seek to revive rhetoric as scientific study. The rising interest in phonology—the analysis of regional pronunciations as well as of the physiology of speech production—had grown out of the Neogrammarian's concern with sound shifts, on the one hand, and out of arguments about the nature and diversity of regional dialects, on the other. By the early decades of the twentieth century, the so-called science of phonology had begun to push speech study away from social education in the arts of eloquence to empirical inquiry into the organs of sound. Speech "science" came to embrace experimental phonology, therapy for the correction of impediments, and, also, oral interpretation. At the 1912 Minneapolis convention of the National Speech Arts Association came the call for a "'science' of persuasion."[65] Speech became, in the terms of the Speech Communication Association, a discipline of "practical, systematic communication." Such moves were designed, in the words of this discipline's historians, "to unify, to place on a solid foundation, and to give academic stature to training in speech which was something more than 'elocution'" (p. 500). By 1926, when the American Academy of Speech Correction was established, it set among its original goals "To secure public recognition of the practice of speech correction as an organized *profession*." "Research into all phenomena of speech and hearing" was the goal of the new speech science (p. 508).

Against this background of scientific language study, several members of the Cornell Department of Speech sought to reassess relationships among expression, writing, rhetoric, and social thought. Beginning in the 1920s, the Cornell group redefined the place of rhetoric in a liberal education.[66] Its goal was a "search for the relation of rhetoric to the modern world and for a definition of [its social] function."[67] And, as part of that search, the group attempted to synthesize the study of past texts and theories with the critique of contemporary modern culture.

The ancients, Gildersleeve had argued, had "to be interpreted into terms of American experience," (*ES*, p. 105), and this, too, seemed the logic of the Cornell group. Concerns with what Gildersleeve had called the "practical" and "systematic" features of American identity found themselves expressed, often backward through historical projection, in the scholarship of the Cornellians. Nowhere is this projection clearer than in the work of Harry Caplan, perhaps the most well-known (and most influential) of the group.

Caplan's first published article, on Latin panegyric, begins in good Ciceronian form by seeking to obtain the benevolence of his audience.[68] Here, it is the potentially hostile readership of the *Quarterly Journal of Speech*, for whom, in 1924, the historical study of rhetoric was a bypath along the road to modern scientific inquiry.

> I am aware that any paper treating of ancient Oratory or Rhetoric is likely to irritate the sensitive feelings of valiant modernists, such as have in our QUARTERLY recently raised the war-cry; "Dam this deluge"—of scribblings by pusillanimous hero-worshippers of the ancient dead. Those of us who are convinced that we have much, very much, to learn from the Rhetoric of high periods of Greece and Rome are smitten hip and thigh, as proper punishment for neglect of the present time, for a deification of men who were but mortal, and whom adulation anyway would do no good. With extreme trepidation, then, do I discuss a product of the civilization of ancient Rome which some critics have considered the most worthless bequest of antiquity. (p. 41)

Caplan begins publicly and oratorically, his very words signaling the triumph of the new study of classical forensics. He is, in short, an *ardent* rhetorician, taking up the pose of Cicero's great orator in *De Oratore*: "It is the part of an orator, when advising on affairs of supreme importance, to unfold his opinion as a man having authority: his duty is to arouse a listless nation, and to curb its unbridled impetuosity. . . . Who more passionately than the orator can encourage to virtuous conduct, or more zealously [*ardentius*] than he reclaim from vicious causes?" (*De Oratore*, 2.8.35). He is aware that he is writing to the unconvinced, and yet he seeks their benevolence, makes them share in both his institutional experience (*our* QUARTERLY), and his fear. He comes to them with trepidation, someone "smitten hip and thigh," like some corporeally punished schoolboy ill fit with his "scribblings" and idolatry to pass before the judgment of readers. Such schoolboy posturing, too, is part and parcel of the essay's matter. Caplan does not take as his subject the work of those "high periods of Greece and Rome." He does not begin at the beginning. Instead, he looks at rhetoric in a period of decline. He looks at Roman imperial literature in its decadent age. And he looks not at the great but at the schoolboys, at texts written by and for the children of late imperial Rome.

By inaugurating his career with a piece on rhetoric in its "decadence," Caplan signals an important scholarly and pedagogical shift of emphasis. The study of rhetorical theory and practice will not be of the great exemplars of the art but of its daily teaching. As he states, the speech that he will study, as one of the "typical products of the activity of the schools, should be of special interest to teachers of Public Speaking." This period, he states, "is made particularly significant to us by the fact that the orators were professors of Rhetoric" (p. 42). We have left the world of philosophers and statesmen and reside throughout this essay at the desks of the classroom.

Caplan thus focuses on the Roman equivalent of academic study—an attempt to figure in the texts of the past the practices of an institutional present. He peppers his essay with affective references to classical and modern locales of authority. For example, the Late Empire is a time when "Senators still harangued and maintained the fiction of a Republic and the image of the old Constitution" (p. 43). This is no "Hyde Park" (p. 43). Professors live for classes and their students, not the public (hence the reference to Latro, who "when suddenly called from his class-room to appear in behalf of a relative, he retired in a funk. He could not endure the open sky" [p. 43]). There is the well-chosen quotation from Petronius, who inveighs against the teachers of rhetoric: "I believe college makes complete fools of our young men. . . . [Y]ou teachers, more than anyone else, have been the ruin of true eloquence" (pp. 44–45). There is the obligatory reference to the Gettysburg Address in discussing the purposes of classical oratory (p. 46). And there are the references, toward the essay's end, to issues in "literary criticism" and the notion of style as necessarily yoked together with content. Here, Caplan argues that the rhetoricians of the Late Empire offer us "eloquence empty of ideas" (p. 51). He notes that, while their Latin is grammatically correct and the diction finished, the works of the panegyrists are examples of mere mannerism, and their authors "specialists in externals" (pp. 50–51).

Caplan challenges the nineteenth-century traditions of that "oratorical culture" that found in rhetoric only the keys to ornament and polish. His imaginary antagonist is not the Midwestern speech scientist among the readership of the *Quarterly Journal of Speech* but rather his academic forbears at Cornell, Harvard, and other institutions of the previous century. The panegyrists of the Late Empire are, in these terms, to be compared with the popular orators of an earlier America. Yet such panegyric survives still, as Caplan avows in the final sentence of his essay: "It is necessary only to hear or read speeches delivered in our own country at inauguration ceremonies, the awarding of advanced degrees, and particularly the nomination of presidential candidates" (p. 52). Like Cicero's orator, whose "duty is to arouse a listless nation," or like Gildersleeve's philologist, whose task is to explain the past through an American present, Caplan establishes the historical background for a modern revival of rhetoric. He wishes to reunify form and content, to grant university teachers and their students public validation, and to claim a pedagogical calling that will remedy Petronius's claim that professors have been "the ruin of true eloquence."

If Caplan's essay inaugurated his professional career, his Loeb Library edition of the *Rhetorica ad Herennium*, published in 1954, capped it. In its historical introduction and its critical apparatus, we may find the fulfillment of these early claims for the professionalization of speech education in America.[69] But the Loeb *Rhetorica ad Herennium* forms also the endpoint of the Cornell school: a manual of public speaking, whose very title, *De Ratione Dicendi*, Caplan translates freely as "On the Theory of Public Speaking." As we open the pages of this text, we can look back to Adams's arguments for *ratio* and *oratoria*, to the debates on theory and practice embedded in the rhetorical traditions as a whole, and to the complex interrelationship of the public and the private that is central to American rhetorical life.

The introduction establishes the nature of the *ad Herennium* as a textbook of rhetorical practice by illustrating, through examples and comparisons, the fundamentally practical quality of the work. Caplan's opening paragraph states succinctly his impressions of the work: "It is a technical manual, systematic and formal in arrangement; its exposition is bald, but in greatest part clear and precise. Indeed the writer's specific aims are to achieve clarity and conciseness, and to complete the exposition of his subject with reasonable speed" (p. vii). From the start, Caplan identifies those ideals not only of rhetorical practice but of scholarly and pedagogical method that had motivated his own work from the first paper on the Latin panegyrics. There is the emphasis on clarity and concision, speed and directness, and the keeping of "practical needs always in view" by avoiding extraneous matter. The vices of the panegyrists (and, by implication, of the earlier American generations of rhetorical and oratorical pedagogics) are absent here. Caplan returns to this ideal, reminding his readers: "We must remark, too, in our author's case the thoroughly practical motives to which he constantly gives expression" (pp. xv–xvi)—again, a phrasing that, by now, should recall Gildersleeve's practical Americans. The *auctor ad Herennium*'s exposition is characterized throughout as systematic (see p. xx), and Caplan avers once more "his primary purpose—technical instruction in the art of rhetoric" (pp. xxiv). Throughout, the *auctor*'s "counsel is for moderation and the considerations of propriety" (p. xx).

That *auctor* was a creature of some question for the nineteenth century: was he Cicero, Cornificius, or some nameless student? Caplan clearly wants the author to be a student of public speaking, but by no means the slavish imitator that earlier scholars had created. He wants him indebted to tradition, but he also wants some originality in his organization of material and selection of examples. He also wants him to be a person and not simply a collection of dedicatory and epidiectic tropes. Caplan announces: "Who, finally, was the real author? We have no evidence to determine that question, and so must assign the work to an *auctor incertus*" (p. xiv). But lack of evidence does not impede the editor's judgment. Caplan wants to argue that the author speaks personally rather than merely rhetorically when he mentions his private life. "We have no reason to believe," he asserts, "that when he speaks of the pressure of private affairs and the demands of his occupations he is merely following a literary convention or indulging in rhetorical fiction" (p. xxii). His examples from political history suggest to Caplan an intimate knowledge and even some partisanship in contemporary affairs. And the author's many examples and patterns of organization also strongly imply, to the editor, an independence from his tutorial model. Note Caplan's own rhetoric here: "We go too far if we assume that the precepts all belong to the teacher and very little more than the Introductions and Conclusions to the author. And one wonders how the teacher would have regarded the release of his own work, even if only for private use, as the work of his pupil" (p. xxiii). Caplan concludes this discussion of the author by continuing this line of belief as argument: "It seems best, however, to grant the author some degree of literary individuality, and to regard his claim to the use of his 'own' examples as at least an honest one" (p. xxxi).

Caplan privileges the personal over the rhetorical, the original over the received, the specific over the general. He imagines a voice and a life for the author: a life modeled along the lines of a kind of advanced student of rhetoric, a kind of Cornell graduate student of the first century B.C., who has culled from his teachers the best in practical rhetoric and who has the maturity or independence of thought to organize and augment material with his own invention. The story told in Caplan's introduction is thus a story of education itself: a move from the imitative childishness of puerile excess to the grown-up security of restraint and decorum. His example of his author's literary criticism may now be reread as a way station on this allegory of maturity. "If we crowd these figures together," wrote the *auctor*, "we shall seem to be taking delight in childish style (*puerili elocutione*)." Such puerile elocution may, Caplan had admitted, be found in the book (pp. xxi–xxii). But, as he said, "not everything labeled as puerile by some critics justifies the label" (p. xxii). The search for what Caplan had signaled "manly independence of thought" (p. xxi) may well now be the critic's charge, as the *ad Herennium* becomes not just a model textbook but a key to growth, a story of a boy become a man.

To find this man, one must find a voice, and Caplan subtly translates the concluding gestures of the *ad Herennium* to present them as a string of first-person avowals in that voice. He creates not just the figure of transcriber or compiler but of narrator. The final paragraph of the work begins with a series of clauses stating what the text has done: *Demonstratum est; dictum est; traditum est; praeceptum est; demonstratum est* (4.56.59). All these third-person perfect indicative passives Caplan translates as first-person perfects: "I have shown; I have told; I have disclosed; I have taught; I have explained" (p. 411). We have, in Caplan's English, the articulations of an individual, one who appears to assert control over his material; one whose powers of systematic organization and clarity of delivery match the ideals that his work espoused.

At moments such as these, Caplan's author speaks in his own voice, and the scholarly goals of his introduction find their voice in the narrative ends of his translation. The repeated concerns with finding "individuality," maturity, and stylistic and organizational control come together at the book's close. So, too, the origins and audience of such an author find expression here. If, as Caplan had stated, "the treatise is . . . an image of school practice" (p. xvii), then the *auctor*, however *incertus*, is a product of the schools, and his treatise is a testimony to the place and purpose of rhetorical education in those schools. If it is a document of its times, it is as well a tract for Caplan's times: an affirmation of the ideals of expository writing and public speaking instruction of the first half of the twentieth century; a text for the Cornell group.

In the end, the Loeb edition of the *Rhetorica ad Herennium* is a textbook of rhetoric for the modern student. Caplan's systematic and clearly organized summary of its contents (with its lists and diagrams [pp. xlv–lviii]) makes the work immediately accessible to that student, and it shows precisely where in the text he or she may go to find the definition of a given trope or the examples of its use. To make his treatise readable and usable by the modern English-speaking student, Caplan favors the use of familiar English terms, even when they may not precisely translate the Latin originals of their Greek sources.

> Inasmuch as a like difficulty attends to the translation of his terms into English, I have thought it my duty to readers to use the terms most familiar to them; accordingly in rendering the names for the figures I have, abandoning strict consistency, used the English derivatives of the author's terms wherever possible, or the accepted English equivalents, and have employed terms of Greek origin where their use was indicated. (p. xxi)

On the one hand, Caplan writes out of "duty," presumably to those students who will wish a textbook for their own scholarly and practical use. But, on the other hand, he historicizes his own practice, offering in a long footnote an essay on the tradition of translating Latin rhetorical terms into English. Look at the scholarship deployed to illustrate a single word: "I follow the practice, perhaps begun by Thomas Wilson, *Arte of Rhetorique* (first ed. 1553), ed. G. H. Mair, Oxford, 1910, p. 89, of translating *constitutio* (or *status* [= stasis], the term used by Cicero, except in De Inv., and by most other rhetoricians) as 'Issue'" (pp. 32–33). And this is only the beginning. The Latin "*constitutio*" translates the Greek term "stasis." "Adumbrated in pre-Aristotelian rhetoric (where it was close to Attic procedure), as well as in Aristotle's Rhetoric, it was developed principally by Hermagoras" (p. 33). Caplan lists a range of sources: an American article in *Speech Monographs*, followed by German doctoral dissertations, articles, and encyclopedia entries, then a reference to "modern students of Roman Law," and then a directive to see yet another one of Caplan's notes, this one to 2.13.19. There, Caplan offers up a disquisition on the origins of "legal custom" (Latin "*iudicatum*," Greek συνηθεια), followed by another daunting bibliography of German, Italian, British, and American scholars (pp. 92–93).

These notes form a microcosm of the Loeb edition of the *Rhetorica ad Herennium*, of the project of the Cornell group, and of the history of the study of rhetoric in the modern world. They bring together scholarship published throughout the world. They juxtapose the learned German dissertation with *Speech Monographs*. They discuss the problem of *status* with reference to pre-Aristotelian traditions, as well as in the work of Aristotle, Hermagoras, Cicero, and Quintilian. They make the discussion relevant to the interest of modern students. Finally, by opening with reference to one of the first sustained and comprehensive treatments of rhetoric in English, Caplan grounds his own enterprise in a scholarly tradition five centuries old. It might be more than coincidence that the first dissertation on the history of rhetoric at Cornell was written in 1928 by Russell Wagner on "Thomas Wilson's 'Arte of Rhetorique'"—and thus Caplan's note hearkens back to the origins of advanced scholarship at Cornell.[70]

These footnotes use the occasion of an etymology to write a genealogy of scholarship. They place the Americans on a par with the Germans, locate a terminological problem in their English language heritage, make the ancient forensic relevant to the modern legal. They are, in short, the epitome of philological rhetoric—a bravura display of learning that reveals the Cornell professor's command of anything the German philologists (or any one else, for that matter) could serve up. If, in the end, there is an *auctor* to the *ad Herennium*, it is Harry Caplan himself: practical and systematic, pressing philological research into a pedagogical imperative, bringing earlier learning to bear on present teachings. And he remains a very American *auctor* at that.

The legacy of Harry Caplan and the Cornell group resides most obviously in those programs in rhetoric and composition that have stressed the classical tradition.[71] But there remains a broader debt in the discourses of late-twentieth-century literary theory. For it lies in the fascinations with the etymologies of tropes that theorists and rhetoricians share a common cause. Words such as "metathesis," or "metaphor," or "catachresis" (to take but the obvious examples) can refer, to the English-speaking student, only to one thing: to the rhetorical device. But once we translate these terms—expose their Greek etymologies, research their Latin equivalents, seek to come up with vernacular English versions—then they no longer pose a simple one-to-one correspondence between term and figure. Instead, they come to narrate stories of manipulation, tales of verbal twists and turns. This question of the figurality of figurative terminology forms the nexus of philology and rhetoric. It governs not just the tradition of a classicizing composition pedagogy but the debates of theory and, by implication, the contemporary study of literature itself.

The most creative response to this legacy of figuralization lies in the deconstructive strain of American literary theory. Derrida's fascination with the turns and figures of rhetorical ornament gave rise to a rhetoricizing or, perhaps more accurately, an allegorizing of rhetoric itself. Rhetorical figures became metaphors for social interaction and the construction of literary meaning. Irony, in particular, became a way of understanding language's relationship to the world and, as a consequence, of literary theory's place in aesthetic evaluation. It came to stand for the estrangement between signifier and thing signified. It embodied the fundamentally non-mimetic nature of linguistic representation. Language did not represent the experience; it represented language. A meditation on the history of irony (as in Paul de Man's "Rhetoric of Temporality") helped generate an awareness of the illusory nature of mimetic representation. Literary language, in this formulation, was, in some sense, always allegorical: not, however, in the sense that it was writing out extended narratives of coded meaning but rather in that it was always telling stories of its own attempts to make meaning. The allegory of literature was, in the terms of another of de Man's titular bequeathals, an allegory of reading.[72]

Theory, in this tradition, queried the very stability of language, be it the language of literature or that of criticism, and, in the process, it potentially undermined the practices of those who would attempt to deploy it. In contrast to the classical conception of rhetoric—that it is socially affirming, ethical in basis, persuasive in purpose, and disciplinarily unifying of the human constituents of *ratio* and *oratio*—the de Manian conception was precisely the opposite. *Allegories of Reading* addressed "the study of tropes and of figures (which is how the term *rhetoric* is used here, and not in the derived sense of comment or of eloquence or persuasion)."[73] By exposing the rhetoricality of all expression, theory of this kind undermined the stability of representation. De Man used Nietzsche's words to argue: "There is no difference between the correct rules of eloquence and the so-called rhetorical figures. Actually, all that is generally called eloquence is figural language. . . . Tropes are not something that can be added or subtracted from language at will; they are its truest nature."[74] And, as he summarized, "The first step of the Nietzschean deconstruction therefore reminds us . . . of the figurality of all language" (p. 111).

Rhetorical reading became a way of pointing out the figurality of all discourses.[75] It centered on locating moments in a text that did not so much affirm as disrupt meaning. Rhetoric was what reading revealed—a dialectic of contradictions, of which the writer may not even have been aware. One contrasting meaning "always lay hidden in the other," de Man wrote in "The Rhetoric of Blindness," "as the sun lies hidden within a shadow, or the truth within error." "Criticism is a metaphor for the act of reading," he noted there, and rhetorical tropes could hold within them the keys to the deconstruction of the narrative text.[76] "The Rhetoric of Temporality" begins with the announcement that "recent developments in criticism reveal the possibility of a rhetoric that would no longer be normative or descriptive but that would more or less openly raise the question of the intentionality of rhetorical figures."[77]

De Man's is a rhetorical philology. A trope's name contains within it a history of meaning or a narrative of estrangement—like the sun hiding within a shadow, or truth within error. But the real issue is the reverse. The etymology of tropes reveals a shadow in the sunlight, or an error in the truth. If "criticism is a metaphor for the act of reading," then, I posit, rhetoric is a metaphor for the act of writing. And this rhetorical turn—with its focus on the etymologies of tropes and the embedded narratives of figurality—is a profoundly philological one. "The turn to theory occurred as a return to philology," de Man wrote in the brief essay of that title, "to an examination of the structure of language prior to the meaning it produces."[78]

Perhaps the most ardent etymologist of the de Manian tradition working now is the Renaissance critic Patricia Parker. Throughout her work, error and etymology control the interpretations of the genre of romance, the ideologies of authorship, the claims of reading.[79] Word histories are never far from Parker's ambit. They become the narratives that often focus her attentions, the true narratives that may displace, or supplement, the literary texts that are the ostensible focus of her claims. Her little essay "Metaphor and Catachresis" is a tour de force of such rhetorical philology.[80] Here, Parker goes back to the etymologies of the rhetorical terms of her title: metaphor means exchange, a placing of one thing in stead of another; catachresis similarly refers to the transferring of terms from one place to another, but, unlike metaphor, it is presented in the rhetorical manuals as an improper transference. Thus Parker calls attention to the Latin word for catachresis, "*abusio*," and exposes it as something of an abuse of language. Catachresis becomes, for her, "a figure of 'abuse'" and thus the occasion for reflecting on the inherent abusiveness of all figurative language—a sense, in other words, that, behind all tropes, behind all expression, lies a defacement, a violence, an act of power.[81]

But behind metaphor and catachresis lies, too, the sense of transfer—what Parker calls a "temporal narrative" behind the *modus transferendi verbi*. Working from Cicero's *De Oratore*, she quotes the discussion about how metaphor "sprang from necessity to the pressure of poverty and deficiency, but it has been subsequently made popular by its agreeable and entertaining quality. For just as clothes were first invented to protect us against cold and afterwards began to be used for the sake of adornment and dignity as well, so the metaphorical employment of words was begun because of poverty, but was brought into common use for the sake of entertainment."[82] Parker finds a story embedded in this sense of transferal or transmission: a movement from something once before to now. "Metaphor," she notes, "*begins* in this little progress narrative *as* catachresis—as a transfer necessitated first by the lack of a sufficient supply of proper terms."[83] It then becomes, as she continues to read the ongoing discussion in *De Oratore*, a problem of control, a question of avoiding overuse or abuse. *Delectatio*, enjoyment, can become (in Parker's reading) *abusio*, not just abuse but now the Latin rhetorical term for the Greek *catachresis*. Parker sets out to expose "metaphor's potential for violence" (p. 67), a potential in line with the Derridean concern for the violence of the letter and the deconstructive commitment to the figurativity of all linguistic utterance.

But what this reading also offers is a narrative of progressive estrangement. The definition offered in *De Oratore* is what Parker calls "the historical narrative," and herein lies a story of civilization told as an allegory of figural language. "Metaphor," we must now remember, is our modern English word for what Cicero calls *modus transferendi verbi*. It exists in this text only in the language of the translator. It may be more familiar for the modern reader, but that familiarity is, in Parker's treatment, rendered an illusion. For, in essence, what Parker does is make metaphor the trope of the violence of the letter and the rhetoric of temporality. She compels her contemporary reader to look back over the seemingly transparent claims of translators such as Caplan to use familiar Anglicized terms and to recognize them as claims not for representation but estrangement. A word such as "metaphor" in English no longer signifies a rhetorical device; rather, it signifies only another string of signifiers—a concatenation of etymologically derived and linguistically translated terms that reveal all the terms of rhetoric to trope into their opposites. *Delectatio* is really *abusio*, pleasure really pain.

As de Man put it, "the one always lay hidden within the other, as the sun lay hidden within a shadow, or the truth within error." And this is how Parker reconceives of metaphor as a form of error. "A noun or verb," wrote Quintilian, in a passage Parker quotes, "is transferred from the place where it properly belongs to another" (p. 62). Words wander from their proper places, and this observations leads Parker to a reflection on the eighteenth-century reflection on the figurality of language. In a vast footnote on this link, she ranges from de Man to Fontannier, to Hugh Blair (who quotes Addison), and back to Cicero. Here is but a sampling.

> One way of approaching the link between eighteenth-century discussions of metaphor—with their delight in its controlled errancy and their concern with the less simply delightful wandering would be to note Blair's citation, in the midst of the discussion of figurative language as "an instrument of the most delicate and refined luxury . . . ," of Addison's passage on the advantages of being entertained with "pleasing shows and apparitions" . . . "In short, our souls are . . . delightfully lost, and bewildered in a pleasing delusion; and we walk about, like the enchanted hero of a romance . . . ." What is here cited by Blair as a masterful use of language . . . becomes in its context a pre-Romantic romance of figuration itself, a kind of darker stand-in for Cicero's description, . . . of metaphor as allowing one's thoughts to be "led to something else . . . without going astray" (*De Oratore* 3.39.160). (p. 221 n. 16)

This note's associations between metaphor and errancy recall Adams's sly remark on the etymology of error as "a wandering of the feet." But what it also recalls is the Caplanesque genealogy of terms, the way he (in his own great footnotes) writes a history of idiom, of scholarship, and of reading. For Parker, that history is all about the indeterminacies of the three: about the errancies behind an etymology, the wanderings of the reader's eye, the deep bewilderment (another word that echoes Adams) of scholarship. Such idioms are, as I noted at this chapter's opening, profoundly transformed in an American context—where the "errand into the wilderness" took on a resonant geography, where Adams, Webster, and anyone after them could always be aware of what was real behind what Henry Tuckerman would later call "the dense and tangled forest of words."

And yet, for Harry Caplan, this whole process is not about indeterminacy but about security. If we return to his great footnote, we see that it is about *status: constitutio*, from the Greek "stasis," all deriving from the root *sto*, to stand, to stick fast, to stop. This is the method of, in Caplan's words, "conjoining . . . two conflicting statements, thus forming the centre of the argument and determining the character of the case."[84] It is not about dialectic but about resolution; not about finding the shadow in the sun, the error in truth, but about resolving something. So, too, the rhetoric of Caplan's own discussion in his footnote is the rhetoric of resolution. A term and its history are in question; Caplan surveys the lexica, the scholarship, the contexts. As the *Rhetorica ad Herennium* put it in the passage that immediately precedes the one under discussion here, "The entire hope of victory and the entire method of persuasion rest on proof and refutation, for when we have submitted our arguments and destroyed those of the opposition, we have, of course, completely fulfilled the speaker's function" (1.10.18, p. 33). This is the very view of rhetoric that de Man—and, by implication, Parker—would refute. And yet it is the logic of the Cornell group, the logic of historical philology and stemmatic textual criticism, the logic of Caplan's footnote. It is the logic of being sure, of taking a stand, the logic behind the etymology of "status" and "*constitutio.*" It is the opposite of *errare.*

And no one took a stand against his errors better than Basil Lanneau Gildersleeve. The concluding lecture of his *Hellas and Hesperia* looked back over the fortunes of classical scholarship in this country. "Time was," he says, "when we of this region were more bent on asserting diversity than unity" (*HH*, p. 90). "But we are all Americans now," and, to this end, he quotes Walt Whitman, voice of Northern passion in the Civil War but, at the time these lectures were delivered (1909), recognized as "the true American poet and prophet; all the others mere echoes of European voices" (*HH*, p. 91). Gildersleeve quotes the passage from *Leaves of Grass* beginning:

> Dead poets, philosophers, priests,
> Martyrs, artists, inventors, governments long since,
> Language shapers on other shores, . . .
> I dare not proceed till I respectfully credit
> What you have left wafted hither.

And the passage concludes, with a line that Gildersleeve will poignantly repeat: "I stand in my place with my own day here." After the errors of this inquiry, the allures of figurality, Gildersleeve can affirm, "I stand in my place." Such is the etymology of "status" and the claim of Harry Caplan's inquiry. Such, too, can be the claim of any etymologist who, weary of wandering, wants something that reminds him or her of home.

> Now the difference between legend and history is in most cases easily perceived by a reasonably experienced reader. It is a difficult matter, requiring careful historical and philological training, to distinguish the true from the synthetic or the biased in a historical presentation; but it is easy to separate the historical from the legendary in general. . . . To write history is so difficult that most historians are forced to make concessions to the technique of legend.
> —Erich Auerbach, *Mimesis*

> Philology is the set of activities that concern themselves systematically with the human language, and in particular with works of art composed in language. . . . The need to constitute authentic texts manifests itself typically when a society becomes conscious of having achieved a high level of civilization, and desires to preserve from the ravages of time the works that constitute its spiritual patrimony.
> —Erich Auerbach, *Introduction aux études de la philologie romane*

CHAPTER FIVE
MAKING MIMESIS:
EXILE, ERRANCY, AND ERICH AUERBACH

Readers of Erich Auerbach's *Mimesis* will remember the first of these epigraphs as a moment in which history and legend fuse to mark the making of his book.[1] The famous story of Odysseus's scar has just been recollected, with its close attention to the detail of its characters and setting; and the story of the sacrifice of Isaac has been retold as a foil for the Homeric style, where the narratives of the Old Testament give us but little of the setting and the motivations of its actors. Auerbach, in his opening chapter, has been distinguishing between the legendary flavor of Homer and the historical feel of the Elohist, when he announces that such a distinction "can be easily perceived by a reasonably experienced reader" (p. 19). But what may not be so apparent, and what stands in the ellipses of my epigraph, is the history behind the making of *Mimesis* itself, and the ways in which that history has been transformed—by Auerbach, by later readers, and by the institutions of professional literary study—into a legend of the writer in exile, remembering the texts and contexts of a past. What interrupts the reading of Odysseus's scar, and what interrupts Auerbach's own career, is "the history which we ourselves are witnessing" (p. 19). "[A]nyone who, for example, evaluates the behavior of individual men and groups of men at the time of the rise of National Socialism in Germany, or the behavior of individual people and states before and during the last war, will feel how difficult it is to represent historical themes in general, and how unfit they are for legend" (pp. 19–20).[2] With the complexity of motives, the bluntness of propaganda, and the ambiguities of political discourse, a simple understanding of these public events becomes nearly unimaginable. No "careful historical and philological training" can distinguish true from false, *das Wahre vom Gefälschten*, in these matters. "To write history," he concludes, "is so difficult that most historians are forced to make concessions to the technique of legend" (p. 20).

Such moments in *Mimesis* contribute to our understanding of the place of exile in philology and, more pointedly, the place of Erich Auerbach in the constructions of the postwar émigré philologist. They share with the writings of his contemporaries Ernst Robert Curtius, Leo Spitzer, and Werner Jaeger—among many others—a recognition that the disciplines of historical philology and literary criticism are inseparably linked to national identity and personal displacement. As Maria-Rosa Menocal has argued in her *Shards of Love: Exile and the Origins of the Lyric*, the study of philology is born in exile. The political, institutional, and aesthetic criteria by which we select the objects and the methods of our inquiry are deeply implicated in the estrangement the philologist feels from the world of experience and the home of learning. And "no story is more famous," she avows, than that of Auerbach in Turkey, writing his *Mimesis*, putting his great book together without libraries or colleagues, the German-Jewish scholar of the Romance languages sitting "helpless at the edge of the desert."[3] This story separates him poignantly from his contemporaries. Though often grouped together as the great exponents of a German philological tradition, they had very different lives. Spitzer is today largely remembered for his impassioned, idiosyncratic teaching at Johns Hopkins (whose faculty he joined in 1936) and his acute application of techniques of *explication de texte* to medieval and Renaissance works. Curtius sat out the war in Switzerland and remains, except to specialists in *Romanistik*, the distant compiler of the topoi that fill *European Literature and the Latin Middle Ages*. Werner Jaeger went to Harvard in the mid-1930s and produced, in his enduring study of Greek educational identity, *Paideia*, as much a historical survey of a culture as a nostalgic blueprint for a university ideal. It is the personal, the self-reflective, in Auerbach that late-twentieth-century readers treasure, as if what marked the *magisterium* of his work was the very suffering that brought him from Marburg, to Istanbul, to Pennsylvania State, and, finally, to Yale, where he died as Sterling Professor of Romance Languages in 1957.[4]

The second epigraph is probably less well known to us.[5] The opening sentences to an introductory handbook of Romance philology, a handbook written originally for Auerbach's Turkish students, they seem, at first glance, to articulate the verities of a tradition rather than the idioms of an individual. Their definition of philology, the importance that they place on textual criticism, and their loose associations between method and cultural understanding would have been familiar to almost any European student at midcentury. With over a hundred years of institutional history behind them, Auerbach's opening lines affirm the centrality of philological investigation to recovering the character of high civilization and its origins.[6] They call to mind such affirmations of the social value of philology as those of Friedrich Diez in 1821 (that the serious study of literature "reveals utterly characteristic directions and tendencies in the mind of man");[7] of Charles Aubertin in 1874 ("L'histoire des origines de la langue est l'histoire même des origines de la nation");[8] and of the many late-nineteenth- and early-twentieth-century French and German attempts to locate the search for national identity in the curricula of language study.[9]

These two quotations, written most likely in the space of the same year, stand at the poles of Auerbach's career. They introduce my reassessment of his place in academic literary study, and they recall, too, the major themes of my own book. Both quotations center on the techniques of recovery; both juxtapose a potentially destructive time against the endurances of culture; and both valorize the power of the philological-historical to distinguish true from false, the originary from the secondary, the authentic from the ersatz. They stimulate our efforts to separate the historical from the legendary in the scholar's work and may become, for such a purpose, subjects of textual inquiry themselves.

Much recent work has focused on the national origins and ideological consequences of the development of European philology: on the tensions between French and German Romanists from the 1820s to World War I, on the agendas of post–World War II American New Criticism and of the German revival of the *Grundriß* project, and on the changing status of medieval studies in the canons of professional training.[10] The past ten years have witnessed something of an Auerbach revival and a renewed set of attempts to place him along the axes of these intellectual developments. The centennial of his birth in 1992 saw at least two major conferences and essay collections, while, more generally, the breakup of the theoretical hegemonies of the previous decades led many to look back—to rhetoric, philology, archival textual criticism—for direction.[11] Moreover, as the temperature of literature departments rose and fell throughout the 1990s, many searched for a moral center to the critical profession: a figure of unassailable impact and integrity.[12] Auerbach in Istanbul and, later, in America presents the figure of the writer in political withdrawal: a Dantesque figure for our time, an Ovid of midcentury, whose *Mimesis* was as *triste* as anything that could be found in the *Tristia*. But Istanbul has, in more recent years, conjured up the aura of orientalism, the European attempt to efface the other or, at the very least, to domesticate it.[13] And Auerbach's exile may not even be what he, or we, would like to believe. In the words of David Damrosch, "far more irrevocably wedded to his present age than he would wish to be, he lives in exile from the past, from the worlds of his beloved texts, which cannot finally provide an Olympian refuge from the dual tyrannies of time and of political pressures."[14]

Auerbach and his émigré contemporaries remain touchstones for the literary academic, and one could well imagine rewriting the history of recent literary criticism as a series of reactions to his work.[15] This task, at least in part, is my concluding purpose in this book: to trace the readings and misreadings that *Mimesis* both encodes and generates. But my goal, too, is to expose its politics of errancy, whether it be found in the techniques of editing a text or in the *Feingefühl* of selecting a passage for review and commentary. *Mimesis* remains a book of errors in all senses of the word. Yet it is, too, a study in synecdoche, of parts for wholes, and, as such, it illuminates the methods and the motives of the history of literary scholarship I have selectively traced here.

From its start, *Mimesis* is a book of exiles, an account of separations and *errores*, of parents and children, and of hoped-for returns home. The famous *Odyssey* chapter that opens the book has been read, taught, and criticized so often that it has attained a canonical status in the classroom almost comparable to the texts it studies.[16] But just what are the stories told here? There is the return of Odysseus and the sacrifice of Isaac. Behind them both, however, lies a similarity of theme and narrative that informs the whole volume.

Chapter 1 is unique in *Mimesis* in that it begins without a quoted text. Instead of a sample passage—selected, it always seems, almost at random, offered in the original language, occasionally noteworthy for its editorial cruces—Auerbach begins with paraphrase. He retells the account of Odysseus's return in book 19 of the *Odyssey* briefly, out of sequence, and wholly in German (there is not a single Greek word in the chapter, even in transliteration). In Auerbach's handling, this is a story totally in the vernacular. It replays all the "touching" (*ergreifenden*) domesticity of Euryclea's discovery of the scar. It focuses on everyday experiences: the activities, rituals, and moments that Homer and, by extension, Auerbach himself "scrupulously" narrate "in leisurely fashion" (*genau ausgeformt und mit Muße erzählt*). One could, in fact, go so far as to say that these opening pages are an essay in vernacularity itself—in the root meaning of the word, from the Latin "*verna*," a slave born in the master's household, hence "*vernaculus*," belonging to the household, domestic (p. 3; p. 7).[17]

At the most obvious level, this is an episode of homecoming. It introduces *Mimesis* explicitly as a book of exiles and returns, and the thematic resonances of the passage have long been noted by the book's readers. But what has not been noticed, perhaps because Auerbach himself subordinates it to the central narrative, is the backstory of Odysseus's scar. Auerbach defers his account of what Homer has done in this scene. In the *Odyssey*, the mention of the scar recalls the tale of young Odysseus's boar hunting during a visit to his grandfather, Autolycus. And there is, within this digression, another remembrance nested inside. For Autolycus had first seen Odysseus as a newborn, when he visited his daughter and was asked to name the child. "Lo, inasmuch as I am come hither as one that has been angered (οδυσσαμενοσ) with many, both men and women, over the fruitful earth, therefore let the name by which the child is named be Odysseus (Οδυσευσ, i.e., 'child of wrath')."[18] Only then does Homer tell the story of Odysseus's boar hunt (now, significantly, another return, this time to see his grandfather). The boy is hunting with Autolycus's sons when they see the animal.

> Then first of all Odysseus rushed on, holding his long spear on high in his stout hand, eager to smite him; but the boar was too quick for

him and struck him above the knee, charging upon him sideways, and with his tusk tore a long gash in the flesh, but did not reach the bone of the man. But Odysseus with sure aim smote him on the right shoulder, and clear through went the point of the bright spear, and the boar fell in the dust with a cry, and his life flew from him.

(19.447–54, 2:259)

I have labored over this passage to focus on what Auerbach elides: a story not of return but of rescue. The young Odysseus is spared from death no less than Isaac is in Genesis. And yet, here, it is Odysseus who becomes the killer, his arm raised with his sharp spear, whose hand is not stayed even in pain and who can thus deliver the sure, fatal stroke to the animal. The Greek boy seems eerily resonant with the Hebrew father, as Abraham will sacrifice a sheep instead of a son.

But even this biblical text is abbreviated in *Mimesis*. Auerbach relies on its familiarity ("everybody knows it" [p. 9]; "ein jeder kennt sie" [p. 13]); he tells us only the part of the story up to Abraham and Isaac's setting forth. "So they went both of them together," he quotes and leaves it at that. "Everything," he avows, "remains unexpressed" (p. 11; "Alles bleibt unausgesprochen" [p. 16]). And so it does for Auerbach himself. These elisions are central to the method of *Mimesis*. By relying on a common literate experience ("Readers will remember" the *Odyssey*, "Abraham gives the well-known answer" in Genesis), he can argue through implication. He counts on readers knowing what is really there, making the connections through only the most allusive, fragmentary hints.

For in his juxtaposing of these two texts, Auerbach now makes it possible to understand them both as tales of filial harm and salvation. The episodes both center on snatching a child from certain death. They encode stories of sacrifice, templates of ritual, against which all subsequent subjects in *Mimesis* will take their measure. If this book remains a collection of exiles and returnees, it is, too, a book of parents and their children, holding (if only barely) to the rituals of everyday, vernacular existence in a threatening world.

Take, for example, scenes of what we might call (giving it an anthropological flavor) ritual ingestion. How many fill the *Odyssey* and Genesis, and how many, too, fill *Mimesis*? There is Trimalchio's great feast (from Petronius and at the heart of chapter 2); the world in Pantagruel's mouth (from Rabelais, in chapter 11); the interrupted supper from

Manon Lescaut (chapter 16); the coffee chatter of *Luise Millerin* (chapter 17); the abbé's thrill at dining with the marquis from Stendahl's *Le rouge et le noir* (chapter 18). And, of course, there is that unforgettable repast, the apple eating of Adam and Eve (in the *Jeu d'Adam*, in chapter 7). Domestic servants abound, from Euryclea to Germinie Lacerteux. And so do families and their quarrels: the willfulness of young Odysseus, the obedience of Isaac, the errancy of Prince Hal, the "middle class tragedy" of *Luise Millerin*, the Ramsays of Virginia Woolf, the Prousts.

"And even if it isn't fine to-morrow, . . . it will be another day." How many times must such a sentence have been uttered? How many exiles, émigrés, or housebound readers far away from home (like Mrs. Ramsay herself) have marked out the passage of their days? This line opens the closing chapter of *Mimesis*, and it presages a poignant future for the writer looking for a reader. "Nothing now remains but to find him—to find the reader, that is," wrote Auerbach in the penultimate sentence of *Mimesis* (p. 577). Why the qualification, though? For whom else could we be looking? Chapter 20 asks these questions in a different way. It takes us back to Homer and the Bible, to the rituals of everyday domestic life, and to the threats and wonders that may shatter childhood and its ease.

As in his opening chapter, Auerbach here uses an analysis of narrative style to reflect on his own method. The central features of high modernism—its selection of the fragmentary portion, its assembly of ruins, its attention to "any random fragment plucked from the course of a life at any time" (p. 547; "dem beliebig Herausgegriffenen des Lebensverlaufs" [p. 488])—may all be thought of as both literary and critical devices. "It is possible to compare this technique of modern writers with that of certain modern philologists who hold that the interpretation of a few passages from *Hamlet*, *Phèdre*, or *Faust* can be made to yield more, and more decisive, information about Shakespeare, Racine, or Goethe and their times than would a systematic and chronological treatment of their lives and works. Indeed, the present book may be cited as an illustration" (p. 548). Much as Mrs. Ramsay had consoled her son—"Let's find another picture to cut out," she says at the end of Auerbach's selected passage—so Auerbach may console himself. But there is something very different about this passage and about its author. For what Auerbach has done is, in the end, locate the authority for his method not in a male but in a female voice. Virginia Woolf becomes the mother of philology—a brilliant recalibration of what Auerbach had elsewhere called the *patrimoine spirituel*—and the paternal relationships so central to *Mimesis*'s opening reframe themselves, at its close, as maternal ones. Rituals of family life hinge now not on hunting or on sacrifice but on artistic play. The journey to the lighthouse, deferred at this moment in Woolf's novel, finds itself replaced by cutting and by knitting. The explorations of great outside spaces will be halted; explorations of interior dimensions may begin.

There is a sense throughout this chapter that the paradigms of European literature that Auerbach has framed throughout his book—the sacrifice, the quest, the revel, the great sin, the social pressures of reform—close down. Fatherhood takes on a complex and muted cast. Mr. Ramsay himself is but a distant and dismissive figure, and, in the passage from Proust that Auerbach apposes to his Woolf, the father appears downright bizarre: "He was still confronting us, an immense figure in his white nightshirt, crowned with the pink and violet scarf of Indian cashmere in which, since he had begun to suffer from neuralgia, he used to tie up his head, standing like Abraham in the engraving after Benozzo Gozzoli which M. Swann had given me, telling Hagar that she must tear herself away from Isaac" (pp. 543–44). I should not say "bizarre" but "bazaar." Proust's father here is something out of a bazaar: an orientalized apparition, a figure not really from life but art, a living presentation of a fantasy about the Bible. For this is the scene, of course, when Abraham reenters *Mimesis*: when the first father of the Jews comes back, from chapter 1, to save his son. But, now, it is a story not of testing faith but of dismissing otherness. Hagar, the emblem of the "oriental," of the Arab, must leave.

And yet Auerbach is wrong. As David Damrosch has perceptively observed, the correct text from Proust's novel has the final phrase as, "telling *Sarah* that she must tear herself away from Isaac."[19] Willard Trask simply alters the Moncrieff translation to conform to Auerbach's misquotation, and, as Damrosch notes, the error has never been corrected. He characterizes the mistake as follows: "This is, however, a resonant slippage of transcription or of memory. Auerbach has not only a secret hope but also a secret fear: that he may most resemble Abraham's other 'first born' son, Ishmael, reprieved from death only to be sent with Hagar into a permanent exile in the wilderness" (p. 115). I agree with Damrosch that this is a resonant mistake, but I locate it elsewhere. The father-son relationship of chapter 1 is now transformed, in chapter 20, into a mother-son one. And European literature becomes refracted through the lens of orientalism. It is as if Auerbach himself, finding himself in the land of Hagar, must affirm his Europeanness—his own identity as Jew, as father, as master of the vernacular (with Hagar now standing, unlike old Euryclea, as the *verna* who must be thrown out). Proust's passage, in this mistranscription (or misremembrance) stands as emblem of the oriental. With the father done up like some potentate—with the Indian cashmere, itself a word coming from Kashmir—Auerbach can confront again the ways in which the oriental may intrude itself even into the most apparently straightforward "European" literary texts. Or, perhaps, a more pointed way of putting it is to say that to read Proust in Istanbul is to find Hagar in it. As Edward Said (who, as far as I can tell, does not discuss this passage) puts it, *Mimesis* "owed its existence to the very fact of Oriental, non-Occidental exile."[20] And as Aamir Mufti summarizes, working from Said's reading of Auerbach, "A major impulse behind the critique of Orientalism is therefore the possibility, the danger, that Orientalist descriptions take hold and repeat themselves in the very societies that they take as their objects."[21] What I would argue is that Hagar, as the emblem of that orientalism, takes hold of this European text; that she becomes, too, an emblem of Auerbach's Oriental exile. Her erroneous, yet powerfully meaningful, presence in this quotation participates in the larger set of challenges, inversions, and paradoxes that close *Mimesis* (and to which I will return at my chapter's close).

Mimesis is a book, then, of familiarities upended; of misquotations; of parts ripped from wholes and made to stand for great traditions; of small boys who, whether they be snatched from death or deprived of a day trip or a kiss, will go on to be writers and readers. "Now nothing remains but to find him." But that "him" is not the reader but the author. Nothing remains but to find myself, to recall the child that must be somewhere hiding in the man, to linger on the memory of a mother. And maybe, too, the answer to that question is not him at all, but her. The mothers are more powerful in chapter 20 than the fathers, far more central to the rites and rituals of everyday experience. "The ends the narrator has in mind," writes Auerbach of Proust, but I think no less of himself, "are not to be seen in them" (that is, the narrative's surfaces). "The way in which the father's death is brought up in the passage cited above—incidentally, allusively, and in anticipation—offers a good example" (p. 547). As Auerbach had put it in his first chapter, "Everything remains unexpressed."

The unexpressed narrative of *Mimesis* is the threat to family security. The paradox of philological inquiry, then, lies in its claim to rescue a *patrimoine spirituel* while at the same time exposing the underminings of that patrimony. What is the legacy that it bequeaths? What happens when the structures of paternity become the models of an intellectual inheritance? If *Mimesis* is framed, then, by tales of parents and children, of removal and return (if only, as in Proust's case, a return by means of memory), it has at its center a tale of our first parents and the original exile. Chapter 7, "Adam and Eve," has many purposes: an education in the arts of scholarly edition, an allegory of collaboration, a plea for the constructive ends of national philology. But much of this is "unexpressed," riding below the surface narrative in Auerbach's critical rhetoric. And much of this, too—the political subtext of this and other chapters of the book—had been effaced by Auerbach's first critics. In what follows, I use Auerbach's own devices of figural interpretation on his own text, seeking to expose a political allegory of philology—to speak what had remained, as he would put it, *unausgesprochen*.

> *I had to dispense with almost all periodicals, with almost all the more recent investigations, and in some cases with reliable critical editions of my texts.*
> —Erich Auerbach, *Mimesis*

"Adam and Eve" begins by trying to establish a text.[22] The opening quotation for this chapter—the dialogue in which Adam and Eve first quarrel, then debate, and then fall—comes from a play "extant in a single manuscript" (pp. 145–46). Of the little that survives of the vernacular, liturgically oriented drama, the play that Auerbach calls the *Mystère d'Adam* is "one of the oldest specimens" (p. 146).[23] Unique and originary, marking both the starting point of a distinctive genre and of a vernacular literary history, the play's text stands here at the opening of "Adam and Eve" in ways far different from the quotations that begin *Mimesis*'s other chapters. It appears not as some randomly selected, exemplary section of a larger work; nor is it one of those "few passages" that, in the phrasing of the book's close, "can be made to yield more, and more decisive, information about [authors] and their times than would a systematic and chronological treatment of their lives and works"

(p. 548). This is a passage carefully selected for its individualities and not its commonplaces. It tells a story of a set of firsts: the first human communication, first sin, first desire, and first text of a tradition that articulates the sublime in colloquial form. It is a story of a loss; yet, in the larger context of *Mimesis*, it provides the occasion for recovery. This passage from the *Mystère d'Adam* enables Auerbach to deploy those few resources of *Zeitschriften* and *Untersuchungen* in his Turkish exile. It enables him to use the techniques of philology to re-create "reliable critical editions" of his texts and, in the process, to restore methodological control over the study of the European Middle Ages.

Because the *Mystère d'Adam* and its manuscript encompass the discussion of first things, Auerbach seems anxious from the start to find its correct and originary form. Textual and literary criticism intertwine themselves here as in no other chapter of *Mimesis*, for the crux of Auerbach's interpretation turns on the correct edition of the manuscript. Adam and Eve speak in what Auerbach defines as the familiar idioms of French life. The first man "calls his wife to account as a French farmer or burgher might have done when, upon returning home, he saw something he did not like," while the first woman responds with "the sort of question which has been asked a thousand times in similar situations by naive, impetuous people who are governed by their instincts: 'How do you know?'" (p. 147). The correct assignment of the dialogue is central to Auerbach's reading, not so much because it governs the play's action but because it helps articulate its characters. The opening paragraphs of the chapter have, in fact, already sketched out the broad contours of those characters: Adam, good, noble, a representative of the French citizenry; Eve, intuitive, childish, even clumsy in her wiles. The text of the *Mystère*—garbled by medieval scribe and confused by modern editor— must be brought into line with the essentials of these characters, their idiom, their motivations, and their sensibilities.

In his *Introduction aux études de philologie romane*, Auerbach sets out the methods of the editor, delineating the procedures for establishing a text beset by problems in transmission.

> As for lacunae and passages that are irreparably corrupt, he [the editor] can try to reconstruct the text by making conjectures, that is, by forming his own hypothesis about the original form of the passage in question; of course, he must indicate, in this case, that he is

making his own reconstruction of the text, and he must also record the conjectures, if there are any, that others have made about the same passage. One sees that the critical edition is, in general, easier to do if there exist few manuscripts or only a single manuscript; in this last case, one only has to have it published, with scrupulous accuracy, and to record any conjectures, if there should be any.[24]

This moment in the *Mystère d'Adam* offers a test case for this advice. The manuscript is, as Auerbach states, "somewhat confused" (p. 148; "ein wenig in Unordnung" [p. 145]). His goal will be to restore "the original form of the passage in question," a task seemingly "easy" when faced with this "unique manuscript." But there is little that is "easy" about the editing of this text. The distributions of these lines has been confused by one S. Etienne who, in a note published in *Romania* in 1922, proposed a new reading of the lines.[25]

> *Adam:* Ne creire ja le traitor!
>   Il est traitre, bien le sai.
> *Eva:* Et tu coment?
> *Adam:* Car l'esaiai!
> *Eva:* De ço que chalt me del veer?
>   Il te fera changer saver.
> *Adam:* Nel fera pas, car nel crerai
>   De nule rien tant que l'asai.
>   Nel laisser mais . . .
>   (280–87 of Auerbach's edition, p. 143)

> *Adam:* Ne creire ja le traitor!
>   Il est traitre.
> *Eva:* Bien le sai.
> *Adam:* Et tu coment?
> *Eva:* Car le'asaiai.
>   De ço que chalt me del veer?
> *Adam:* Il te ferra changer saver.
> *Eva:* Nel fera pas, car nel crerai
>   De nule rien tant que l'asai.
> *Adam:* Nel laisser mais . . .
>   (280–87 of Etienne's edition, p. 148)

This is, to Auerbach, clearly no "reconstruction of the text" but a complete misunderstanding; from a manuscript only "somewhat confused," Etienne constructs a reading now "completely confused" (*völlig durcheinandergemischt*). The problem with the manuscript lay in the assignation of the parts, signaled by the scribe with a capital *A* and *E* for the respective speakers. Now, in Etienne's note, this particular passage "ont embarrassé la critique." It is "très curieux," presenting a problem in what Etienne calls the psychological continuity of the speakers.[26] What seems clear to him is that the scribe has mangled the assignment of the lines, shifting radically the tone of Adam and Eve. Etienne's goal, therefore, is to rescue the text from its copyist's mistakes; in Auerbach's terms, defined in the first page of the *Introduction aux études de philologie romane*, "to preserve them not only from oblivion, but also from the changes, mutilations, and additions that necessarily result from popular consumption or the negligence of copyists."[27]

For Auerbach, however, there is no "negligence of copyists" in the text of the *Mystère d'Adam*. Rather, it is Etienne who misconstrues both the characters and the themes of the drama. Eve, in Etienne's edition, is far too knowing for Auerbach, far too skillful and self-assured. The emendation presents a dynamic of seduction and control, where the serpent's intercession simply augments Eve's advance. To Auerbach, though, it is the serpent who masterminds the Fall. Eve is clumsy (*ungeschikt*), "for without the Devil's special help she is but a weak—though curious and hence sinful—creature, far inferior to her husband and clearly guided by him" (p. 149). Adam, the good French citizen ("ein braver Mann, ein französischer Bürger oder Bauer" [p. 147]) must be approached "where he is weak," must be confused into compliance. After the devil's intercession, Eve can take control; only after taking counsel from the serpent can she master the situation. "The Devil has taught her how to get the better of her man; he has showed her where her strength is greater than his: in unconsidered action, in her lack of any innate moral sense, so that she transgresses the restriction with the foolhardiness of a child as soon as the man loses his hold (*sa discipline*) upon her" (pp. 150–51). Eve's character, for Auerbach, remains stable, even though her actions shift in form and direction. Before and after her encounter with the serpent, she is childish, impetuous. Her earlier question was akin to that of "kindlichen, sprunghaften, instinktgebundenen Menschen"; here she has the "Tollkühnheit des Unmündigen," the rashness of the underaged. By contrast, Adam is always adult, always the head of the household. His fall, in these terms, is the fall of the grown-up trapped by games of the child. The pathos of his situation lies in this vision of a "poor confused, uprooted Adam" with whom Eve plays (*spielt*). She eats, as if to goad him into playing—"und dann ist es geschehen," and then all is over and the game is won (p. 151; p. 148).

Auerbach offers this analysis as a case study of the way in which the Christian drama of redemption gives voice to sublime ideas in simple form. The juxtaposings of the learned and the popular, the Latin and the Old French, illustrate how vernacular literary experience becomes the vehicle for moral truth. The profundity of the Fall resounds in a scene of "everyday reality," a dialogue "in simple, low style." Its pathos and its power look back to those moments in the *sermo humilis* of Augustine while they anticipate the Tuscan idioms of Dante. The possibilities for figural interpretation—here, as in nearly all the medieval texts Auerbach handles—lie precisely in this nexus of the high and low. God, the *figura* of the *Mystère d'Adam*, is both judge and savior, legal officer and spiritual father. He embodies the capacity of medieval literature to use historical or biblical personae to prefigure spiritual forms while holding both distinct as historical realities. The simple surfaces of medieval Christian drama simultaneously shadow and reveal the underlying patterns of Creation, Incarnation, Passion, and Last Judgment that define what Auerbach identifies as "the very truth of the figural structure of universal history" (p. 158).

> The everyday and real is thus an essential element of medieval Christian art and especially of the Christian drama. In contrast to the feudal literature of the courtly romance, which leads away from the reality of the life of its class into a world of heroic fable and adventure [*Sage und . . . Abenteuer*], here there is a movement in the opposite direction, from distant legend and its figural interpretation into everyday contemporary reality [*aus der fernen Legende und ihrer figürlichen Ausdeutung in die alltäglich-zeitgenössische*].
>
> (p. 159; p. 155)

But what precisely is this everyday contemporary reality for Auerbach? As he reminds us at the close of *Mimesis*, it is a scholar's life without the tools of scholarship: the journals, studies, and editions of the philological profession. As he announces at the opening, it is an exile's life without a nation, a moment when political and military action so challenges relations between truth and falsehood that "most historians are forced to make concessions to the techniques of legend" (*Konzessionen an die Sagentechnik zu machen*).

These similarities of phrasing blur the line between the philological and the political. Read in tandem, they point toward the construction of a scholarly *figura* of their own, a recognition that debates on the establishment of texts may adumbrate the arguments of nations. The high and low are not just styles of literature but styles of scholarship as well. The place of the sublime in the colloquial becomes an issue not just for the story of the Fall but for the narrative of its edition. To paraphrase the reading of the drama, we might say that "Adam and Eve" moves from distant readings and their scholarly interpretations into the language of everyday contemporary reality.

Throughout the chapter, technical analyses are couched in the colloquial expressions of feeling. Arrestingly informal, the conversational gambit that opens the discussion of the play disarms the reader: "Now let us examine" (p. 147). But we are really asked, in Auerbach's "Betrachten wir nun" (p. 144), to reflect and meditate, to move in that realm of impression and response that early German reviewers of *Mimesis* found characteristic of its *Feingefühl*, its almost belletristic sensitivity. Auerbach asks us to share his imagination of the everyday. The ordinariness of his French Adam is translated into language full of idiom and commonplace. Eve's question, we are told, is asked a thousand times. We are, in his translations and his paraphrases, on familiar turf here, much as we are in Auerbach's own analysis. "I find this impossible" (p. 148; "Mir scheint das unmöglich" [p. 145]), he rejoinds to Etienne's emendation. Exclamations, rhetorical questions, appeals to common sense—these are the argumentative devices of this scholar. "I know from experience": this might as well be Auerbach's as well as Adam's line. Indeed, it might as well be that of the reader of *Mimesis*, for what the scholar is relying on here is not so much a refined ability with ancient languages but simple clear-headed observation. Experience is what is at the heart of "Adam and Eve," an experience of how people react, of how men speak to women, and of how the stories from the past can resonate with present lives. Eve is, after the serpent's tuition, "Herrin der Lage" (p. 147), idiomatically master of the situation. She is "to use the language of sport . . . in great form" (p. 150; "wie man in der Sportsprache sagt, in großer Form," [p. 148]), and, as she plays (*spielt*) with her confused husband, we can see the transformation not only of the Fall into a game but of the discipline of textual edition into sportsmanship.

For it is Auerbach himself who is *in großer Form* here, Auerbach who deploys all the clichés of *his* everyday reality to offer up a *sermo humilis* of philological control whose simple, low style may conceal the subtleties of criticism. The quarrel with Etienne replays the quarrel of his Eve and Adam: a quarrel about what we know, about the control of *sa discipline*, about what might be thought of as the spiritual patrimony of high civilization. There is an allegory to the philological. Textual recovery becomes a kind of restitution, and these pages in *Mimesis* work out, in practical form, the directives of the *Introduction aux études de philologie romane*. Philology saves texts not only from oblivion but from the changes, mutilations, and additions that popular usage or the carelessness of copyists necessarily brings to them. The emendation of Etienne, and its acceptance and reprinting in the published text of Chamard, presents a fallen text to Auerbach. Its misassignments of the dialogue place Eve over her husband, rewrite, in effect, the challenge of serpentine guile in the subversions of the first couple. Eve may play here, may be in the fine form of the competitor, may be the master of the situation, yet it must remain for Auerbach to show *his* form, to reaffirm the competitive edge of textual criticism, to become the master of the interpretive situation. Auerbach, in short, replays a competition between French and German critics and philologists charged with the politics of the academy.

The story of Romance philology is a distinctively German story, as the discipline arose "in a period in which German intellectuals were accustomed to taking the French to task as effete (*Welsche*)."[28] The origins of *Romanistik* worked in tandem with the origins of European nation states, and a good deal of the institutional support for literary studies hinged on the recovery of a cultural patrimony to the emerging political entities. The character of literature and the character of a people came to stand as elements in an equation whose solution was a national identity conceived through educational structures. Philology, to paraphrase von Clausewitz, became a form of politics by other means; indeed, it could become a form of war by other means. The French responses to the so-called German science often couched themselves in military terms. Leon Gautier could write of his defeated countrymen in 1870: "We find before us a nation which makes war scientifically.... For the Prussian fights in the same way he criticizes a text, with the same precision and method."[29] And in 1913 Henry Massis could complain: "[T]here is a clear, logical link between our system of classical studies and the capitulation of Metz, as, of course, between the methodology of German universities and the invasion of Paris."[30] The rise of chairs of literature in France, the establishment of journals dedicated to medieval culture (*Romania* being among the first), all contributed to what Gaston Paris could think of as a medieval literature emanating from French soil: *plantes indigènes*.[31]

What was Auerbach to make of all this? He had been compelled, as a Jew, to leave his appointment at Marburg, the very university town where, Gautier had complained nearly seventy years before, "there were more Germans working on the chanson de geste than were French scholars in all of France."[32] For Auerbach, the anxieties of exile go beyond the mere lament for journals, up-to-date investigations, and reliable editions. They embrace something of the taint of having been a part of the ongoing war with France and French philology. Thus the quarrel with Etienne, on the surface, seems to recapitulate these national philology wars, seems to revile the scholar in *Romania* for constructing an interpretation of the *Mystère d'Adam* that is *Welsche*, even feminized, in its imaginations of a controlled and controlling Eve. But only on the surface. Rather than reinvest in the rhetoric of military conquest, Auerbach recasts his quarrel with philology and, in turn, his reading of the play as a story of collaboration. In reading his analysis of Eve, we find not the "invasion of Paris" but the infiltration of the French countryside. We find her assault on her husband—called, almost pathetically now, "ein braver Mann, ein französischer Bürger oder Bauer"—worked not by the machinery of all-out war but in the machinations of betrayal.

Eve's claims, in her discussion with her husband, always rely on appeals to the here and now. She wishes for their betterment, speaks of experience in its most commonplace terms, and queries Adam on his understanding of the hard facts of life. Hers is the language of betrayal, and much of Auerbach's discussion hinges on Eve's failure to appreciate the line between her realistic questioning and her real betrayal. "*Verrat*," "*Verräter*," and "*verraten*": these are the words that predominate in Auerbach's German. For Adam himself, the idiom is always that of being led astray: "*verführen*" is the operational verb, as Satan becomes the *Verführer* of the cause. The heart of Auerbach's objection to Etienne's reading is that Eve cannot be the "extremely skillful and diplomatic person" generated by his emendation. Diplomacy is far from Auerbach's concerns here. Eve's discussions with the serpent, and her temptation of Adam, do not go on in the realm of skill or political savvy. They transpire in the worlds of instinct, of impression, and of a blithe unawareness of the historical (if not the spiritual) consequences of her acts.

The picture of the Fall drawn here fits neatly in the terms of another, exiled essayist of collaboration. In his "Qu'est-ce qu'un collaborateur?" published first in New York in August 1945, Jean-Paul Sartre defines the logic of collaboration as the logic of realism.[33] Sartre's paradigmatic collaborator succumbs to the "tentations de la defait," the temptations not just of defeat but of defeatism. What he identifies as the "réalisme" of collaborationist thought devolves to a sense of the fait accompli, a sense that what is about to happen has already happened. "Réalisme," he writes, is the "refus de l'universel et de la loi" (p. 60). It signals a confusion between judgment and experience. Instead of judging facts in the light of the law, the realist collaborator judges the law in the light of facts. He evidences an odd sort of passivity; indeed, he is not necessarily a *he* at all. There is a certain "féminité" about collaboration, not simply a docility in the face of facts but a participation in the subversion of natural laws and hierarchies. Femininity might be thought of here as a figure for the fait accompli itself, and this precisely is how Auerbach defines the serpent's swaying of Eve in her Edenic collaboration. His counsel to the woman "upsets the order of things established by God, . . . makes the woman the man's master, and so leads both to ruin." He continues: "The serpent accomplishes this by advising Eve to break off the theoretical discussion [of sin and treason] and to confront Adam with a wholly unexpected *fait accompli*." Adam's knowledge of the law, his sense of right now inextricably a part of his condition as a good Frenchman, finds its subversions in the claims of Eve. "Manjue, Adam," eat Adam, she implores, until she eats the fruit herself "and it is all over" (p. 149).[34]

Auerbach tells the story of the Fall as the figural narrative of collaboration for specific pedagogical as well as political goals. It is not so much that he wishes to condemn Eve as much as he wants to save Adam. Again and again, the character of Adam is affirmed as good, as noble, and as French. This sense of character is what bridges the political and the philological. Etienne's misunderstanding of the characters of the *Mystère* now may be seen as standing for that larger misinterpretation of the French themselves and of the national characters of all the European peoples. What is "völlig durcheinandergemischt," completely confused, is the notion of responsibility in the face of political challenge. How do we evaluate, as Auerbach had put it in "Odysseus's Scar," "the behavior of individual men and groups of men at the time of the rise of National Socialism in Germany" (p. 19)? To whom do we assign blame? What is the relationship between the national character and the individuals who live and act within, and sometimes for, those nations?

Such questions find their answers in the course of Auerbach's whole chapter, a sequence of brief assessments and long quotations designed to illustrate the humble and sublime in the religious literatures of the thirteenth century. From the *Mystère d'Adam*, we traverse the works of Bernard of Clairvaux, St. Francis of Assisi, and a range of early French and Italian dramas. Unlike the other chapters of *Mimesis*, in which ancillary texts appear as foils for the declared subject—the Old Testament to Homer, Proust to Virginia Woolf—here, we seem to lose sight of the focus. The reader moves through a variety of European Latin and vernacular texts, from anonymous plays in unique manuscripts to named, canonical authors writing at their most authoritative. What remains a constant in this panoply is the editor. Each text, no matter how exemplary or marginal, receives its full citation. Editors are acknowledged: Förster-Koschwitz, Ferdinand Brunot, H. Boehmer, P. Eduardus Alenconiensis, E. Monaci. The volumes build, each with their comprehensive titles of the past half-century of learning: *Übungsbuch, Histoire, Analekten, Crestomazia*. German, French, Latin, and Italian stand side by side, as Auerbach re-creates on these pages the European resources he had abandoned. Now, in this chapter and only in this chapter, we get the range of *Zeitschriften, Untersuchungen,* and *zuverlässige-kritische Ausgabe* whose loss he had lamented at *Mimesis*'s end.

"Adam and Eve" recites a literary history not in the narratives of the textbook but in the selections of the anthology. It compiles a chrestomathy in miniature, a selection whose illustrative texts may complement the story told in the *Introduction aux études de philologie romane*. As in that work, the telos of "Adam and Eve" is the restoration of a *patrimoine spirituel* for high civilization, or, as Auerbach puts it in the final paragraph of the chapter, "the character of the people" (p. 173; "das

Charakter des Volkes" [p. 168]). "Adam and Eve" thus answers questions about national character and individual motivation not by meditating on politics but by doing philology. By offering a miniature anthology of European texts, it recovers and sets out in clear order a moral conscience for a medieval and a modern Europe. By locating "das Charakter des Volkes" in the idioms of the vernacular, it illustrates the power of philology to find the ethic that inheres in nations. And, finally, by couching this discussion in the old debates between the national philologies, it realigns relations between literary origins and political types. Auerbach does more than seek to reclaim Romance philology from the French; he seeks to reclaim it from the Germans. He seeks a politically pacifist philology, one that restores the possibilities of language study and literary criticism to a humanist agenda. He is not depoliticizing scholarship, as later critics hoped to do. Rather, he repoliticizes it. The allegory of collaboration behind the *Mystère d'Adam* and its interpretation, by the chapter's end, takes as its moral the belief in the inherent goodness of the European peoples. We need not blame the good French like Adam, only the childish, instinct-governed, impetuous French like Eve, who would succumb to the temptations of a satanic *Verführer*.

"Sed inimici hominis domestici eius," but a man's enemies are the men of his own house. These are Bernard of Clairvaux's words, quoted in this chapter, as a guide against "the prickings of temptation" (p. 163).[35] And when St. Francis of Assisi speaks, he gives voice to the very theme and method of the whole of Auerbach's enterprise. Developing the observation that the bulk of the saint's sentences, in one of his letters to Brother Leo, all begin with *et*, Auerbach notes (speaking as much, perhaps, for himself as for Francis): "But the person who writes these hurried lines is obviously so inspired by his theme, it fills him so completely, and the desire to communicate himself and to be understood is so overwhelming, that parataxis becomes a weapon of eloquence [*zu einer Waffe der Beredsamkeit wird*]" (p. 166; p. 162). "Adam and Eve" may well be seen as something of an armory of those weapons of eloquence, an education in the powers of philology both to read and write figurally. It teaches us that the political occasions of linguistic study can, in themselves, come to be the subject of scholarly erudition. It teaches, too, that allegory may become a mode of writing far more historical than history itself, for to find the historical resonance of "Adam and Eve"—to discern its political subtext—we need to read the chapter allegorically, as if it were itself a text in need of figural interpretation.

This allegorico-political *Mimesis* I have outlined seems far from the version of the book imagined by its early readers. The vision painted of Auerbach in the legends of the European and American academy is of a scholar almost willfully detached from social activism. The various interpretations advocated for the origins of Auerbach's projects—their Hegelianism, their Viconianism, their commitments to a humanist philology—are, in their own way, curiously removed from the history of German university life between the world wars.[36] And, to a certain extent, the criticisms of *Mimesis*'s reception in America after the war, and of its embrace by the formalist New Critics, hinge on the criticism of the work itself: its lack of a self-conscious methodology, its apparent garbling of the theoretical and the historical.[37] This apprehension of the book is due largely to its first reviews by German and American readers. As Paul Bové has argued, the original reviews in American journals were by German émigrés who, apparently unfamiliar with Auerbach's work on Dante and figuralism, considered *Mimesis* an idiosyncratic collection of essays without guiding principles of method or style (pp. 96–113).[38] The historical moment of its making, and its thematic and ideological consequences for the book, were lost on (or ignored by) early readers, who saw Auerbach's exile more as impediment than challenge to his project.[39] To Helmut Hatzfeld, who wrote the first American review in 1949, "The book was doomed to remain eclectic because of the working conditions of the author in Istanbul."[40] And, to the audiences who heard him in the first Princeton Seminar in Literary Criticism (later to be called the Gauss Seminars), in the fall of 1949, Auerbach's personal experience was almost crassly heroic. "A Jew, an *émigré* from Germany, for years homeless, putting his big book together in Istanbul without benefit of the great libraries he longed for, Auerbach had faced with his flesh and blood the reality of evil force; the extremity of Pascal's thought [the subject of the first seminar] answered, for him, an extremity of experience."[41]

These two sides to the book's early reception—the one flat, the other romantic—share nonetheless a predilection for effacing the political subtext to Auerbach's reflections. The Turkish exile is externalized, made either a problem in research or a badge of honor, yet nowhere relocated in the critic's narratives.[42] This depoliticizing of *Mimesis* is in the interest of the institutions of postwar academic criticism. To find its origins, we need to turn not to the critic's early reception in America but to the responses of Auerbach's German contemporaries in the first years after the war. The second number of the 1948 volume of *Romanische Forschungen*—perhaps the premier organ of German *Romanistik*—opens with a long review essay by Gerhard Hess of Heidelberg, "Mimesis: Zu Erich Auerbachs Geschichte des abendländischen Realismus" (pp. 173–211); the volume's third number closes with a brief notice of the *Introduction aux études de philologie romane* by Peter M. Schon of Mainz. Sandwiched between them is a full review by Auerbach himself of Leo Spitzer's *Essays in Historical Semantics* and his *Linguistics and Literary History*. This volume of the journal represents Auerbach's postwar debut in the media of German scholarship: *Mimesis* had appeared, in Bern, in 1946, and, with the exception of a piece in *Speculum* of that year, all Auerbach's other publications from the end of the war until the Spitzer review appeared in Turkish volumes.[43] To call it a debut, though, or even a reemergence would be a misnomer, for the overall impression of these contributions to *Romanische Forschungen* is that, quite simply, there was nothing from which to emerge.

Hess's is certainly the most positive of the early reviews (it is certainly the longest), and it appears from Auerbach's "Epilegomena zu *Mimesis*" of 1953 that he did not consider it one of the negative assessments full of "Mißverständnisse" and in need of rebuttal.[44] What makes this review distinctive, however, is less its outright praise for the book—it is a little muted—than its desire to ground it in a tradition of a certain kind of scholarship. Hess begins by placing *Mimesis* not in the locus of the author's exile but in the genealogies of academic scholarship. There are, he begins, few "Außergewöhnliche Bücher . . . in den geisteswissenschaftlichen Disciplinen" (p. 173), few truly unusual examples of scholarly work, such as Eduard Norden's *Antike Kunstprosa* and, before that, Erwin Rohde's *Griechischer Roman*. Norden and Rohde stand as exemplars of a nineteenth-century scholarly control, a blend of an "unermüdichen philologischen Fleißes und literarischen Feingefühls" (an untiring philological industry and a literary sensitivity). They also appear as teachers, and Norden himself, as Auerbach's old teacher, stands as a fitting opening to this forthcoming account of the student's book. The legacies of scholarship present themselves as legacies of student and master, as the paternity of learning.

Now, Auerbach's *Mimesis* is, to Hess's mind, not quite up to the model of these masters: it seems a little spotty in its coverage, familiar in its choice of major texts, and relatively unimaginative in its focus on the old question of the representation of reality and its choice of a primarily *soziologische* mode of inquiry. Yet Hess's impression (*Eindruck*) is of a singular mind at work in *Mimesis*, an impression of "einer überlegenen, kunstverständigen, geschmackssicheren, im guten Sinne gebildeten Persönlichkeit" (a personality judicious, connoisseurial, sure of its tastes, and brought up with good sense [p. 173]). Auerbach has a literary talent, one discernible from the book's opening pages, but not one that imposes itself through polemic or dogmatic judgments. "Der Leser lebt in einer wohltuend humanen Atmosphäre"—The reader lives in a comforting, humane atmosphere (p. 174).

This attention to the humane atmosphere, to the more belletristic rather than the primarily scholarly features of *Mimesis*, leads off Hess's chapter-by-chapter summary of the book. Though he begins with an allusive reference to "die Geschichte des Buchs" and to the writings of Auerbach's "Istanbuler Zeit" (p. 174), there is no mention of the difficulties of his exile, no attention to the details of that *Geschichte* or to the contours of that *Zeit*. Hess's review preoccupies itself with placing *Mimesis* in its traditions—scholarly, institutional, and literary—rather than in its time. Its goal is to bring Auerbach back into the official organs of *Geistesgeschichte* by emphasizing the continuities, genealogies, and detachments that enable *der Leser* to read *Mimesis* in the study. Instead of the fissures of exile, the limitations of a Turkish library, or the personal reflection on political conditions, Hess proffers the unbroken flow of learning.

The emphases on sensitivity and belletrism here—and, I would argue, in many of the early reviews—is not simply a misunderstanding on the part of Auerbach's contemporaries. It represents a conscious strategy to efface the disturbing political and personal themes of *Mimesis*: to make it safe for the reader in the study, the student in the library, the connoisseur in that literary gallery where we may all breathe the "humane atmosphere" of intellectual comfort. More informed than the American reviewers of the late 1940s and early 1950s, Hess relates *Mimesis* to Auerbach's other work on Dante and on *figura* (p. 189). He recognizes that certain chapters, especially the Flaubert section, bring together work that Auerbach had written earlier. And he compares the work on Old French texts to scholarship by Curtius and Voretzsch (pp. 181–186, 187). These citations do not necessarily imply that Hess's is a more objective account of the book than those by Hatzfeld, Ludwig Edelstein, or others. It is a more *informed* account, but one whose display of information presents an ideal of the worker in the institutions of the academy, where each book, each essay, has a place in the trajectory of apprenticeship, journeyman work, and mastery. The review, as a whole, papers over the hiatus of exile and the political subtexts of *Mimesis*'s readings. It brings the book back into the ambience of scholarship as if nothing had arrived to interrupt it or as if even such an interruption ("die Istanbuler Zeit") could be safely tucked away in the vagaries of euphemism. Discontinuities exist: discontinuities of style, of method, and of technical approach. But, in spite of this apparent eclecticism of *Mimesis*, Hess writes, "hat der Leser nie das Gefühl der Uneinheitlichkeit. Ein klarer Geist durchdringt und verbindet scheinbar Disparates" (pp. 175–76). A clear and guiding spirit binds together all that seems disparate. For this, too, is Hess's purpose, to unite together the disparate periods and products of Auerbach's career as part of a genealogy of *Geisteswissenschaft* at whose heart may lie that *Geist* that has no history or politics.

The pages of *Romanische Forschungen* that follow Hess's opening review article similarly leave us with a sense of academic business as usual. Studies of etymology, dialects, phonology, and literary topoi fill the volume in a manner hardly different from anything that had appeared before or during the Second World War. The tone of scholarly detachment similarly permeates Auerbach's review of Spitzer's books, the first entry in the *Besprechungen* section of the volume. For the most part, Auerbach concerns himself with narrating the contents of Spitzer's volumes and with defining his particular method and its strengths and limitations. Only occasionally is there a reference to the personal in this review: to what, for example, Auerbach identifies as the "teilweise autobiographischen" (occasionally autobiographical) introduction to *Linguistics and Literary History* (p. 398) or to the letter from an American student, quoted in the book, criticizing Spitzer's approach as personal and intuitive. The differences between the German review of this book and the one in English Auerbach published in the first volume of *Comparative Literature* (1949) are subtly instructive in this regard. Though the American review is somewhat shorter than the one in *Romanische Forschungen*, it closes with a substantial reflection on the personal in academic study and teaching. Commenting on the idiosyncratic possibilities of Spitzer's method in his hands, Auerbach notes that we should not condemn the approach because of the excesses of the user.

> But it would be a great mistake not to study the method because of the imperfections of those who use it; or because, on the contrary, it requires so high a level of knowledge and so large an horizon that it is not adaptable to practical teaching or even to average research work. I have had excellent results in using it on a very modest level, in Germany as well as Turkey. Our students learn too much biographical and other textbook material; they are like people who listen to lectures on fruits, but almost never get hold of an apple or a grape. . . . For such teaching [i.e., in national literature courses] Spitzer's book can serve as an excellent introduction, although practice would have to be simpler and less personal.[45]

For Auerbach writing in the pages of *Romanische Forschungen*, however, the practice has to be simpler and less personal. There are no comparable reflections in the German review, nothing of the "teilweise autobiographischen" that he attributes to Spitzer himself. Only in America, and only in English, could he give voice to the personal and political concerns behind the practice of scholarship. For the readers of *Romanische Forschungen*, such concerns can only be slipped in, allusively, in other forms and other languages. Witness the curious, unique English quotation in the discussion of Spitzer on Racine: "Racine's main purpose was to show us the collapse of the world order as revealed to Thesée" (*RF*, p. 400). Or witness the moment, in the otherwise purely descriptive, brief review by Peter Schon of Auerbach's *Introduction aux études de philologie romane*, where the circumstances of the book's production can only be quoted in the French ("Ce petit livre fut écrit à Istanbul . . . pendant la guerre . . . loin des bibliothèques européennes et américaines" [*RF*, p. 490]).

The Auerbachiana of these volumes of *Romanische Forschungen* take us far from the political allusions or the personal reflections of *Mimesis*—so far that when Auerbach eventually came to publish his "Epilegomena zu Mimesis" in the 1953 volume of that journal, he set out to rehistoricize the book. This essay, which opens the volume, offers an occasion to respond to queries about individual interpretations by catching up on current scholarship. Yet, in the course of his responses to reviewers published,

Auerbach grows more personal. He reminds the readers of the period in Istanbul (p. 5), recalls his youthful training in Germany (p. 15), and, at the close, explicitly addresses the historical and biographical moment in which the book took shape: "*Mimesis* ist ganz bewußt ein Buch, das ein bestimmter Mensch, in einer bestimmten Lage, zu Anfang der 1940er Jahre geschrieben hat" (p. 18). A certain man, at a certain time, in a certain "situation" (*Lage*)—this is the closing key to understanding *Mimesis*, to reading its *figurae* of the person and the present. Auerbach's phrasing takes us back to the chapter on Adam and Eve, where Eve herself, "Herrin der Lage," overthrows the order of her God and man; and it reminds us, too, of Auerbach's quarrel with Etienne over who will be the master of the editorial situation.

It would be rewarding to name Auerbach the winner in that quarrel and to show that, in spite of all the manglings of *Mimesis* in the early reviews and the later appropriation of Auerbach himself into the canons of literary studies, his editorial decisions on the *Mystère d'Adam* stood up to professional approval. But, apparently, they do not. He is, perhaps, as much in error here as he was in his Proust quotation. The critical edition of the play by Paul Aebischer, published in the Textes Littéraires Français series in 1963, accepts without question Etienne's distribution of the lines between Adam and Eve.[46] And, while the diplomatic edition of Leif Sletsjöe, published with a facing-page facsimile of the manuscript in 1968, does not print the text of the speeches as Etienne edits them, it does state in a note to line 283 that Adam probably should speak this line and that the *A* used by the scribe to signal the speaker has probably been lost from the margin of the manuscript.[47] Sletsjöe and Aebischer both cite Etienne approvingly, and, while their spellings of the individual words of the text may differ from the earlier scholar's, they both confirm an ordering of speeches first suggested on the pages of *Romania* in 1922. So powerful has been this editorial tradition that, in the definitive American anthology of medieval drama edited by David Bevington, Etienne's version appears without question. And yet so powerful is Auerbach's example for the institutions of American medieval studies that Bevington can quote his interpretation of the play as received wisdom.[48]

This fissure in a classroom anthology, perhaps more precisely than the record of the histories of scholarship, shows the paradox of the place of Auerbach's *Mimesis* in the academy. On the one hand, it accepts the critical interpretation, treasures its appreciation of the humble and the everyday in the articulations of the sublime in order to breathe in fully that atmosphere of humanistic scholarship. On the other hand, it rejects—or, better yet, ignores—the textual interpretation, bypasses the very heart of Auerbach's display of philological erudition that enables him to recover the character of European peoples and to write their literary history. One can only speculate on why Auerbach never went back to this passage, never revised his reading in the light of further textual scholarship (especially once he reached America).[49] Such speculation, too, might take us back to the very style of Auerbach's chapter and to the paradoxes of *Mimesis* itself. The colloquialism of the presentation in "Adam and Eve" shifts scholarly attention away from the details of his editorial technique and toward the sensitivities of belletrism. Ironically, it may be Auerbach himself who seems to lack the precision of method he demanded in the *Introduction aux études de philologie romane*. The paradoxes of *Mimesis* lie in the tensions between the scholarly and the colloquial, between the learned techniques of *Geisteswissenschaft* and the felt experience of *Feingefühl*, between what Auerbach defined as the historical and the legendary. "Again and again, I have the purpose of writing history."[50] This widely quoted passage has been used throughout much recent scholarship on Auerbach to emphasize the theory of historical understanding that grounds even his most affective of readings. But, as I have suggested here, we might do well to find his purpose in writing not *Geschichte* but *Sage* and to recall, as he asks us, that in times such as those in which he wrote *Mimesis*, "most historians are forced to make concessions to the technique of legend."

If most historians are forced to make concessions to the technique of legend, then so, too, are most literary critics. Erich Auerbach himself has become something of a legend, and the critical reception of his work in the past decade, as I have already noted, skirts the fine line between *Sage* and *Geschichte*: between exemplary valorization and historical framing. Certainly, by the time he had ensconced himself at Yale (whose faculty he joined in 1950), he was already legendary. Curtius himself complained, during a visit to America in the late 1940s, "one hardly hears anything but *Mimesis*."[51] Early American reviews waxed orphic over its great range and scope. No one, it would appear, had read as much, or with such insight, as Auerbach had. And, at Yale, whose New Critical formalism had, by the early 1950s, come to dominate the teaching of, at least, English literature, the apparently formalist close reading of *Mimesis* seemed a welcome confirmation of the local pedagogy. Carl Landauer has wittily reviewed "how New Haven stole the idea of *Mimesis*." What he has called "the virtuoso performer" of that book—the rhetorically constructed narrator we see throughout its chapters—"played perfectly to American audiences of the 1950s." Landauer goes on: "For the mid-century attempt to apotheosize culture, in a sense to create an Americanized *Kultur*, *Mimesis* was an exemplary text" (p. 180).[52]

Landauer and others have done much to trace the impact of the book, and of Auerbach himself, on American readers, and the blend of formalist close reading and high literary cultural appreciation still, for some, embodies the ideal of literary study.[53] But even the history of Auerbach's seven years at Yale has been transformed into a legend. Who can really say just what went on; who can draw lines between *Sage* and *Geschichte* among memories now half a century old? Almost everyone, it seems, wants something of his legacy, his imprimatur. Stephen G. Nichols reminisces about taking tea with Auerbach's widow in the late 1950s, while he was a graduate student at Yale, going through old notes and papers, "each one seeming to recall a special occasion whose background and significance Mrs. Auerbach would gloss with reminiscences of university politics and intellectual quarrels from Weimar Germany (she did not much care to discuss their years in Istanbul)."[54] More recently, Alvin Kernan has also sought his place, quite literally, at Auerbach's table, as he recalls his years in the mid-1950s at Branford College, Yale, when the dining room would be "graced sometimes by Erich Auerbach." *Mimesis*, Kernan reminds us, was written "with only his small personal library available to him."

> Now that he was at Yale he felt that he had to make use of the vast resources of Sterling Library. Ironically, the result of riches was a dreary book on rhetoric, read and used by few; *Mimesis*, however, with its exquisite explorations of the way reality was perceived and rendered in texts from the Bible to the present, has become one of the literary classics of our time. It was at the Branford fellows' table that Auerbach one day had a stroke, from which he later died, and was carried down to the red leather couch in my office just off the stairway to the hall.[55]

I have no idea just what "dreary book on rhetoric" is on Kernan's mind. Perhaps he is thinking of *Literary Language and Its Public*, the collection of essays assembled in the 1950s and published posthumously in German in 1958, though soon translated into English and, in fact, regarded as one of the most important critical assessments of the literary culture of late antiquity.[56] Of course, it is in Kernan's interest to imagine a contrast between the brilliant *Mimesis* (the product of exile and almost intuitive literary skill) and the scholarly "book on rhetoric" (the product of a research library and a book, apparently, for specialists). Of course, too, it is in Kernan's interest to associate himself with such an author, who should find himself not just in Auerbach's dying presence but be instrumental in the scene. There is, in fact, a curiously Auerbachian quality to both the reminiscences of Nichols and Kernan. Both focus on scenes of repast—the domestic tea, the faculty lunch—and both lovingly linger over the everyday details that grant larger meaning to the scene. One could well imagine Kernan's memoir of the moment, "The Red Leather Couch," as something of his own "Brown Stocking" chapter. Or perhaps, too, "The Interrupted Supper" of *Mimesis* now becomes the interrupted lunch.

So, other than the techniques of close reading or the patina of humanistic scholarship or a collection of self-serving anecdotes, just what *did* New Haven steal from *Mimesis*? I would suggest that there remains another strand of influence, one not explicitly (or perhaps one might better say ingenuously) acknowledged by its practitioners, and one that has had an impact on more recent modes of inquiry in the academy. What the Yale critics of the 1970s (not just the 1950s) learned from Auerbach was the technique of synecdochic reading, of selecting apparently random quotations from literary works in order both to illustrate the larger stylistic and aesthetic qualities of those works and to illuminate the broader social environments and literary periods in which those works were written and read. There lies, behind this technique, a project in cultural etymology, and Auerbach's other heirs have their tie to the modern ardent etymologists who closed my previous chapter.

Perhaps the best example of these later Auerbachian engagements is that succinct manifesto of American deconstruction, J. Hills Miller's "The Critic as Host," published in 1979 when Miller was professor of English at Yale.[57] This essay works through a series of etymological feints. It writes a cultural philology of Romanticism, yet it performs its

Auerbachian maneuvers not only on literary texts but on critical ones as well. Its opening selection of quotations—the apparent guise of randomness, the performance of a kind of *sortes* of the critics—functions much like the *Mimesis* technique of selection. The whole point of this process, in Miller as well as in Auerbach, is to create the rhetorical impression not that random samplings necessarily exemplify larger textual structures but that there is something in the gift or talent of this particular selector, this particular reader, that enables him to select, quite simply, better than you or I can. Look at the way Miller begins.

> At one point in "Rationality and Imagination in Cultural History," M. H. Abrams cites Wayne Booth's assertion that the "deconstructionist" reading of a given work is "plainly and simply parasitical" on "the obvious or univocal reading." The latter is Abram's phrase, the former Booth's. My citation of a citation is an example of a kind of chain which it will be part of my intention here to interrogate. What happens when a critical essay extracts a "passage" and "cites" it? Is this different from a citation, echo, or allusion within a poem? Is citation an alien parasite within the body of the main text, or is the interpretive text the parasite which surrounds and strangles the citation which is its host? (p. 452)

Miller brilliantly stands Auerbach on his head. Central, as we remember, to *Mimesis* is that there are no citations: that the work was written without access to a major library, without access to "almost all the more recent investigations." We know this now to be a pose.[58] And so, too, Miller's is a pose, for here the subject matter is the set of "recent investigations" themselves. Miller effectively inverts the hierarchical relationship of text and critic by performing the Auerbachian move on critical rather than authorial works. And he proceeds, in what immediately follows, to perform a similar bit of critical magic on the philological tradition itself. His etymological play with the word "parasite" (here, though redolent as much of Freud on the uncanny as it is of any professional philologist) leads him to argue (in terms that might resonate with Auerbach or, for that matter, with William Dwight Whitney) that "[a] curious system of thought, or of language, or of social organization (in fact all three at once) is implicit in the word parasite" (p. 453). Cultural history through philology.

But there is more. Midway through Miller's essay, as he turns from etymology and criticism to the reading of Romantic poetry, he introduces texts in ways distinctively reminiscent of the rhetoric of *Mimesis*. Look at the way Shelley enters: "One of the most striking 'episodes' of *The Triumph of Life* is the scene of self-destructive erotic love" (p. 459). This could be the opening sentence of any chapter of *Mimesis*—except for the way in which Miller ironizes it by placing the word "episodes" in scare quotes. The very notion of the critical selection here, the very gesture of exemplary reading, is called into question, exposed as the feint of the critic rather than the genius of the writer. After the passage from Shelley, when Miller returns to the rhetoric of awe, we cannot, I think, read it wholly straight: "This magnificent passage is the culmination of a series of passages writing and rewriting the same materials in a chain of repetitions beginning with *Queen Mab*. In the earlier versions the word 'parasite' characteristically appears, like a discreet identifying mark *woven into the texture of the verbal fabric*" (p. 460; emphases mine). If we did not know what the "Brown Stocking" meant in Auerbach, we know it now. And if, in some sense, *Mimesis* really is a modernist novel—a verbal version of Mrs. Ramsay's injunction to "find another picture to cut out," where individual fragments are selected and reconfigured into a compelling yet self-consciously artificial whole—then Miller's version of things is a postmodernist fiction. As such, it is a fiction that leads not to success but to failure. Shelly's poetry concerns itself with "narcissism and incest, the conflict of generations, struggles for political power, the motifs of the sun and the moon, the fountain, the brook, the caverned enclosure, ruined tower, or woodland dell, the dilapidation of man's constructions by nature, and the failure of the poetic quest" (p. 459).

Miller's "Critic as Host" represents a possible response to the philological tradition as exemplified by Auerbach. It exposes *as rhetoric* the devices of selection, close reading, aesthetic evaluation, and etymological reading that motivate that tradition. In this project, it works out what Frederic Jameson (who was Miller's Yale contemporary, teaching French there from 1976 to 1983) recognized as the fiction of etymology: "For etymology . . . is to be considered not so much a scientific fact as a rhetorical form, the illicit use of historical causality to support the drawing of logical consequences." And then, quoting an authoritative source—Jean Paulhan "in an ingenious little book"—Jameson continues: "the word itself tells us so:

etymology *etumos logos*, authentic meaning. Thus etymology advertises itself, and sends us back to itself as its own first principle."[59] Jameson here, in the opening pages of *The Prison-House of Language*, is reviewing the Saussurian inheritance in critical theory, and he argues (in the passage just before the one I quote) that "Saussure's is in a sense an existential perception"—that is, that behind Saussure's notion of the sign lies an awareness that, for all the history behind individual words, such history is irrelevant to the speaker of a language. This observation was, as I noted in my previous chapter, central to Whitney's notion of the arbitrary and conventional nature of communication (and, in turn, his claim that appeals to etymology could have a rhetorical effect but really were not useful in language of the everyday). But it is here, in Jameson, pressed into the service of a kind of existential criticism itself. "Only for the speaker, at any moment in the history of the language, one meaning alone exists, the current one: words have no memory."[60]

If words have no memory, people do. The memory of texts and readings is of primary concern to Auerbach and those who write in his wake ("Readers will remember," begins *Mimesis*). And this concern, too, lies just beneath the surface of *The Prison-House of Language*. A little later in the book, when he is reviewing the idea of defamiliarization and the Russian critical term "*ostranenie*," Jameson illustrates the idea with a passage from the seventeenth-century French writer La Bruyère. He quotes from La Bruyère's description of the peasantry, with its depiction of those people as "ferocious animals," who only have "a sort of articulate voice," and who, upon standing up, the viewer recognizes as people. It is a long and terrifying passage, and Jameson reflects: "This horrifying text, one of the first explicit descriptions of the peasantry in modern French literature, no longer directs our attention to the natural and metaphysical conditions of human life, but rather to its unjustifiable social structure, which we have come to take for granted as something natural and eternal, and which therefore cries out for defamiliarization" (pp. 56–57). But the attention of the reader of *The Prison-House of Language* is, in fact, directed someplace else. Go to the bottom of the page, and find La Bruyère's text cited as follows: "Quoted in Erich Auerbach, *Mimesis* (trans. Willard Trask [Princeton, New Jersey, 1968], p. 366" (p. 57 n. 10). Certainly, Jameson could have found the passage on his own. But he did not. Like Miller's "Critic as Host," Jameson's book here questions the very problem of quotation and citation. The point is not just Jameson's laziness but rather that the passage stands as part of the critical consciousness because Auerbach had quoted it. And he had quoted it with an attention-getting commentary of his own. "I should also like to quote the well-known and strangely arresting passage on the peasantry," is how Auerbach introduces it, and then he writes: "Although this important passage is clearly of its century through its moralizing emphasis, it yet would seem to stand alone in the belles-lettres of the time. . . . I prefer to assume that he was also thinking of himself and the general political and aesthetic situation. . . . [P]olitical reasons and aesthetic reasons are interrelated" (pp. 366–67).

The interrelatedness of the political and the aesthetic is a key theme throughout Jameson's work. It is the very argument of *Prison-House* (as it would be for the much later *Political Unconscious*). And so, here, it is the authority of Auerbach, the commentary behind the quotation, that grants Jameson the entry into his discussion of the "unjustifiable social structure." The text, and its politico-aesthetic reading, has been sanctioned by *Mimesis*, and yet Jameson can take that reading one step further by enfolding it into the legacy of Russian formalism. What is being defamiliarized here, in other words, is not just the "phenomena of social life" presented in La Bruyère but the phenomena of critical life as represented in Auerbach.

The old philology, then, lurks always in the background not just of New Criticism but high theory. And, most recently, it has come out of the shadows to be acknowledged in the New Historicism. At the beginning of their *Practicing New Historicism*, Catherine Gallagher and Stephen Greenblatt offer Auerbach as nothing less than the inspiration for their project. *Mimesis* is a book of "textual fragments," informed by "a profoundly melancholy sense that the centuries-long project [Auerbach] chronicles is close to exhaustion, disintegration, or irrelevance" (pp. 32–33). There is, in *Mimesis*, too, a "buried Hegelian plot," not, perhaps "finally realized" but certainly informing Auerbach's fascination with "the secularized representations of human destiny." But what does this enterprise have to do with the claims of the New Historicism?

> Those of us who began writing literary history in the 1970s had a strong affinity both with Auerbach's existential pessimism and with

his method, a method by which many of us were, from the beginning, influenced and that we self-consciously imitated. The influence is most striking in the adaptation of Auerbach's characteristic opening gambit: the isolation of a resonant textual fragment that is revealed, under the pressure of analysis, to represent the work from which it is drawn and the particular culture in which that work was produced and consumed.... The new historicist anecdote as many of us deployed it is an Auerbachian device. (p. 35)

Unlike the critics of Kernan's generation, there is no appeal here to the direct influence of the master. Auerbach was dead two decades before Gallagher and Greenblatt and their peers were "writing literary history in the 1970s." This is a kind of metareminiscence: a remembrance not of the author but of the text, a nostalgia for a time not when the literary works were read but when the literary critics were—a time, by implication, when literary criticism *mattered*. The New Historicist anecdote now has a genealogy of its own, one that goes back to the method of selection and discussion raised, almost to an art, by Auerbach. What was, then, "so appealing about Auerbach's strategy" was that it "enabled critics to illuminate extremely complex and ... long works without exhausting themselves or their readers" (p. 36).

But there remains, it seems to me, something profoundly disingenuous about this critical appeal. "Auerbach can say convincing and fresh things about texts like the Bible, the *Odyssey*, the *Inferno*, ... because he has liberated himself from the task of writing a full 'history,' because his analyses have the kind of intensity and detail more typically associated with readings of Shakespeare sonnets or Donne lyrics" (pp. 36–37). In other words, Auerbach could say fresh things because his techniques looked like classical New Criticism: intense, detailed readings of rich Renaissance texts. But the point remains: Auerbach can say convincing and fresh things because *he is Auerbach*. His insights come not from some "conjuring trick," as Gallagher and Greenblatt insouciantly imply (p. 38), but from a blend of immense learning and intense reflection. The New Historicists, as Gallagher and Greenblatt do acknowledge, were, in fact, "for the most part vastly less learned than Auerbach" (p. 45). Moreover, they were reading texts he would not care to read: texts not framed in the canon of great Western literature. Had canonical literature exhausted itself? Had the times so changed that rereadings of the classics simply would not do? Had the question of reality revealed in style become unanswerable? "The turn to the historical anecdote," Gallagher and Greenblatt write, "in literary study promised both an escape from conventional canonicity and a revival of the canon, both a transgression against the domestic and a safe return to it" (p. 47).

In these, and the many other passages in *Practicing New Historicism* that reflect on Auerbach's influence, there remains a curious defensiveness, a need to justify a project through an appeal to the method and example of the master. But more than adherence to a method, the pressure of this claim is to *participate in the moral fiction of* Mimesis: in the story of exile and dismissal, the fantasy of homecoming and its parent-child relationships. *Practicing New Historicism* seeks a parent for its project, one safely dead who cannot query the methods or motives of his heirs. "We suspect that Auerbach would have disliked this characterization of his work," an aside that makes sense only in the larger rhetoric of approval that these writers play (p. 37). What *Mimesis* itself inscribes within it is the fundamentally paternalistic quality of the philological tradition and, in turn, of that very need for authoritative approval. Auerbach rhetorically constructs himself as an exiled prodigal son, whose return is metaphorically adumbrated in its chapters. Odysseus comes home, and Isaac is spared; Mrs. Ramsay smoothes her young boy's hair; and so on.

Mimesis may be a paternalistic text, and Gallagher and Greenblatt are but the most recent appellants to its approval. And, as such appellants, they are complicit in the reading, or the reconstruction, of *Mimesis* as a book of fathers. Their account of Auerbach's engagement with Virginia Woolf—"virtually the only female author accorded sustained attention . . . , and then as an emblem of dissolution and decadence" (p. 45)— misses the point. She is, in many ways, the telos of *Mimesis*. As I have suggested, she emerges as the maternal figure of philology, the voice through which the method of the book itself is posited ("let's find another picture to cut out"), the entrée for a final chapter that takes all the paradigms of literary canonicity (male, European, Christian) and inverts them. Gallagher and Greenblatt fail to notice the women who populate the volume. Indeed, one could make the claim that *Mimesis* stands as book of female figures at the center of the literary tradition.

Let us imagine such a project. Let us think of the book's first reader not as that "him" that Auerbach would seek but as a her. Euryclea becomes the motivating reader of the *Odyssey*, the true interpreter of signs and marks. Odysseus's scar is an inscription; like so many marks on skin and bone throughout the epic, it is written on the body (the word used to describe such scars is often επιγραψε). As Haun Saussy has shown in great detail, Euryclea's reading of the scar is really that: the recognition of a written sign, its meaning, and its bearer. Her recognition recalls many other moments in the epic when the incised mark or scratch provokes an understanding. For an oral poem, such scenes of epigraphy break in, revealing not just the fissures in our own, historical conception of the poem and its circulation (are there really literate figures in its narrative?) but in Homer's, too. Euryclea becomes *the* reader who remembers, even though her expression of that memory is stifled as Odysseus goes for her throat and silences her.[61]

Let us imagine all the women of *Mimesis* longing for a voice. Amid the bustle of Petronius, there is Fortunata, who has risen from nothing to a position of such power that "[i]f she tells [Trimalchio] at high noon it's dark, he'll agree." "Sed haec lupatria providet omnia," a phrase translated in the English as "But that bitch looks out for everything." Perhaps she is a forerunner of Adam's Eve in chapter 7, who would similarly aspire to control, to be "Herrin der Lage." And there are Madame du Chastel, Lady Macbeth (who comes in only briefly and already dead [p. 326]), the Dulcinea of Don Quixote's desire, Esther in Racine's play of that name (treated in the context of "The Faux Dévot," chapter 15), Manon Lescaut, Luise Millerin, Madame Vauquer, Germinie Lacerteux. Throughout, the book is moving, almost aching, for a fully fledged female authority, one that may speak or write without fear of censure, dismissal, or death. And that is where Virginia Woolf comes in.

"Had we but world enough and time . . . ." This phrase from Andrew Marvell stands as the epigraph to *Mimesis* (right on the title page of the German but deferred to a later page of its own in the English). It has long been valued for its melancholy: its enduring sense that, if we only had enough time, all things would resolve, the great projects would emerge, and readers and scholars would reunite in a world literature. And yet this epigraph comes from a poem about not melancholy but desire. It is a plea "To His Coy Mistress," and perhaps, so is *Mimesis* itself. For now, philology is that coy mistress—that Lady Philology of the medieval allegories—as are, perhaps, the many women (some coy, some not) who populate its chapters. Read this phrase not as an epigraph but as a dedication to another kind of reader, and restore it to its context.

> Had we but World enough and Time,
> This coyness Lady were no crime.
> We would sit down, and think which way
> To walk, and pass our long Loves Day.
> Thou by the Indian Ganges side
> Should'st Rubies find: I by the Tide
> Of Humber would complain. I would
> Love you ten years before the Flood:
> And you should if you please refuse
> Till the Conversion of the Jews.[62]

Marvell's lines telescope all earth and all time into narrow space. And so does Auerbach. Can we imagine him, if not by the Indian Ganges, then some place similarly (at least for the European reader) at the end of the earth—or should we say that instead of the Indian Ganges there lies that touch of the "oriental" in the Indian cashmere of Proust's remembered father? And how could anyone who, in Auerbach's words, "evaluates the behavior of individual men and groups of men at the time of the rise of National Socialism in Germany" (p. 19) read Marvell's line on the "Conversion of the Jews" and not shudder? Had we but world enough and time, certain behaviors would be no crime; but in these times and this place, just being who you were was criminal.

I leave *Mimesis* as a paradox: a book of sons and fathers that inscribes a female reading in it; a work of a European written in the "orient"; a book that aspires to correct editions and right readings and yet is shot through with error. Let me say, more to the point, that it lies in this book, and not in the work of later critics, that we find "both a transgression against the domestic and a safe return to it." No better phrase, it seems to me, could be deployed to describe many of the literary narratives *Mimesis* brings together. And no better phrase could stand as epigraph to those traditions of philology and rhetoric I trace throughout my book. For if *Mimesis* is a story of synecdoche, then so is almost everything I study here. Errata sheets take bits and pieces out of books, call them to our attention, and then alter them—in the process, not simply correcting a local error but forever altering our way of reading an entire book. The history of Anglo-Saxon literature is a history of fragments, whether they be the surviving leaves of a near-lost vernacular tradition or the exemplary passages selected by historians and critics from George Hickes to Tolkien and beyond. Casaubon's barely legible notes, the explicitly named "errant fragments," seek to construct a history of thought but, in the end, lead only to despair. And the ardent etymologies of American rhetoricians and philologists aspire, from the eighteenth century to the present, to explain a history of reading, nationhood, or scholarly identity in a single word.

The Oxford English Dictionary had built its history of the language out of well-selected bits and pieces. Book reviewing, literary criticism, even reading itself uses parts for wholes. The great reader is one who can recall a quote, make aphorisms, epigraphs, or anecdotes out of a text (perhaps "Auerbach can say convincing and fresh things," in large part, because he can select fresher passages than anybody else). And "text" itself, from "*textus*," something woven (hence, our modern word "textile") finds itself etymologically brought to life, not only in Virginia Woolf's brown stocking but in the anonymous review of a mid-nineteenth-century forgotten dictionary: "The authorship or compilership of a dictionary which has gone through numerous editions is, indeed, a question like that of the identity of the darned and redarned stockings with the original pair." I made much of this quotation in chapter 3, showing both how the *OED* had truncated it and how it may be read, both in the *Dictionary* and in its original context, as something of a statement about authorship itself. Is any work of criticism little more than a redarned stocking, a patchwork of the fabric of others? What happens when we wrap the old in fabrics fresh or strange? Like Proust's father, turbaned in his Indian cashmere, philology has always come so sheathed: wrapped in the trappings of the orientalist, embedded in the memories of childhood, fearful of fathers. And, in what may be the most dazzling compilation of fragments, the concatenation of Shakespearean quotations drawn, as Auerbach himself says, "at random" and full of mothers, fathers, kings, and servants, there appears this comment.

> But something else is to be noted here besides the great variety of phenomena to which we referred above and the ever-varied nuances of the profoundly human mixture of high and low, sublime and trivial, tragic and comic. It is the conception, so difficult to formulate

in clear terms although everywhere to be observed in its effects, of a basic fabric of the world [*Weltgrundes*], perpetually weaving [*webenden*] itself, renewing itself, and connected in all its parts [*in all seinen Teilen zusammenhängenden*], from which all this arises and which makes it impossible to isolate any one event or level of style.

(p. 327; p. 313)

And then he quotes Prospero from *The Tempest* on the "baseless fabric of this vision."

At moments such as this one, Auerbach anticipates the ending of his book. The fabric of the world, the fabric of this vision, look ahead to the knitting of the stocking. And the "little life" that Prospero finds "rounded with a sleep" looks forward, too, to all our bedtime stories, not the least those of one who "used to go to bed early" and whose remembrance of bedtime comes complete with structures "long ago demolished." *Mimesis* closes, as we all know, with an appeal to the future. "Nothing now remains but to find him—to find the reader, that is." I return to this line now to reread it not as a problem in gender (as I had suggested earlier) but in referent. Perhaps the claim is not to find the reader but to find the author. Nothing now remains but to find *him*. I've searched throughout my book to find them—scholars, that is—and I think I have. Their errancies and errors, like my own, help us to find them and to find ourselves. Nothing now remains but to find him. "Mi ritrovai per una selva oscura." I found myself, as Auerbach's beloved Dante put it. If that search goes on by recalling our pasts, it also transpires in the search for our futures, and my final foray into this inquiry lies with one imagination of such a future. For, if Auerbach imagines Prospero, at least implicitly, as his philologist in exile, then so did his contemporaries. My epilogue looks at a popular account of such an exile, the movie *Forbidden Planet*, released just a year before Auerbach's death. It scripts out an errand into a wilderness both domestic and weird, familiar and familial, grounded in *The Tempest* and yet driven by an image of the émigré philologist and his uncomprehending, all-too-American students.

*The philologist of the future as skeptic of our whole culture,
and thereby the destroyer of professional philology.*
—Nietzsche, *Wir Philologen*

EPILOGUE

FORBIDDEN PLANET AND THE TERRORS OF PHILOLOGY

The émigré experience took many forms. For some, positions in America lay waiting. The Princeton Institute for Advanced Study, Johns Hopkins, the University of Chicago, the New School for Social Research, and some other institutions seemed to have first pick of the Jewish intellectuals streaming out of Europe in the 1930s.[1] For others, the way out was harder. Istanbul had become a place of refuge, not just for Auerbach but (for a time) for Leo Spitzer, Herbert Dieckmann, Paul Hindemith, and many others.[2] Some scholars had to make their way through smaller schools in North America: the classicist Friedrich Solmsen went from Berlin and Cambridge to Olivet College in Michigan; the art historian Richard Krautheimer went from Marburg to Louisville; the artists Josef and Anni Albers went from the Bauhaus to Black Mountain College.[3] And for still others, the emigration—regardless of how prestigious the landing site—remained fraught with anxiety. The political scientist Franz Neumann found himself at Columbia and, by the late 1940s, in the words of his memoirist,

> seemed to be fully absorbed in American life: for more than a decade he had made the United States his home; he was married and had

two young children; he lived in a prosperous suburb, to outward appearance thoroughly *embourgeoisé*.

Yet the new fit was never complete. Whatever Neumann's academic success—and it was very great—however warmly he might speak of the openness of American social and university life, he remained curiously detached from his surroundings. And by the same token he became increasingly melancholy.[4]

As Neumann himself wrote of his, and his peers', American sojourn: "The German exile, bred in the veneration of theory and history, and contempt for empiricism and pragmatism, entered a diametrically opposed intellectual climate: optimistic, empirically oriented, ahistorical, but also self-righteous."[5] The émigré became, for some, not just a resident alien but an alienated resident, a kind of marginal figure, in the words of the sociologist Paul Lazarsfeld, "who is part of two different cultures."[6]

The historiography of émigré intellectuals has thus split along two lines. On the one hand, there are the celebrations, often written by acquaintances, or spouses, or students: chronicles of what Laura Fermi called the "Illustrious Immigrants" in her book of that title.[7] Even the collection edited by Donald Fleming and Bernard Bailyn, *The Intellectual Migration*, for all its contributors' sensitivities to the difficulties of transition, remains a paean to the transforming contribution of the émigré to American life. On the other hand, though, there are the dark memories and cultural reflections. Neumann's case is but the most explicit, and it colors the collection of responses to which he contributed in 1953, *The Cultural Migration*.

To my mind, the most engaging of such dark reflections on the émigré experience may be found not in the memoirs of the intellectuals but in an artifact of popular culture. Perhaps the most esteemed science fiction movie of the 1950s, *Forbidden Planet* (released in December 1956), has long been appreciated for its blend of high culture allusion and high camp effects. With its narrative spine taken from Shakespeare's *Tempest*, its investment in a vision of nuclear power, and its dramatic twist pendant on Freudian psychoanalysis, the movie seems replete with all the cultural commodities that the postwar decade saw as central to a learned life. But with its jokey dialogue, arch monsters, and near-cartoon characters (stretching from the stiff American Captain Adams, played by the young Leslie Nielsen, to the lithe beauty Altaira, played by the even younger

Anne Francis, and including, quite literally, the cartoon animated "monster from the id"), *Forbidden Planet* comes off as a rich repository of the kitsch of that same decade. Few films have seemed as funny or as dark, as forward-looking and as retrograde, as richly textured and as hokey; and it is no wonder that it has attained a status within both the intellectual discourses of the university and the cult fandom of the Website.

Much has been made of all these elements.[8] But little, if anything, has been said about the central character of Dr. Morbius (played by Walter Pidgeon) and his profession: philologist. Dr. Morbius embodies a popular American response to the incursions of an émigré literary study into the academy and popular culture of the 1950s. His visage, his bearing, his pursuits, and his demise all constellate around a set of social and historical events that were reshaping literary and linguistic study in the postwar period. One way of coming to this well-known film afresh—and one way of coming to the close of my book on the scholarly imagination—will be to understand the movie as a story of contemporary anxieties about learning and literature, the American and the alien. *Forbidden Planet* offers up an allegory of the émigré philologist—an allegory that was being played out, too, in some of the most important writings of the time by philologists themselves. In Erich Auerbach's *Mimesis*, Ernst Robert Curtius's *European Literature and the Latin Middle Ages*, the essays of Leo Spitzer, and the teaching of the classicist Werner Jaeger, the disciplines of historical philology and literary criticism are inseparably linked to notions of national identity and personal exile.

Such is the story, too, of Dr. Morbius. His movie is a legend of the ambiguities of learning, ambiguities that extend to the émigré himself. Exile or collaborator? asked the American academy of him and his ilk. Had survival depended on luck and industry, or on guile and deceit? When Morbius at the movie's end recognizes his own responsibility for the monster that destroyed his shipmates and threatens to destroy his daughter ("Guilty, guilty!" he cries just before he swoons), he voices a larger concern about the guilt of those who made it out. Such is the theme of scholarship not just for the mid-twentieth century but for the early twenty-first, as we still work in the legacy of those whose wartime wiles have been exposed and whose critical practices and theoretical stances bear the stigma of collaboration.

The future of philology looks all too much like its past. And yet, before I turn to this particular future, I want to pause to note how science fiction and philology have long shared an uneasy alliance. In George Orwell's *1984*, the ill-fortuned Syme appears as the philological specialist in Newspeak. Charged with the compilation of the eleventh edition of the Newspeak dictionary (perhaps in mocking obeisance to the iconic eleventh edition of the *Encyclopedia Britannica*), Syme boasts how he and his colleagues are "getting the language into its final shape. . . . You think, I dare say, that our chief job is inventing new words. But not a bit of it! We're destroying words—scores of them, hundreds of them, every day. We're cutting language down to the bone." And he avers, warming to his theme, "It's a beautiful thing, the destruction of words."[9] Such philological state terror hinges, as we all know, on the Newspeakers' ability to make the old word seem is exact opposite: to transfer Peace to War, Love to Hate, Fact to Fiction. As O'Brien will phrase it later in the novel, when he speaks of historical textuality in terms oddly premonitive of more recent academic argument: "Past events . . . have no objective existence, but survive only in written records and in human memories. The past is whatever the records and the memories agree upon" (p. 176).

But such historical and philological free-handedness is no mere Orwellian fantasy. It is the central tenet of what might be thought of as the archetypal foray into science fiction itself: Freud's 1919 essay "The Uncanny."[10] There, after a magisterial display of lexicographical research and philological acumen, Freud can—as we now all know—assert that the *unheimlich* and the *heimlich* are but one and the same: that what we think is most alien is, in fact, most at home, most domestic. With its close reading of E. T. A. Hoffmann's "The Sandman," Freud's essay stands as something of a template for an understanding of the science fictional. Androids haunt our imagination after reading it (how can we not see the inheritor of its mechanical Olympia as Pris in the 1984 movie *Blade Runner*?). Mad scientists of our imagination all seem to go back to Coppelius, not just the terrifying cryptocastrator of Freud's interpretation but the anti-Semitic caricature of Hoffmann's. Freud's reading, which has, too, become the subject of much critical interpretation, reveals etymology's ability to terrify; it places literary scholarship at the service of explicating haunting dreams or comic and macabre texts. Together with Orwell's *1984*, it shows how the ministrations of our monsters, whether they be creatures of the state or phantoms of our minds, are laid bare before the philological.

The story of *Forbidden Planet* is the story of the exile. The ship of Captain J. J. Adams, seeking to recover the remaining crew and colonists of the *Bellerophon*—sent out to Altair IV some twenty years before—finds only one survivor. In a cold and condescending voice, Dr. Morbius radios the ship as it approaches, warning them to stay away. Yet, when they do land, and he sends his robot out to fetch them, Morbius is all decorum and delight. He has them brought to his elegantly appointed house, feeds them exquisite food and drink, and tells them how most of the crew of the *Bellerophon* was killed off on the surface by some strange planetary force. When three barely surviving members of the crew had tried to take off in the ship, they, too, were destroyed, "vaporized," he says, in midair. Only he and his wife (dead now, he says, of "natural causes") were spared, perhaps immune to the force. Only their great love for the planet separated them from the others. Morbius's daughter enters after lunch, surprising and stimulating the young men. She shows them her Edenic paradise of animal friends, and they return to the ship, only to face a series of unexplained intrusions, sabotages, and later killings of the crew.

Of course, they must return to Morbius, who tells them of the Krell, the race who once inhabited the planet (Morbius consistently uses the word "race" to describe them); he shows them their technology, their works, their writings. He takes them on a tour of Krell magnificence: everything is of an immense scale, from the "plastic educator" that enhances mental ability, to the generators that produce a seemingly infinite amount of power, to the nearly endless rows of machinery deep in the planet that maintain the power. The Krell had vanished in a single night, just on the verge of some immense discovery.

And, as we later learn, the Krell had, in fact, made such a discovery: the complete transformation of matter by thought without any instrumentality. But, having unleashed the potential for immediate transmutation, what the Krell unleashed, too, were the unconscious appetites that they had superficially conquered. "Monsters from the id," announces Doctor Ostrow, just before he dies after having surreptitiously taken the brain boost from the plastic educator. The darkest powers of the id had been unleashed upon the Krell, just as the hidden id of Morbius himself had killed off the *Bellerophon* party and was now threatening the crew of Captain Adams. Once Altaira falls in love with Adams, Morbius's secret anger lashes out at them as well: only by acknowledging his own responsibility for such a monster ("Guilty, guilty," Morbius cries, as the invisible creature melts through the seemingly indestructible Krell metal protecting the three of them in the lab) can he call off the attack. He lets the captain and his daughter go, but not before initiating the overload of the planet's thermonuclear reactors and assuring its, and his own, self-destruction.

Even this bare-bones outline illustrates the problematic of the intellectual in American society. The secret of the Krell, in fact, is not just technological advancement but brain building. The plastic educator is both IQ meter and IQ enhancer. The first scene with the captain and the doctor shows how conscious they all are of the measurability of intelligence: just what is the relationship between quantifiable brainpower and the ability to learn, command, feel, understand? The doctor is amazed that, with a measured IQ of 167, he can only raise the meter half has high as Morbius (who had himself taken the brain boost almost as soon as he had arrived on the planet), while Morbius remarks that the captain really doesn't need a high IQ, "just a good strong voice." But, of course, this is not a vision of the future but a mirror of the present. Debates on measurable intelligence were at the heart of 1950s notions of society and education. IQ testing had long been an established feature of public school life, and individual IQ had come to stand as a defining mark of potential for anyone at school or work. And yet intelligence testing served not just to advance, or hinder, academic progress; it was intimately linked with access to America itself. From the 1920s on, IQ became the marker of admission to the country—a device for separating out desirable and undesirable aliens, a supposedly quantifiable assessment of the quality of immigrant potential (and, in particular, of central European immigrant potential).[11]

But just where does a bigger brain get you? For the linguistically trained Morbius, it enables him to read the Krell, to decipher their writings, understand—at least, in part—their vast technology, and build his robot servant. Morbius is, as Captain Adams remarks, only a "philologist, a specialist in words, their origins and meanings." Robby the Robot, though, represents a technological advance far beyond that of current human culture. "Child's play," sniffs Morbius. And yet, when Morbius sits down himself before the captain and the doctor at the plastic educator, what he conjures up is not some marvel of his learning but a moving statue of his daughter. She spins to life out of the smoke of his imagination in this scene. The men express astonishment; Morbius calmly explains that she comes to life here simply because she is "alive from microsecond to microsecond" in his mind. Much has been made by recent critics of this moment. It has been linked to a potential incest theme for the movie, as Morbius's jealousy becomes murderous, and as the Freudian subtext behind the id monster teases the viewer: is she the vision of a father's lovely child or the seductive statue of a fantasist? Altaira postures just as much for Morbius's delectation as for Adams's and the doctor's. Morbius is a fantasist of learning, one whose dark side will soon be evident in monsters from the id, but, right here, one whose vision gives us something of a foretaste of what lurks in the imagination of an old recluse.

But I think more than just inviting speculation on the prurience of their relationship, or on the fantasies spun by the movie's captain or its critics, we must see this as a problem in philology. What are the subjects of the scholar? What does the old philologist do when he sits alone in his study? What is the nature of desire, the relationship of text and sexuality, and the paternalism of the professorial in academic life? Such questions have long been asked by practitioners of this profession. Consider, for example, Max Müller, whose powers of linguistic and cultural arbitration found themselves sapped by emotional despondency following the loss of *his* daughter.[12] Or, better, think of Leo Spitzer, who defined philology itself as a subset of love, where the desire for interpretation and the pleasures of aesthetics clash with the rationality and technocratics of the modern world. Writing in 1960, he could claim:

> [P]hilology is the *love* for works written in a particular *language*. And if the methods of a critic must be applicable to works in all languages in order that the criticism be convincing, the critic, at least at the moment when he is discussing the poem, must love *that* language and *that* poem more than anything else in the world. In the final analysis, the critic, beneath the cold rationality of the professional, is not an automaton or a robot but a sentient being, with his own contradictions and spontaneous impulses.[13]

Such love may seem willfully out of step with the mechanized culture of postwar America—much as, one might add, Spitzer's notions of a cultural elite in an American democracy might lead to a similar pervasive sense of out-of-placeness. "You may have decided that," he addressed the MLA convention in 1950, given my criticism of the life actually led by our young scholars in our university system, a system so intimately connected with national ideals, I am criticizing these ideals themselves and that, consequently, as the phrase goes, "I should go back where I came from." But I do not wish to go back, I wish to stay in this country which I *love*. Is it not understandable that a relationship deliberately based on choice may inspire, at the same time, more *passion* and more criticism than an inherited relationship?[14]

But even in the prewar Europe of the Spitzerian education, such passion was not always seen as fitting. Erich Auerbach found his contemporary's idiom—if not his id—deeply distasteful, and, if Spitzer's postwar protestations of his love of country resonate, in an odd way, with Morbius's protestations about his "great love for this planet" and his own refusal to return to Earth, then Auerbach's complaints strike at the heart of those relationships among desire, discipline, pedagogy, and paternalism that may stand not only in the background of *Forbidden Planet* but in the forefront of the profession of philology itself. Writing to his friend Ludwig Binswanger in 1930, Auerbach offers this caricature of Spitzer (but no less a caricature than, as I will suggest shortly, we see in Morbius and his prototypes).

> Spitzer is the son of a Viennese Jew and an opera singer. He is full of activity and tactlessness, he has very lively ideas and not even a shadow of culture and true critical spirit, he is very cordial, very malicious, very presumptuous, very insecure, very emotional, he is open-hearted beyond belief, and a born comedian. He is incapable of sitting still for a moment, he must always work, dance, love, move, and set others into motion. In general, I like him fine, and I can learn a lot from him. But he does not have the slightest idea of what I am like; both in his admiration and his critique he always fails, and our friendship is a tissue of misunderstandings. At the same time, he believes it to be his right and mission to educate me. You should see him. The face of a comedian, always ahead, a long and baroque nose, with his curls beginning to turn gray, always on the street with a coat that is too short [*Ein Schauspielergesicht, Kopf vor, mit langer Barocknase und schon etwas grauen Locken, auf der Strasse einen viel zu kurzen Mantel*]. And this man loves his students,

is wooing them for their sympathy, gives them his whole heart, and relies on their judgment.¹⁵

What Auerbach finds so distasteful in his colleague is the unbridled passion of the pedagogue: his manic action, his barely suppressed eroticism, his need for love. The passions of *Forbidden Planet* find, I think, a telling antecedent here, as what is forbidden about both are forms of excessive desire and misdirected passion (indeed, Morbius is the one who forbids what, for 1950s audiences, would have been the proper passionate relationship in the film, that between the handsome and controlling Captain Adams and the brainy but ultimately submissive Altaira).

Auerbach's portrait, too, raises some more disturbing points of contact with the movie and, more generally, with what would become a later émigré condition of the academic. For here we have not just a condemnation of desire but a physiognomy of fear. Spitzer becomes a stage Jew in this portrait—a child of a performer and a bearer of the iconography anti-Semitic caricature with his "baroque nose," the curls, the ill-fitting cloak. These are the very characteristics of an earlier literary horror, one equally at home with fantasies of the forbidden: Coppelius in Hoffman's "The Sandman." Compare the vision of *his* big nose, growing over his lip ("über di Oberlippe gezogener Nase"); his greasy, perhaps pomaded curls (*Kleblocken*); and his ash-gray coat, cut in an outmoded style ("altmodish zugeschnittenen aschgrauen Rocke"). Coppelius enters the child Nathaniel's world as the emblem of repulsiveness itself, a hateful, spectral monster ("ein häßlicher, gespenstischer Unhold"), whose visage would haunt the dreams of scholars from the early-nineteenth through the mid-twentieth century.¹⁶

Auerbach's portrait of Spitzer transforms the philologist into a nightmare creature of the Jewish other, a predatory monster, an invasive and invading id. And the terms of this portrait share in both a literary legacy and a political afterlife: a construction, as it were, of the iconography of academic aliens. For if Spitzer comes off as a Viennese stage creature, then so, too, is Morbius theatricalized: a Hollywood philologist. In contrast to the clean-cut crew, all openness and brilliant color, Morbius is bearded, dark, elusive. Dressed in black, with that Mephistophelean goatee and widow's peak, he is the very icon of death that is the etymon of his name. Our suspicions are made explicit in the movie's novelization by W. J. Stuart: "We stared at him. He was a big man, and striking, with a head of greying dark hair and a neat forked beard which lent the impassive face of an effect partly Oriental, partly satanic."[17] True, Morbius may be, for readers of the 1950s, more Fu Man Chu than philologue. But I cannot help seeing behind that word "Oriental," once again, the code word of Jewishness that stretches back to Heinrich Heine's formulation, noted, too, by George Eliot: "Judea always seemed to me like a piece of the Occident lost in the Orient." But there is also the satanic. Compare the novelization's phrasing with the Spitzer who would reemerge in America in, for example, the characteristically devilish reminiscences of John Freccero, who, writing of his teacher at Hopkins in the 1950s, noted: "In those days of crew cuts and white bucks, the figure of the continental virtuoso challenged every canon of male decorum."[18] More fully, Paul Zumthor's recollections of Auerbach and Spitzer mark perfectly the iconology of the philologist.

> No one would deny the long-term impact effected in our discipline at certain times by the major personal traits of some scholar who managed to imprint upon it, as it were, the features of his own character. The work of the gentle Auerbach, with his large eyes and his expression of timid goodness, marked a generation, otherwise but no less than the work of the brilliant Spitzer, that great conversationalist, self-confident and beloved by women. One could cite many other names; I am only recalling a few impressions to which I was particularly sensitive because of the happenstances of my career. And of the many whom I have known, I prefer to evoke only those who are now among the dead.[19]

What of those dead? Look at their pictures: Auerbach, with those sad eyes staring from the posthumous collection of essays; Spitzer, full of vision and of life; or Curtius, with that open face, beaming from the bench of a Heidelberg walkway.[20] None of them really looks like Morbius (indeed, Spitzer bears little resemblance either to Auerbach's or to Freccero's portraits of him), and that is precisely the point. For Morbius is not an accurate representation of the émigrés who entered the academy in the 1950s. Instead, he is a fantastic evocation of the Europeans who had taught them, Europeans of the late nineteenth and early twentieth centuries: near mythic figures of repose and eminence. I search the library and find, almost at random, a clutch of illustrated *Festschriften*:

Wilhelm Streitberg, all wing collar and goatee, staring out of his *Festschrift* portrait of 1924; Eduard Sievers, lost in thought before his bookshelf, similarly goateed in a 1925 photograph; Albert Debrunner, staring out beside the title page of his 1954 *Festschrift, Sprachgeschichte und Wortbedeutung* (a title, by the way, as clear a definition of the philologist's calling as Captain Adams's is), with the same hirsuted visage.[21] These are the icons of academic fantasy, a look of European middle-aged intellectualism that is as much a part of what we might call the postwar theater of philology as Auerbach's Hoffmannesque caricature was of an earlier age.

For such philologists, the study was the stage. Morbius's great desk, set before a mural of a wild galactic field, juts out like some proscenium of pedagogy. When Captain Adams and the doctor enter, they find all the stage props of the discipline: the manuscript, the magnifier, and the map. We see the text but for an instant in the movie, just before Morbius returns to his study to find the two astronauts intruding on his work. "You'll find the family silver in the cabinet and my daughter's jewelry on her dresser," he sardonically snaps. But, then, what would one say to any intruder—come take the money, take the jewels, but leave me, leave my work. And the surprise: we're not interested in the money; we're interested in the work. How many would have heard these words, heard these responses, as the treasured work of decades is appropriated, stolen, ripped apart? Turn to a Website for *Forbidden Planet*, and one lingers over this manuscript long enough to see it modeled on the manuscripts of old—to see Morbius's new philology directed to deciphering what Auerbach himself had called "the spiritual patrimony of a culture."[22] When Morbius offers his tour of Krell bibliography, he sounds more like the European university professor he appears to be than the mad scientist of films that he denies he is. His benighted vision of the Krell is not unlike the émigré classicist's imagination of a long-dead civilization—one where pettiness and want have been dismissed in favor of an elevated cultivation.

Writing about the classicist Werner Jaeger's "humanism" of the 1930s, Moses Hadas could look back from the vantage point of 1960 with a colder eye: "What humanism seems to amount to, in Professor Jaeger's conception, is a mystical and exclusive cult to which only a spiritual elite can have access, but which alone, in turn, can produce such an elite. Its perfect and permanent paradigm is classical Athens, where an elite conscious of the obligations of its own nobility selflessly cultivated the most exalted reaches of human potentiality. The preciosity of such a view is not so sympathetic to 1960 America."[23] Would 1956 America had found Morbius's view so precious? Again and again, Morbius calls his Krell a noble race, an "all-but-divine race," whose crystal towers reached to heaven. In the novelization of the movie, Morbius is given an extended paean to this species that explicitly turns his Krell into something like Jaeger's Athenians:

> "Their explorations ended . . . the Krell appear to have achieved the very last pinnacles of knowledge, with only the ultimate peak left to ascend and conquer. But then"—my voice shook uncontrollably—"but then at this crowning point in their great, their truly miraculous history, this godlike race was destroyed. In one night of unknown, unimaginable disaster they were wiped from existence. . . . Even their cities, with their cloud-piercing towers of glittering translucent metal—even these have crumbled back into the soil."[24]

Such sad nostalgia fits precisely with the Jaegerian fantasies of a Paedeia-driven Athens and, in turn, of a resentful, cultureless America. Morbius's fascination with his Krell is part and parcel of his abiding rejection of Earth—a place he still remembers, and which the astronauts exemplify, as one of arid anti-intellectualism. "Without the abiding respect for the antique idea of humanity in human culture," Jaeger himself wrote in 1960, in the penultimate year of his life, "the study of classical antiquity vanishes into thin air" (*schwebt die klassische Altertumswissenschaft in der luft*). "Whoever does not see this should come to America and let himself bear witness to the progress of the denouement of classical studies."[25]

The irony, of course, is that what Morbius has re-created on his stage set of discovery is nothing less than the American dream: a southern California–style high-modernist household, complete with landscape, furnishings, and elevations right out of, say, the work of Marcel Breuer, Mies van der Rohe, or Richard Neutra. Of course, this is a southern California house, a Hollywood stage set itself designed out of the building blocks of émigré modernism.[26] The movie's plans, meticulously reproduced in the 1979 special issue of the magazine *Cinefantastique* devoted to the making of *Forbidden Planet*, are nothing if not brilliant mock-ups of this international-style contemporaneity. Indeed, the very landscape of the film's forbidden planet—in spite of its double moon and pink sky—is a papier-mâché metamorphosis of southern California wilderness (if one has any doubt, recall the moment when the id monster approaches at night and the radar man reports, "It's just stopped at the head of the arroyo," a word that was opaque to me until I spent a research year in Pasadena and lived near one). Morbius, in short, lives with all the trappings of postwar émigré knowledge and technology: philology, modernist architecture, nuclear physics, aleatory music. It is a household only superficially American (the doctor, like a figure out of Donna Reed, first assumes that "Mrs. Morbius" is not at home), whose domesticities are, in the end, defined not by *domestici* but *alieni*.

"Sed inimici hominis domestici eius." But a man's enemies are the men of his own house. There are the words of the prophet Micah, used by Bernard of Clairvaux and quoted by Erich Auerbach in the "Adam and Eve" chapter of *Mimesis*. I suggested in my last chapter that this phrase stands as the fulcrum of an essay on philology and collaboration, an exercise in autoallegory where the story of the devil's tempting of our Edenic first parents may be understood as the occasion for reflecting on the nature of collaboration, on the politics of philological inquiry, and on the relationships between the autobiographical and the historical in writing literary scholarship. I return to these words now to show us Morbius himself confronted with the same scholarly and political dilemma. "My evil self is at the door," he cries. Spent in his study, twisted after two decades of self-absorption, steeped in the texts of Krell philology and the tableaux vivants of an old plastic educator, Morbius comes, too late, to realize his own guilt. The thing that killed his colleagues is not, as he would aver, some "planetary force" but the *inimicus* of his own house.

"Guilty, guilty," he cries, as the monster from his own repressed subconscious comes to kill his daughter and her love. But what is guilt? We bring our horrors with us. Twenty years before, Morbius stood by as his crew was murdered and only he and his wife saved. Twenty years before—that is, twenty years before 1956—came the first waves of exile. In 1936 Auerbach was dismissed from Marburg and went to Istanbul; Curtius had left Istanbul and arrived at Hopkins; Jaeger showed up at Chicago (and would, by 1939, be at Harvard). For the film's living audience, the invocation of two decades passing could not help recalling the horrors of another planet, when the monsters from submerged selves came out to shatter their own crystalline cities (in the novelization, Morbius explicitly refers to the destruction of his crew two decades earlier as "the holocaust," [p. 43]). So, what is Morbius afraid of? He had left the confines of a sullen earth, sought refuge in a world apart from strife and anger, where he could be but a recluse, as he put it early in the film. What is the guilt here? For it is not simply that his id had vanquished those who would remove him from his paradise. Morbius and his family are not just "immune," as he put it, from the planetary force. They are collaborators.

Those who were not touched by violence and removal were long seen as those collaborating with the enemy. Whose houses were not burnt, whose glass was not broken in that crystal night? The guilt of Morbius—whose name now most assuredly is death itself—is the guilt of the collaborator. He's turned them all in, named names, fingered friends and family. What he brings with him in two decades of nightmares is the stain of collusion, and this guilt, precisely, is the guilt all émigrés and exiles must confront.

In the end, what is the difference between emigration and exile? For Erich Auerbach, the émigré experience may have seemed, at first glance, a simple exile. But Auerbach himself was married to a daughter of a director of the Deutsche Bank; he was in touch, throughout the war, with family and friends. True, he was there in Istanbul, without his books, and later, at Penn State and in New Haven, re-creating, still in German, the *Weltliteratur* of a fallen *Welt*. And yet, still, anxiousness remains.[27] The world of Auerbach's connections may never have left him. *Mimesis* was reviewed, in the German philological journals, almost immediately after its publication—a German work by a German scholar, with almost (I stress "almost") no mention of its author's removal and exile. Soon, everyone would show up. Behind the mute tranquillity of an American pastoral—memoirs of the seminar with Spitzer, of tea with Mrs. Auerbach—lie still the nightmares of twenty years before.

The id (in Freud's German, *es*) that comes to crash this alien Edenic world is maybe not so much the creature of an orthodox Freudian subconscious but, as I have suggested throughout this epilogue, the creature of the émigré's experience itself. Writing of the phenomenon in his 1944 autobiography *Die Welt von Gestern*, Stefan Zweig put his finger on the pulse of emigration. The émigré experiences, he wrote, a disturbance of equilibrium (*Gleichgewichtsstörung*), where, as he states, "I just don't feel that I belong together with myself anymore. Something of the inborn identity with my original and proper *Ich* remains forever disrupted."[28] I leave that *Ich* untranslated, as it is Freud's word for what we would come to know as the ego. *Ich* und *es*, the émigré now splits the parts of selfhood, and the old philologist well schooled in texts of ancient and of alien desires, cannot find himself at home in an America of Adams and new Eves. And as we leave the theater, or I close this book, we may come to see that the truly forbidden planet is not somewhere in the stars but always right beneath our feet.

NOTES

Introduction.
The Pursuit of Error: Philology, Rhetoric, and the History of Scholarship

1. For the idea of the counterhistory, see Catherine Gallagher and Stephen Greenblatt, *Practicing New Historicism* (Chicago: University of Chicago Press, 2000), p. 52 and p. 214 n. 4.

2. Friedrich Nietzsche: "The eighth of April, 1777, when F. A. Wolf invented for himself the name of *stud. philol.*, is the birthday of philology" (*Wir Philologen* 3[2], trans. William Arrowsmith, in William Arrowsmith, "Nietzsche: Notes for 'We Philologists,'" *Arion*, n.s. 1/2 [1973/1974]: 281). On Wolf's matriculation at Göttingen as "Philologia Studiosus," see Mark Pattison, "F. A. Wolf," in *Essays by the Late Mark Pattison*, ed. Henry Nettleship (Oxford: Oxford University Press, 1889), 1:343. But see, too, the discussion in E. J. Kenney, *The Classical Text* (Berkeley: University of California Press, 1974), p. 98 n. 1, who notes that, in fact, Wolf "had predecessors as far back as 1736" for his choice of philological study. On Wolf and his milieu—the history of classical philology in eighteenth-century German universities, the relationship between Homeric scholarship and Romanticism, the beginnings of scholarly professionalism in Europe—see the introduction and bibliographical essays in *F. A. Wolf: Prolegomena to Homer, 1795*, trans., intro., and ann. Anthony Grafton, Glenn W. Most, and James E. G. Zetzel (Princeton: Princeton University Press, 1985), pp. 3–36, 249–54.

3. Gregory Nagy, "Death of a Schoolboy: The Early Greek Beginning of a Crisis in Philology," in *On Philology*, ed. Jan Ziolkowski (University Park: Pennsylvania State University Press, 1991), pp. 37–48.

4. Roberta Frank, "The Unbearable Lightness of Being a Philologist," *Journal of English and Germanic Philology* 100 (1997): 487, citing Bacon, *Novum Organum* (London: Reeves, 1879), 2:505.

5. Friedrich Schlegel, "On the Language and Custom of the Indians," quoted in Michel Foucault, *The Order of Things* (New York: Vintage, 1970), p. 280.

6. William Dwight Whitney, *The Life and Growth of Language* (New York: Appleton, 1875), p. 315.

7. Ferdinand de Saussure, *Course de linguistique générale*, ed. Charles Bally and Albert Sechehaye, rev. Tullio de Mauro (Paris: Payot, 1982); idem *Course in General Linguistics*, trans. Roy Harris (London: Duckworth, 1983). The opening chapter is "A Brief Survey of the History of Linguistics" (*Course in General Linguistics*, pp. 1–5; "Coup d'oeil sur l'histoire de la linguistique," *Course de linguistique générale*, pp. 13–19). For the story of the making of the *Course* and its relationship to Saussure's lectures, see Roy Harris, *Reading Saussure: A Critical Commentary on the* Cours de linguistique générale (London: Duckworth, 1987); and Jonathan Culler, *Ferdinand de Saussure*, rev. ed. (Ithaca: Cornell University Press, 1986).

8. Harris, *Reading Saussure*, p. 5.

9. The heart of the discussion is *Gorgias*, 462–63. I use the translation of Walter Hamilton (Harmondsworth: Penguin, 1960), where the discussion appears on pp. 42–44. A convenient guide to the argument and subsequent bibliography is George A. Kennedy, *A New History of Classical Rhetoric* (Princeton: Princeton University Press, 1994), pp. 35–39. See, too, Thomas M. Conley, *Rhetoric in the European Tradition* (Chicago: University of Chicago Press, 1990), pp. 8–11; and, for a characteristically wide-ranging and idiosyncratic account of the Platonic tradition generally, Brian Vickers, *In Defense of Rhetoric* (Oxford: Oxford University Press, 1987).

10. Kennedy, *New History*, p. 3.

11. Carole Blair, "Contested Histories of Rhetoric: The Politics of Preservation, Progress, and Change," *Quarterly Journal of Speech* 78 (1992): 403. For an extended argument about the need for the discipline of rhetoric to historicize itself, see James L. Kastely, *Rethinking the Rhetorical Tradition: From Plato to Postmodernism* (New Haven: Yale University Press, 1997).

12. John Quincy Adams, *Lectures on Rhetoric and Oratory* (Cambridge, Mass.: Hilliard and Metcalf, 1810; reprint, New York: Russell and Russell, 1962), 1:12. For Cicero, see *De Inventione*, ed. and trans. H. M. Hubbell, Loeb Library (Cambridge: Harvard University Press, 1949), I.i.2, pp. 4–5.

13. See Karl Weick, *The Social Psychology of Organizing* (Reading, Mass.: Addison-Wesley, 1969); D. M. Boje, "The Storytelling Organization," *Administrative Science Quarterly* 36 (1991): 106–26; Charlotte Linde, *Life Stories* (Oxford: Oxford University Press, 1994).

14. Friedrich Nietzsche, notes for the unfinished book *Wir Philologen*, published as *Nachgelassene Fragmente*, in Friedrich Nietzsche, *Sämtliche Werke*, ed. Giorgio Colli and

Mazzino Montinari (Berlin: de Gruyter, 1980), vol. 8, 5[187]. The English translation of this material is available in William Arrowsmith, "Nietzsche: Notes for 'We Philologists,'" *Arion*, n.s. 1/2 (1973/1974): 279–380, with each fragment keyed to the number in the Colli and Montinari edition. Further references to these notes from *Wir Philologen* will be cited by number in the edition of Colli and Montinari and the translation of Arrowsmith.

15. See Mary Carruthers, *The Book of Memory* (Cambridge: Cambridge University Press, 1990).

16. Pseudo-Cicero, *Rhetorica ad Herennium*, ed. and trans. Harry Caplan, Loeb Library (Cambridge: Harvard University Press, 1954), 3.22.35, pp. 218–19.

17. Paul de Man, "The Return to Philology," *Times Literary Supplement*, December 10, 1982, pp. 1355–56, reprinted in idem, *The Resistance to Theory* (Minneapolis: University of Minnesota Press, 1986), pp. 21–26. For de Man's concerns with rhetorical reading and his investment in the history of Western rhetoric, see idem, *Blindness and Insight: Essays in the Rhetoric of Contemporary Criticism*, 2d ed. (Minneapolis: University of Minnesota Press, 1983); and Kastely, *Rethinking the Rhetorical Tradition*, pp. 195–220.

18. De Man, "Return to Philology," in *Resistance to Theory*, p. 23.

19. René Wellek, "Memories of the Profession," in *Building a Profession: Autobiographical Perspectives on the History of Comparative Literature in the United States*, ed. Lionel Gossman and Mihai Spariosu (Albany: State University of New York Press, 1994), pp. 1–11.

20. Erich Auerbach, *Mimesis: The Representation of Reality in Western Literature*, trans. Willard R. Trask (Princeton: Princeton University Press, 1953), p. 525.

21. See Neal Gilbert, *Renaissance Concepts of Method* (New York: Columbia University Press, 1960), pp. 48–55. I have discussed the idea and the etymology of "method" in detail in my *Boethius and Dialogue: Literary Method in the Consolation of Philosophy* (Princeton: Princeton University Press, 1985).

22. Saussure, *Course in General Linguistics*, p. 1; idem, *Course de linguistique générale*, p. 13.

23. "From a methodological point of view, however, it is of some interest to be acquainted with these errors [*erreurs*]. The mistakes [*les fautes*] a science makes in its initial stages present a magnified picture of the mistakes made by individuals starting out on scientific research" (p. 4; pp. 17–18).

24. "Der Lese- und Schreiblehrer und der Corrector sind die ersten Typen des Philologen" (5[189]).

25. For discussion of the genesis and reception of *Wir Philologen*, see William Arrowsmith, "Nietzsche on Classics and Classicists (Part II)," *Arion* 2 (1963): 5–27.

26. Arrowsmith, "Nietzsche on Classics and Classicists," p. 8.

1. Errata: Mistakes and Masters in the Early Modern Book

1. Stephen Greenblatt, *Renaissance Self-Fashioning: More to Shakespeare* (Chicago: University of Chicago Press, 1980), chap. 2, pp. 74–114.

2. "The Work of Art in the Age of Mechanical Reproduction," in *Illuminations*, ed. Hannah Arendt, trans. Harry Zohn (New York: Schocken, 1969), pp. 217–51.

3. Tyndale had an English translation printed in Cologne, probably in the summer of 1525, but printing was stopped midway through the book. All that has survived from this aborted print run is one copy of the translation of chapter 22 of the Book of Matthew (now in the British Library). The entire New Testament in English was eventually printed in early 1526, at Worms. Only two copies survive, and only one (the Bristol Baptist College copy, now held in the British Library), is complete. Tyndale's Pentateuch was printed in Amsterdam in 1530, and a revised version of the New Testament appeared in 1534. See David Daniell, *William Tyndale: A Biography* (New Haven: Yale University Press, 1994), pp. 109–11, 134–51, and 283–315.

4. Greenblatt, *Renaissance Self-Fashioning*, pp. 97, 95, and 99.

5. Elizabeth Eisenstein, *The Printing Press as an Agent of Change*, 2 vols. (Cambridge: Cambridge University Press, 1979).

6. See Anthony Grafton, "The Importance of Being Printed," *Journal of Interdisciplinary History* 11 (1980): 265–86; Michael Warner, *Letters of the Republic* (Cambridge: Harvard University Press, 1987); and Adrian Johns, *The Nature of the Book: Print and Knowledge in the Making* (Chicago: University of Chicago Press, 1999).

7. See Lucien Febvre and Henri-Jean Martin, *L'apparition du livre* (Paris: Albin-Michel, 1958); Roger Chartier and Henri-Jean Martin, eds., *Histoire de l'édition française*, 4 vols. (Paris: Fayard, 1982); Roger Chartier, ed., *L'usage de l'imprimé* (Paris: Fayard, 1987), published in English as *The Culture of Print*, trans. Lydia Cochrane (Princeton: Princeton University Press, 1989). American scholars associated with this movement include Natalie Davis (see, esp., her *Society and Politics in Early Modern France* [Stanford: Stanford University Press, 1975], and *Fiction in the Archives* [Stanford: Stanford University Press, 1987]); Robert Darnton (see, esp., *The Literary Underground of the Old Regime* [Cambridge: Harvard University Press, 1982]); and Paul Saenger (see, esp., *Space Between Words: The Origins of Silent Reading* [Stanford: Stanford University Press, 1999]).

8. Johns, *The Nature of the Book*, p. 5.

9. Warner, *Letters of the Republic*, p. 7.

10. For English typefaces and manuscript models, see my discussion in *Chaucer and His Readers* (Princeton: Princeton University Press, 1993), pp. 160 and 270 n. 31. For the influence of humanist scripts on the development of italic type by Aldus Manutius and his contemporaries, see Nicolas Barker, "The Aldine Italic," in *A Millennium of the Book*, ed. Robin Myers and Michael Harris (New Castle, Del.: Oak Knoll, 1994), pp. 45–60.

11. Several recent studies of humanist bookmaking inform my account here: John F. D'Amico, *Theory and Practice in Renaissance Textual Criticism* (Berkeley: University of California Press, 1988); Paolo Trovato, *Con ogni diligenza corretto: La stampa e le revisioni editoriali dei testi letterari italiani (1470–1570)* (Bologna: Il Mulino, 1991); Anthony Grafton, *Defenders of the Text: Traditions of Scholarship in an Age of Science, 1450–1800* (Cambridge: Harvard University Press, 1991); David Carlson, *English Humanist Books:*

Writers and Patrons, Manuscript and Print, 1475–1525 (Toronto: University of Toronto Press, 1993); Lisa Jardine, *Erasmus: Man of Letters* (Princeton: Princeton University Press, 1993); Brian Richardson, *Print Culture in Renaissance Italy: The Editor and the Vernacular Text, 1470–1600* (Cambridge: Cambridge University Press, 1994). For some reflections on the culture of correction in the period immediately after the one I survey here, see Andrew Murphy, "'Came errour here by myss of man': Editing and the Metaphysics of Presence," *Yearbook of English Studies* 29 (1999): 118–37.

12. See Hans Widmann, "Die Lektüre unendlichen Korrekturen," *Archiv für Geschichte des Buchwesens* 5 (1964): 778–826.

13. Epigrams of Martial that address directly the relationship of author to scribe, the problems of error, and the control of correct texts include 1.101, 2.6, 2.8, 4.10, 7.11.

14. See *Cassiodorus Senator: An Introduction to Divine and Human Readings*, trans. L. W. Jones (New York: Columbia University Press, 1946).

15. See Karlheinz Hilbert, *Baldricus Burgulianus Carmina* (Heidelberg: Winter, 1979), poems numbered 9, 10, 84, 85, 92, 105, 108, 144, 148, 196.

16. See *Petrarch: Four Dialogues for Scholars*, ed. and trans. C. H. Rawski (Cleveland: Western Reserve University Press, 1967), pp. 34–37.

17. Larry D. Benson, gen. ed., *The Riverside Chaucer* (Boston: Houghton Mifflin, 1987), p. 650.

18. See R. B. McKerrow, *An Introduction to Bibliography* (Oxford: Oxford University Press, 1927); Fredson Bowers, *Principles of Bibliographical Description* (New York: Russell and Russell, 1962), esp. pp. 42, 46–47 n. 6; Philip Gaskell, *A New Introduction to Bibliography* (Oxford: Oxford University Press, 1972), esp. p. 354. For more specific accounts, see Joseph A. Dane, "'On Correctness': A Note on Some Press Variants in Thynne's 1532 Edition of Chaucer," *The Library*, 6th ser., 17 (1995): 156–67; and Joseph A. Dane and Seth Lerer, "Press Variants in John Stow's Chaucer (1561) and the Text of 'Adam Scriveyn,'" *Transactions of the Cambridge Bibliographical Society* 11 (1999): 468–79.

19. Elizabeth Eisenstein offers a few brief remarks on the origin and impact of the errata sheet in *The Printing Press as an Agent of Change*, pp. 80–81, 85. Elsewhere, she credits the Venetian printer Erhard Ratdolt with the "innovation" of the "first list of errata" (pp. 587–88), but I can find no evidence to support this claim.

20. Noted in Gabriele Paolo Carosi, *Da Magonza a Subiaco: L'introduzione della stampa in Italia* (n.p.: Bramante, 1982), p. 30; see, too, Trovato, *Con ogni diligenza*, pp. 87–88.

21. Richardson, *Print Culture*, p. 45.

22. See Trovato, *Con ogni diligenza*, pp. 86–93.

23. Horace, *Opera* (Florence: Antonius Miscominus, 1482), pp. 265v–266r in the modern pagination (Huntington Library Copy).

24. "Siqui uel desint / uel perperam notati sint in grecis dictionibus accentus: eos eruditi uel restituant / uel emendent pro iudico. Siqua etiam preter hec mendosa lector inuenies / que propera[n]tes oculos nostros subterfugerint / ea quo[que] [pro] tuo iudicio eme[n]dabis; nec [quodcunque] putabis nostrum quod parum sit rectum: Errata

aut[em] omnia uel impressoribus adscribes / uel curatoribus: Na[m] si mea esse hic errata ulla credes: tunc ego te credam cordis habere nihil" (Politian, *Miscellanea* [Florence: Antonius Miscominus, 1489], Huntington Library copy). On Politian's scholarship generally, see the chapter "The Scholarship of Poliziano and Its Context," in Grafton, *Defenders of the Text*, pp. 47–75; the comments in D'Amico, *Textual Criticism in the Renaissance*, pp. 23–27; and, for more specifics, see Joseph Dane, "'Si vis archetypas habere nugas': Authorial Subscriptions in the Houghton Library and Huntington Library Copies of Politian, *Miscellanea* (Florence: Miscomini, 1489)," *Harvard Library Bulletin*, n.s., 10 (1999): 12–22.

25. See Trovato, *Con ogni diligenza*.

26. For Caxton's remarks, see *Canterbury Tales* prologue and *Eneydos* prologue, in *The Prologues and Epilogues of William Caxton*, ed. J. B. Crotch, Early English Text Society, Original Series, 176 (London: Oxford University Press, 1928), pp. 91 and 109, respectively. For the word "oversee" as specifically meaning proof correcting, see Percy Simpson, *Proofreading in the Sixteenth and Seventeenth Centuries* (London: Oxford University Press, 1935), pp. 1–3.

27. John Constable, *Epigrammata* (London: Bercula [Berthelett], 1520), sig. d4. My attention was drawn to this publication by John M. Headley, ed., *Responsio ad Lutherum*, in *The Complete Works of St. Thomas More*, vol. 5, part 2 (New Haven: Yale University Press, 1969), p. 836 n. 3.

28. Quoted in Simpson, *Proofreading*, pp. 46–47. Pynson apparently had a paid corrector at the press as early as 1499, as indicated in a petition (dated 1506) apparently referring to the 1499 publication of the *Abbreuiamentum statutorum* (see p. 111).

29. Headley, *Responsio ad Lutherum*, pp. 832–41, where the complex history of the printing of this text is detailed. The work was first published in early 1523, but it was seen as defective; More apparently reworked the text in response to new publications by Luther. A second issue appeared from Pynson probably in December 1523 (according to Headley, the first issue is not in *A Short-Title Catalogue of Books Printed in England, Scotland, and Ireland, 1475–1640* [hereafter *STC*], 2d ed., ed. W. A. Jackson, F. S. Ferguson, and Katharine Pantzer, 3 vols. [London: Bibliographical Society, 1976–1991]; the second is, however). Headley presents evidence and arguments that the errata list it contains was compiled by More himself.

30. See Clarence H. Miller, "The Texts," in Frank Manly, ed., *Letter to Bugenhagen, Supplication of Souls, Letter Against Frith*, in *The Complete Works of St. Thomas More*, vol. 7 (New Haven: Yale University Press, 1990), pp. clxi–clxviii. These editions are undated but are datable on external evidence to before October 1525 (p. clxi).

31. J. B. Trapp, ed., *The Apology*, in *The Complete Works of St. Thomas More*, vol. 9 (New Haven: Yale University Press, 1979), pp. lxxxix–xci.

32. Miller, *Supplication*, pp. clxiv, clxvi.

33. Thomas M. Lawler, ed., *A Dialogue Concerning Heresies*, in *The Complete Works of St. Thomas More*, vol. 6, part 2 (New Haven: Yale University Press, 1981), pp. 548–87.

34. See Simpson, *Proofreading*, pp. 3–4; and Lawler, *Dialogue*.

35. See the discussion in Lawler, *Dialogue*, pp. 556 ff.

36. Fisher's sermon against Luther, delivered at St. Paul's, February 11, 1526, quoted and discussed in Lawler, *Dialogue*, p. 440.

37. More's attention to the multiple reviews of his text may also resonate with the claims of European printers' colophons that touted the high quality of the proofreaders (or correctors of the press) they employed.

38. Louis A. Schuster, ed., *The Confutation of Tyndale's Answer*, in *The Complete Works of St. Thomas More*, vol. 8, part 1 (New Haven: Yale University Press, 1972), 8:36.

39. Translated and quoted in Headley, *Responsio*, p. 837.

40. From the printer's advertisement for the 1576 edition of Gascoigne's *The Droome of Doomes Day*, reproduced in Simpson, *Proofreading*, p. 9; see pp. 3–45.

41. Among the vast collection of researches on Tyndale and his Bible, the endpoints may be marked by Edward Arber, *The First Printed English New Testament* (London: Constable, 1871; reprint, London: Constable, 1895), and David Daniell, whose researches have been summarized in *William Tyndale: A Biography* (which also contains a full bibliography on the subject). For a collection of primary documents relating to the making and reception of the English Bible generally and Tyndale's version in particular, see Alfred W. Pollard, *Records of the English Bible* (London: Oxford University Press, 1911).

42. My study of the 1526 New Testament is based on the facsimile of the unique, complete edition (Banbury: Henry Stone and Son, 1976), with an afterword by F. F. Bruce, though unfortunately, as the afterword states, "any marginalia added by readers have been removed" in the photographic reproduction.

43. Daniell mentions them without comment (*William Tyndale*, p. 146). Many other misprints and distinctive wordings in the 1526 New Testament have been recorded and compared with the revised 1534 edition (and its misprints) in N. Hardy Wallis, ed., *The New Testament Translated by William Tyndale, 1534* (Cambridge: Cambridge University Press, 1938), pp. 613–28.

44. See Trovato, *Con ogni diligenza*.

45. "William Tindale, yet once more to the christen reader," the supplementary preface to the 1534 version of the New Testament. The text is available in Wallis, *The New Testament*, pp. 15–19; and in Pollard, *Records of the English Bible*, pp. 178–84. In this same preface, Tyndale reviews George Joye's unauthorized revision of the earlier New Testament translation, remarking sarcastically on how Joye's version was "diligentlye oversene and correct." When Joye's text was brought before him, Tyndale seemed astonished to find that it purported to have "diligent correction[s]" in it.

46. "An Expert Criticism of Tyndale's Version," is the title given by Pollard to the text of Ridley's letter to Henry Gold, February 24, 1527 (BL MS Cotton Cleopatra E. v. 362r, reproduced in Pollard, *Records of the English Bible*, pp. 122–26; the quotation is from p. 124).

47. *OED*, s.v., "fault," def. 5b, which offers a 1523 quotation from the Lord Berners translation of Froissart as the first use of the term meaning "a slip, error, mistake" and offers several examples up through a 1633 citation of an errata sheet titled "Faults escaped." The *OED* also notes, in defining *escape* (def 2b), "To issue unawares or involuntary from" and goes on, "Perhaps the obj. was originally dative. . . . Cr. Fr. *Il lui est*

échappé une sottise." It seems likely that the "faults escaped" idiom is a French one, while the "errors committed" phrase is Latin.

48. *OED*, s.v., "commit," def III, "to perpetrate or perform (in a bad sense)," a meaning that the editors state "existed in Latin from the earliest period." The word appears to enter English in this sense in the late fifteenth century, but the *OED* offers references for the subdefinition (6b), to commit "a folly, an error," only from 1596.

49. According to the *OED*, the earliest appearance of the word "folio" in English is in More's *Debellation* (1533), and the *Dictionary*'s editors state, "in the early instances the word may have been regarded as Latin" (s.v., "folio," def. A.I.1).

50. The actual errors recorded are almost exclusively typographical, that is, dropped letters and wrong letters, transpositions, and an occasional word left out. There are what may be substantive changes in replacing the word "obtayne" with "attayne" and in changing the phrase "humblenes off angles" to "humblenes and holynes of angels." It is worth comparing the 1535 English Bible of Matthew Coverdale, which on its final page lists only one erratum: "A faute escaped in pryntinge the New Testament. / Vpon the fourth leafe, the first syde, in the sixte chapter of S. Mathew. / Seke ye first the kyngdome of heaven: &c / Reade / Seke ye first the kyngdome of God:&c." This change may represent a substantive alteration of the text rather than a printer's error, but it is interesting that Coverdale uses the "faults escaped" idiom for recording it. I use the facsimile edition, *The Coverdale Bible, 1535*, intro. S. L. Greenslade (Folkstone: Dawson, 1975).

51. In Pollard, *Records of the English Bible*, p. 123. By "first print," Ridley most likely is referring to the incomplete version of the Gospels printed in Cologne in 1525, which appeared with prefaces and heavy glossing.

52. The *OED* uses this quotation to illustrate the meaning of "frenzy" as "agitation . . . wild folly, distraction, craziness" (s.v. "frenzy," def. A2).

53. Pollard, *Records*, p. 124.

54. See the discussion in Greenblatt, *Renaissance Self-Fashioning*, p. 94.

55. Pollard, *Records*, p. 124.

56. More's remark is from the *Dialogue Concerning Heresies*, book 3, chap. 8 (Lawler, p. 285).

57. Pollard, *Records*, pp. 123–24.

58. All references to Elyot's *Dictionary* are to the facsimile edition reproducing the copy in the Bodleian Library, Oxford (Menston: Scolar, 1970).

59. See G. R. Elton, *Policy and Police: The Enforcement of the Reformation in the Age of Thomas Cromwell* (Cambridge: Cambridge University Press, 1972); David Starkey, "Representation Through Intimacy," in Ioan Lewis, ed., *Symbols and Sentiments* (London: Academic, 1977), pp. 187–244; and idem, "Intimacy and Innovation: The Rise of the Privy Chamber, 1485–1547," in *The English Court: From the Wars of the Roses to the Civil War*, ed. David Starkey (London: Longman, 1987), pp. 71–118. See, too, my discussion in *Courtly Letters in the Age of Henry VIII* (Cambridge: Cambridge University Press, 1997), pp. 115–16, 133–35.

60. Stephen Merriam Foley, "Coming to Terms: Thomas Elyot's Definitions and the Particularity of Human Letters," *ELH: A Journal of English Literary History* 61 (1994): 214.

61. See the accounts in Starkey, "Representation Through Intimacy" and "Intimacy and Innovation."

62. Starkey, "Representation Through Intimacy," p. 198.

63. Quoted and discussed in Starkey, "Representation Through Intimacy," p. 207.

64. Foley, "Coming to Terms," p. 212.

65. Lawler, *Dialogue*, p. 450.

66. P. S. Allen, ed., *Opus Epistolarum Des. Erasmi Roterodami* (Oxford: Oxford University Press, Clarendon, 1910), letter number 325, 2:52. Translation from R. A. B. Mynors and D. F. S. Thomson, *The Correspondence of Erasmus*, in *The Collected Works of Erasmus* (Toronto: University of Toronto Press, 1976), 3:65.

67. Thomson, *Correspondence*, 3:67; Allen, *Opus Epist.*, 2:53.

68. *Oxford Latin Dictionary*, s.v., "mendum," "menda," "mendose."

69. Thomson, *Correspondence*, 3:276; Allen, *Opus Epist.*, 2:228.

70. See Elaine Fantham, "Imitation and Evolution: The Discussion of Rhetorical Imitation in Cicero *De Oratore* 2.87–97 and Some Related Problems of Ciceronian Theory," *Classical Philology* 73 (1978): 1–16.

71. Thomson, *Correspondence*, 3:276; Allen, *Opus Epist.*, 2:228–29.

72. Stephen M. Foley, *Sir Thomas Wyatt* (Boston: Twayne, 1990), p. 37.

73. Jardine, *Erasmus*, pp. 27–53. For further details, see the notes and discussion in my *Courtly Letters*, pp. 97–99, 232.

74. Clouet's portrait, now in the Metropolitan Museum of Art, New York City, is reproduced in Thomson, *Correspondence*, 3:274.

75. Thomson, *Correspondence*, 3:277; Allen, *Opus Epist.*, 2:229.

76. See Charlton T. Lewis and Charles Short, *A Latin Dictionary* (Oxford: Oxford University Press, Clarendon, 1879), s.v., "solvo," def. I.A.1.e, p. 1725.

77. Thomson, *Correspondence*, 3:278; Allen, *Opus Epist.*, 2:231.

78. David Greetham, "Textual Forensics," *PMLA* 111 (1996): 32–51. Material in this section of my chapter develops, with substantial changes of emphasis, augmentation of detail, and correction of error, arguments I made in *Courtly Letters in the Age of Henry VIII*, pp. 183–201.

79. See the account in Kenneth Muir, *The Life and Letters of Sir Thomas Wyatt* (Liverpool: Liverpool University Press, 1963), pp. 172–78; Perez Zagorin, "Sir Thomas Wyatt and the Court of Henry VIII: The Courtier's Ambitions," *Journal of Medieval and Renaissance Studies* 23 (1993): 113–41, esp. pp. 122–23, 132–33; Stephen M. Foley, *Sir Thomas Wyatt*, pp. 76–77.

80. Muir, *Life and Letters*, p. 186.

81. The two texts are preserved in British Library MS Harley 78, fols. 5–15, and edited versions appear in Muir, *Life and Letters* (*Declaration*, pp. 178–84; *Defence*, pp. 187–209). The reasons Wyatt did not deliver these speeches remain unclear, though Zagorin argues that Wyatt "went through the motions of confession and petitioning for mercy in order to save his life and regain his freedom" ("Sir Thomas Wyatt and the Court," p. 135).

82. Muir, *Life and Letters*, p. 178. All subsequent references will be cited in the text.

83. See the repeated remarks on letters sent and received in Muir, *Life and Letters*, pp. 179–80.

84. On the humanist uses of collation, see Grafton, *Defenders of the Text*, pp. 47–75; and Trovato, *Con ogni diligenza*, esp. pp. 93–96.

85. I quote from the facsimile edition: Derek Brewer, ed., *Geoffrey Chaucer: The Works, 1532* . . . (Menston: Scolar, 1969), sig. Aii v. The *OED* cites this passage as the first appearance in English of the word "collation" used in textual criticism (s.v., "collation," def. 3). "To collate," "to confer," and "to compare" are linked together in the example offered next by the *OED*, a 1568 reference to H. Campbell, ed., *Love Letters of Mary Queen of Scots*, app. 52: "The originals . . . were duly *conferred* and *compared* . . . with sundry other lettres . . . in *collation* whereof no difference was found" (emphases mine). The *OED* also notes, s.v., "confer," def. 4, "to bring into comparison, compare, collate (exceedingly common from 1530 to 1650)," and offers a citation from 1533 as the first appearance of the word. "Collation," however, appears in More's 1532 *Dialogue* in precisely these textual-critical terms (uncited by the *OED*): Scripture "maye be well vnderstanden / by the collacyon . . . of one texte wyth an other" (Lawler, *Dialogue*, p. 451).

86. See W. A. Sessions, "Surrey's Wyatt: Autumn 1542 and the New Poet," in *Rethinking the Henrician Era*, ed. Peter G. Herman (Urbana: University of Illinois Press, 1994), p. 175.

87. All quotations from Wyatt's poetry are from Kenneth Muir and Patricia Thompson, *The Collected Poems of Sir Thomas Wyatt* (Liverpool: Liverpool University Press, 1969), cited by number in my text.

88. Jonathan Crewe, *Trials of Authorship* (Berkeley: University of California Press, 1990), p. 22.

89. R. A. Rebholz, ed., Sir Thomas Wyatt: *The Complete Poems* (Harmondsworth: Penguin, 1978), pp. 14–15.

90. Lerer, *Courtly Letters in the Age of Henry VIII*, pp. 191–97.

91. Quoted in Simpson, *Proofreading*, p. 47.

92. Compare Skelton's indictment of Wolsey and King in *Why Come Ye Nat to Courte?* in *John Skelton: The Complete English Poems*, ed. John Scattergood (New Haven: Yale University Press, 1979): "He sayth the kynge doth wryte, / And writeth he wottith nat what" (lines 678–79).

93. Simpson, *Proofreading*, p. 55.

94. Quoted in Simpson, *Proofreading*, p. 5. See, too, Murphy, "'Came errour here by mysse of man.'"

95. Pseudo-Cicero, *Rhetorica ad Herennium*, ed. and trans. Harry Caplan (Cambridge: Harvard University Press, 1954), 3.16.28, pp. 204–5.

2. Sublime Philology: An Elegy for Anglo-Saxon Studies

1. Daniel Calder, "Histories and Surveys of Old English Literature: A Chronological Review," *Anglo-Saxon England* 10 (1982): 244, quoted and discussed in Allen Frantzen,

Desire for Origins: New Language, Old English, and Teaching the Tradition (New Brunswick: Rutgers University Press, 1990), p. 58. But Frantzen reports that Calder later "identified these remarks as insertions by Professor Peter Clemoes, editor of the journal in which this article appears" (p. 235 n. 110).

2. Michael Lapidge, "Textual Criticism and the Literature of Anglo-Saxon England," *Bulletin of the John Rylands Memorial Library* 73 (1991): 17–45, these quotations from p. 17, quoting Housman, *The Classical Papers of A. E. Housman*, ed. J. Diggle and F. R. D. Goodyear (Cambridge: Cambridge University Press, 1972), 3:1058.

3. See Frantzen, *Desire for Origins*; his introduction to his edited collection, *Speaking Two Languages* (Albany: State University of New York Press, 1991); and his subsequent essay, "The Fragmentation of Cultural Studies and the Fragments of Anglo-Saxon England," *Anglia* 114 (1996): 310–39. See, too, the volume edited by Frantzen and John D. Niles, *Anglo-Saxonism and the Construction of Social Identity* (Gainesville: University of Florida Press, 1997). For a particularly vivid exchange on the history, ideology, and potential direction of the field (something of a microcosm of the argumentativeness of Anglo-Saxonists of the mid-1990s), see Frantzen and Gillian Overing, letter to the editor, *PMLA* 108 (1993): 1177–78, on Michael Near, "Anticipating Alienation: *Beowulf* and the Intrusion of Literacy," *PMLA* 108 (1993): 320–32.

4. For approaches drawing on a deconstructionist tradition, see John P. Hermann, *Allegories of War* (Ann Arbor: University of Michigan Press, 1989); for work in sign theory and Foucauldian history, see Martin Irvine, *The Making of Textual Culture: "Grammatica" and Literary Theory, 350–1100* (Cambridge: Cambridge University Press, 1994); for psychoanalytic approaches, see James Earl, *Thinking About Beowulf* (Stanford: Stanford University Press, 1994), and, to a lesser extent, John M. Hill, *The Cultural World in Beowulf* (Toronto: University of Toronto Press, 1995); for a cultural studies approach, see Frantzen, "The Fragmentation of Cultural Studies"; for a variety of feminist approaches, see Jane Chance, *Woman as Hero in Old English Literature* (Syracuse: Syracuse University Press, 1986); Helen Damico and Alexandra Hennesey Olsen, eds., *New Readings on Women in Old English Literature* (Bloomington: Indiana University Press, 1990); Gillian Overing, *Language, Sign, and Gender in Beowulf* (Carbondale: Southern Illinois University Press, 1990); Gillian Overing and Clare Lees, "Before History: Bodies, Metaphor, and the Church in Anglo-Saxon England," *Yale Journal of Criticism* 11 (1999): 315–34.

5. Representative reviews and exchanges include Joyce Hill, review of Frantzen, *Desire for Origins*, in *Anglia* 111 (1993): 161–64; Frantzen's reply, "Who Do These Anglo-Saxonists Think They Are, Anyway," *Æstel* 2 (1994):1–43; Alexandra Hennesey Olsen's review of Overing, *Language, Sign, and Gender*, in *Speculum* 67 (1992): 1024–26; Joseph Harris's review of Hermann, *Allegories of War*, in *Speculum* 67 (1992): 983–86; Gernot Wieland's review of Irvine's *Making of Textual Culture*, in the online *Bryn Mawr Medieval Review* 95.2.10 (February 10, 1995); and Irvine's response in the same forum, 95.3.12 (April 12, 1995), together with Wieland's later response, 95.5.22 (May 22, 1995). Not all such reviews, however, were negative. For a review of the rhetoric of criticism in Old English studies of the mid-1990s, see John P. Hermann, "Why Anglo-Saxonists Can't Read; or, Who Took the Mead out of Medieval Studies?" *Exemplaria* 7 (1995): 9–26.

6. Steven Zwicker, *Lines of Authority: Politics and English Literary Culture, 1649–1689* (Ithaca: Cornell University Press, 1993), p. 7.

7. Available in facsimile as no. 248 in the series English Linguistics, 1500–1800, ed. R. C. Alston (Menston: Scolar, 1970), published in two volumes (all references are to this edition, henceforth referred to as *Thesaurus*). To my knowledge, there exists no complete translation into English of the *Thesaurus*. An abridged version of its grammatical material (not including the critical and historical portions I discuss here) was prepared by William Wotton, *Linguarum vett. Septentrionalium thesauri grammatico-critici, et archaeologici, auctore Georgio Hickesio, conspectus brevis* (London, 1708), and translated into English by Maurice Shelton, *Wotton's Short View of G. Hickes's Grammatico-Critical and Archaeological Treasure of the ancient northern-languages* (London, 1735).

8. The fullest account of Hickes's life and works is Richard L. Harris, *A Chorus of Grammars: The Correspondence of George Hickes and His Collaborators on the* Thesaurus linguarum septentrionalium (Toronto: University of Toronto Press, 1992), whose critical and biographical materials augment its collection of letters to paint a vivid personal portrait. Earlier accounts of Hickes include David Charles Douglas, *English Scholars, 1660–1730* (London: Eyre and Spottiswode, 1939; rev. ed, 1951), pp. 77–97; J. A. W. Bennett, "Hickes's *Thesaurus*: A Study in Oxford Book-Production," *English Studies 1948* [*Essays and Studies*, n.s., 1] (1948): 28–45; and Shaun F. Hughes, "The Anglo-Saxon Grammars of George Hickes and Elizabeth Elstob," in *Anglo-Saxon Scholarship: The First Three Centuries*, ed. Carl Berkhout and Milton McC. Gatch (Boston: Hall, 1982), pp. 119–47. It was Edward Thwaites who dedicated his *Heptateuchus, Liber Job et Evangelium Nicodemi: Anglo-Saxonice* (London, 1698) to Hickes, addressing his preface to "Viro summo, Georgio Hickesio, S. T. P. Literaturae Anglo-Saxonicae Instauratori."

9. Bennett, "Hickes's *Thesaurus*," pp. 28–29 and (on Mabillon's response), p. 43.

10. Letter to the Revd. Dr. John Smith, December 6, 1703, in Harris, *Chorus*, letter 251, p. 390; also quoted and discussed in Bennett, "Hickes's *Thesaurus*," p. 37.

11. For a brief review of this chapter, without, however, reference to the materials I discuss here, see Harris, *Chorus*, pp. 77–79. For a fuller discussion of Hickes and Pindar, together with the bibliographical materials on Hickes's reading and editing practices, see Seth Lerer, "The Anglo-Saxon Pindar: Old English Scholarship and Augustan Criticism in George Hickes's *Thesaurus*," *Modern Philology* 99 (2001): 26–65.

12. Harris, *Chorus*, p. 28.

13. Joseph Levine, *The Battle of the Books* (Ithaca: Cornell University Press, 1991), pp. 327–417, much of whose discussion is explicitly indebted to Harris's researches.

14. Headnote to "The Second Olympique Ode of Pindar," in *The English Writings of Abraham Cowley* (hereafter referred to as Waller), ed. A. R. Waller (Cambridge: Cambridge University Press, 1905–1906), 1:157.

15. Respectively, Cowley's note 1 to "The Resurrection" (Waller, 1:183); and his preface to his *Writings* (Waller, 1:11).

16. Harvey D. Goldstein, "*Anglorum Pindarus*: Model and Milieu," *Comparative Literature* 17 (1965): 309.

17. John Dennis, "The Grounds of Criticism in Poetry," in *The Critical Works of John Dennis*, ed. Edward Niles Hooker, 2 vols. (Baltimore: Johns Hopkins University Press, 1939), esp. the discussion at 1:332.

18. Thomas Sprat, *The Life and Writings of Abraham Cowley*, in *Critical Essays of the Seventeenth Century*, ed. J. E. Spingarn (1908; reprint, Bloomington: Indiana University Press, 1957), 2:131.

19. In 1677 Dryden appealed to Cowley's example in his claim for the importance of "boldness of figures" in poetry. See Norman Maclean, "From Action to Image," in *Critics and Criticism*, ed. R. S. Crane (Chicago: University of Chicago Press, 1952), p. 419. Dryden, "The Author's Apology for Heroic Poetry and Poetic Licence," in *Essays of John Dryden*, ed. W. P. Ker (Oxford: Oxford University Press, 1926), 1:185–86. The 1680 preface to the *Translation of Ovid's Epistles* reiterates these claims and finds in Cowley's Pindar a translator's precedent for what Dryden would seek to do with Ovid (1:237).

20. Dryden, *Essays*, 1:267. Similarly, in the preface to *Albion and Albianus* (1685), Dryden considers Cowley to have "admirably restored" Pindar "in our language [and] ought for ever to be the standard of them" (*Essays*, 1:272). Such praise, however, was not without criticism. Dryden himself, in the passage quoted above, noted that not all the Pindarists were as controlled as Cowley. A decade later, John Dennis found a slew of excesses in the *Pindarique Odes* that would unduly influence the poets of his own time. See, for example, his remarks in the preface to *Miscellanies in Verse and Prose* (1693) and the preface to the *Court of Death* (1695), in *The Critical Works of John Dennis*, 1:6, 1:42. By the turn of the century, the vogue for the Pindaric had produced what William Congreve would call, writing in 1706, "a Bundle of rambling incoherent Thoughts, express'd in a like Parcel of irregular Stanzas, which also consist of such another Complication of disproportion'd, uncertain and perplex'd Verses and Rhimes" ("A Discourse on the Pindarique Ode," in William Congreve, *Letters and Documents*, ed. John C. Hodges [New York: Harcourt Brace, 1964], p. 214).

21. See Steven Shankman, *In Search of the Classic* (University Park: Pennsylvania State University Press, 1994), pp. 219–44; Howard Weinbrot, *Britannia's Issue* (Cambridge: Cambridge University Press, 1993), pp. 334–58; Joshua Scodel, *The English Poetic Epitaph* (Ithaca: Cornell University Press, 1991), pp. 272 ff; and idem, "Lyric Forms," in *The Cambridge Companion to English Literature, 1650–1740* (Cambridge: Cambridge University Press, 1998), pp. 120–142.

22. Penelope Wilson, "'High Pindaricks Upon Stilts': A Case Study in the Eighteenth-Century Classical Tradition," in *Rediscovering Hellenism*, ed. G. W. Clark and J. C. Eade (Cambridge: Cambridge University Press, 1989), p. 28.

23. Cowley, "To Mr. Hobs," 3.10–15, in Waller, 1:189.

24. As the English translator of Wotton's abridgment recognized, calling it the *Grammatico-Critical and Archaeological Treasure*.

25. "Imo in nonnullis carminibus & carminum locis, praesertim asyndetis, ubi incalescens poeta praecipitare videtur orationem, multi tetrasyllabi, & pentasyllabi continuo leguntur, hic illic raro interpositis plurium syllabarum versibus: ut moris plerunque est apud metrorum *Boethianorum* translatorem in uersionibus *Cottoniensis*, &

non raro apud *Caedmonem*, p. 72. Quemadmodum ista ostendunt, quae disjunctim hic infra ponuntur, more *Pindaricorum*, quibus haud usque adeo absimilia sunt" (*Thesaurus*, 1:180).

26. "The Author's Apology for Heroic Poetry and Poetic License," in Dryden, *Essays*, 1:196.

27. *Exodus*, lines 447–51, in *Thesaurus*, 1:180. Hickes prints Old English in half-lines in a single column, each line beginning with a capital letter and ending with a period (or a colon). For purposes of space, I have realigned these half-lines into full lines corresponding to the lineation of modern editions. But I have kept Hickes's spellings, even when they differ from modern editions. The standard, modern text of *Exodus* and other Old English poems can be found in George Philip Krapp and Elliott Van Kirk Dobbie, eds., *The Anglo-Saxon Poetic Records*, 6 vols. (New York: Columbia University Press, 1936–52). All references to lineation are to this edition.

28. Metrum 3.2–3 and Metrum 20.210b–224a, from *Meters of Boethius*, in *Thesaurus*, 1:177, 1:178. Hickes prints all of Metrum 4 (*Thesaurus*, 1:185); the phrasing I discuss appears at lines 21b–26a of the poem. He also prints all of Metrum 6 (*Thesaurus*, 1:182); the phrasing I discuss appears at lines 11–15 of the poem.

29. *Durham*, 1–5, in *Thesaurus* 1:178. Hickes prints the entire poem with a Latin translation in a parallel column.

30. I have discussed *Durham*'s thematic and structural issues of landscape and control in my *Literacy and Power in Anglo-Saxon Literature* (Lincoln: University of Nebraska Press, 1991), pp. 199–204, adapted and developed in a larger context in my "Old English and Its Afterlife," in *The Cambridge History of Medieval English Literature*, ed. David Wallace (Cambridge: Cambridge University Press, 1999), pp. 7–34.

31. See Horace, ode 4.2.5–8 and 27–32. Compare Cowley's version of these lines in "The Praise of Pindar," especially the phrasing of "all inferior beauteous things" (4.12, in Waller, 1:179).

32. "Secundo, hoc ut credam facit, in *Anglo-Saxonum*, si dicam, *Pindaricis* audax illa & libera vocum, non solum a simpliciter loquentium, sed ab ornate dicentium ratione inter oratores maxime aliena transpositio, qua opus, ut videtur, non foret, nisi lex aliqua metri diversorum temporum & pedum observationem requirens, eam a Poetis postularet" (*Thesaurus*, 1:187).

33. Ode 4.2.10–12. "Whether he rolls new words through daring dithyrambs and is borne along in measures freed from rule."

34. Cowley's note to "To Dr. Scarborough," in Waller, 1:200.

35. Sprat, *Life and Writings*, 2:132. Hickes's notion of *transpositio* may have something to do with the separations of parts of speech in verse lines or, more generally, with what Dryden called the "disordered connexion of discourse" in the Pindaric ode. Indeed, Dryden's terms are designed to translate *hyperbaton*, what the *Rhetorica ad Herennium* had defined as the "transposition" (*transiectio*), or separation, of adjectives from the nouns they modify: a device that, when used properly, could enable the arrangement of words "in such a way as to approximate a poetic rhythm" (*poeticum numerum*). See Dryden, "The Author's Apology," in *Essays*, 1:186. For the *Rhetorica ad Herennium* discus-

sion, see Pseudo-Cicero, *Rhetorica ad Herennium*, ed. Harry Caplan (Cambridge: Harvard University Press, 1954), 3.32.44, pp. 338–39.

36. *Meters of Boethius* 9, Genesis, 2850–2922, and Exodus, 447–58a, 506b–14a, in *Thesaurus*, 1:184, 182–83, 180.

37. Weinbrot, *Britannia's Issue*, p. 347.

38. "Denique nullae in hisce carminibus, etsi lyricorum plane speciem prae se ferant, quas ego invenire potui, strophae, antistrophae vel epodi sunt, ex certo versuum numero constantes" (*Thesaurus*, 1:181).

39. *Finnsburh Fragment*, 35b–36, in *Thesaurus* 1:192.

40. *Thesaurus*, 1:192. Hickes quotes from Pindar, *Olympian I*, as published in *Pindari Olympia, Nemea, Pythia, Isthmia, Una cum Latina omnium Versione Carmine Lyrico per Nicolaum Sudorum*, ed. Richard West and Robert Welsted (Oxford: Clarendon, 1697), p. 1. For details on Hickes's use of this volume, see my "Anglo-Saxon Pindar." My English translations of Pindar's phrasings modernize and adapt those in *The Odes of Pindar, Including the Principal Fragments*, ed. and trans. John Sandys (Cambridge: Harvard University Press, 1961), pp. 4–7.

41. "Hoc quasi *Pindaricum, Lyricumve* genus carminis, si non invenit verus ille *Caedmon*, dictante numine, saltem, numine dictante, eo prius a vetustioribus *Scaldis* invento usus est; ut ex fragmento supra citato manifestum est. *Lyricum* autem genus carminis voco, quod lyrae & cantui aptum, pro veri carminis genio ac indole, ab inspirato Poeta cantari solebat, suorum poematum vel odarum cantore. Idem enim & carmina condere & canere erudiente spiritu docebatur" (*Thesaurus*, 1:189)

42. See, for example, Congreve's association of Pindaric poetry with lyric when he notes that the odes "were sung by a Chorus, and adapted to the Lyre, and sometimes ot the Lyre and Pipe" ("Discourse on the Pindaric Ode," p. 214).

43. Dryden, *Essays* 1:268.

44. I have examined in detail these quotations and their larger thematic, political, and bibliographical contexts in my "Anglo-Saxon Pindar."

45. Jonathan Kramnick, *Making the English Canon* (Cambridge: Cambridge University Press, 1999), p. 19.

46. For complete details on these selections, see my "Anglo-Saxon Pindar," pp. 48–57.

47. Hickes to Edmund Gibson, April 24, 1691, quoted and discussed in Harris, *Chorus*, p. 36. For "*exauctorat*" (meaning "deprived of office or divested of authority"), a form of the word Hickes may have coined, see *OED*, s.v. "exauctorate" (which cites a 1680 sermon by Hickes as the first usage) and "exauctoration" (which cites a 1625 sermon by Donne for its first appearance).

48. George Hickes, *A Sermon Preached at the Cathedral Church of Worcester*... (London: R. E., for Walter Kettilby, 1684), p. 9.

49. "Now let us really move on to those things which occur in their poems, the first of which offered for observation is the not infrequent use of words beginning with the same initial letter, which seems to enhance and to govern in a certain way the harmony of the poem. Now, in this matter, the following examples show just how our Anglo-Saxons

imitated the poets (Anglo-Saxons, Greeks, and Latins), and also how—more to the point—all the poets do the same thing following those masters, the Muses, when the consonance of initial letters is heard in the poems of all peoples" ("Jam vero ad ea, quae eorum carminibus accidunt, progrediamur; quorum imprimis se observandum offert dictionum ab eadem initiali litera incipientium usus non infrequens, quae harmoniam carminis augere & quodammodo regere videtur. In hoc autem *Anglo-Saxones* & *Graecos* & *Latinos*, quemadmodum nostri *Anglo-Saxonum* Poetas imitantur; vel potius *Musis* ipsis magistris, omnes idem faciunt, quum in omnibus omnium gentium poematis initialium illa consonantia auditur, ut sequentia ostendunt" [*Thesaurus*, 1:195]). After offering his string of literary examples of alliteration, Hickes concludes: "So, too, through the inspiration of the Muses, the poets of the Anglo-Saxons rejoiced in (or praised by means of) the harmony of sounds that came from the same initial letter. This is the kind [of expression] that one finds in the real Caedmon, inspired by the divine spirit" ("Sic musis inspirantibus etiam *Anglo-Saxonum* Poetae vocum ab iisdem initialibus incipientiu[m] harmonia gaudebant. id genus sunt, in vero *Caedmone*, numine afflato" [*Thesaurus*, 1:197]).

50. Sermons that bear directly on these issues include his *Spirit of Enthusiasm Exorcised* ... (London: Walter Kettilby, 1681) and *The True Notion of Persecution Stated* ... (London: Walter Kettilby, 1681). For a brief review of some of these concerns, see David Gunto, "Kicking the Emperor: Some Problems of Restoration Parallel History," *1650–1850: Ideas, Aesthetics, and Inquiries in the Early Modern Era* 3 (1997): 109–27.

51. Dennis, *Critical Writings of John Dennis*, 1:370.

52. Maclean, "From Action to Image," p. 420.

53. Nathaniel Noel, *Bibliotheca Hickesiana; or, A Catalogue of the Library of the Reverend Dr. George Hickes* (London, 1716), lists "Dryden's Virgil with Cuts, 1698."

54. Dennis, *Critical Writings of John Dennis*, 1:267.

55. *Genesis*, 1–4, in *Thesaurus*, 1:188, printing the Old English in short columns and the Latin as prose below. The entire passage is reproduced here.

56. Dennis, *Critical Works of John Dennis*, 1:216.

57. "Calendario jam finito subjungitur hoc carmen quasi *dithyrambicum*, cujus primus versus in majusculis miniatis exaratus nitet. In eo autem mores hominum, affectus animantium & inanimatorum naturae; res itidem alius generis, civiles, ethicae, theologicae describuntur in gnomis & sententiis asyndetis, quarum elegantia, splendor & proprietas *Latine* exhiberi non possunt" (*Thesaurus*, 1:207). In a letter to William Nicholson, dated April 25, 1699, Hickes refers to the "rambling dithyrambs" of this poem (Harris, *Chorus*, letter 122, p. 290).

58. T. A. Shippey, *Poems of Wisdom and Learning in Old English* (Cambridge: D. S. Brewer, 1976), p. 15.

59. Shippey states that "these poems have been described as 'gnomic' at least since 1826, when J. J. Conybeare used the term" (p. 12, referring to Conybeare, *Illustrations of Anglo-Saxon Poetry* [London, 1826]).

60. Paul Fry, *The Poet's Calling in the English Ode* (New Haven: Yale University Press, 1980).

61. Roberta Frank, "The Search for the Anglo-Saxon Oral Poet," *Bulletin of the John Rylands University Library* 75 (1993): 11–36.

62. Fry, *The Poet's Calling*, p. 2.

63. Edmund Gibson to Arthur Charlett, January 10, 1695, quoted in Harris, *Chorus*, p. 79; emphases mine.

64. Hughes, "The Anglo-Saxon Grammars of George Hickes and Elizabeth Elstob"; Mechtild Gretch, "Elizabeth Elstob: A Scholar's Fight for Anglo-Saxon Studies," *Anglia* 177 (1999): 163–200, 481–524.

65. Harris, *Chorus*, p. 106. Over one hundred copies of the *Thesaurus* remained unsold as of 1713.

66. Joseph Henley, *An Introduction to an English Grammar* (London, 1726), p. xxxi, quoted in Samuel Kliger, "Neo-Classical Views of Old English Poetry," *Journal of English and Germanic Philology* 49 (1950): 520.

67. John Campbell, *Rational Amusement* (London, 1753), pp. 247, 263, 270, quoted in Kliger, "Neo-Classical Views," p. 521. See, too, the brief (and bibliographically confusing) discussion in T. A. Birrell, "Society of Antiquaries," *Neophilologus* 50 (1966): 110, on something called *The Polite Correspondence* (dated 1730), which refers to "a Saxon or a Greek ode" and offers comparisons between them.

68. Frank, "Search for the Anglo-Saxon Oral Poet," p. 20.

69. Thomas Warton, *A History of English Poetry* (London, 1774), facsimile reprinting, ed. David Fairer (London: Routledge, 1998). The discussion in dissertation 1, "Of the origin of romantic fiction in Europe," runs from sig. d3r to e4v, with footnotes to Hickes throughout. After his translation of *Brunanburh* (which Warton does not title as such but which he cites as coming from Hickes), he notes: "This piece, and many other Saxon odes and songs now remaining, are written in a metre much resembling that of the scaldic dialogue at the tomb of Angantyr. . . . The extemporaneous effusions of the glowing bard seem naturally to have fallen into this measure, and it was probably more easily suited to the voice or harp" (sig. e4v).

70. See Birrell, "Society of Antiquaries"; and even Frank, "Search," which considers "the second half of the eighteenth century" to be one of the key periods in the formation "of the Saxon singer we know today" (p. 14). For an interesting twist on this tradition, arguing that it is, in fact, Scandinavian scholarship (Thorkelin, Grundtvig, and their heirs) that shapes the modern study of Old English literature, see Robert E. Bjork, "Nineteenth-Century Scandinavia and the Birth of Anglo-Saxon Studies," in Frantzen and Niles, *Anglo-Saxonism*, pp. 111–32.

71. See Kramnick, *Making the English Canon*; Trevor Ross, *The Making of the English Canon* (Montreal: McGill-Queens, 1999); and Johns, *The Nature of the Book*.

72. T. A. Shippey, *J. R. R. Tolkien: Author of the Century* (London: HarperCollins, 2000).

73. T. A. Shippey, *The Road to Middle Earth* (London: Allen and Unwin, 1982), p. 32.

74. The standard biography remains Humphrey Carpenter, *J. R. R. Tolkien: A Biography* (London: Allen and Unwin, 1977). *J. R. R. Tolkien: Scholar and Storyteller*, ed. Mary Salu and Robert T. Farrell (Ithaca: Cornell University Press, 1979), offers essays

in appreciation and analysis, as well as some scholarly contributions on medieval literature inspired by Tolkien's researches. The journal *Mythlore* is devoted to the study of Tolkien and his contemporaries; articles of particular relevance to my account here include Bruce Mitchell, "J. R. R. Tolkien and Old English Studies: An Appreciation," *Mythlore* 80 (1995): 206–12; and David Sandner, "The Fantastic Sublime: Tolkien's 'On Fairy-Stories' and the Romantic Sublime," *Mythlore* 33 (1997): 4–7. In addition, a selection of letters has been edited by Carpenter and Tolkien's son, Christopher, *Letters of J. R. R. Tolkien* (London: Allen and Unwin, 1981).

75. Read to the British Academy on November 25, 1936, and published in *Proceedings of the British Academy* 22 (1936): 245–96. It was separately published as a pamphlet by Oxford University Press (1936; reprint, 1958), and it has been frequently reprinted. I use the separately printed Oxford University Press pamphlet.

76. For a stimulating analysis of the lecture and its reception and response in Old English scholarship, see T. A. Shippey, "Structure and Unity," in *A Beowulf Handbook*, ed. Robert E. Bjork and John D. Niles (Lincoln: University of Nebraska Press, 1997), pp. 149–74.

77. *Julius Caesar*, 5.5.68–75, ed. William and Barbara Rosen, in *The Complete Signet Classic Shakespeare*, ed. Sylvan Barnet (New York: Harcourt Brace Jovanovich, 1972).

78. *Troilus and Criseyde*, 5.1811–15, in *The Riverside Chaucer*, ed. Larry D. Benson, 3d ed. (Boston: Houghton Mifflin, 1987).

79. Stanley Greenfield and Fred Robinson, *A Bibliography of Publications on Old English Literature to the End of 1972* (Toronto: University of Toronto Press, 1980), p. xii.

80. *Essays and Studies*, n.s., 6 (1953): 1–18.

81. "To the Electors of the Rawlinson and Bosworth Professorship of Anglo-Saxon, University of Oxford," June 27, 1925, in *Letters*, pp. 12–13.

82. "The Homecoming of Beorhtnoth Beorhthelm's Son," p. 2.

83. The poem was published without line numbers.

84. "From a Letter to Christopher Tolkien," February 21, 1958, in *Letters*, p. 264.

85. See my *Literacy and Power*, pp. 158–94; Frantzen, *Desire for Origins*, pp. 184–90; Overing, *Language, Sign, and Gender in Beowulf*, pp. 33–67; Near, "Anticipating Alienation"; James I. McNelis III, "Hrothgar's Hilt, Theory, and Philology," in *Studies in English Language and Literature: "Doubt Wisely," Papers in Honour of E. G. Stanley* (London: Routledge, 1996), pp. 175–85.

86. Seth Lerer, "*Beowulf* and Contemporary Critical Theory," in *A Beowulf Handbook*, ed. Robert Bjork and John D. Niles (Lincoln: University of Nebraska Press, 1997), pp. 329–44. See, too, my "Grendel's Glove," *ELH: A Journal of English Literary History* 61 (1994): 721–51.

87. H. Aram Veeser, introduction to *The New Historicism*, ed. H. Aram Vesser (New York: Routledge, 1989), p. xi.

88. Seamus Heaney, *Beowulf: A New Verse Translation* (New York: Farrar, Straus, and Giroux, 2000), with the Old English text reproduced from the edition of C. L. Wrenn and W. F. Bolton, *Beowulf, with the Finnsburgh Fragment* (London: Harrap, 1973).

89. Meyer Abrams, gen. ed., and Stephen Greenblatt, assoc. gen. ed., *The Norton Anthology of English Literature*, 7th ed. (New York: Norton, 2000).

90. All quotations from Heaney's poetry are from *Seamus Heaney: Poems, 1965–1975* (New York: Farrar, Straus, and Giroux, 1980), cited by title.

91. T. A. Shippey, "*Beowulf* for the Big-Voiced Scullions," *Times Literary Supplement*, October 1, 1999, pp. 9–10.

92. Nicholas Howe, "Scullionspeak," *New Republic*, February 28, 2000, pp. 32–37.

93. *Longinus*, ed. and trans. W. R. Roberts (Cambridge: Cambridge University Press, 1935), 7.2, pp. 54–55.

94. Pseudo-Cicero, *Rhetorica ad Herennium*, 3.22.35, p. 219.

3. My Casaubon: The Novel of Scholarship and Victorian Philology

1. George Eliot, *Middlemarch* (New York: Modern Library, 1994), chap. 2, p. 13. All quotations are from this edition, henceforth cited by chapter number and page number in my text.

2. On John Horne Tooke (1736–1812), see Hans Aarsleff, *The Study of Language in England, 1780–1860* (Princeton: Princeton University Press, 1967; rev. ed., Minneapolis: University of Minnesota Press, 1983); Olivia Smith, *The Politics of Language, 1791–1819* (Oxford: Oxford University Press, Clarendon, 1984); Daniel Rosenberg, "'A New Sort of Logick and Critick': Etymological Interpretation in Horne Tooke's *The Diversions of Purley*," in *Language, Self, and Society*, ed. Peter Burke and Roy Porter (Cambridge: Polity, 1991), pp. 300–29.

3. Gordon Haight, *George Eliot: A Biography* (New York: Oxford University Press, 1968), pp. 448–50 and 563–65; and his "Poor Mr. Casaubon," in *Nineteenth-Century Literary Perspectives*, ed. Clyde de L. Ryals and John Clubb (Durham, N.C.: Duke University Press, 1974), pp. 255–70.

4. See Haight, *George Eliot*, pp. 448–49. Eliot's review of Mackay originally appeared in the *Westminster Review* 54 (January 1851): 353–68 and is reprinted in *Essays of George Eliot*, ed. Thomas Pinney (New York: Columbia University Press, 1963), pp. 27–45, with notes calling attention to resonances with Casaubon and *Middlemarch* generally.

5. Haight, *George Eliot*, pp. 49–51 (quotation from p. 51).

6. F. W. H. Meyers, "George Eliot," *Century Magazine* 23 (November 1881): 60, quoted and discussed in Haight, *George Eliot*, p. 450. For more associations between Casaubon and Eliot herself, drawing on remarks made in her letters and journals, see Alan Mintz, *George Eliot and the Novel of Vocation* (Cambridge: Harvard University Press, 1978), pp. 115–21.

7. See W. J. Harvey, "The Intellectual Background of the Novel: Casaubon and Lydgate," in *Middlemarch: Critical Approaches to the Novel*, ed. Barbara Hardy (New York: Oxford University Press, 1967), pp. 25–37, as well as Anna Theresa Kitchel, ed., *Quarry for Middlemarch* (Berkeley: University of California Press, 1950); John Clark Pratt and Victor A. Neufeldt, eds., *George Eliot's Middlemarch Notebooks* (Berkeley: University of

California Press, 1979); Joseph Wiesenfarth, ed., *George Eliot: A Writer's Notebook, 1854–79, and Uncollected Writings* (Charlottesville: University Press of Virginia, 1981), esp. pp. xxxii–xxxvi and 86–135.

8. On the thematics of authorship in the novel, see Mintz, *George Eliot and the Novel of Vocation*; and Leah Price, *The Anthology and the Rise of the Novel* (Cambridge: Cambridge University Press, 2000), pp. 105–56. On readers and writers and the problem of textuality, see J. Hillis Miller, "Narrative and History," *ELH: A Journal of English Literary History* 41 (1974): 455–73; and idem, "Optic and Semiotic in *Middlemarch*," in *The Worlds of Victorian Fiction*, ed. Jerome H. Buckley, Harvard English Studies 6 (Cambridge: Harvard University Press, 1975), pp. 125–45; Neil Hertz, "Recognizing Casaubon," in *The End of the Line: Essays on Psychoanalysis and the Sublime* (New York: Columbia University Press, 1985), pp. 75–96.

9. See Hertz, "Recognizing Casaubon."

10. On Casaubon as a failure and for suggestive remarks on the theme of failure generally in the novel, see Pratt and Neufeldt, *George Eliot's Middlemarch Notebooks*, p. xlvii.

11. Gordon Haight, ed. *The George Eliot Letters*, 9 vols. (New Haven: Yale University Press, 1954–78); Margaret Harris and Judith Johnston, eds., *The Journals of George Eliot* (Cambridge: Cambridge University Press, 1998); Jerome Beatty, *"Middlemarch" from Notebook to Novel: A Study in George Eliot's Creative Method* (Urbana: University of Illinois Press, 1960).

12. Miller, "Optic and Semiotic," p. 140. For the impact of Miller's work on a sustained reading of *Middlemarch*, see Patricia McKee, *Heroic Commitment in Richardson, Eliot, and James* (Princeton: Princeton University Press, 1986), pp. 150–207.

13. Hertz, "Recognizing Casaubon," p. 92.

14. Haight, "Poor. Mr. Casaubon," p. 255.

15. Hertz, "Recognizing Casaubon," pp. 75, 90.

16. Catherine Maxwell, "The Brooking of Desire: Dorothea and Deferment in *Middlemarch*," *Yearbook of English Studies* 26 (1996): 116.

17. See Peter Carlton, "Rereading *Middlemarch*, Rereading Myself," in *The Intimate Critique: Autobiographical Literary Criticism*, ed. Diane P. Freedman (Durham, N.C.: Duke University Press, 1993), pp. 237–44.

18. In addition to Aarsleff's still unsurpassed *Study of Language*, see K. M. Elisabeth Murray, *Caught in the Web of Words: James A. H. Murray and the Oxford English Dictionary* (New Haven: Yale University Press, 1977); John Willinsky, *Empire of Words: The Reign of the OED* (Princeton: Princeton University Press, 1994); Lynda Mugglestone, *Lexicography and the* OED*: Pioneers in the Untrodden Forest* (Oxford: Oxford University Press, 2000); Simon Winchester, *The Professor and the Madman: A Tale of Murder, Insanity, and the Making of the Oxford English Dictionary* (New York: HarperCollins, 1998).

19. Linda Dowling, *Language and Decadence in the Victorian Fin de Siècle* (Princeton: Princeton University Press, 1986); Cary H. Plotkin, *The Tenth Muse: Victorian Philology and the Genesis of the Poetic Language of Gerard Manley Hopkins* (Carbondale: South-

ern Illinois University Press, 1989); Dennis Taylor, *Hardy's Literary Language and Victorian Philology* (Oxford: Oxford University Press, Clarendon, 1993).

20. Quoted in Willinsky, *Empire of Words*, p. 119.

21. "The Philological Society's English Dictionary" (unsigned), *Academy*, May 10, 1879, p. 413.

22. In addition to the printed editions of the *Oxford English Dictionary* (which appeared in fascicles from 1888 to 1928 under the title *The New English Dictionary*, then as *The Oxford English Dictionary* in the entire, multivolume publication of 1933, and then in the second edition of 1989), I have used the online version that incorporates revisions and supplementary material through the third edition (*http://dictionary.oed.com*). The online concordance to *Middlemarch* is *http://princeton.edu/batke/eliot/middle*.

23. George Lewes to John Blackwood, July 13, 1872, in *Letters*, 5:291, quoted in Haight, *George Eliot*, p. 445.

24. For the history and etymology of "author," see A. J. Minnis, *Medieval Theory of Authorship* (London: Scolar, 1984).

25. See Willinsky, *Empire of Words*, esp. pp. 92–112. But see E. G. Stanley's review, *Review of English Studies*, n.s., 48 (1997): 218–20; and Charlotte Brewer, "*OED* Sources," in *Lexicography and the OED*, pp. 40–58.

26. Willinsky, *Empire of Words*, p. 103. On Scott's status in the nineteenth century and his relationships to later authors, see Judith Wilt, "Steamboat Surfacing: Scott and the English Novelists," *Nineteenth-Century Fiction* 35 (1981): 459–86; Harry Shaw, *The Forms of Historical Fiction: Sir Walter Scott and His Successors* (Ithaca: Cornell University Press, 1993).

27. Quoted in Willinsky, *Empire of Words*, p. 103.

28. Mintz, *George Eliot and the Novel of Vocation*, p. 119; Rosemarie Bodenheimer, *The Real Life of Mary Ann Evans* (Ithaca: Cornell University Press, 1994); Price, *The Anthology and the Rise of the Novel*, pp. 105–56.

29. Quoted in Bodenheimer, *Real Life*, p. 174, from "Authorship," a late fragment probably intended for *Theophrastus Such*, reprinted in *Essays*, pp. 437–42.

30. Eliot to Stowe, May 8, 1868, in *Letters*, 5:29; Eliot to Main, December 28, 1871, in *Letters*, 5:229; both quoted and discussed in Mintz, *George Eliot*, p. 120.

31. Quoted in Haight, *George Eliot*, p. 433; see now Harris and Johnston, *Journals*, p. 142.

32. Haight, *George Eliot*, p. 433.

33. *Letters*, 5:185, 212, quoted and discussed in Bodenheimer, *Real Life*, p. 175.

34. For the details of *Middlemarch*'s publication and Lewes's plans for its serial appearance, see the discussion in Haight, *George Eliot*, pp. 431–38, which quotes the correspondence.

35. On Scott and Eliot, see Haight, *George Eliot*, passim; Price, *Anthology*, esp. pp. 117–18; and Harry Shaw, *Naming Reality: Austen, Scott, Eliot* (Ithaca: Cornell University Press, 1999).

36. Eliot to Main, August 9, 1871, in *Letters*, 5:175. August 1871 also saw the centenary of Scott's birth, and Eliot was invited to sit at the head table at the celebration in

Edinburgh—though she eventually declined the invitation. No matter, Gordon Haight notes: "She celebrated Scott's birthday by working quietly on *Middlemarch*" (*George Eliot*, p. 439).

37. Haight, *George Eliot*, p. 7. See, too, Price, *Anthology*, pp. 117–18 and p. 186 n. 49.

38. Haight, *George Eliot*, respectively pp. 58, 271, 319, 327.

39. Unsigned review, "A Dictionary of Biography," *Spectator*, December 14, 1867, p. 1423.

40. Aarsleff, *Study of Language*, p. 255.

41. See Richard W. Bailey, "'This Unique and Peerless Specimen': The Reputation of the *OED*," in *Lexicography and the OED*, pp. 207–27, esp. pp. 216–20 on Whitney and the *Century Dictionary*.

42. Trench, *On Some Deficiencies in our English Dictionaries*, quoted in Aarsleff, *Study of Language*, pp. 261–62.

43. The *Spectator* reviews, all unsigned, appeared as follows: December 16, 1871, pp. 1528–29; February 3, 1872, pp. 147–48; March 30, 1872, pp. 404–6; December 7, 1872, pp. 1554–55. A fifth, general review appeared under the title "George Eliot's Moral Anatomy," October 5, 1872, pp. 1262–64. See W. J. Harvey, "Criticism of the Novel: Contemporary Reception," in *Middlemarch: Critical Approaches to the Novel*, pp. 125–47. For a complete list of all contemporary reviews, see Carol A. Martin, *George Eliot's Serial Fiction* (Columbus: Ohio State University Press, 1994), pp. 270–73.

44. *Spectator*, December 16, 1871, p. 1528; February 3, 1872, p. 147.

45. *Spectator*, March 30, 1872, p. 404.

46. *Spectator*, December 7, 1872, pp. 1555–56.

47. Henry James, unsigned review, *Galaxy*, March 1873, p. 428.

48. Quoted in Haight, *George Eliot*, pp. 467–68.

49. James A. H. Murray, "President's Address," *Transactions of the Philological Society*, 1879: 575.

50. "Pronunciation," in the introduction to the *OED*.

51. See Bodenheimer, *Real Life*, p. 243. See, too, Lewes to John Blackwood, July 13, 1872, in *Letters*, 5:291: "The shadow of old Casaubon hangs over me and I fear my 'Key to all Psychologies' will have to be left to Dorothea."

52. See Harvey, "Intellectual Background"; U. C. Knoepflmacher, "Fusing Fact and Myth: The New Reality of *Middlemarch*," in *This Particular Web: Essays on Middlemarch*, ed. Ian Adam (Toronto: University of Toronto Press, 1975), pp. 43–72. For some specifics, see Pratt and Neufeldt, *George Eliot's Middlemarch Notebooks*, pp. 100, 109, 133–39, 165, 245, 258, 262, 265, 267.

53. For a detailed accounting of Eliot's reading in mythography, philology, and history, as well as other disciplines, all bearing on the texture of *Middlemarch*, see Pratt and Neufeldt, *George Eliot's Middlemarch Notebooks*, pp. xvii–xlii. On Eliot's use of Max Müller, Henry Sumner Maine, and Friedrich Creuzer, see pp. xxvi–xxvii, xlii–liii. See, too, the "Check List of George Eliot's Reading: January 1868 to December 1871," pp. 279–88).

54. Review of *The Progress of the Intellect*, *Westminster Review* 54 (January 1851): 353–68, in *Essays*, pp. 27–45.

55. See Harvey, "Intellectual Background."

56. See the discussion in Haight, *George Eliot*, pp. 563–65.

57. For the first remark, see *George Eliot*, p. 449; for the second, see "Poor Mr. Casaubon," p. 266.

58. The material is summarized in Haight, *George Eliot*, pp. 49–52; and repeated in "Poor Mr. Casaubon."

59. Haight, *George Eliot*, p. 50.

60. Eliza Lynn Linton, *My Literary Life* (London: Hodder and Stoughton, 1899), p. 43. Haight quotes this passage, though without the introductory reference to Landor, in *George Eliot*, pp. 50–51; and "Poor Mr. Casaubon," p. 268.

61. Haight, *George Eliot and John Chapman, with Chapman's Diaries* (New Haven: Yale University Press, 1940), p. 25 and n. 17 there. Nowhere does he actually quote from Layton's book.

62. George Soames Layton, *Mrs. Lynn Linton* (London, 1901), p. 67 n. 1.

63. Note, in particular, Casaubon's remark, "I am fastidious in voices" (chap. 2, pp. 13–14).

64. *Spectator*, December 16, 1871, p. 1528 ("dry and formal," "cobwebby"); December 7, 1872, p. 1555 ("a dried-up formalist," "pedant").

65. *Athenaeum*, December 2, 1871, p. 713.

66. James, unsigned review, p. 426.

67. *OED*, s.v. "repoussoir."

68. *OED*, s.v. "ungauged," where the quotation from *Middlemarch* is one of only three to illustrate the word.

69. *OED*, s.v. "manqué." The quotation is from *The Great Tradition* (1948).

70. Hertz, "Recognizing Casaubon," p. 90.

71. James, unsigned review, p. 426.

72. Haight reviews the "usual pedants pointing out little errors" of legal, medical, and historical fact immediately after *Middlemarch*'s publication (*George Eliot*, pp. 446–47).

73. *Academy*, January 1, 1873, p. 3; Harvey, "Criticism of the Novel," p. 189 n. 1.

74. See the discussions in Miller, "Optic and Semiotic" and "Narrative and History."

75. *Writer's Notebook*, pp. 115–16.

76. I reproduce the text as Eliot transcribed it, without correcting for spelling or capitalization.

77. Eliot to John Blackwood, September 25, 1861, in *Letters*, 7:291, quoted in David Carroll, ed., *Middlemarch* (Oxford: Oxford University Press, Clarendon, 1986), p. v.

78. Miller, "Narrative and History," p. 466; quoted and discussed in Hertz, "Recognizing Casaubon," p. 77.

79. Eliot to Alexander Main, January 9, 1873, in *Letters*, 5:366, quoted and discussed in Carroll, *Middlemarch*, p. lx; and Allan C. Dooley, *Author and Printer in Victorian England* (Charlottesville: University Press of Virginia, 1992), pp. 76–77.

80. Eliot to John Blackwood, September 19, 1873, in *Letters*, 5:441, quoted and discussed in Carroll, *Middlemarch*, p. lxi.

81. Quoted in Jerome Beatty, "The Text of the Novel: A Study of the Proof," in *Middlemarch: Critical Approaches*, p. 38, with fuller discussion in Beatty, *Middlemarch, from Notebook to Novel*, pp. 106–7.

82. The passages are taken from Beatty, "The Text of the Novel," pp. 59–60.

83. Eliot to John Blackwood, November 5, 1873, in *Letters*, 5:454, quoted in Dooley, *Author and Printer*, p. 86.

84. For a full discussion of Main's errata hunting, see Dooley, *Author and Printer*, pp. 76–77. Dooley shows that Eliot was far more aware of the technologies of publishing and the status of her own text than she let on to Main and that her famous responses to his letters offer little more than a "genteel brush-off."

85. Eliot to Main, January 9, 1873, in *Letters*, 5:366, discussed in Dooley, *Author and Printer*, p. 76.

86. Dooley, *Author and Printer*, pp. 76–77.

87. These texts are from Beatty, "Text of the Novel," pp. 61–62.

88. Aarsleff, *Study of Language*, p. 35.

89. Reprinted in facsimile in two volumes as no. 127 in the series English Linguistics, 1500–1800, ed. R. C. Alston (Menston: Scolar, 1968), from which my quotations are taken.

90. Aarsleff, *Study of Language*, p. 64.

91. For Eliot's record of Tooke's death, see *Writer's Notebook*, p. 30.

92. For this history, see Aarsleff, *Study of Language*; Dowling, *Language and Decadence*, and her earlier essay, "Victorian Oxford and the Science of Language," *PMLA* 97 (1982): 160–78; Taylor, *Hardy's Literary Language*, esp. pp. 207–52; and Holger Pedersen, *Linguistic Science in the Nineteenth Century*, trans. John W. Spargo (Cambridge: Harvard University Press, 1931).

93. Pedersen, *Linguistic Science*, p. 240.

94. Franz Bopp, *Vergleichende Grammatik* (1833), published in English as *A Comparative Grammar*, trans. Edward B. Eastwick (London: Williams and Northgate, 1845; rev., 1856). My quotations are from the 1856 edition. For the organicist vocabulary mentioned here, see pp. vi–viii.

95. Murray, "President's Address," p. 585.

96. Knoepflmacher, "Fusing Fact and Myth," p. 45. For more details, see Pratt and Neufeldt, *George Eliot's Middlemarch Notebooks*, pp. xxviii–xxx.

97. On Schleicher and his family tree of languages, see the discussion in Pedersen, *Linguistic Science*, pp. 311–14, and, more generally, pp. 265–72. Schleicher's *Compendium der vergleichenden Grammatik der indogermanischen Sprachen* appeared in 1861–1862 and was soon translated (in abridged form) into English: *A Compendium of the Comparative Grammar of the Indo-European, Sanskrit, Greek and Latin Languages*, trans. Herbert Bendall, 2 vols. (London: Trübner, 1874, 1877). For the family tree, see 1:8. For the relationships between historical philology and evolutionary biology in the nineteenth century, with special reference to the figurations of the family tree, see Stephen G. Alter, *Darwinism and the Linguistic Image* (Baltimore: Johns Hopkins University Press, 1999),

pp. 108–45 (with reproductions of a remarkable set of nineteenth-century "trees," linguistic, biological, and racial).

98. *Writer's Notebook*, p. 87.

99. A. J. Engel, *From Clergyman to Don: The Rise of the Academic Profession in Nineteenth-Century Oxford* (Oxford: Oxford University Press, Clarendon, 1983).

100. Aarsleff, *Study of Language*, p. 180, quoting August Boeckh. See, too, Rudolph Pfeiffer, *Die Klassische Philologie von Petrarca bis Mommsen* (Munich: Beck, 1982).

101. The discussion is attributed to R. Newton, principal of Hart Hall, Oxford, in 1750. Quoted and discussed in Engel, *From Clergyman to Don*, p. 15.

102. From the *Edinburgh Review* 14 (July 1809): 431, quoted and discussed in Engel, *From Clergyman to Don*, p. 16.

103. *Edinburgh Review* 54 (December 1831): 486, quoted and discussed in Engel, *From Clergyman to Don*, p. 21.

104. "The Legality of the Present Academic System . . ." (Oxford, 1832), pp. 22–23, quoted and discussed in Engel, *From Clergyman to Don*, p. 22.

105. *Eclectic Review*, 4th ser., 2 (August 1837): 125, quoted and discussed in Engel, *From Clergyman to Don*, p. 21.

106. "A Word for the Germans," *Pall Mall Gazette* 1 (March 7, 1865): 201, in *Essays*, pp. 386–90.

107. Note, too, Madame de Stael's comment on the perfection of the German academic system: "L'éducation intellectuelle est parfaite en Allemagne, mais tout s'y passe en théorie" (quoted in Aarsleff, *Study of Language*, p. 181).

108. See Haruko Momma, "A Man on the Cusp: Sir William Jones's 'Philology' and 'Oriental Studies,'" *Texas Studies in Language and Literature* 41 (1999): 160–79.

109. Aarsleff, *Study of Language*, p. 126.

110. Franz Bopp, *A Comparative Grammar*, trans. Edward B. Eastwick, rev. ed. (London: Williams and Northgate, 1856), p. vi.

111. On Müller, see Dowling, "Victorian Oxford and the Science of Language."

112. Max Müller, "Comparative Mythology" (1856), in *Selected Essays on Language, Mythology and Religion* (London: Longmans, 1881), 1:299–451.

113. Müller does not identify the poem.

114. Max Müller, *Lectures on the Science of Language* (New York: Scribner's, 1862), 1:35–36, quoted in Dowling, "Victorian Oxford," p. 166.

115. She read Müller's *History of Sanskrit Literature* between August and October 1869 (*Writer's Notebook*, p. xli n. 41). For details of her reading, see Pratt and Neufeldt, *George Eliot's Middlemarch Notebook*, pp. xvii–xlii, 279–88; and the discussion throughout *A Writer's Notebook*.

116. *Writer's Notebook*, pp. 115–16. The passage was copied from Müller's "Buddhist Pilgrims, 1857," in *Chips from a German Workshop*, probably in early 1868 (see Wiesenfarth's commentary, *Writer's Notebook*, p. 209).

117. I argue for its relevance to *Middlemarch* even though Eliot copied out the passage, as Wiesenfarth notes, as part of her reading for *Felix Holt*.

118. *Letters* 1:29, quoted in Bodenheimer, *Real Life*, p. 39.

119. *Writer's Notebook*, pp. 86–87, 92, 100, 118–19, 120, 121, 122–23. For the list-making process that helped organize the plot of the novel, which is recorded in Eliot's *Quarry for Middlemarch*, see Carroll, *Middlemarch*, pp. xliii–lvii.

120. *New English Dictionary*, vol. 7 (1909).

121. Murray, *Caught in the Web of Words*, p. 136.

122. Murray, "President's Address," p. 568.

123. Jennett Humphreys, "English: Its Ancestors, Its Progeny," *Fraser's Magazine*, n.s., 26 (1882): 429–57. For Humphreys, see Mugglestone, *Lexicography and the OED*, p. 240.

124. "The Philological Society's English Dictionary," p. 413.

125. George Eliot, "Silly Novels by Lady Novelists," *Westminster Review*, October 1856, quoted and discussed in Price, *Anthology*, p. 125.

126. Thackeray, "Mr. and Mrs. Frank Berry," *Fraser's Magazine*, March 1843, quoted and discussed in Price, *Anthology*, pp. 125–26, 189 n. 81.

127. Dickens, "Our English Watering-Place," quoted and discussed in Price, *Anthology*, p. 128.

128. Andrew Lang, "Mrs. Radcliffe's Novels," *Cornhill Magazine*, n.s., 9 (1900): 24–43, quoted and discussed in Price, *Anthology*, p. 128.

129. Price, *Anthology*, p. 128.

130. This quotation stands, too, as the epigraph to Lynda Mugglestone, "'Pioneers in the Untrodden Forest': The New English Dictionary," in *Lexicography and the OED*, pp. 2–21, though Mugglestone curiously replaces the word "white" with an ellipsis (p. 1).

131. George Eliot, *Silas Marner* (London: Oxford University Press, 1964), chap. 2, p. 21. The *OED* quotation offers only, "Thought was arrested by utter bewilderment."

132. Ephraim Chambers, *Cyclopaedia; or, An Universal Dictionary of Arts and Sciences*, 2 vols. (London: J. and J. Knapton, 1728).

133. Humphreys, "English," p. 432.

134. James, unsigned review, p. 428.

135. Adams Sherman Hill, *Principles of Rhetoric*, new ed. (New York: American Book Company, 1895). Extracts from *Middlemarch* are printed and discussed on pp. 16, 53, 104, 116, 195.

136. As praised in Basil Lanneau Gildersleeve, "Classics and Colleges," in *Essays and Studies* (New York: Stechert, 1924), p. 62 (this essay was originally written in the late 1860s).

137. William Dwight Whitney, *The Life and Growth of Language* (New York: D. Appleton, 1875; reprint, New York: Dover, 1979), pp. 318–19.

138. William Dwight Whitney, "Müller's Chips from a German Workshop," in *Oriental and Linguistic Studies*, 2d ser. (New York: Scribners, 1874), pp. 137, 148.

139. William Dwight Whitney, "Müller's Lectures on Language," in *Oriental and Linguistic Studies*, 1st ser. (New York: Scribners, 1872), p. 260.

140. William Dwight Whitney, *Max Müller and the Science of Language* (New York: Appleton, 1892), p. 75.

4. Ardent Etymologies: American Rhetorical Philology, from Adams to De Man

1. H. L. Mencken, *The American Language*, 4th ed., abr. and ed. Raven I. McDavid Jr. (New York: Knopf, 1963), p. 99.
2. Jay Fliegelman, *Declaring Independence: Jefferson, Natural Language, and the Culture of Performance* (Stanford: Stanford University Press, 1993).
3. Mason Locke Weems, *The Life of Washington*, ed. Marcus Cunliffe (Cambridge: Harvard University Press, 1962), p. 2, quoted and discussed in Fliegelman, *Declaring Independence*, p. 122.
4. Fliegelman, *Declaring Independence*, p. 122.
5. William Thornton, *Cadmus; or, a Treatise on the Elements of Written Language* (Philadelphia, 1793), pp. v–vii, quoted in David Simpson, *The Politics of American English, 1776–1865* (Oxford: Oxford University Press, 1986), p. 25.
6. John Quincy Adams, *Lectures on Rhetoric and Oratory* (Cambridge, Mass.: Hilliard and Metcalf, 1810; reprint, New York: Russell and Russell, 1962), 2:281.
7. Henry Tuckerman, *Characteristics of Literature Illustrated by the Genius of Distinguished Writers* (Philadelphia, 1851), p. 116, quoted in Olivia Smith, *The Politics of Language, 1791–1819* (Oxford: Oxford University Press, Clarendon, 1984), p. 149.
8. On the concept of manifest destiny (the phrase apparently coined in 1845) and American conceptions of language, see Julie Tetel Andresen, *Linguistics in America, 1769–1924* (London: Routledge, 1990), p. 125. Among the many studies of the place of language study in the American tradition, see, in particular, Thomas Gustafson, *Representative Words: Politics, Literature, and the American Language, 1776–1850* (Cambridge: Cambridge University Press, 1992); Michael Kramer, *Imagining Language in America: From the Revolution to the Civil War* (Princeton: Princeton University Press, 1992); Gavin Jones, *Strange Talk: The Politics of Dialect Literature in Gilded Age America* (Berkeley: University of California Press, 1999); Michael West, *Transcendental Wordplay: America's Romantic Punsters and the Search for the Language of Nature* (Athens: Ohio University Press, 2000).
9. George Kennedy, *A New History of Classical Rhetoric* (Princeton: Princeton University Press, 1994), p. xi.
10. Albert S. Cook, "The Province of English Philology," *PMLA* 12 (1898), reprinted in part in *Origins of Literary Studies in America*, ed. Gerald Graff and Michael Warner (New York: Routledge, 1989) p. 99.
11. Adams, *Lectures*, 1:50–51; Gildersleeve, "Abstract of Presidential Address to the American Philological Association," *Transactions of the American Philological Association* 40 (1909): xxxvii, xxxix.
12. *De Oratore*, ed. and trans. E. W. Sutton and H. Rackham (Cambridge: Harvard University Press, 1942), 2.44.188, 190.
13. Samuel Johnson, preface to *Dictionary of the English Language* (London, 1755), B2v.
14. For the history of the Boylston professorship and the institutional contexts that shaped its teaching of rhetoric, see Ronald F. Reid, "The Boylston Professorship of Rhetoric and Oratory, 1806–1904: A Case Study in Changing Concepts of Rhetoric and

Pedagogy," *Quarterly Journal of Speech* 45 (1959): 239–57; Donald M. Goodfellow, "The First Boylston Professor of Rhetoric and Oratory," *New England Quarterly* 19 (1946): 372–89; Paul E. Ried, "The First and Fifth Boylston Professors: A View of Two Worlds," *Quarterly Journal of Speech* 74 (1988): 229–40; and James A. Berlin, *Writing Instruction in Nineteenth-Century American Colleges* (Carbondale: Southern Illinois University Press, 1984).

15. For Adams's use of Cicero's *Tusculans*, see Greg Russell, "John Quincy Adams: Virtue and the Tragedy of the Statesman," *New England Quarterly* 69 (1996): 68–69. For a general review of Adams's debts to Cicero, especially *De Oratore*, see Lousene G. Rousseau, "The Rhetorical Principles of Cicero and Adams," *Quarterly Journal of Speech* 2 (1916): 397–409. For the impact of Cicero on American rhetorical theory and practice, see Fliegelman, *Declaring Independence*; and, for more particulars, Mary Rosner, "Reflections on Cicero in Nineteenth-Century England and America," *Rhetorica* 4 (1986): 153–82.

16. Adams, *Lectures*, 1:12–13, ellipses in original. Future references will be cited by volume and page number in the text.

17. Cicero, *De Inventione*, ed. and trans. H. M. Hubbell, Loeb Library (Cambridge: Harvard University Press, 1949), 1.1.2, pp. 4–5. Future references in text.

18. Horne Tooke, *The Diversions of Purley* (London: J. Johnson's, 1798), 1:40, quoted and discussed in Daniel Rosenberg, "'A New Sort of Logick and Critick': Etymological Interpretation in Horne Tooke's *The Diversions of Purley*," in *Language Self and Society*, ed. Peter Burke and Roy Porter (Cambridge: Polity, 1991), p. 306.

19. Quoted in Simpson, *Politics of American English*, p. 82.

20. On Tooke's American reception, see Simpson, *Politics of American English*, pp. 81–90.

21. Quoted in Simpson, *Politics of American English*, p. 81.

22. See Simpson, *Politics of American English*, pp. 83–84.

23. See Michael Kramer, *Imagining Language in America: From the Revolution to the Civil War*, p. 62; and Simpson, *Politics of American English*, p. 83.

24. Jay Fliegelman, *Prodigals and Pilgrims: The American Revolution Against Patriarchal Authority, 1750–1800* (Cambridge: Cambridge University Press, 1982), esp. pp. 197–98.

25. Adams does not specify the source, stating only that it is a passage "which you have all heard a thousand times." It is *Midsummer Night's Dream*, 5.1.12–17.

26. See Simpson, *Politics of American English*, pp. 204–5.

27. Tooke, *Diversions*, 1:399, quoted and discussed in Olivia Smith, *The Politics of Language of Language, 1791–1819* (Oxford: Oxford University Press, Clarendon, 1984), pp. 123–34.

28. Tooke, *Diversions*, 1:51, quoted and discussed in Hans Aarsleff, *The Study of Language in England, 1780–1860* (Princeton: Princeton University Press, 1967; rev. ed., Minneapolis: University of Minnesota Press, 1983), p. 13.

29. Aarsleff, *Study of Language*, p. 48: "[Abbreviation] was the great discovery which to his contemporaries made Horne Tooke the immortal 'philologer.'"

30. *Port Folio*, 3d ser., 4 (August 1810): 122–36. For the political conflicts that may stand behind this review (most likely by the journal's editor, Joseph Dennie) and the broader relationships between the journal and the Adams family, see Linda K. Kerber and Walter John Morris, "Politics and Literature: The Adams Family and the *Port Folio*," *William and Mary Quarterly*, 3d ser., 23 (1966): 450–76; and William C. Dowling, *Literary Federalism in the Age of Jefferson: Joseph Dennie and the Port Folio, 1801–1812* (Columbia, S.C.: University of South Carolina Press, 1999), esp. p. 97 n. 1.

31. See Reid, "Boylston Professorship"; Ried, "First and Fifth Boylston Professors."

32. Ibid.

33. Adams Sherman Hill, *The Principles of Rhetoric*, new ed. (New York: American Book, 1895), p. v.

34. James Morgan Hart, "College Course in English Literature," in *Origins of Literary Studies*, ed. Gerald Graff and Michael Warner, p. 35.

35. Cook, "Province of English Philology," p. 99.

36. While Americans had been attending German universities since the end of the eighteenth century, men of the generation of Whitney, Gildersleeve, and Child were the first to return and make significant academic careers, especially in philology, at major American universities. On Whitney's German experience in particular, see Carl Diehl, *Americans and German Scholarship* (New Haven: Yale University Press, 1978), pp. 119–30.

37. For general surveys of the life and work, see Brigitte Nerlich, *Change in Language: Whitney, Bréal and Wegener* (London: Routledge, 1990); and Andresen, *Linguistics in America*, pp. 135–68. For detailed reviews of Saussure's debts to Whitney, see Roman Jakobson, "The World Response to Whitney's Principles of Linguistic Science," in *Whitney on Language*, ed. Michael Silverstein (Cambridge, Mass.: MIT Press, 1971), pp. xxv–xlv; and Richard W. Bailey, "William Dwight Whitney and the Origins of Semiotics," in *The Sign: Semiotics Around the World*, ed. R. W. Bailey (Ann Arbor: Michigan Slavic Publications, 1978), pp. 68–80. Linda Dowling has developed the argument about Whitney's "clairvoyant glimpse" of structuralist linguistic principles, especially in the context of the Neogrammarian work of the 1870s. See her *Language and Decadence in the Victorian Fin de Siècle* (Princeton: Princeton University Press, 1986), pp. 80–81. For an important review of Whitney's work on American dialects in the larger context of nineteenth-century American philological reflection, see Jones, *Strange Talk*, pp. 14–36.

38. William Dwight Whitney, "Müller's Rig-Veda Translation," in *Oriental and Linguistic Studies*, 1st ser. (New York: Scribner's, 1872), p. 139 (hereafter *OLS* I). For an argument that Whitney's work is really indebted to that of the earlier scholar Johann Madvig (and therefore that Whitney is not the originator of the Saussurian notions of the arbitrariness of the sign or the conventionality of language), see Hans Aarsleff, *From Locke To Saussure* (Minneapolis: University of Minnesota Press, 1982), pp. 293–334.

39. William Dwight Whitney, *Language and the Study of Language* (New York: Scribner's, 1889), p. 129 (hereafter *LSL*).

40. E. W. Hopkins, "Max Müller," *Nation*, November 1, 1900, pp. 343–44, quoted in Linda Dowling, "Victorian Oxford and the Science of Language," *PMLA* 97 (1982): 175.

41. "Müller's History of Vedic Literature," in *OLS* I, p. 96.
42. "Müller's Lectures on Language," in *OLS* I, p. 240.
43. "Müller's Chips from a German Workshop," in *Oriental and Linguistic Studies*, 2d ser. (New York: Scribner's 1874), p. 136 (hereafter *OLS* II).
44. William Dwight Whitney, *Max Müller and the Science of Language* (New York: Appleton, 1892), p. 75.
45. "The Elements of English Pronunciation," in *OLS* II, pp. 202–76; "Alford's Queen's English," in *OLS* II, pp. 166–80, (quotation from p. 167).
46. "How Shall We Spell," in *OLS* II, pp. 181–201 (quotations from pp. 181, 199).
47. Webster, *Dissertations* (Boston, 1789), p. 34, quoted and discussed in Simpson, *Politics of American English*, p. 59.
48. Anonymous (Archibald Campbell), *Lexiphanes* (London, 1767), quoted and discussed in Simpson, *Politics of American English*, p. 59.
49. "Elements of English Pronunciation," in *OLS* II, p. 203, emphases mine.
50. Webster, *Compendious Dictionary* (Hartford and New Haven, 1806), p. xvi, quoted and discussed in Simpson, *Politics of American English*, p. 69.
51. Basil Lanneau Gildersleeve, "Grammar and Aesthetics," in *Essays and Studies* (New York: Stechert, 1924), p. 141 (hereafter *ES*).
52. Basil Lanneau Gildersleeve, *Hellas and Hesperia* (New York: Henry Holt, 1909), p. 119 (hereafter *HH*).
53. George Eliot, "A Word for the Germans," in *Essays of George Eliot*, ed. Thomas Pinney (New York: Columbia University Press, 1963), p. 390.
54. For Gildersleeve's life and work, see the essays collected in Ward W. Briggs Jr. and Herbert W. Benario, eds., *Basil Lanneau Gildersleeve* (Baltimore: Johns Hopkins University Press, 1986).
55. Basil Lanneau Gildersleeve, "Formative Influences," *Forum* 10 (February, 1891): 608, quoted in Deborah Reeves Hopkins, "Basil Lanneau Gildersleeve: The Charleston Background," in *Gildersleeve*, p. 6.
56. See Ward W. Briggs, Jr., "Basil Lanneau Gildersleeve and the University of Virginia," in *Gildersleeve*, pp. 9–20; Stephen Newmyer, "Gildersleeve on the Study of the Classics," in ibid., pp. 27–35; George A. Kennedy, "Gildersleeve, *The Journal*, and Philology in America," in ibid., pp. 42–49, esp. p. 44, on Gildersleeve's desire to be buried in Charlottesville.
57. *The Creed of the Old South, 1865–1915* (Baltimore: Johns Hopkins University Press, 1915), esp. p. 14.
58. Hopkins, "Charleston Background," p. 5.
59. See Gregory A. VanHoosier-Carey, "Byrhtnoth in Dixie: The Emergence of Anglo-Saxon Studies in the Postbellum South," in *Anglo-Saxonism and the Construction of Social Identity*, ed. Allen J. Frantzen and John D. Niles (Gainesville: University of Florida Press, 1997), pp. 157–72.
60. J. B. Henneman, "The Study of English in the South," *Sewanee Review* 2 (1894): 180–197.
61. Quoted in Kennedy, "Gildersleeve, *The Journal*, and Philology in America," p. 44.

62. Gildersleeve, *The Creed of the Old South*, pp. 113–14 (hereafter *Creed*).
63. "Müller's Rig-Veda Translation," in *OLS* I, p. 139; *LSL*, p. 238.
64. Hart, "College Course in English Literature," p. 35.
65. Frank M. Rarig and Halbert S. Greaves, "National Speech Organizations and Speech Education," in *History of Speech Education in America*, ed. Karl Wallace (New York: Appleton-Century-Crofts, 1954), p. 496.
66. On the Cornell school, see Theodore Otto Windt Jr., "Everett Lee Hunt on Rhetoric," *Speech Teacher* 21 (1972): 177–92; and idem, "Hoyt H. Hudson: Spokesman for the Cornell School of Rhetoric," *Quarterly Journal of Speech* 68 (1982): 186–200. See, too, the more personal survey of Edward P. J. Corbett, "The Cornell School of Rhetoric," *Rhetoric Review* 4 (1985): 4–14. Two collections of essays representative of the school are A. M. Drummond, ed., *Studies in Rhetoric and Public Speaking in Honor of James Albert Winans* (1925; reprint, New York: Russell and Russell, 1962); and Donald C. Bryant, ed., *The Rhetorical Idiom: Essays in Rhetoric, Oratory, Language, and Drama Presented to Herbert August Wichelns* (Ithaca: Cornell University Press, 1958).
67. Windt, "Hoyt H. Hudson," p. 192.
68. Harry Caplan, "Latin Panegyrics of the Empire," *Quarterly Journal of Speech* 10 (1924): 41–52.
69. [Cicero], *Ad C. Herennium*, ed. and trans. Harry Caplan (Cambridge: Harvard University Press, 1954).
70. See Franklin H. Knower, "Graduate Theses—An Index of Graduate Work in the Field of Speech from 1902–1934," *Speech Monographs* 2 (1935): 7.
71. See, in particular, E. J. Corbett, *Classical Rhetoric for the Modern Student* (Oxford: Oxford University Press, 1965; 3d ed., 1990).
72. See Frank Lentricchia, *After the New Criticism* (Chicago: University of Chicago Press, 1980), esp. pp. 282–317; Victoria A. Kahn, "Humanism and the Resistance to Theory," in *Literary Theory / Renaissance Texts*, ed. Patricia Parker and David Quint (Baltimore: Johns Hopkins University Press, 1986), pp. 373–96; John Guillory, *Cultural Capital* (Chicago: University of Chicago Press, 1993), pp. 176–265; James Kastely, *Rethinking the Rhetorical Tradition: From Plato to Postmodernism* (New Haven: Yale University Press, 1997), pp. 195–220.
73. Paul de Man, *Allegories of Reading* (New Haven: Yale University Press, 1979), p. 6.
74. Ibid., p. 105–6, quoting Nietzsche's notes on rhetoric as published in *Gesammelte Werke* (Munich: Musarion, 1922), 5:300.
75. See David Lehman, *Signs of the Times: Deconstruction and the Fall of Paul De Man* (New York: Poseidon, 1991); and John Bender and David E. Wellbery, "Rhetoricality: On the Modernist Return of Rhetoric," in *The Ends of Rhetoric*, ed. Bender and Wellbery (Stanford: Stanford University Press, 1991).
76. "The Rhetoric of Blindness," in *Blindness and Insight*, 2d ed. (Minneapolis: University of Minnesota Press, 1983), p. 103.
77. "The Rhetoric of Temporality," in *Blindness and Insight*, pp. 186–87.
78. "The Return to Philology," in *The Resistance to Theory* (Minneapolis: University of Minnesota Press, 1986), p. 24.

79. Patricia Parker, *Inescapable Romance* (Princeton: Princeton University Press, 1979); idem, *Shakespeare From the Margins* (Chicago: University of Chicago Press, 1996).

80. In *The Ends of Rhetoric*, pp. 60–73, 219–22.

81. Parker, "Metaphor and Catachresis," p. 61.

82. Cicero, *De Oratore*, 3. 38. 155, pp. 121–23, quoted in Parker, "Metaphor and Catachresis," p. 66. My quotation here is from Rackham's translation, without the parenthetical Latin original phrases in Parker's quotation.

83. Parker, "Metaphor and Catachresis," p. 66.

84. [Cicero], *Ad C. Herennium*, p. 32.

5. Making Mimesis: Exile, Errancy, and Erich Auerbach

1. Erich Auerbach, *Mimesis: The Representation of Reality in Western Literature*, trans. Willard R. Trask (Princeton: Princeton University Press, 1953), pp. 19–20. The original German reads:

> Nun ist der Unterschied zwischen Sage und Geschichte für einen etwas erfahrenen Leser in den meisten Fällen leicht zu entdecken. So schwer est ist, und so sorgfältiger historisch-philologischer Ausbildung es bedarf, um innerhalb eines geschichtlichen Berichts das Wahre vom Gefälschten oder einseitig Beleuchteten zu unterscheiden, so leicht ist es im allgemeinen, Sage und Geschichte überhaupt auseinanderzuhalten. . . . Geschichte zu schreiben ist so schwierig, daß die meisten Geschichtsschreiber genötigt sind, Konzessionen an die Sagentechnik zu machen.
>
> (Erich Auerbach, *Mimesis: Dargestellte Wirklichkeit in der abendländischen Literatur* [Bern: Francke, 1946], pp. 24–25)

Throughout this chapter, when I occasionally attend to Auerbach's German, all quotations will be from this edition. When I cite both the English translation and the German, the first reference is to the English, the second to the German, except where otherwise noted.

2. In German: "[W]er etwa das Verhalten der einzelnen Menschen und Menschengruppen beim Aufkommen des Nationalsozialismus in Deutschland, oder das Verhalten der einzelnen Völker und Staaten vor und während des gegenwärtigen (1942) Krieges erwägt, der wird fühlen, wie schwer darstellbar geschichtliche Gegenstände überhaupt, und wie unbrauchbar sie für die Sage sind" (p. 25).

3. Maria Rosa Menocal, *Shards of Love: Exile and the Origins of the Lyric* (Durham, N.C.: Duke University Press, 1994), p. 106.

4. For Spitzer, see *Leo Spitzer: Representative Essays*, ed. Alban Forcione, Herbert Lindenberger, and Madeline Sutherland (Stanford: Stanford University Press, 1988), especially John Freccero's foreword on Spitzer as teacher (pp. xi–xx). Spitzer and Auerbach

are often paired in the impressions of mid-century German émigré medievalists. See, for example, the reflections of Paul Zumthor: "The work of the gentle Auerbach, with his large eyes and his expression of timid goodness, marked a generation, otherwise but no less than the work of the brilliant Spitzer, that great conversationalist, self-confident and beloved by women" (*Speaking of the Middle Ages*, trans. Sarah White [Lincoln: University of Nebraska Press, 1985], p. 21). See, too, Harry Levin, "Two *Romanisten* in America," in *The Intellectual Migration: Europe and America, 1930–1960*, ed. Donald Fleming and Bernard Bailyn (Cambridge: Harvard University Press, 1969), pp. 467–83. On Curtius and Auerbach, see Geoffrey Green, *Literary Criticism and the Structures of History: Erich Auerbach and Leo Spitzer* (Lincoln: University of Nebraska Press, 1982). For a discussion of Auerbach's response to Curtius's *European Literature and the Latin Middle Ages* in his "Philologie der Weltliteratur" of 1952, see Paul Bové, *Intellectuals in Power* (New York: Columbia University Press, 1986), pp. 205–6. For an amusing anecdote about Auerbach's encounter with Curtius in Princeton in 1949, related as an icon of their respective scholarly and emotional personalities, see Robert Fitzgerald, *Enlarging the Change: The Princeton Seminars in Literary Criticism, 1949–1951* (Boston: Northeastern University Press, 1985), pp. 21–22. For Jaeger, see the essays collected in *Werner Jaeger Reconsidered*, ed. William M. Calder III, Illinois Classical Studies, supp. 3 (Atlanta: Scholars, 1992).

5. Erich Auerbach, *Introduction aux études de la philologie romane* (Frankfurt am Main: Vittorio Klostermann, 1949), p. 9. The original French reads: "La philologie est l'ensemble des activités qui s'occupent méthodiquement du langage de l'homme, et des oeuvres d'art composées dans ce langage. . . . Le besoin de constituer des textes authentiques se fait sentir quand un peuple d'une haute civilisation prend conscience de cette civilisation, et qu'il veut préserver des ravages du temps les oeuvres qui constituent son patrimoine spirituel." Page numbers following subsequent quotations from this work refer to this edition.

6. See Hans Ulrich Gumbrecht, "'Un Souffle d'Allemagne ayant passé': Friedrich Diez, Gaston Paris, and the Genesis of National Philologies," *Romance Philology* 40 (1986): 1–37 (with a full bibliography of primary and secondary sources); and the following contributions to the special "New Philology" volume of *Speculum* 65, no. 1 (1990): Stephen G. Nichols, "Introduction: Philology in a Manuscript Culture" (pp. 1–10); R. Howard Bloch, "New Philology and Old French" (pp. 38–58); Lee Patterson, "On the Margin: Postmodernism, Ironic History, and Medieval Studies" (pp. 87–108).

7. From Diez's remarks on his candidacy for a lectureship at the University of Bonn, quoted in Gumbrecht, "'Un Souffle d'Allemagne ayant passé,'" p. 18.

8. From the opening of Aubertin's *Histoire de la langue et de la littérature française au moyen age d'après les travaux les plus récents*, quoted in Gumbrecht, "'Un Souffle d'Allemagne ayant passé,'" pp. 26–27.

9. For a chronicle of these attempts, see Gumbrecht, "'Un Souffle d'Allemagne ayant passé,'"; and Bloch, "New Philology and Old French."

10. In addition to the contributions to the *Speculum* "New Philology" issue, see William D. Paden, ed., *The Future of the Past* (Gainesville: University of Florida Press,

1994); and R. Howard Bloch and Stephen G. Nichols, eds., *Medievalism and the Modernist Temper* (Baltimore: Johns Hopkins University Press, 1996).

11. Volumes published from those conferences are Seth Lerer, ed., *Literary History and the Challenge of Philology: The Legacy of Erich Auerbach* (Stanford: Stanford University Press, 1996); and the special issue of *Poetics Today*, "Erich Auerbach and Literary Representation," 20, no. 1 (1999). In addition to these volumes (which together discuss the full previous critical bibliography on Auerbach), see Michael Holquist, "The Last European: Erich Auerbach as Precursor in the History of Cultural Criticism," *Modern Language Quarterly* 54 (1993): 371–91; David Damrosch, "Auerbach in Exile," *Comparative Literature* 47 (1995): 97–117. For a chronicle of Auerbach's reception—from the first reviews of *Mimesis* through the 1980s—see Herbert Lindenberger, "On the Reception of *Mimesis*," in *Literary History*, pp. 195–215.

12. See Catherine Gallagher and Stephen Greenblatt, *Practicing New Historicism* (Chicago: University of Chicago Press, 2000), pp. 31–47; and my discussion at the close of this chapter.

13. See Aamir R. Mufti, "Auerbach in Istanbul: Edward Said, Secular Criticism, and the Question of Minority Culture," *Critical Inquiry* 25 (1998): 95–125, especially this remark: "The German Jewish critic in ('Oriental') exile becomes for Said the paradigmatic figure for modern criticism" (p. 104).

14. Damrosch, "Auerbach in Exile," p. 115.

15. See Bové, *Intellectuals in Power*.

16. See Egbert J. Bakker, "Mimesis as Performance: Rereading Auerbach's First Chapter," *Poetics Today* 20 (1999): 11–26; Damrosch, "Auerbach in Exile"; Luiz Costa-Lima, "Auerbach and Literary History," in *Literary History*, pp. 50–60; Jesse Gellrich, "Figura, Allegory, and the Question of History," in *Literary History*, pp. 108–23.

17. For the Latin roots of "*vernacular*," see the *Oxford Latin Dictionary*, s.v. "verna," "vernaculus."

18. Homer, *The Odyssey*, 19.407–9, ed. and trans. A. T. Murray (London: Heinemann, 1919), 2:256–59 (the quotation is from pp. 257–58).

19. Damrosch, "Auerbach in Exile," p. 114.

20. Edward Said, *The World, the Text, and the Critic* (Cambridge: Harvard University Press, 1983), p. 7.

21. Mufti, "Auerbach in Istanbul," p. 110.

22. The original German of the epigraph for this section reads: "so daß ich auf fast alle Zeitschriften, auf die meisten neueren Untersuchungen, ja zuweilen selbst auf eine zuverlässige kritische Ausgabe meiner Texte verzichten mußte" (p. 497; English translation, p. 557). On the "Adam and Eve" chapter, see, too, Stephen G. Nichols, "Philology in Auerbach's Drama of (Literary) History," in *Literary History*, pp. 63–77; and Suzanne Fleischman, "Medieval Vernaculars and the Myth of Monoglossia: A Conspiracy of Linguistics and Philology," in *Literary History*, pp. 92–104.

23. Early in the twentieth century, the play was known as the *Mystère*; more recently, it is referred to as the *Jeu d'Adam*; those who locate it primarily in its liturgical setting call it the *Ordo Representationis Ade*.

24. In French:

> Quant aux lacunes et aux passage irrémédiablement corrumpus, il peut essayer d'en reconstituer le texte par des conjectures, c'est-à-dire par sa propre hypothèse sur la forme originale du passage en question; bien entendu, il faut indiquer, dans ce cas, qu'il s'agit de sa propre reconstitution du texte, et il faut y ajouter encore les conjectures que d'autres ont faites pour le même passage, s'il y en a. On voit que l'édition critique est, en general, plus facile à faire s'il y a peu de manuscrits ou seulement un manuscrit unique; dans ce dernier cas, on n'a qu'à le faire imprimer, avec une exactitude scrupuleuse, et à y ajouter, le cas échéant, des conjectures. (p. 12)

25. S. Etienne, "Note sur les verse 279–287 du *Jeu d'Adam*," *Romania* 48 (1922): 592–95. For a complete review of the textual problems of this passage, together with an account of Auerbach's probable sources, editions, and critical discussions available to him, see Nichols, "Philology in Auerbach's Drama," pp. 75–77.

26. Etienne, "Note," pp. 592, 593.

27. In French: "les sauver non seulement de l'oubli, mais aussi de changements, mutilations et additions que l'usage populaire ou l'insouciance des copistes y apportent nécessairement" (p. 9).

28. Gumbrecht, "'Un Souffle d'Allemagne ayant passé,'" p. 2.

29. Léon Gautier, "Chronique," *Revue des questions historiques* 9 (1870): 496, translated and discussed in Bloch, "New Philology and Old French," p. 40.

30. Henri Massis, *Les jeunes gens d'aujourd'hui* (Paris, 1913), p. 107, translated and discussed in Bloch, "New Philology and Old French," p. 40.

31. For the rise of chairs of literature in France and Germany in the nineteenth century, see Gumbrecht, "'Un Souffle d'Allemagne,'" pp. 31–32. For the rise "of a new paradigm in the history of French scholarship, which will create its own publication outlets in *Romania* (from 1872 on) and the *Société des Anciens Textes Français* (from 1875)," see ibid., p. 27. For the phrasings of Gaston Paris, see his *Contges orientaux dans la littérature français du moyen age* (Paris, 1875), quoted in Bloch, "New Philology and Old French," pp. 41–42.

32. Bloch, "New Philology and Old French," p. 40.

33. Jean-Paul Sartre, "Qu'est-ce qu'un collaborateur?" in *Situations III* (Paris: Gallimard, 1949), pp. 43–61.

34. Auerbach, *Mimesis*, p. 151; p. 148.

35. Actually, they are the words of the Book of Micah 7:6, as quoted by Bernard.

36. See, for example, Timothy Bahti, "Vico, Auerbach, and Literary History," in *Vico Past and Present*, ed. Giorgio Tagliacozzo (Atlantic Highlands, N.J.: Humanities, 1981), pp. 249–66; Edward Said, *Beginnings: Intention and Method* (New York: Basic, 1975), p. 363 (where Said calls Auerbach "Vico's principal and most profound literary student"); Luiz Costa-Lima, "Erich Auerbach: History and Metahistory," *New Literary History* 19 (1988): 467–99; idem, "Auerbach and Literary History," in *Literary History*, pp. 50–60;

Claus Uhlig, "Auerbach's 'Hidden' (?) Theory of History," in *Literary History*, pp. 36–49.

37. See Bové, *Intellectuals in Power*, pp. 79–208.

38. See, too, Herbert Lindenberger, "On the Reception of *Mimesis*," in *Literary History*, pp. 195–213; and Carl Landauer, "Auerbach's Performance and the American Academy; or, How New Haven Stole the Idea of *Mimesis*," in *Literary History*, pp. 195–213.

39. One exception to this dehistoricized *Mimesis* among the early reviews is René Wellek, "Auerbach's Special Realism," *Kenyon Review* 16 (1954): 299–306.

40. *Romance Philology* 2 (1949): 338.

41. Robert Fitzgerald, *Enlarging the Change*, pp. 21–22.

42. See Liselotte Dieckmann, "Akademische Emigranten in der Türkei," in *Verbannung: Aufzeichnungen deutscher Schriftsteller im Exil*, ed. Egon Schwarz and Matthias Wegner (Hamburg: Christian Wegner, 1964), pp. 122–26. But we now know that Auerbach's situation in Istanbul was much more complex. He may have, in fact, had access to major research collections. His personal correspondence reveals that, at least on one occasion, he formally requested an extension of his stay in Turkey from the German government. And, throughout his letters, there emerges what has been called an "air of irony" about his stay. See Hans Ulrich Gumbrecht, "'Pathos of the Earthly Progress': Auerbach's Everydays," in *Literary History*, pp. 13–35; and Jesse Gellrich, "*Figura*, Allegory, and the Question of History," in *Literary History*, pp. 109–23, esp. pp. 110–11. In 1939 Auerbach could write to Martin Hellweg: "Haben Sie die Arbeiten von E. R. Curtius über M[ittel] A[lter] gelesen, die in der Z[eitschrift] [für] Rom[anische] Ph[ilologie] . . . erscheinen sint?" (letter of May 22, 1939, in *Erich Auerbachs Briefe an Martin Hellweg (1939–1950)*, ed. Martin Vialon [Tübingen: Francke, 1997], p. 57)—implying, I take it, that Auerbach *had* seen it.

43. For the details of Auerbach's publications from 1946 to 1948, see the bibliography of his writings in Erich Auerbach, *Literary Language and Its Public in Late Antiquity and the Middle Ages*, trans. Ralph Mannheim, with a new foreword by Jan Ziolkowski (Princeton: Princeton University Press, 1993), pp. 399–400.

44. "Epilegomena zu *Mimesis*," *Romanische Forschungen* 65 (1953): 1–18.

45. *Comparative Literature* 1 (1949): 83–84. It cannot escape notice that Spitzer's now most famous essay, also published in 1949, was "American Advertising Explained as Popular Art," with its brilliant close reading of the rhetoric of Sunkist Orange posters—a lecture on fruits if ever there was one. And it cannot escape notice, too, that Adam and Eve had themselves received something of a lecture on fruits and did get hold of an apple. Spitzer's essay is reprinted in *Leo Spitzer: Representative Essays*, pp. 327–56.

46. Paul Aebischer, ed., *Le Mystère d'Adam* (Geneva: Droz, 1963), pp. 51–52.

47. Leif Sletsjöe, ed., *Le Mystère d'Adam* (Paris: Klincksieck, 1968), pp. 21, 85. For additional information on manuscripts and editions, see Nichols, "Philology in Auerbach's Drama," pp. 75–77.

48. David Bevington, ed., *Medieval Drama* (Boston: Houghton Mifflin, 1975), text on p. 94, discussion on p. 79, quoting Auerbach's discussion of the everyday element of

the play's realism (from Trask's translation of *Mimesis*, p. 151) in support of an argument that the play was "intended for an audience of ordinary men and women." For a counterargument to this tradition of interpretation, reading the play as primarily a liturgical, Latin occasion rather than a popular, vernacular one, see Steven Justice, "The Authority of Ritual in the *Jeu d'Adam*," *Speculum* 62 (1987): 851–64.

49. Nichols speculates that "[h]is general inattentiveness to textual questions, in the technical sense of the term, suggests a philological perspective . . . more fixed on the 'historical horizon' than on textual studies. The best text for Auerbach was the one that most accurately could convey an image of the medieval imagination that was most exciting, most satisfying to modern sensibilities" ("Philology in Auerbach's Drama," p. 76).

50. From Auerbach, *Literary Language and Its Public*, p. 20. This passage generates the discussion of Auerbach's method in Thomas M. De Pietro, "Literary Criticism as History: The Example of Auerbach's *Mimesis*," *Clio* 8 (1979): 377–87; and it forms the point of argument for the critique of Auerbach's "understanding of humanism's contradictory development" in Bové's *Intellectuals in Power*, pp. 206–7. Auerbach's claim to write history also forms the basis of the foreword to the reprinting of *Literary Language* by Jan Ziolkowski (pp. ix–xxxii), which, among other things, avers that "readers should not exaggerate the topicality—or the ideological elements" of Auerbach's work (p. xxii) and offers a vision of "the constancy of Auerbach in his self-understanding and in his lifelong engagement with European literature" as an "indeed attractive" alternative to the situation of "our days" in which "the self-definitions of the professors—and the professionals—who are hired to teach and write about literature change with dizzying rapidity" (p. xxvii).

51. Quoted in Landauer, "Auerbach's Performance and the American Academy," p. 187 and p. 288 n. 20.

52. For discussion of the early American reviews and the larger contexts for *Mimesis*'s absorption into academic practice, see Landauer's entire essay, pp. 179–94.

53. Most notably in Jan Ziolkowski's foreword to the reprinting of Auerbach, *Literary Language and Its Public*. For another reminiscence of Auerbach and his place in a broader postwar humanist ideal, see Thomas R. Hart, "Literature as Language: Auerbach, Spitzer, Jakobson," in *Literary History*, pp. 227–39.

54. Nichols, "Philology in Auerbach's Drama," p. 63.

55. Alvin Kernan, *In Plato's Cave* (New Haven: Yale University Press, 1999), p. 108.

56. The book was originally published in German as *Literatursprache und Publikum in der lateinischen Spätantike und im Mittelalter* (Bern: Francke, 1958) and in English translation in 1965. The only other book published by Auerbach in his Yale years is *Typologische Motive in der mittelalterlichen Literatur* (Cologne: Petrarca-Institut, 1953), a work not really concerned with "rhetoric" and probably so arcane that even Kernan did not know about it.

57. Originally published in short form in *Critical Inquiry* 3 (1976): 439–47; and expanded and printed in *Deconstruction and Criticism*, ed. Harold Bloom (New York: Seabury, 1979). I use the version as it appears in Hazard Adams and Leroy Searle, eds., *Critical Theory Since 1965* (Gainesville: University of Florida Press, 1986), pp. 452–68.

58. See the discussion above, in n. 35.

59. The book in question is *La preuve par l'étymologie* (Paris, 1953), with Jameson quoting from p. 12.

60. Frederic Jameson, *The Prison-House of Language: A Critical Account of Structuralism and Russian Formalism* (Princeton: Princeton University Press, 1972), p. 6.

61. See Haun Saussy, "Writing in the *Odyssey*: Eurykleia, Parry, Jousse, and the Opening of Letter from Homer," *Arethusa* 29 (1996): 299–338, esp. the discussion on pp. 300–304. Even Saussy cannot discuss this passage without reference to Auerbach (p. 302), whose observations find themselves pressed into the service of enhancing Saussy's largely deconstructive reading (that is, that writing is already present in the oral epic).

62. *The Poems and Letters of Andrew Marvell*, ed. Ed. H. M. Margoliouth (Oxford: Oxford University Press, Clarendon, 1971), 1:27, lines 1–10.

Epilogue: Forbidden Planet *and the Terrors of Philology*

1. See Donald Fleming and Bernard Bailyn, eds., *The Intellectual Migration: Europe and America, 1930–1960* (Cambridge: Harvard University Press, 1969), especially the capsule biographies of the "300 Notable Emigrés" that close the volume (pp. 675–718). Among more recent books, see Anthony Heilbut, *Exiled in Paradise: German Refugee Artists and Intellectuals in America: From the 1930s to the Present* (New York: Viking, 1983); Lewis A. Coser, *Refugee Scholars in America: Their Impact and Their Experiences* (New Haven: Yale University Press, 1984); Martin Jay, *Permanent Exiles: Essays on the Intellectual Migration from Germany to America* (New York: Columbia University Press, 1986). Still valuable for its firsthand accounts is W. Rex Crawford, ed., *The Cultural Migration: The European Scholar in America* (Philadelphia: University of Pennsylvania Press, 1953), with contributions by Franz Neumann, Henri Peyre, Erwin Panofsky, Wolfgang Köhler, and Paul Tillich. For a German perspective on this history, see Helge Pross, *Die deutsche akademische Emigration nach den Vereinigsten Staaten, 1933–1941* (Berlin: Duncker und Humblot, 1955).

2. See Liselotte Dieckmann, "Akademische Emigranten in der Türkei," in *Verbannung: Aufzeichnungen deutscher Schriftsteller im Exil*, ed. Egon Schwarz and Matthias Wegner (Hamburg: Christian Wegner, 1964), pp. 122–26.

3. See the information in the capsule biographies of these figures and the corresponding discussions in the essays in *The Intellectual Migration*.

4. H. Stuart Hughes, "Franz Neumann Between Marxism and Liberal Democracy," in *Intellectual Migration*, p. 449.

5. Franz Neumann, "The Social Sciences," in *The Cultural Migration*, p. 19. This passage is discussed in Jean Matter Mandler and George Mandler, "The Diaspora of Experimental Psychology," in *Intellectual Migration*, p. 379.

6. Quoted in Donald Fleming and Bernard Bailyn, introduction to The *Intellectual Migration*, p. 7.

7. Laura Fermi, *Illustrious Immigrants: The Intellectual Migration from Europe, 1930–41*, 2d ed. (Chicago: University of Chicago Press, 1971).

8. For a complete production history of the film and a review of some of its sources and early responses, see the special issue of *Cinefantastique* 8 (1979): 1–2.

9. George Orwell, *1984* (New York: Signet, 1950), p. 45.

10. In *The Standard Edition of the Works of Sigmund Freud*, ed. James Strachey (London: Hogarth, 1955), 17:218–56. The essay originally appeared in German in *Imago* 5 (1919): 297–324.

11. See Henry L. Minton, *Lewis M. Terman: Pioneer in Psychological Testing* (New York: New York University Press, 1988), esp. p. 265:

In essence, what Terman and the other testing advocates accomplished was to provide a scientific mode of thought and practice that served the interests of maintaining social order and organizational efficiency. With few exceptions, the distribution of tested intelligence reflected the opportunity structure of the social hierarchy. Those identified as most meritorious came primarily from the most privileged strata; those judged to be least meritorious, by virtue of tested IQ, were disproportionately members of the lowest rungs on the social ladder—often racial minorities or recent immigrants.

12. See Linda Dowling, "Victorian Oxford and the Science of Language," *PMLA* 97 (1982): 160.

13. "Development of a Method," in *Leo Spitzer: Representative Essays*, ed. Alban Forcione, Herbert Lindenberger, and Madeline Sutherland (Stanford: Stanford University Press, 1988), p. 448.

14. "The Formation of the American Humanist," *PMLA* 66 (1951): 47; emphases mine.

15. Auerbach to Binswanger, March 3, 1930, quoted and translated in Hans Ulrich Gumbrecht, "'Pathos of the Earthly Progress': Erich Auerbach's Everydays," in *Literary History and the Challenge of Philology: The Legacy of Erich Auerbach*, ed. Seth Lerer (Stanford: Stanford University Press, 1996), pp. 23–24. I am grateful to Professor Gumbrecht for providing me with a copy of the original German letter. Gumbrecht considers this a "caricature," and his extended assay in providing a more textured portrait of the critic is *Leo Spitzers Stil* (Tübingen: Narr, 2001).

16. E. T. A. Hoffmann, "Der Sandman," in *Sämtliche poetischen Werke* (Berlin: Tempel, 1963), pp. 612–13

17. W. J. Stuart, *Forbidden Planet* (New York: Farrar, Strauss, 1956), p. 35.

18. John Freccero, foreword to *Leo Spitzer: Representative Essays*, p. xii.

19. Paul Zumthor, *Speaking of the Middle Ages*, trans. Sarah White (Lincoln: University of Nebraska Press, 1984), p. 21. For another portrait in contrasts, see Harry Levin, "Two *Romanisten* in America: Spitzer and Auerbach," in *Intellectual Migration*, pp. 463–84.

20. Auerbach's picture appears as the frontispiece to *Gesammelte Aufsätze zur romanischen Philologie* (Bern: Francke, 1967) and also appears on the cover of Martin

Vialon, ed., *Erich Auerbachs Briefe an Martin Hellweg (1939–1950)* (Tübingen: Francke, 1997). Spitzer's appears as the frontispiece to *Classical and Christian Ideas of World Harmony* (Baltimore: Johns Hopkins University Press, 1963). Curtius's is printed as the frontispiece to *Ernst Robert Curtius: Werk, Wirkung, Zukunftsperspectiven*, ed. Walter Berschin and Arnold Rothe (Heidelberg: Winter, 1989).

21. *Stand und Aufgaben der Sprachwissenschaft: Festschrift für Wilhelm Streitberg* (Heidelberg: Winter, 1924); *Germanica: Eduard Sievers zum 75. Geburtstage 25. November 1925* (Halle: Niemeyer, 1925); *Sprachgeschichte und Wortbedeutung: Festschrift Albert Debrunner gewidmet von Schülern, Freunden und Kollegen* (Bern: Francke, 1954).

22. *http://sfstation.members.easyspace.com/fbkrel.htm*, which reproduces a page of Krell writing, together with an imaginary translation key.

23. Moses Hadas, review of the second edition of Jaeger's *Humanistische Reden und Vorträge*, *Classical Journal* 56 (1960): 284.

24. Stuart, *Forbidden Planet*, pp. 101–2.

25. "Zur Einführung," *Scripta Minora* (Rome: Edizioni di Storia e letteratura, 1960), 1:xxvi.

26. See William H. Jordy, "The Aftermath of the Bauhaus in America: Gropius, Mies, and Breuer," in *Intellectual Migration*, pp. 485–544. For an account of Neutra's modernism, with designs and photographs of homes that recall those of Dr. Morbius, see Esther McCoy, *Richard Neutra* (New York: Braziller, 1960). Neutra also designed the so-called Chemosphere House, off Mulholland Drive in Los Angeles, in 1960; with its saucer-shaped living space and its tall pedestal of a foundation, this striking house became a fixture of early 1960s futurism and appeared frequently in science fiction television of that decade.

27. For details, see Gumbrecht, "'Pathos of the Earthly Progress.'"

28. "Jede Form vom Emigration verursacht an sich schon unvermeidlicher—weise eine Art von Gleichgewichtsstörung. . . . [I]ch mich nie mehr ganz als mit mir zusammengehörig empfand. Etwas von der natürlichen Identität mit meinem ursprünglichen und eigentlichen Ich blieb für immer zerstört" (quoted as the epigraph to A. B. Malgarini, "Werner Jaeger in the United States," in *Werner Jaeger Reconsidered*, ed. W. M. Calder III [Atlanta: Scholars, 1992], p. 107; my translation).

INDEX

Abraham, in *Mimesis*, 226, 228–29
Absalom and Achitophel (Dryden), political aspects of, 69–70
"Adam and Eve," in *Mimesis*, 230–41, 246–47, 256, 273–75
Adams, John Quincy, 8–9, 177–79; compared to Cicero, 179–81, 186; contemporary reviews of, 190–91; rhetorical practice of, 183–90
ad Herennium. *See Rhetorica ad Herennium*
"adoption," in *OED*, 182–83
"Advancement and Reformation of Poetry, The" (Dennis), 71
Aebischer, Paul, 246
alliteration, in Anglo-Saxon poetry, 68–69, 72, 92–93
American, in imaginary lexicon, 172–74
American dream, the, 272–73
American Language, The (Mencken), 175–76

American philology, 3–4, 175–79, 207–8; and Caplan, 208–15; and de Man, 215–20; and Gildersleeve, 195, 199–207; and Hill, 191–99; and Whitney, 195–99. *See also* Adams, John Quincy
American vocabulary, growth of, 175–77
Anglo-Saxon Pindarics, 65–69, 75–76
Anglo-Saxon studies, 3, 55–58, 75–78, 81–83, 90–94, 100–101, 193, 287nn. 4–5. *See also* Hickes, George; Old English verse
"annex," in *OED*, 182
Annotations on the Pandects (Budé), 38–40
antiauthor, Dorothea as, 117–18
antifeminism, 126, 156–57
antipioneer, Casaubon as, 159–61, 163–65
antisublime, Casaubon as, 165–72
Arrowsmith, William, 14
atta, 90–91

attila, 90–91
Aubertin, Charles, 223
audax, in Anglo-Saxon Pindarics, 65–67
Auerbach, Erich, 4, 11, 221–24, 268–71, 273–75, 308n. 4; early critics of, 241–47, 274; and faulty scribes, 231–33, 246; later critics of, 247–55. *See also Mimesis*
author: compared with compiler, 118–21; corrections by (*see* errata; proofreading); and despondency, 112–13, 164–65; failed (*see* Casaubon, Edward, as failure); and identity, 2, 112–18; and vanity, 112. *See also author, authorship*, in imaginary lexicon
author, authorship, in imaginary lexicon, 110–22
authority, literary, in *OED*, 111–12
"Authorship" (Eliot), 112

Bacon, Franics, 6
"Barbarians and Citizens" (C. Tolkien), 90–91
Battle of Bruanburh, 75
Baudri of Bourgeuil, 19
Bellerophon, 92
Bellerophon (spaceship), 265
Bennet, Arnold, 108
Bennett, J. A. W., 58
Beorhtnoth, 83, 85–91
Beowulf, 84, 90; Heaney's translation of, 57, 94–101; sword hilt in, 92–94; Tolkien's lecture on, 57, 77–83, 90
"*Beowulf*: The Monsters and the Critics" (Tolkien), 57, 77–83, 90
"bewilderment," in *OED*, 164–65
Bible. *See* scripture
Bibliography of Publications on Old English Literature, A (Greenfield and Robinson), 81–83
Bonner, Edmund, 41

Bopp, Franz, 139–40, 142, 148
Bosworth, Joseph, 78
Brabant, Robert Herbert, as model for Casaubon, 104, 126–27
Brooke, Arthur, 159–62; and pigeonholing, 151–55
Brooke, Dorothea. *See* Dorothea
Bryan, Jacob, 124
Budé, Guillaume, 3, 36–41, 54

Cadmus (Thornton), 176–77, 199
Caedmon, 73–74, 85
Campbell, John, 74–75
Caplan, Harry, 208–10, 219–20; and Loeb edition of *ad Herennium*, 210–15, 220
Carlyle, Thomas, 111
Casaubon, Edward, 3, 103–10, 121–23; as antipioneer, 159–61, 163–65; as antisublime, 165–72; and error, 130–38; as failure, 105–7, 112–14, 117–18, 120–21, 124, 144, 148; historical model for, 104–5, 124–29; and orientalism, 147–51; and pigeonholing, 151–52, 154, 156–57; and scholarship, 144–47
Casaubon, in imaginary lexicon, 122–29. *See also* Casaubon, Edward
Cassiodorus, and faulty scribes, 18–19
Catalogue of Manuscripts Containing Anglo-Saxon (Ker), 58
Cates, W. L. R., *A Dictionary of General Biography*, 118–20
Caxton, William, and errata, 21–22, 26
censorship. *See* Wyatt, Thomas, modernization of
Chaucer, Geoffrey, 44–45; and faulty scribes, 19
Child, Francis, 194
Cicero, 178, 217–20; compared to Adams, 179–81, 186
Clouet, Jean, portrait by, of Budé, 38
Coleridge, Herbert, 153, 169–70

INDEX   319

"collation," first attested use of, 44, 286n. 85
compiler, compared with author, 118–21
Confutation of Tyndale (More), 24–26, 28
Cook, Albert S., 177, 194–95
Copland, Robert, 51–52
Cornell group. *See* Caplan, Harry
correction, authorial. *See* errata; proofreading
Cowley, Abraham. *See* Cowleyan Pindaric
Cowleyan Pindaric, 60–69, 72–74, 98–99, 289n. 20, 290n. 35
Creed of the Old South (Gildersleeve), 203
"Critic as Host, The" (Miller), 249–51
criticism: early, of Auerbach, 241–47, 274; later, of Auerbach, 247–55; literary, 81, 83, 85–91; textual, 34–36, 55
Cromwell, Oliver, 32
Curtius, Ernst Robert, 222, 247–48, 270

Damrosch, David, 228–29
David, Alfred, 100
Death of Edgar, 75
Debrunner, Albert, 271
Declaration . . . of his Innocence . . . , A (Wyatt), 41–46
De falsa legatione (Demosthenes), 40
Defence To the Iudges after the Indictement and the evidence (Wyatt), 41–46
Deloynes, François, 38
de Man, Paul, 10, 93, 178, 215–20
Demosthenes, *De falsa legatione*, 40
Dennis, John, 60, 70–71
Denny, Anthony, 31–32
"De Poetica Anglo-Saxonum" (Hickes), 59, 62–69, 71–74
despondency, authorial, 112–13, 164–65
de Worde, Wynkyn, 22

Dialogue Concerning Heresies (More), 22–24, 34
Dickens, Charles, 157
Dictionary (Elyot), 30–34
Dictionary of General Biography, A (ed. Cates), 118–20
Diez, Friedrich, 223
diligence. *See* proofreading
Dissertations on the English Language (Webster), 182
Diversions of Purley (Tooke), 138–39, 181–82
Dorothea, 103, 105–7, 109, 112–13, 120; as antiauthor, 117–18; and error, 130–38; and pigeonholing, 151–52, 156–57; as pioneer, 159, 164–65; and scholarship, 145–47
Dr. Morbius. *See* Morbius, Edward
Dryden, John, 60–61, 68–69, 71
Durham, 64–65, 72, 75
"dylygently ouerseen." *See* proofreading

Eisenstein, Elizabeth, 16
"Elements of English Pronunciation" (Whitney), 198–99
Eliot, George, 103–10, 122–23, 156–57, 164–65; and German scholarship, 143–47, 158, 201; as model for Casaubon, 104–5, 129; and mythography, 124–25; and orientalism, 147–51; and pilgrimage motif, 131–32, 149–51; and proofreading, 132–38, 300n. 84; Scott's influence on, 114–16. *See also* Evans, Mary Ann; Mackay, Robert William; *Middlemarch* (Eliot)
Elstob, Elizabeth, 74
Elton, G. R., 32
Elyot, Thomas, 44, 53–54; and errata, 30–34
émigrés (exiles), 10–14, 221–25, 234–42, 244, 261–62, 273–75, 308n. 4. *See also Forbidden Planet* (movie)

Erasmus, 53–54; and Budé, 36–41; and textual criticism, 34–36
errata, 2; early history of, 17–22, 26, 281n. 19, 282n. 29; Elyot's, 30–34; More's, 22–29, 282n. 29; Tyndale's, 17, 26–29. See also proofreading
error, 1–2; doctrinal, 23–26; in imaginary lexicon, 129–38; in *Mimesis*, 228–29. See also errata; scribes, faulty
Etienne, S., 232–34, 238–39, 246
etymologies, 215–20; and Adams, 183–90; and Caplan, 213–15; and Gildersleeve, 202–3, 206–7; and Hill, 192–93; and Whitney, 196–99. See also *etymology*, in imaginary lexicon
etymology, in imaginary lexicon, 138–43. See also etymologies
Evans, Mary Ann, 104, 116, 126–27, 152. See also Eliot, George
exiles. See émigrés (exiles)

"fault," 27; in *OED*, 283n. 47. See also errata
feminism. See antifeminism; *Mimesis*, gender issues in
Finnsburh Fragment, 59, 67, 72–73, 80, 94
Fisher, John, 24
Fiske, John, 122–24
Fliegelman, Jay, 176, 198
Foley, Stephen Merriam, 31, 33–34, 38
Forbidden Planet (movie), 4, 259, 262–65; and philology, 263, 267–75; plot of, 265–67
Frank, Roberta, 73–75
Freud, Sigmund, 262, 264, 274–75
Fry, Paul, 73
"funds," in *OED*, 183

Gallagher, Catherine, 253–57
Garth, Caleb, 166–67, 171
George Eliot and John Chapman (Haight), 127

Germans, in imaginary lexicon, 143–47
Gibson, Edmund, 73–74
Gildersleeve, Basil Lanneau, 173, 178, 195, 199–207, 220
Greenblatt, Stephen, 15, 253–57
Greenfield, Stanley, 81–83
Greetham, David, 41
Grimm Brothers, 139–40

Hadas, Moses, 271–72
Hagar, in *Mimesis*, 228–29
Haight, Gordon, 106–7, 113–14, 125–27
Hamilton, Sir William, 144
Hart, James Morgan, 194, 207
Harvey, W. J., 130
Hatzfeld, Helmut, 241
Heaney, Seamus, 56–57, 94–101
hearsay, defined, 24
Henley, Joseph, 74
Henneman, J. B., 204–5
Henry, Robert, 75
Henry VIII: and Elyot, 30–34; and Tuke, 45; and Wyatt, 41–46
Hertz, Neil, 106–7, 128–29, 132
Hess, Gerhard, 242–44
Heywood, Jasper, 52–54
Hickes, George, 56–57, 76–77, 80, 85, 94, 178; biographical sketch of, 58–59; lyric poetry defined by, 167–69; *Menologium* considered by, 71–72; on meter, 62–66; and the sublime, 70–74. See also *Thesaurus* (Hickes)
Highland Widow, The (Scott), 114
Hill, Adams Sherman, 173, 191–99
History of English Poetry (Warton), 75
History of Great Britain, The (Henry), 75
Hoffmann, E. T. A., 264, 269
"Homecoming of Beorhtnoth Beorhthelm's Son, The" (Tolkien), 83, 85–91
Housman, A. E., 55
Howe, Nicholas, 95

Hrothgar, 92–93
Humphreys, Jennett: and pigeonholing, 154–57; and the sublime, 168–71
Hymn (Caedmon), 73–74
Hypnerotomachia Poliphili, 21

identity: authorial, 2, 112–18; Jewish, 4, 10–11, 268–71
Introduction to an English Grammar (Henley), 74
IQ testing, 266, 315n. 11
Isaac, in *Mimesis*, 221, 225–29, 255

Jaeger, Werner, 222, 271–73
James, Henry, and *Middlemarch*, 3, 121–22, 124, 128–29, 172
James II, and Hickes, 59
Jameson, Frederic, 251–53
Jardine, Lisa, 35–38
Johns, Adrian, 16
Johnson, Samuel, 178, 183, 185
Jones, Sir William, 12, 139, 147–48

Kennedy, George, 8, 177
Ker, N. R., 58
Kernan, Alvin, 248–49
"Key to All Mythologies." *See* Casaubon, Edward, as failure
Kramnick, Jonathan, 69

Ladislaw, Will, 130, 150–51; as pioneer, 158–64
Lady of the Lake, The (Scott), 114
Landauer, Carl, 248
Landor, Walter Savage, 126–27, 192–93
Lang, Andrew, 157
"Lawrenny, H." (Edith Simcox), 130
Layton, George Soames, 127
Lazarsfeld, Paul, 262
Leaves of Grass (Whitman), 220
Lectures on Rhetoric and Oratory (Adams), 179–81
Leland, John, 31

letter of application, Tolkien's, 83–86, 90
Lewes, George Henry, 104, 109, 113–14, 124
lexicography, and *Middlemarch*, 118–22, 160–61
lexicon, imaginary: American, 172–74; author, authorship, 110–22; Casaubon, 122–29; error, 129–38; etymology, 138–43; Germans, 143–47; orientalist, 147–51; pigeonhole, 151–57; pioneer, 158–65; sublime, 165–72
libera, in Anglo-Saxon Pindarics, 65–67
Life and Growth of Languages, The (Whitney), 7
Life and Writings of Abraham Cowley (Sprat), 60
Life of Scott (Lockhart), 114
Linguarum Vett. Septentrionalium Thesaurus Grammatico-Criticus et Archaeologicus. *See Thesaurus* (Hickes)
Linguistic Science in the Nineteenth Century (Pedersen), 139–40
Linton, Eliza Lynn, 104, 126–27
literary criticism, Tolkien's, 81, 83, 85–91
literature, social function of, 92–94
Loeb edition of *Rhetorica ad Herennium*, 210–15, 220
Longinus, 70–71
Lucubrationes (Seneca), 34–38, 40–41
Lydgate, Tertius, 130, 146; as pioneer, 158, 161, 163, 165, 172; and the sublime, 167–68
lyric poetry, defined by Hickes, 67–69

Mabillon, Jean, 58
Mackay, Robert William: Eliot's review of, 124–25, 158–59, 171–72; as model for Casaubon, 104
Main, Alexander, and Eliot, 113, 133, 136, 300n. 84
manqué, in *OED*, 128

Manutius, Aldus, 21
marginalia, 156–57
Marshall, John, 183
Martial, and faulty scribes, 18–19
Marvell, Andrew, 256–57
Maxwell, Catherine, 107
memory, 9–14; Wyatt's focus on, 42–46
Mencken, H. L., 175–76
Menocal, Maria-Rosa, 222
Menologium, Hickes's consideration of, 71–72
Meredith, George, 155, 157
"Metaphor and Catachresis" (Parker), 217–20
meter, in Old English verse, 62–66
Middlemarch (Eliot), 3, 103–10; American reading of, 3, 172–73; and authorial identity, 112–18; as book of errors, 129–38; and etymology, 138–43; idealism of, 172; and lexicography, 118–22, 160–61; as a novel of pioneers, 158–65, 172; organization as theme in, 151–57; pronunciation in, 166–68; and sublimity, 165–72; and "volume," 113–14; wordplay in, 141–43. *See also* Casaubon, Edward; Eliot, George; James, Henry, and *Middlemarch*
Middlemarch Pioneer, 159–61
Miller, J. Hillis, 106, 132, 249–51
Mill on the Floss, The (Eliot), 115
Mimesis: "Adam and Eve" in, 230–41, 246–47, 256, 273–75; as book of exiles, 4, 224–25; and error, 228–29; and familial relationships, 225–31, 255–59; gender issues in, 4, 227–29, 238, 255–59; and homecomings, 4, 225–26; Isaac in, 221, 225–29, 255; and methods of the editor, 231–36, 239–40; Odysseus in, 221–22, 224–26, 255–56; paradoxes of, 246–47, 257–59. *See also* Auerbach, Erich

Miscellanea (Politian), 20
Miscomini, Antonio, 20–21
"Monsters and the Critics, The." *See* "*Beowulf*: The Monsters and the Critics" (Tolkien)
Morbius, Edward, 4, 263, 265–67, 269–75
More, Thomas, 34, 53; and errata, 22–29, 282n. 29
Mrs. Lynn Linton (Layton), 127
Müller, Max, 148–51, 173, 196–98, 267
Murray, James A. H., 3, 108, 123, 140; and pigeonholing, 152–57; as pioneer, 163–65, 172, 206; and sublime pursuit of philology, 168–72. *See also Oxford English Dictionary (OED)*
Murray, K. M. Elisabeth, 153
My Literary Life (Linton), 126–27
Mystère d'Adam. See "Adam and Eve," in *Mimesis*
mythography, 124–25, 148–49

Nagy, Gregory, 5–6
naming: Heaney's, 95–96; Tolkien's, 78
Nature of the Book, The (Johns), 16
Neogrammarians, 13
Neumann, Franz, 261–62
Neutra, Richard, 272, 316n. 26
New Criticism, 247–54
New Historicism, 92–94, 253–57
Nichols, Stephen G., 248–49
Nietzsche, Friedrich, 13–14
1984 (Orwell), 264
nonjurors (seventeenth century), 59
Norden, Eduard, 242
Norton Anthology of English Literature, The, 94, 100
Novum instrumentum (Erasmus), 37–39

Odysseus, in *Mimesis*, 221–22, 224–26, 255–56

OED. See Oxford English Dictionary (OED)
ofermod, 83, 85, 88–89
Old English verse: *Durham*, 64–65; *Exodus*, 63–64; meter in, 62–66. See also Anglo-Saxon Pindarics; Anglo-Saxon studies; Cowleyan Pindaric
On the Sublime (Longinus), 71
orientalism, 140, 145, 229, 270. See also *orientalist*, in imaginary lexicon
orientalist, in imaginary lexicon, 147–51. See also orientalism
Orwell, George, 264
Oxford English Dictionary (OED), 3, 108–10, 128, 258; "adoption," 182–83; "annex," 182; "bewilderment," 164–65; "funds," 183; literary authority in, 111–12; *manqué*, 128; "orientalist," 147; "pigeonhole," 152–57; "pioneer," 158, 162–65; "plash," 167; *repoussoir*, 122, 128; "retrogressive," 159–61; role of pronunciation in, 123–24; Scott cited in, 111–12, 114, 167; "sublime," 168. See also Murray, James A. H.

Palsgrave, John, and proofreading, 22
paradoxes, of *Mimesis*, 246–47, 257–59
Parker, Patricia, 217–20
Passow, Franz, 119
Pattison, Mark, as model for Casaubon, 104, 125–26
Pedersen, Holger, 139–40
performance: culture of, 176; nature of, 92–94
Petrarch, 19
Philological Society, 182
philology: comparative, 12–13, 139–43, 148, 173–74, 300n. 97; and *Forbidden Planet*, 263, 267–75; function of, 177; and German scholarship, 143–47, 173, 277n. 2; Heaney's vision of, 95–101; history of, 5–7, 9–14, 277n. 2; and mythography, 124–25; and politics (*see under* politics); sublime pursuit of, 168–72; Tolkien's vision of, 85–91. See also American philology
phonology, so-called science of, 207–8
pigeonhole, in imaginary lexicon, 151–57
pilgrimage motif, in Eliot, 131–32, 149–51
Pindar. See Cowleyan Pindaric
Pindarique Odes (Cowley). See Cowleyan Pindaric
pioneer: in imaginary lexicon, 158–65; in *OED*, 158, 162–65. See also pioneers
pioneers, 172–74; and politics, 163–65, 206–7. See also *pioneer*
"plash," in *OED*, 167
poetry: alliteration in, 68–69, 72, 92–93; Heaney's, 94–97; lyric, defined, 67–69; and politics (*see under* politics). See also Anglo-Saxon Pindarics; *Beowulf*; Cowleyan Pindaric; Hickes, George
Policy and Police (Elton), 32
Politian, *Miscellanea*, 20
politics: and philology, 181–83, 235–41, 253 (*see also* Adams, John Quincy; American philology); and pioneers, 163–65, 206–7; and poetry, 59–60, 69–70, 97–101
Practicing New Historicism (Gallagher and Greenblatt), 253–57
Price, Leah, 147
Principles of Rhetoric, The (Hill), 173, 191–92
printers, 51–54; English, and errata, 21–22, 282n. 29; Italian, and errata, 20–21, 26
printing, early history of, 15–17, 19–20. See also printers
Printing Press as an Agent of Change, The (Eisenstein), 16
Prison-House of Language, The (Jameson), 252–53

Progress of the Intellect, The (Mackay), Eliot's review of, 124–25, 158–59, 171–72
pronunciation: in *Middlemarch*, 166–68; in *OED*, 123–24; and phonology, 207–8
proofreading, 21–23, 51–54, 282nn. 26, 28, 29; Eliot's, 132–38, 300n. 84; self-correction as, 25–30. *See also* errata
Proust, Marcel, 228–30
Pynson, Richard, and proofreading, 22, 51, 282nn. 28, 29

Rask, Rasmus, 139, 141
Rational Amusement (Campbell), 74
Rawlinson and Bosworth Chair (Oxford). *See* letter of application, Tolkien's
Rebholz, R. A., and modernization of Wyatt, 46–51
reform, university, 144–45
Renaissance Self-Fashioning (Greenblatt), 15
repoussoir, in *OED*, 122, 128
"retrogressive," in *OED*, 159–61
Rhetorica ad Herennium, 99–100, 210–15, 220
rhetoricians, 7–9, 12. *See also* Adams, John Quincy; American philology
Richardson, Brian, 20
Ridley, Robert, 27–29, 44, 53–54
Robinson, Fred, 81–83
Rohde, Erwin, 242
Romanische Forschungen, 242–47
Ruthall, Thomas, Erasmus's letter to, 34–36

"Sandman, The" (Hoffmann), 264, 269
Sartre, Jean-Paul, 238
Saussure, Ferdinand de, 7, 12–13
Schlegel, Friedrich, 6–7

scholarship: English, 173; German, 143–47, 158, 173, 200–201, 236–37, 305n. 36; and self-reflection, 5–7; Southern, 203–7
science fiction. *See Forbidden Planet* (movie)
Scott, Sir Walter: influence of, on Eliot, 114–16; in *OED*, 111–12, 114, 167
scribes, faulty, 18–19, 53, 231–33, 246
scripture, 15–17, 26–29, 280n. 3; and doctrinal error, 23–26
self-correction, 25–30
self-reflection, in disciplinary scholarship, 5–7
Seneca, *Lucubrationes*, 34–38, 40–41
Shakespeare, William, 111, 258–59, 262
Shards of Love: Exile and the Origins of Lyric (Menocal), 222
Shippey, T. A., 72, 76–77, 95
Sievers, Eduard, 271
Silas Marner (Eliot), 164–65
"Silly Novels by Lady Novelists" (Eliot), 156–57
Simcox, Edith ("H. Lawrenny"), 130
Socrates, 7–8
Sparrow, John, 125–26
Spitzer, Leo, 222, 244–45, 267–70, 308n. 4
Sprat, Thomas, 60
Starkey, David, 31
Stowe, Harriet Beecher, Eliot's letter to, 113
Streitberg, Wilhelm, 271
sublime: in imaginary lexicon, 165–72; in *OED*, 168. *See also* sublime, the
sublime, the: Casaubon as negation of, 106; and Heaney, 95–101; and Hickes, 70–74; search for, 91–94; and Tolkien, 80, 89–91. *See also sublime*
Supplication (More), 22
Surgeon's Daughter, The (Scott), 114
Sweynheim and Pannarz, atelier of, 20
sword hilt, in *Beowulf*, 92–94

swurd-leoma, 67, 80, 94
synecdochic reading, technique of, 249–53

"Taxation no Tyranny" (Johnson), 185
textual criticism: Erasmus's comments on, 34–36; Housman's definition of, 55
"textual forensics," 41
Thesaurus (Hickes), 57, 73–76; "De Poetica Anglo-Saxonum," 59, 62–69, 71–74
þolian, 99
Thornton, William, 176–77, 199
Thynne, William, 44
Tidwald, and Torhthelm, 85–91
Tolkien, Christopher, 90–91
Tolkien, J. R. R., 56–57, 76–77, 91–94; "*Beowulf*: The Monsters and the Critics," 57, 77–83, 90; "Homecoming of Beorhtnoth Beorhthelm's Son, The," 83, 85–91; letter of application, 83–86, 90; and literary criticism, 81, 83, 85–91; and philology, 85–91; and the sublime, 80, 89–91
tombs, in *Middlemarch*, 117, 120, 137
"To Mr. Hobs" (Cowley), 61–62
Tooke, John Horne, 138–40, 177, 181–82, 186–87
Torhthelm. and Tidwald, 85–91
Tottel, Richard, 52
Trench, Richard Chenevix, 110, 120, 169
Trovato, Paolo, 21
Tuckerman, Henry, 177
Tuke, Brian, 44–45
Tyndale, William, 53–54; Bible, 15, 17, 280n. 3; and errata, 17, 26–29

"Uncanny, The" (Freud), 264

vanity, authorial, 112
Vaughn, Thomas, 144
Veeser, Aram, 93
Vincy, Fred, 117
Vincy, Mary, 117
vocabulary, American, growth of, 175–77
"volume," and *Middlemarch*, 113–14

Warner, Michael, 16
Warton, Thomas, 75, 293n. 69
Waverley (Scott), 114–15
Webster, Noah, 182
Weems, Parson, 176
Weinbrot, Howard, 66–67
Wellek, René, 10–11
Whitman, Walt, 220
Whitney, William Dwight, 7, 173, 195–99, 250, 305nn. 37–38
Wilson, Penelope, 61
Wolf, F. A., 5, 277n. 2
Woodford, Samuel, 60
Woolf, Virginia, 227–28, 258
"Word for the Germans, A" (Eliot), 145–47, 201
wordplay, in *Middlemarch*, 141–43
Wordsworth, William, 148–49
Wülker, Richard, 82
Wyatt, Thomas, 14, 51–54; declaration of innocence, 41–46; modernization of, 46–51

Yale University, 10, 247–53
Yeats, W. B., 97

Zumthor, Paul, 270
Zweig, Stefan, 274–75

GPSR Authorized Representative: Easy Access System Europe, Mustamäe tee
50, 10621 Tallinn, Estonia, gpsr.requests@easproject.com

www.ingramcontent.com/pod-product-compliance
Lightning Source LLC
Chambersburg PA
CBHW031544300426
44111CB00006BA/172